N BRANCH
Kitchen Princess

5

Natsumi Ando

Story by Miyuki Kobayashi

Translated by Satsuki Yamashita

Adapted by Nunzio DeFilippis and Christina Weir

Lettered by North Market Street Graphics

Ballantine Books • New York

A Del Rey Manga/Kodansha Trade Paperback Original

Kitchen Princess copyright © 2006 by Natsumi Ando and Miyuki Kobayashi
English translation copyright © 2008 by Natsumi Ando and Miyuki Kobayashi

Published in the United States by Del Rey Books, an imprint of The Random House Publishing Group, a division of Random House, Inc., New York.

DEL REY is a registered trademark and the Del Rey colophon is a trademark of Random House, Inc.

Publication rights arranged through Kodansha Ltd.

First published in Japan in 2006 by Kodansha Ltd., Tokyo

ISBN 978-0-345-49885-4

Printed in the United States of America

www.delreymanga.com

9 8 7 6 5 4 3

Translator: Satsuki Yamashita
Adaptors: Nunzio DeFilippis and Christina Weir
Lettering: North Market Street Graphics
Original cover design by Akiko Omo

Contents

Honorifics Explained

Throughout the Del Rey Manga books, you will find Japanese honorifics left intact in the translations. For those not familiar with how the Japanese use honorifics and, more important, how they differ from American honorifics, we present this brief overview.

Politeness has always been a critical facet of Japanese culture. Ever since the feudal era, when Japan was a highly stratified society, use of honorifics—which can be defined as polite speech that indicates relationship or status—has played an essential role in the Japanese language. When addressing someone in Japanese, an honorific usually takes the form of a suffix attached to one's name (example: "Asuna-san"), is used as a title at the end of one's name, or appears in place of the name itself (example: "Negi-sensei," or simply "Sensei!").

Honorifics can be expressions of respect or endearment. In the context of manga and anime, honorifics give insight into the nature of the relationship between characters. Many English translations leave out these important honorifics and therefore distort the feel of the original Japanese. Because Japanese honorifics contain nuances that English honorifics lack, it is our policy at Del Rey not to translate them. Here, instead, is a guide to some of the honorifics you may encounter in Del Rey Manga.

-san: This is the most common honorific and is equivalent to Mr., Miss, Ms., or Mrs. It is the all-purpose honorific and can be used in any situation where politeness is required.

-sama: This is one level higher than "-san" and is used to confer great respect.

-dono: This comes from the word "tono," which means "lord." It is an even higher level than "-sama" and confers utmost respect.

-kun: This suffix is used at the end of boys' names to express familiarity or endearment. It is also sometimes used by men among friends, or when addressing someone younger or of a lower station.

-chan: This is used to express endearment, mostly toward girls. It is also used for little boys, pets, and even among lovers. It gives a sense of childish cuteness.

Bozu: This is an informal way to refer to a boy, similar to the English terms "kid" and "squirt."

Sempai/ Senpai: This title suggests that the addressee is one's senior in a group or organization. It is most often used in a school setting, where underclassmen refer to their upperclassmen as "sempai." It can also be used in the workplace, such as when a newer employee addresses an employee who has seniority in the company.

Kohai: This is the opposite of "sempai" and is used toward underclassmen in school or newcomers in the workplace. It connotes that the addressee is of a lower station.

Sensei: Literally meaning "one who has come before," this title is used for teachers, doctors, or masters of any profession or art.

-[blank]: This is usually forgotten in these lists, but it is perhaps the most significant difference between Japanese and English. The lack of honorific means that the speaker has permission to address the person in a very intimate way. Usually, only family, spouses, or very close friends have this kind of permission. Known as *yobisute*, it can be gratifying when someone who has earned the intimacy starts to call one by one's name without an honorific. But when that intimacy hasn't been earned, it can be very insulting.

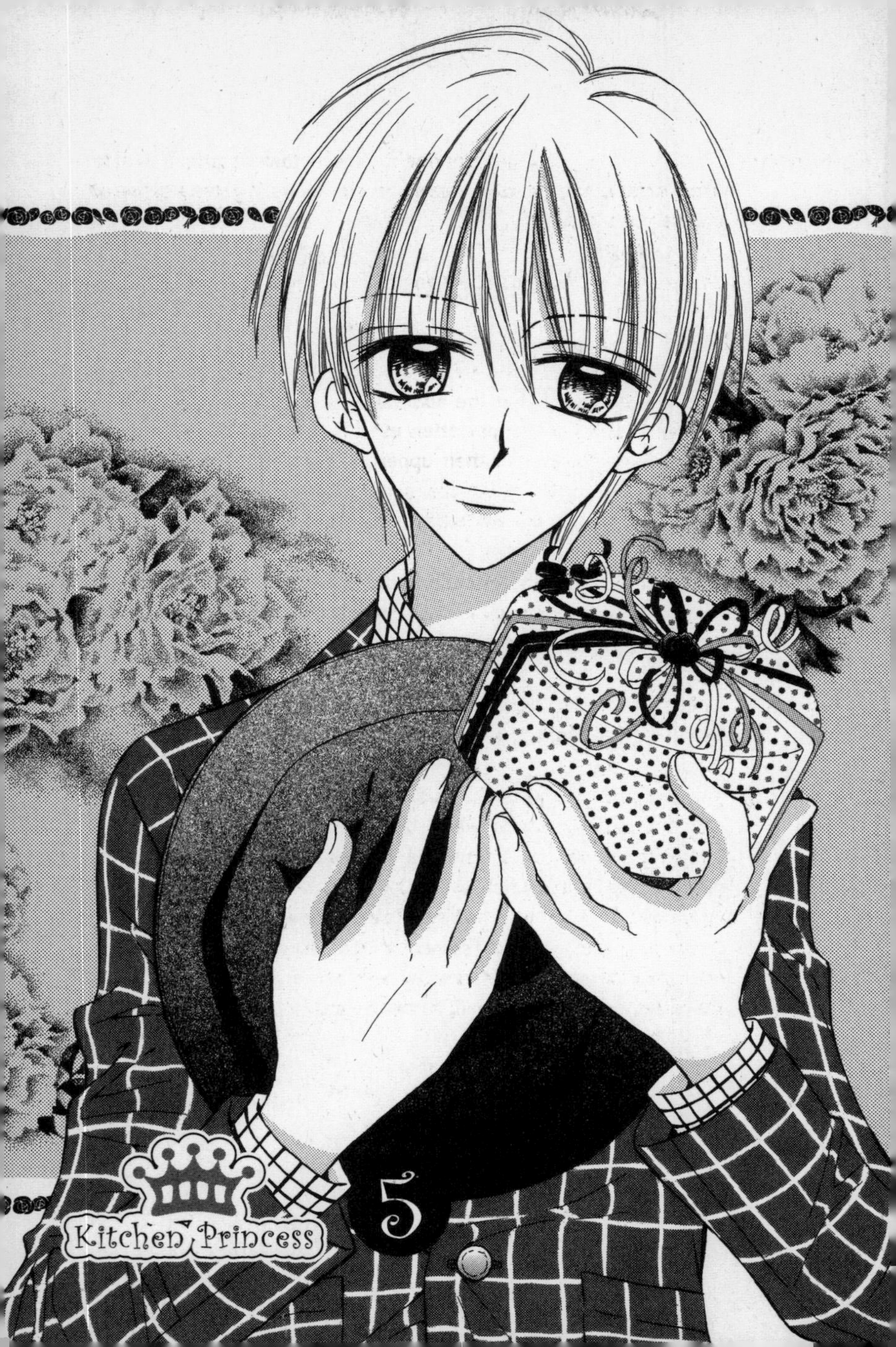
Kitchen Princess
5

Kitchen Princess

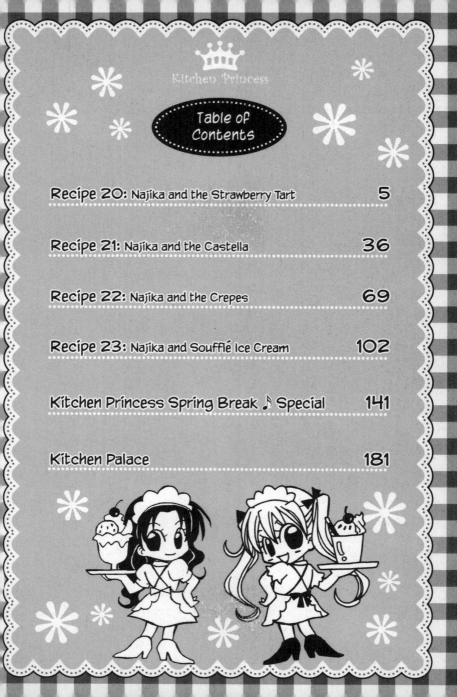

Table of Contents

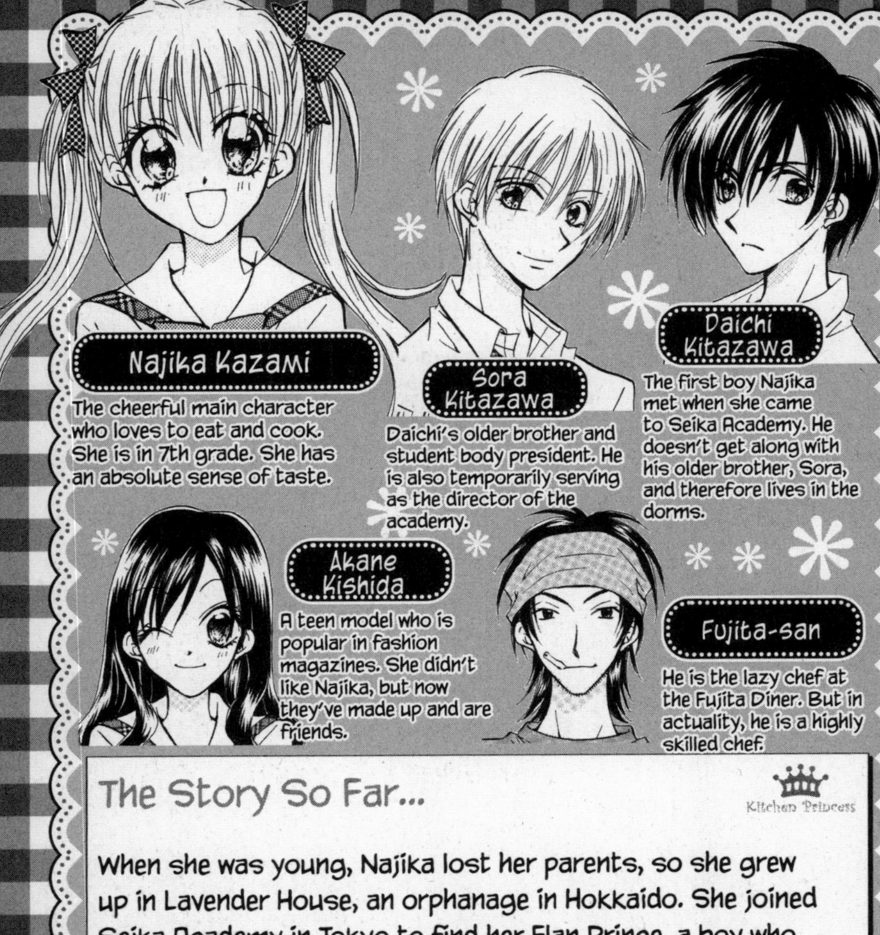
Najika Kazami
The cheerful main character who loves to eat and cook. She is in 7th grade. She has an absolute sense of taste.
Sora Kitazawa
Daichi's older brother and student body president. He is also temporarily serving as the director of the academy.
Daichi Kitazawa
The first boy Najika met when she came to Seika Academy. He doesn't get along with his older brother, Sora, and therefore lives in the dorms.
Akane Kishida
A teen model who is popular in fashion magazines. She didn't like Najika, but now they've made up and are friends.
Fujita-san
He is the lazy chef at the Fujita Diner. But in actuality, he is a highly skilled chef.

The Story So Far...

Kitchen Princess

When she was young, Najika lost her parents, so she grew up in Lavender House, an orphanage in Hokkaido. She joined Seika Academy in Tokyo to find her Flan Prince, a boy who saved her from drowning when she was young. Najika slowly started to fall in love with Sora, but Daichi was attracted to Najika. However, thanks to interference from Akane, who has feelings for Daichi, he wound up hurting Najika's feelings. Sora comforted her and told her that he was the Flan Prince, and Najika's love for Sora grew further. She decided to compete in the national confectionary competition, hoping to tell Sora about her feelings when the competition was over. But then Daichi suddenly kissed her!

Hello

"Kitchen Princess" is already at Volume 5.

Having a manga series reach five volumes is a *first* for me! And I was amazed that this manga won the 30th Kodansha Manga Award.

It's all thanks to the readers who support me!!

I would like to use this space to say...

Thank you very much!!

Natsumi Ando

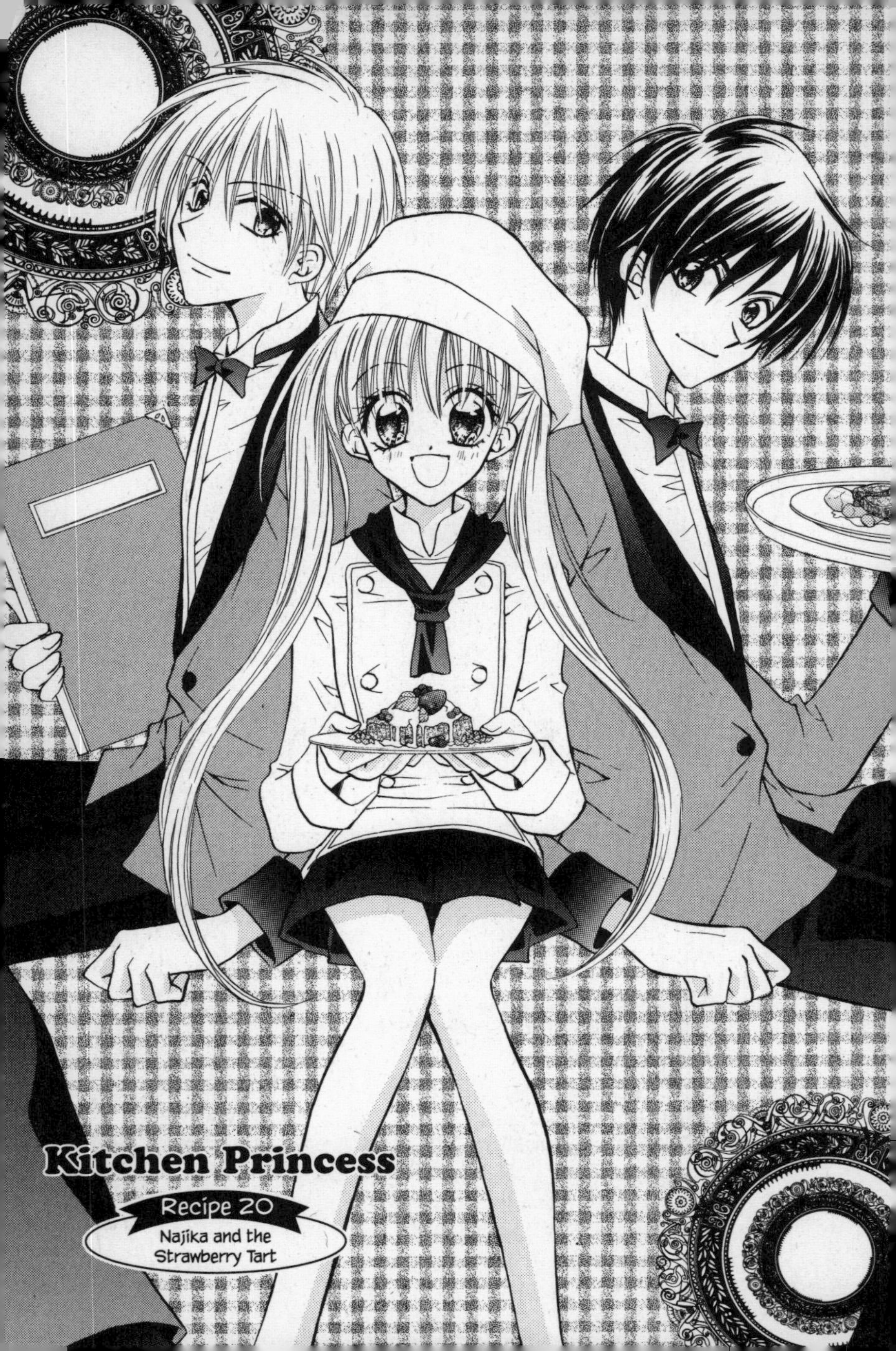
Kitchen Princess
Recipe 20
Najika and the Strawberry Tart

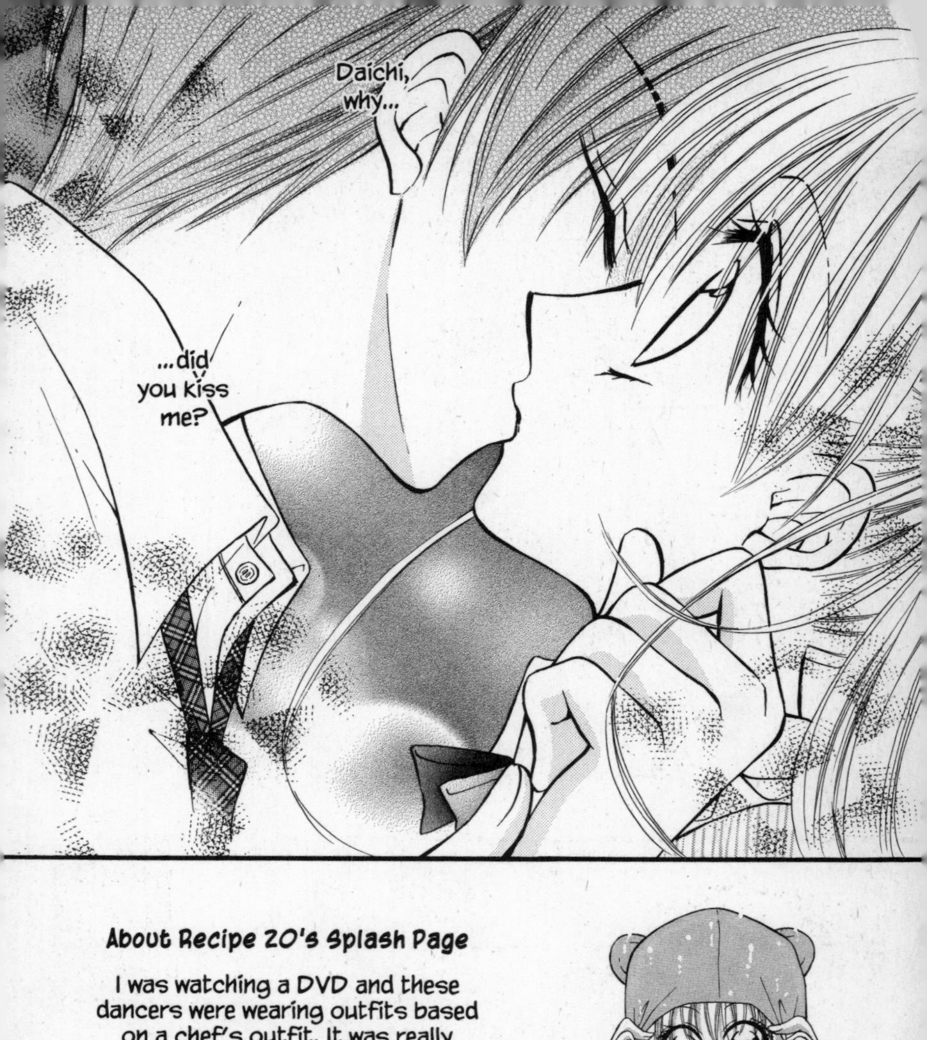
Daichi, why...
...did you kiss me?

About Recipe 20's Splash Page

I was watching a DVD and these dancers were wearing outfits based on a chef's outfit. It was really cute, so I used it as inspiration for the trio's clothes.

The actual outfits were very short and were very sexy (I'm sure they're wearing shorts underneath.♪)

A chef's outfit can be very cute, once you make a few small adjustments here and there.

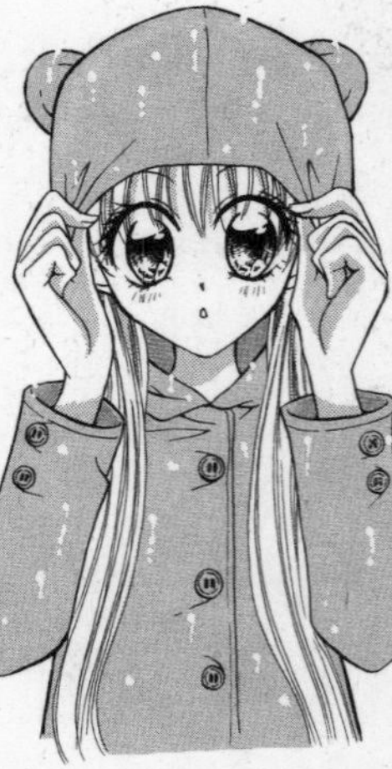

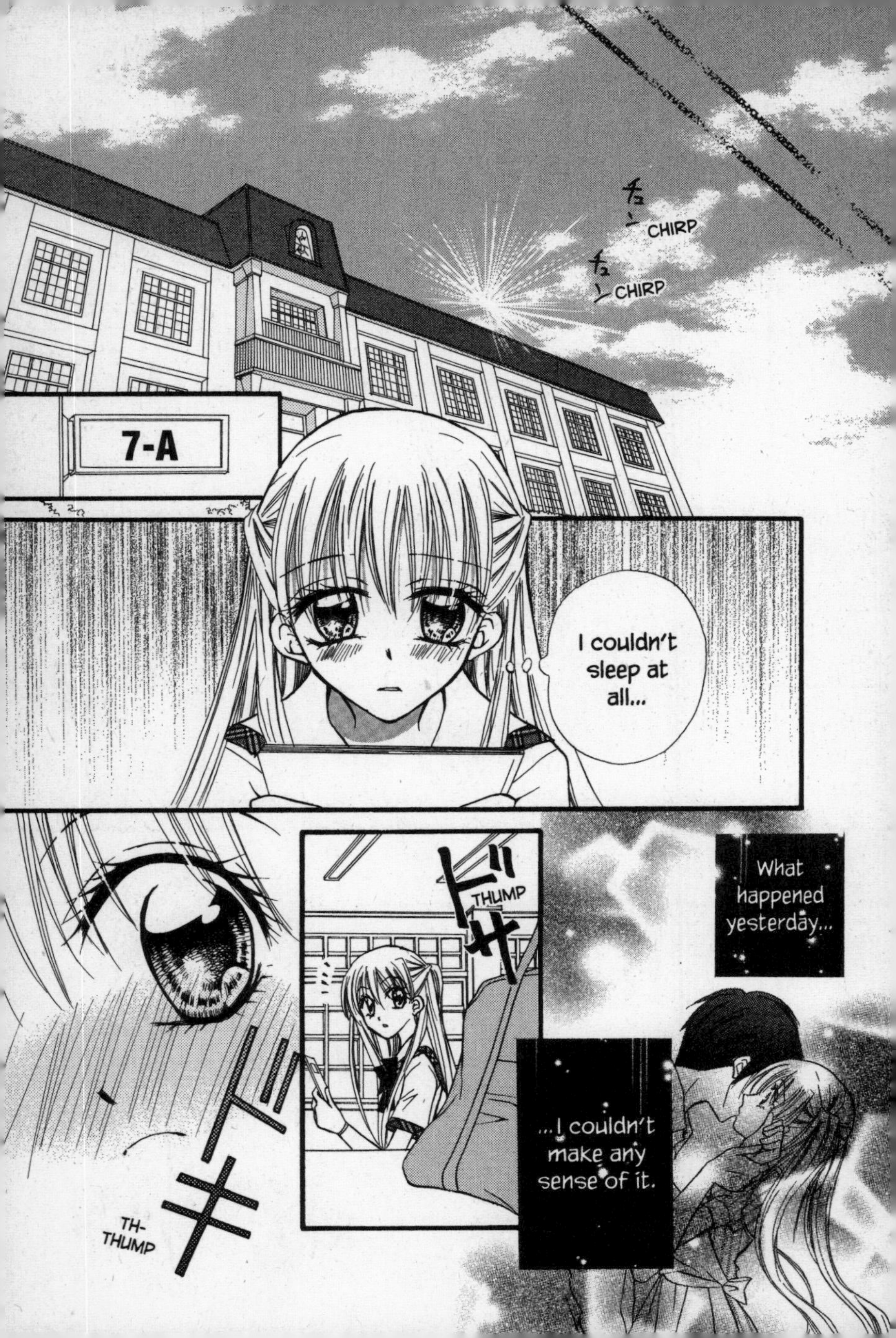

チュン CHIRP
チュン CHIRP
7-A
I couldn't sleep at all...
What happened yesterday...
...I couldn't make any sense of it.
ドキ THUMP
ドキ TH-THUMP

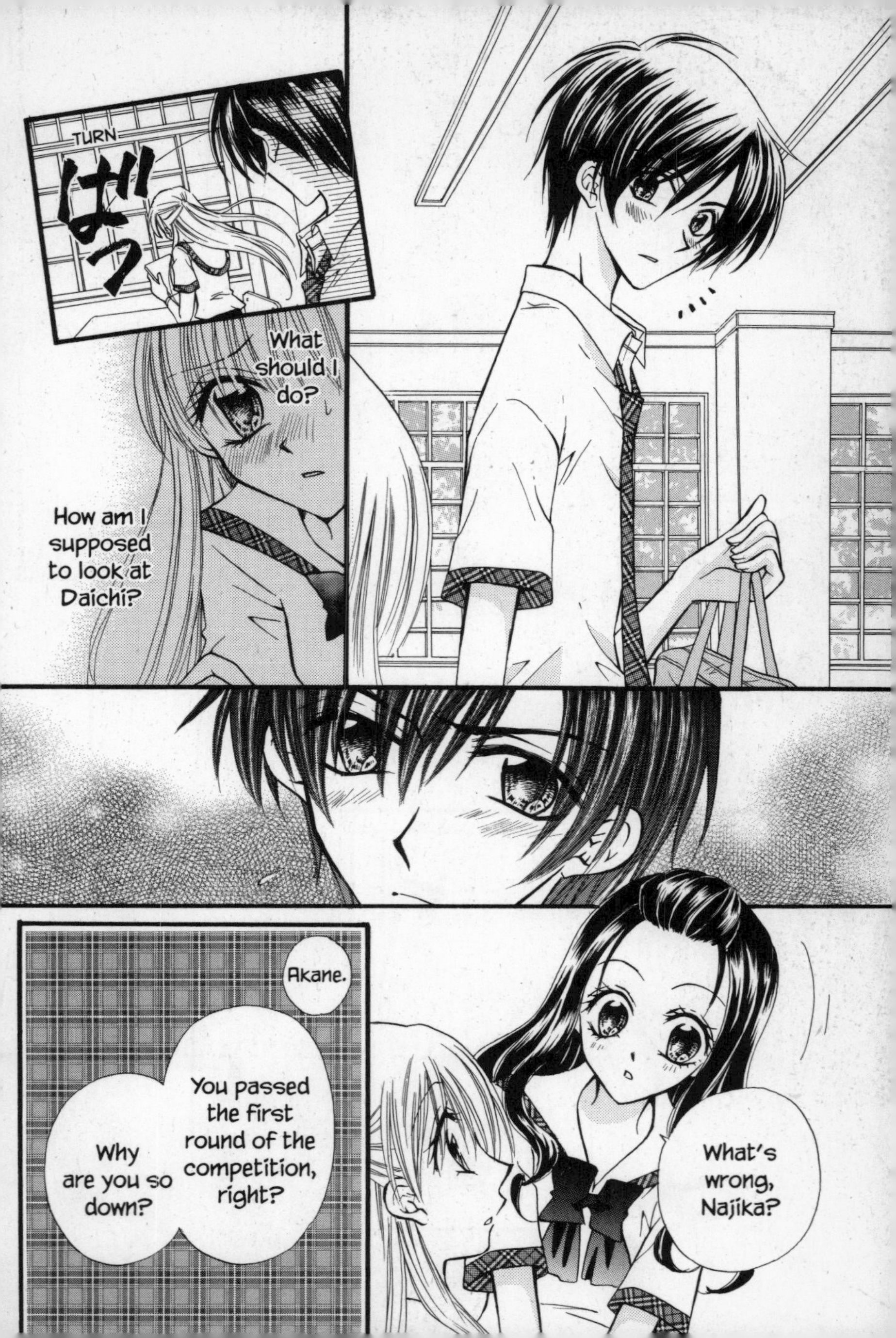
TURN
ばっ
What should I do?
How am I supposed to look at Daichi?
Akane.
What's wrong, Najika?
You passed the first round of the competition, right?
Why are you so down?

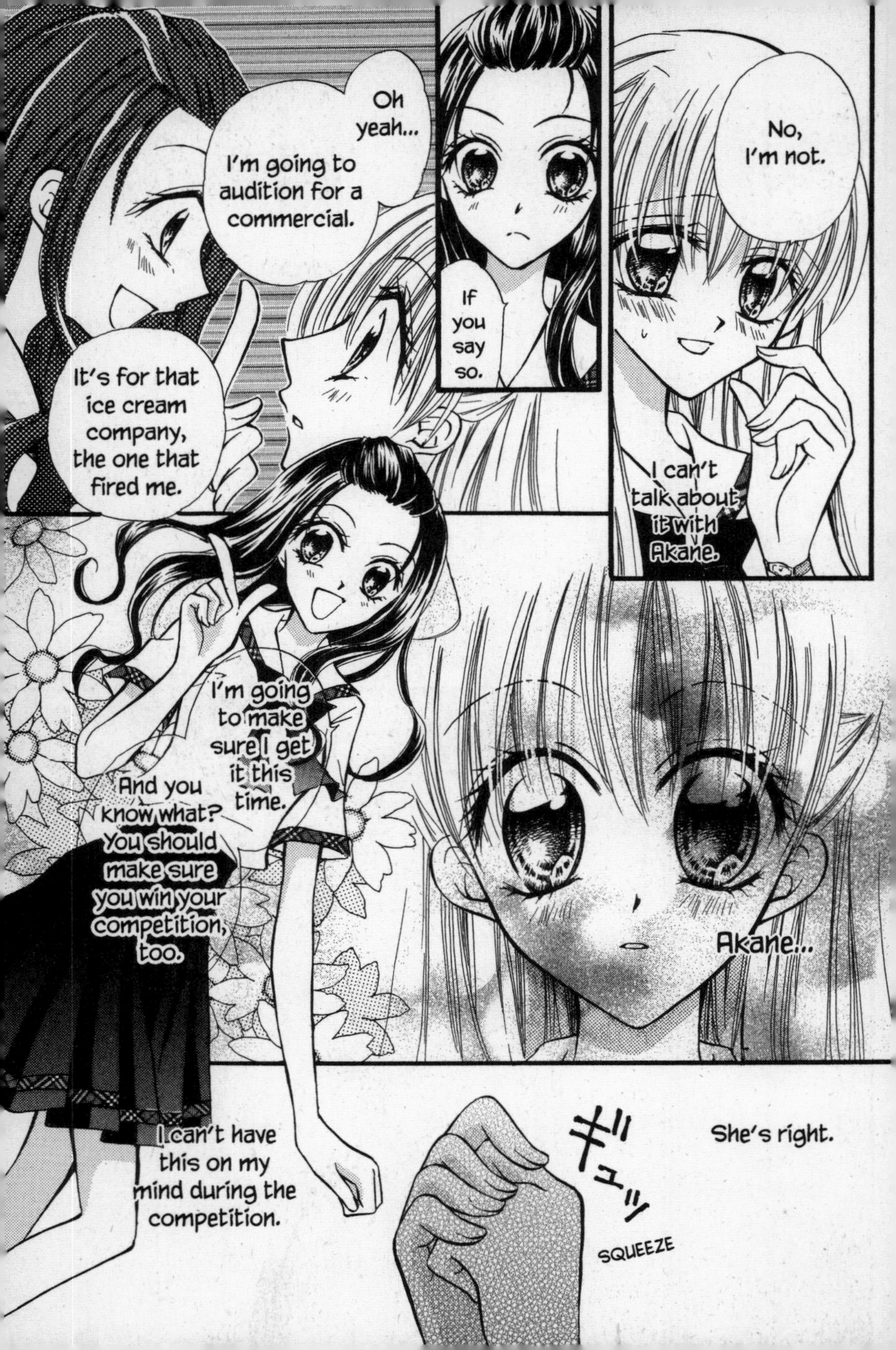
No, I'm not.
I can't talk about it with Akane.
If you say so.
Oh yeah...
I'm going to audition for a commercial.
It's for that ice cream company, the one that fired me.
I'm going to make sure I get it this time.
And you know what? You should make sure you win your competition, too.
Akane...
She's right.
ギュッ
SQUEEZE
I can't have this on my mind during the competition.

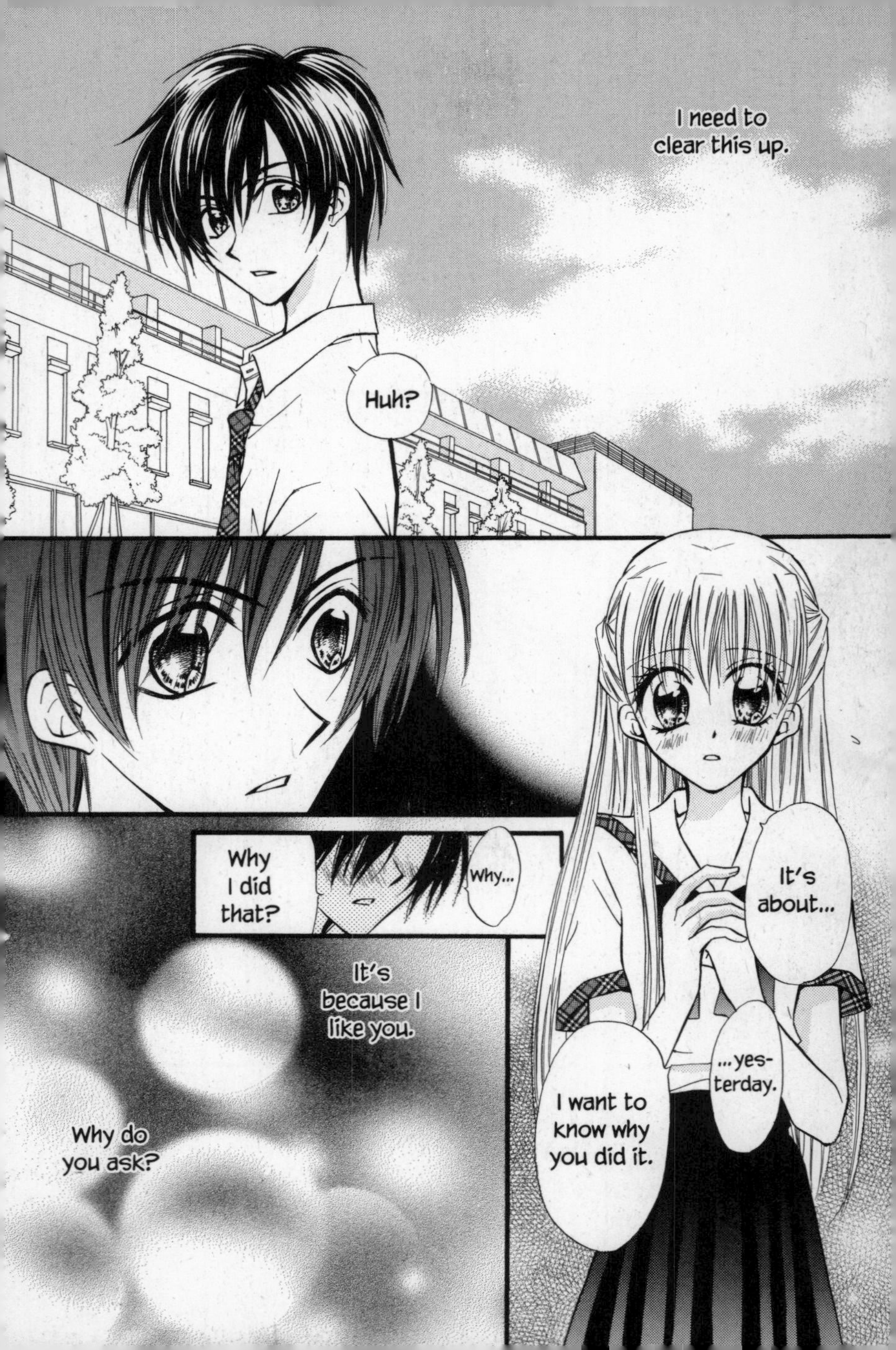
I need to clear this up.
Huh?
It's about...
...yes-terday.
I want to know why you did it.
Why...
Why I did that?
It's because I like you.
Why do you ask?

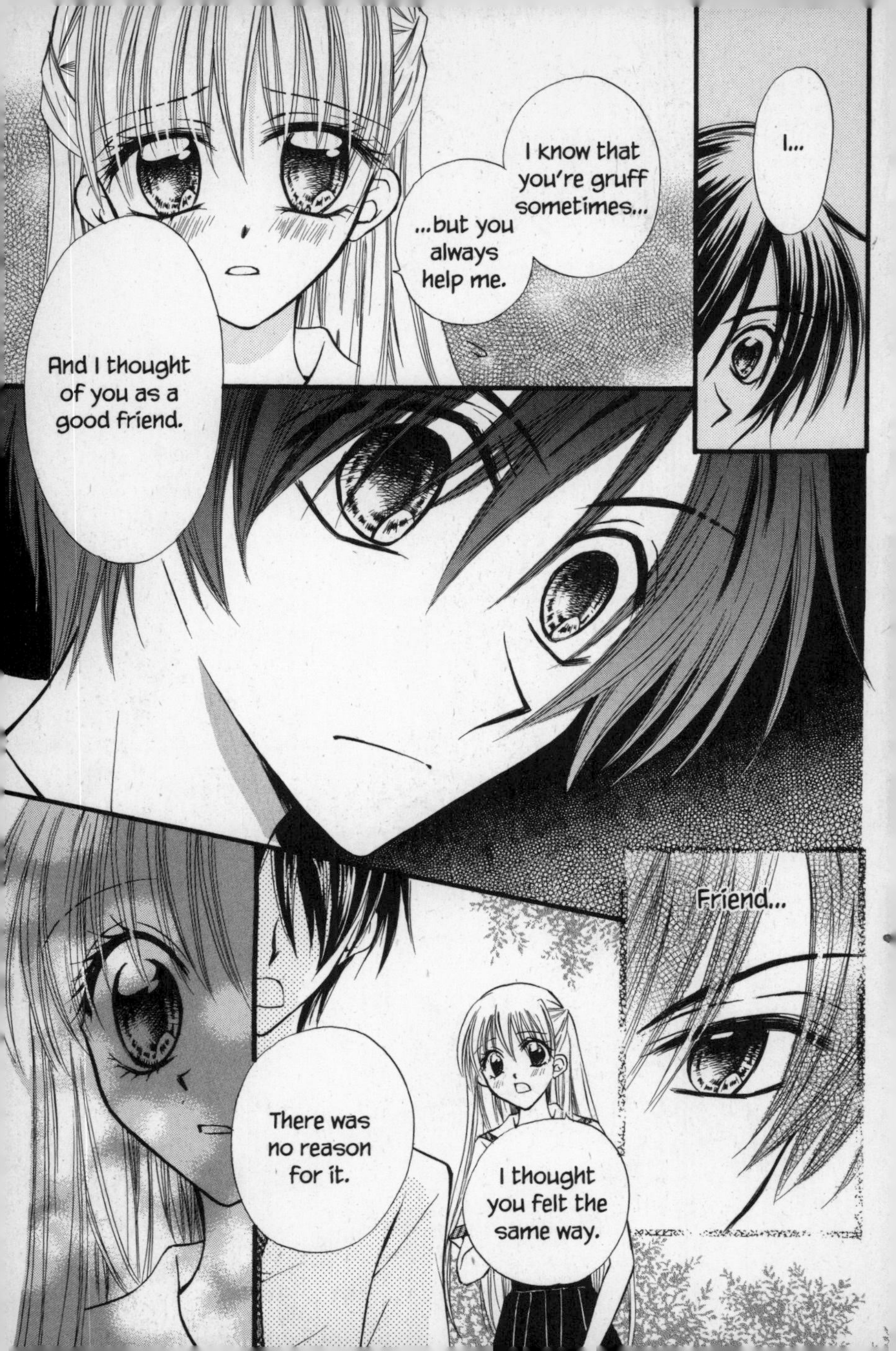
I...
I know that you're gruff sometimes...
...but you always help me.
And I thought of you as a good friend.
Friend...
I thought you felt the same way.
There was no reason for it.

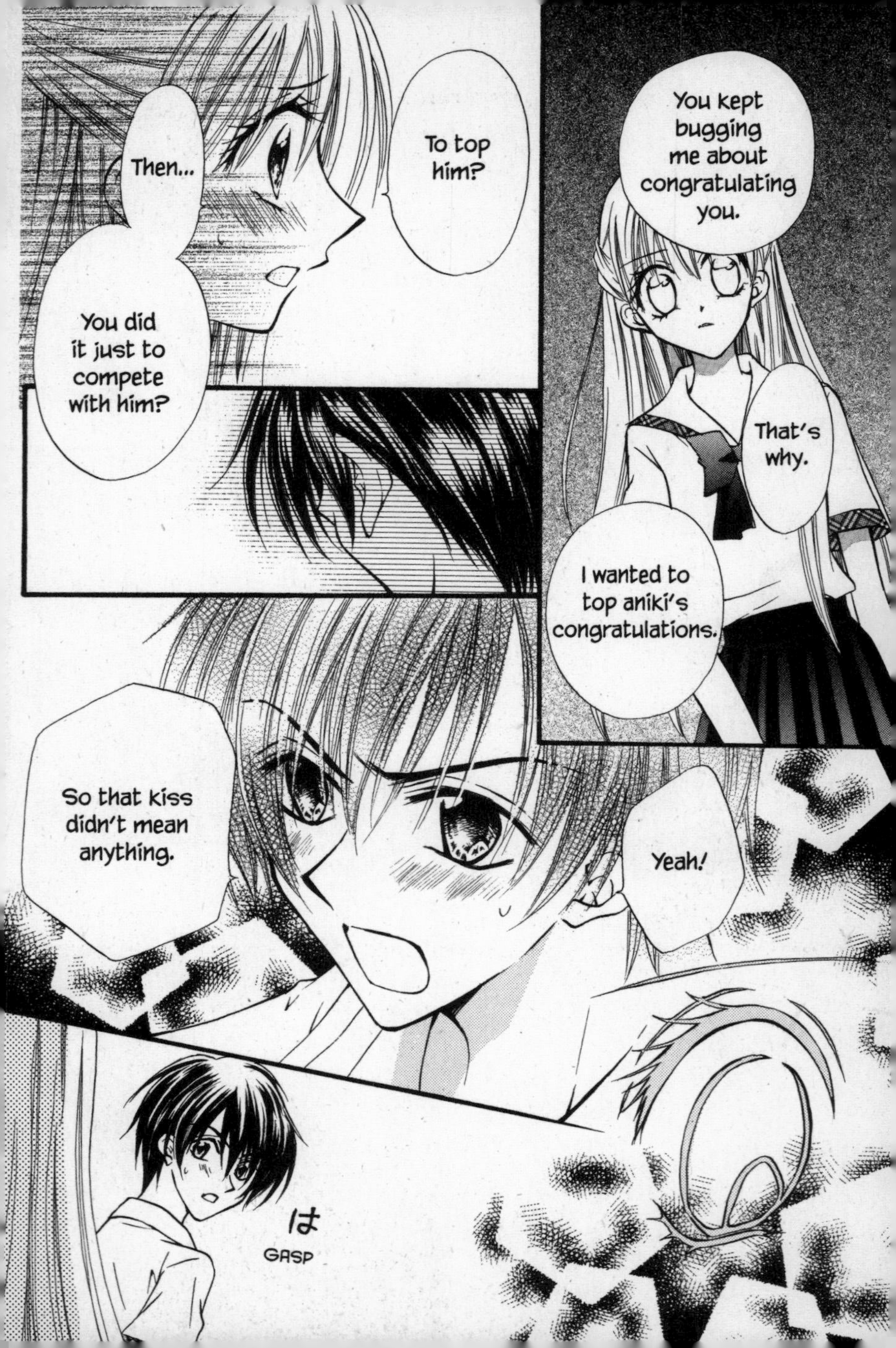
You kept bugging me about congratulating you.
That's why.
I wanted to top aniki's congratulations.
To top him?
Then...
You did it just to compete with him?
Yeah!
So that kiss didn't mean anything.
は
GASP

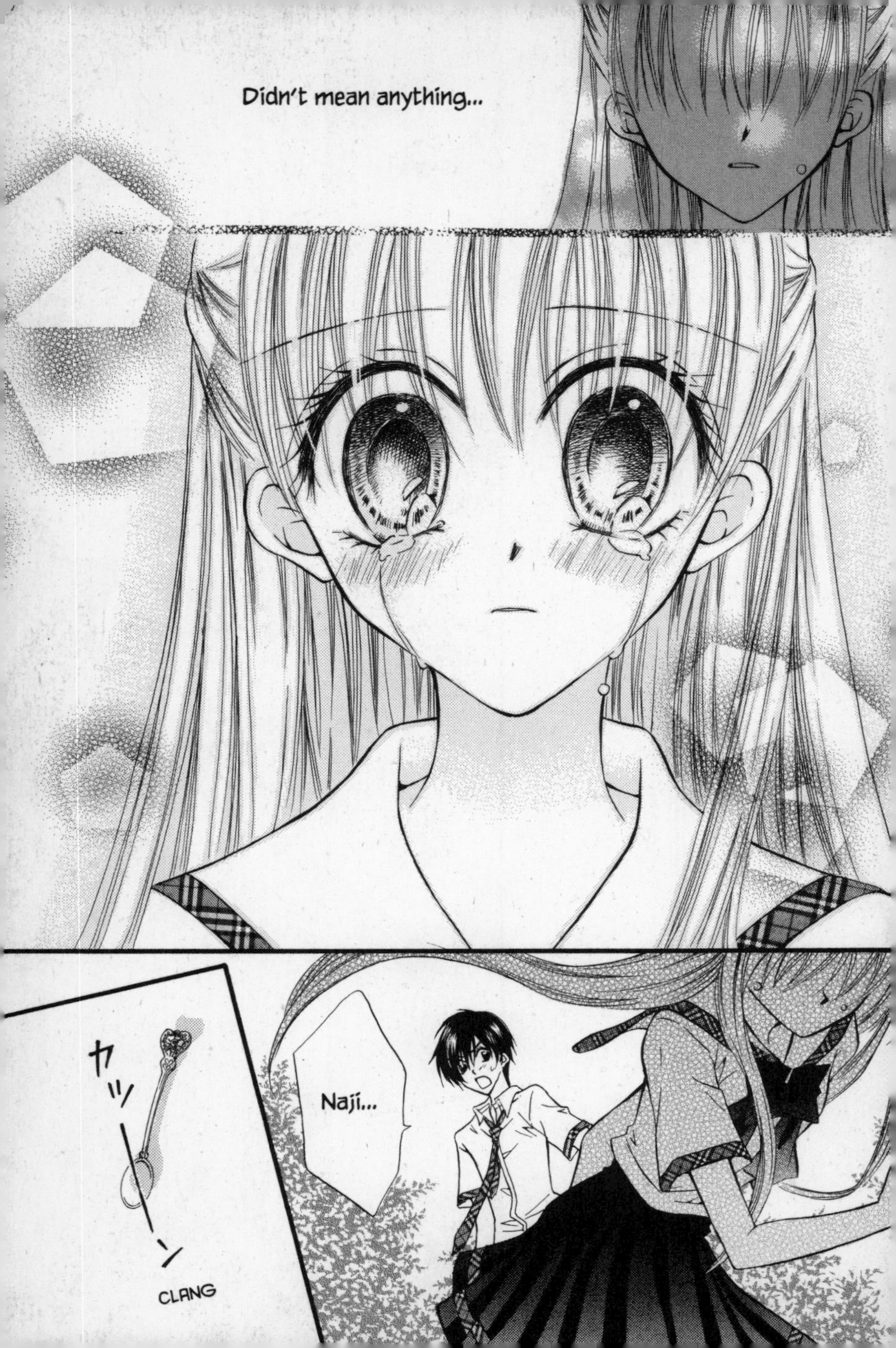
Didn't mean anything...
Naji...
カツーン
CLANG

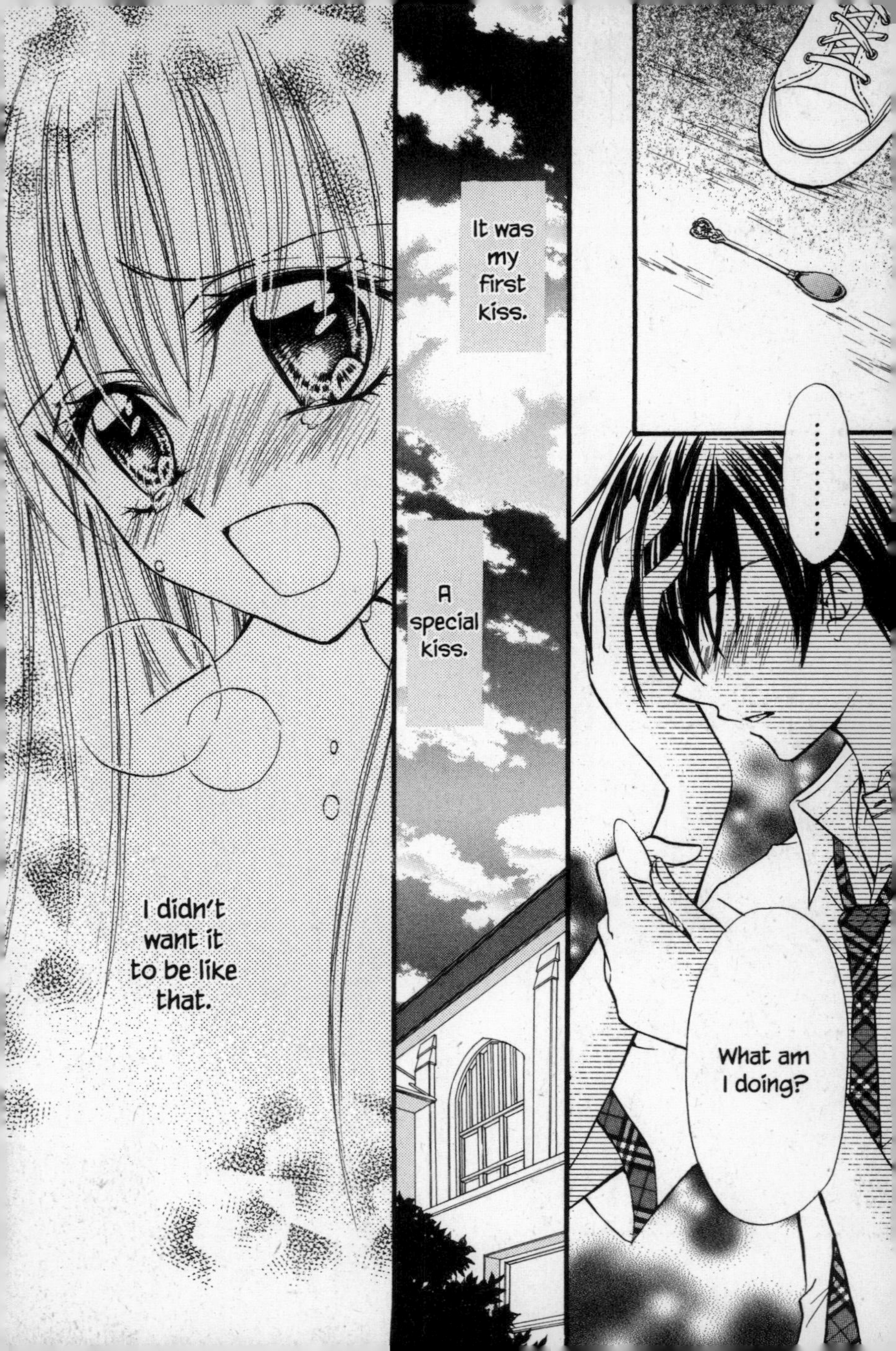
……
What am I doing?
It was my first kiss.
A special kiss.
I didn't want it to be like that.

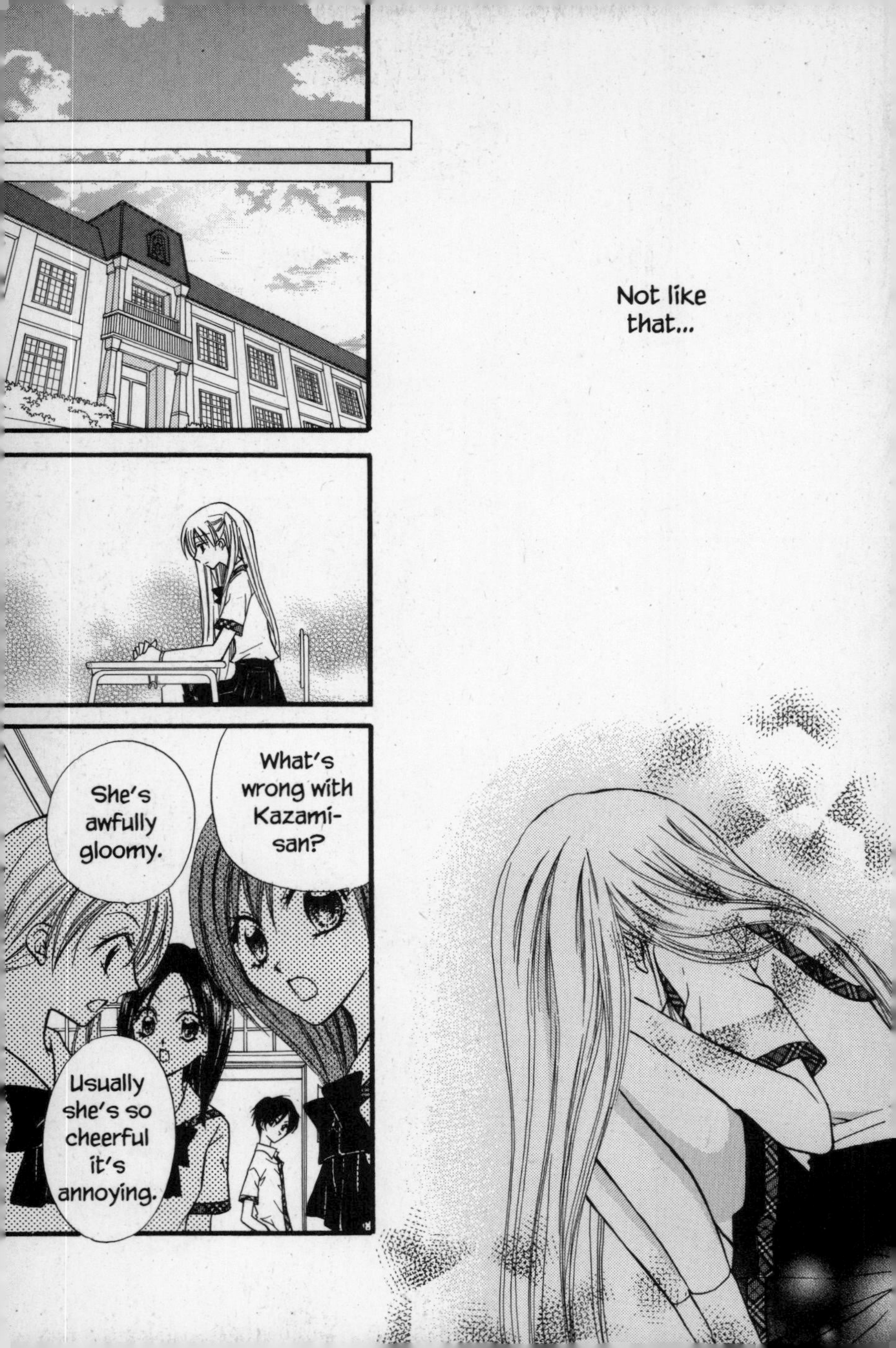
Not like that...
What's wrong with Kazami-san?
She's awfully gloomy.
Usually she's so cheerful it's annoying.

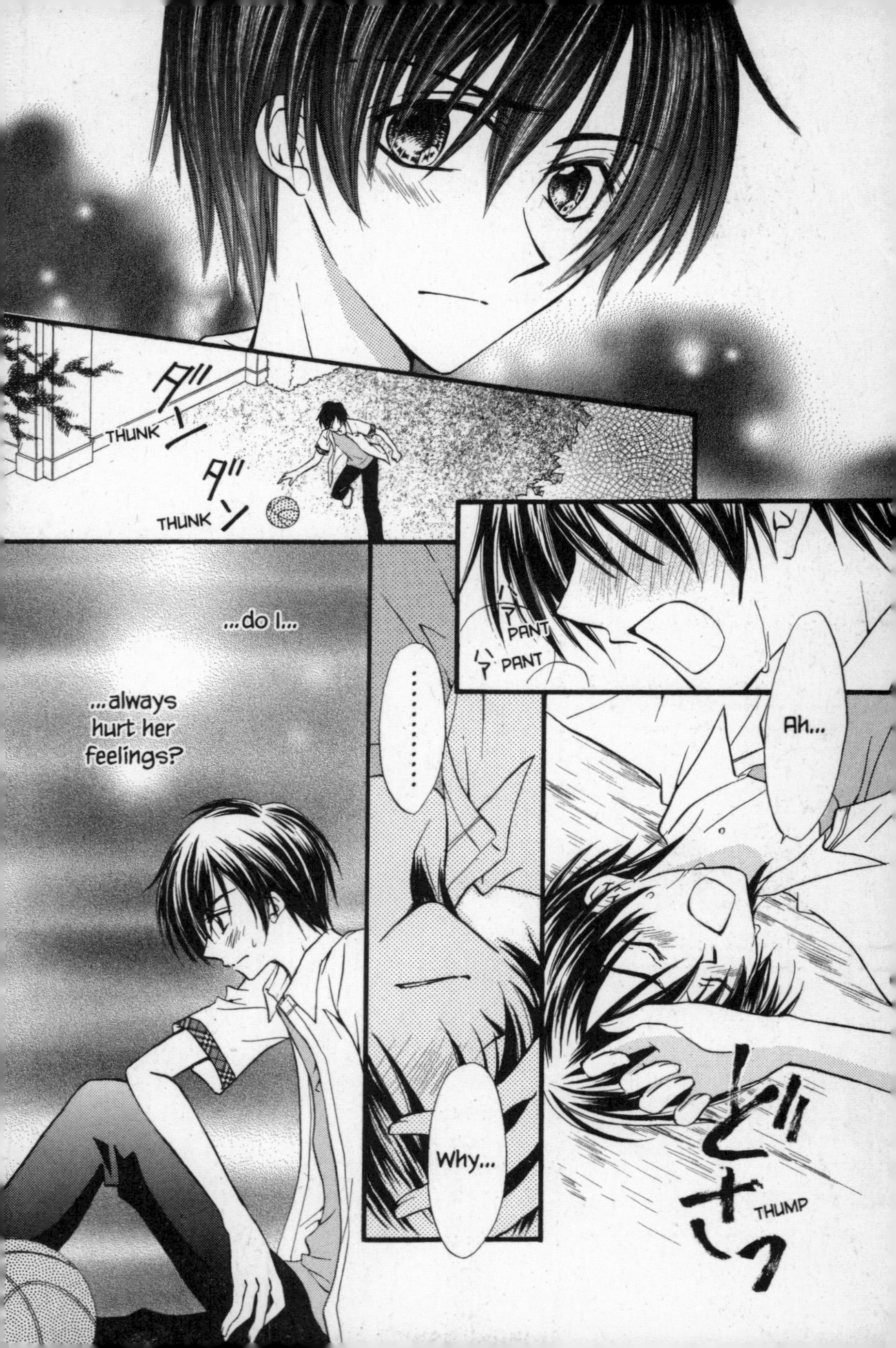

ダン THUNK
ダン THUNK
ハア PANT
ハア PANT
Ah...
どさっ THUMP
......
Why...
...do I...
...always hurt her feelings?

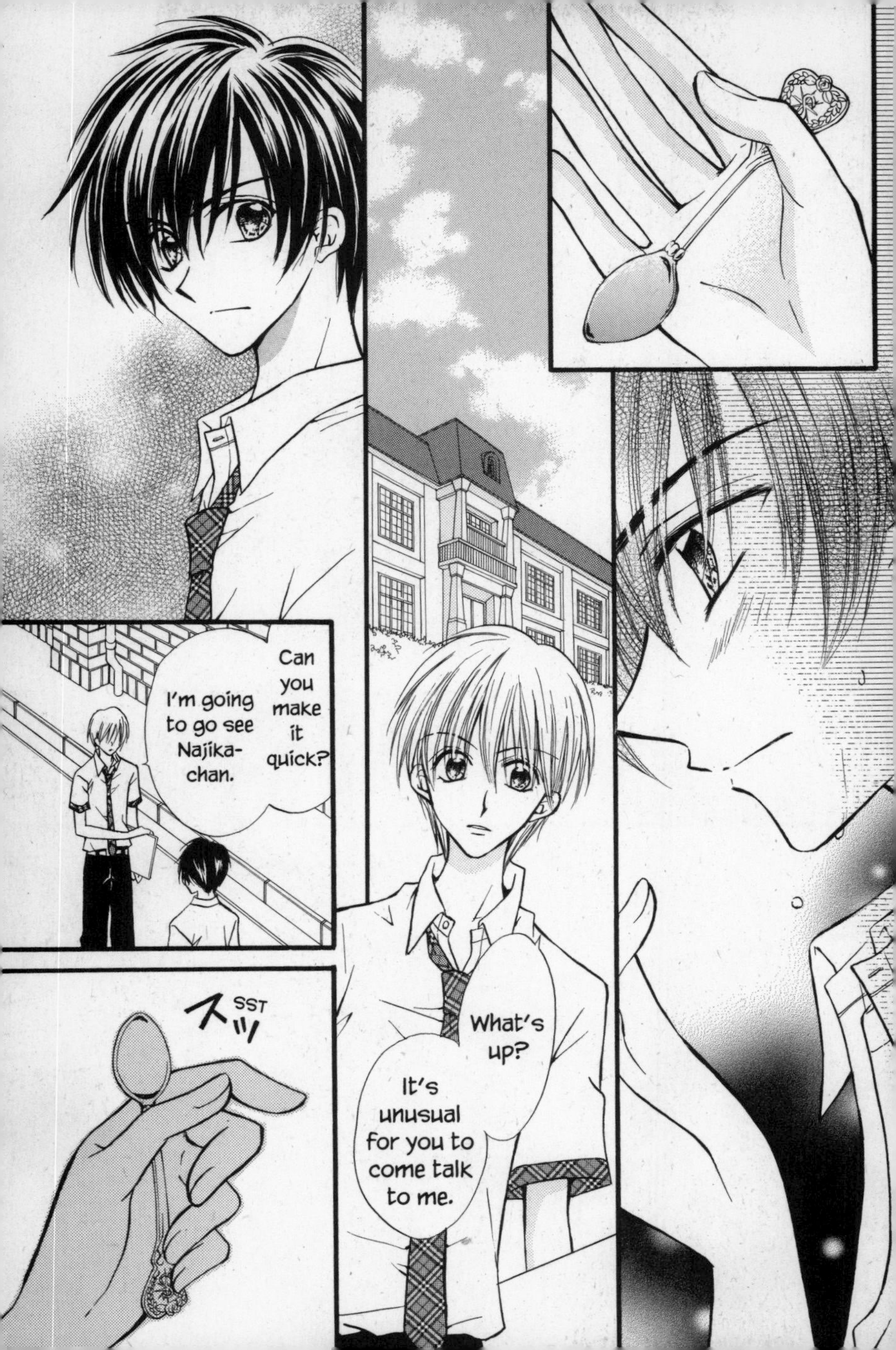
What's up?
It's unusual for you to come talk to me.
Can you make it quick?
I'm going to go see Najika-chan.
スッ SST

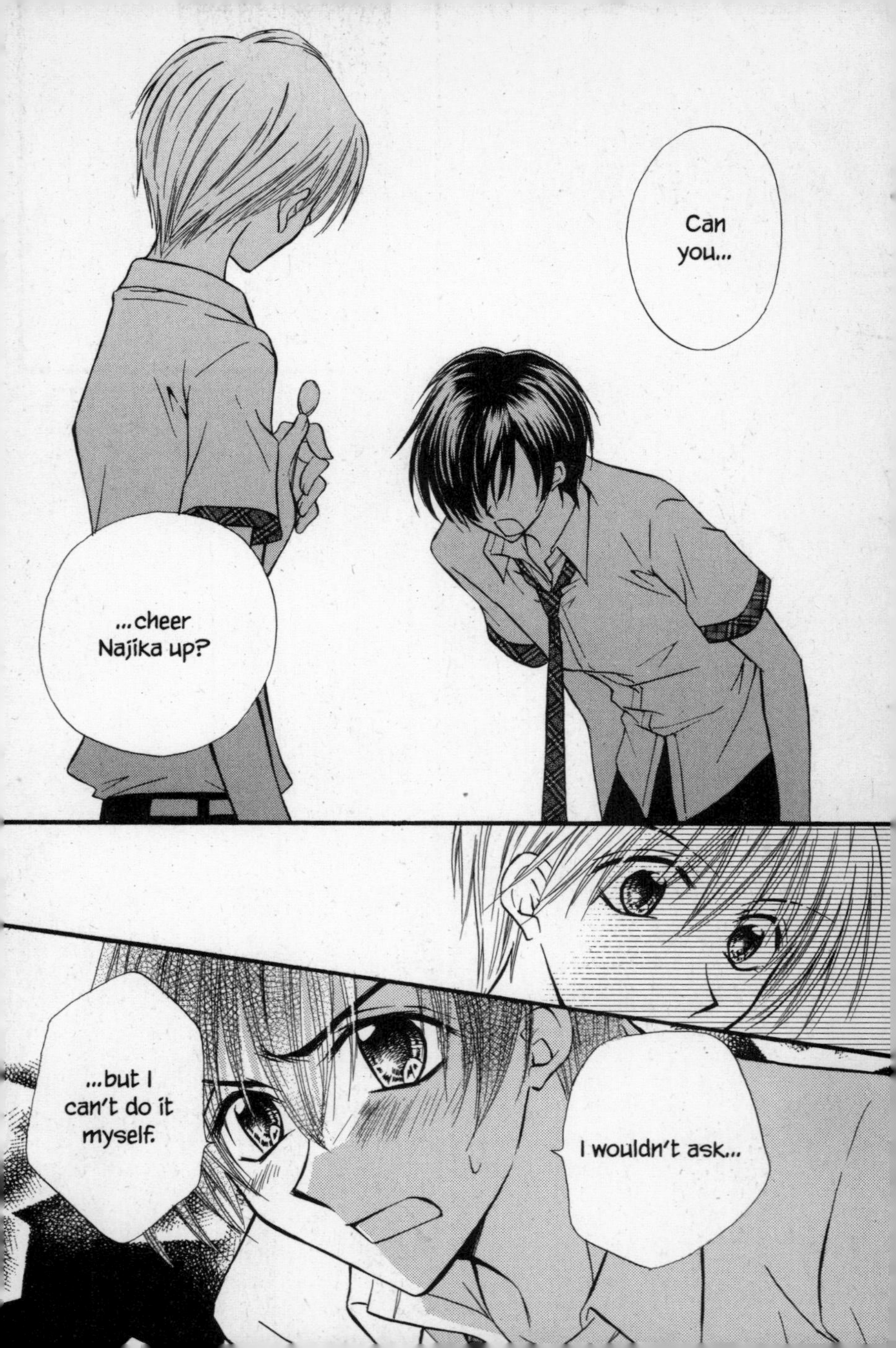
Can you...
...cheer Najika up?
I wouldn't ask...
...but I can't do it myself.

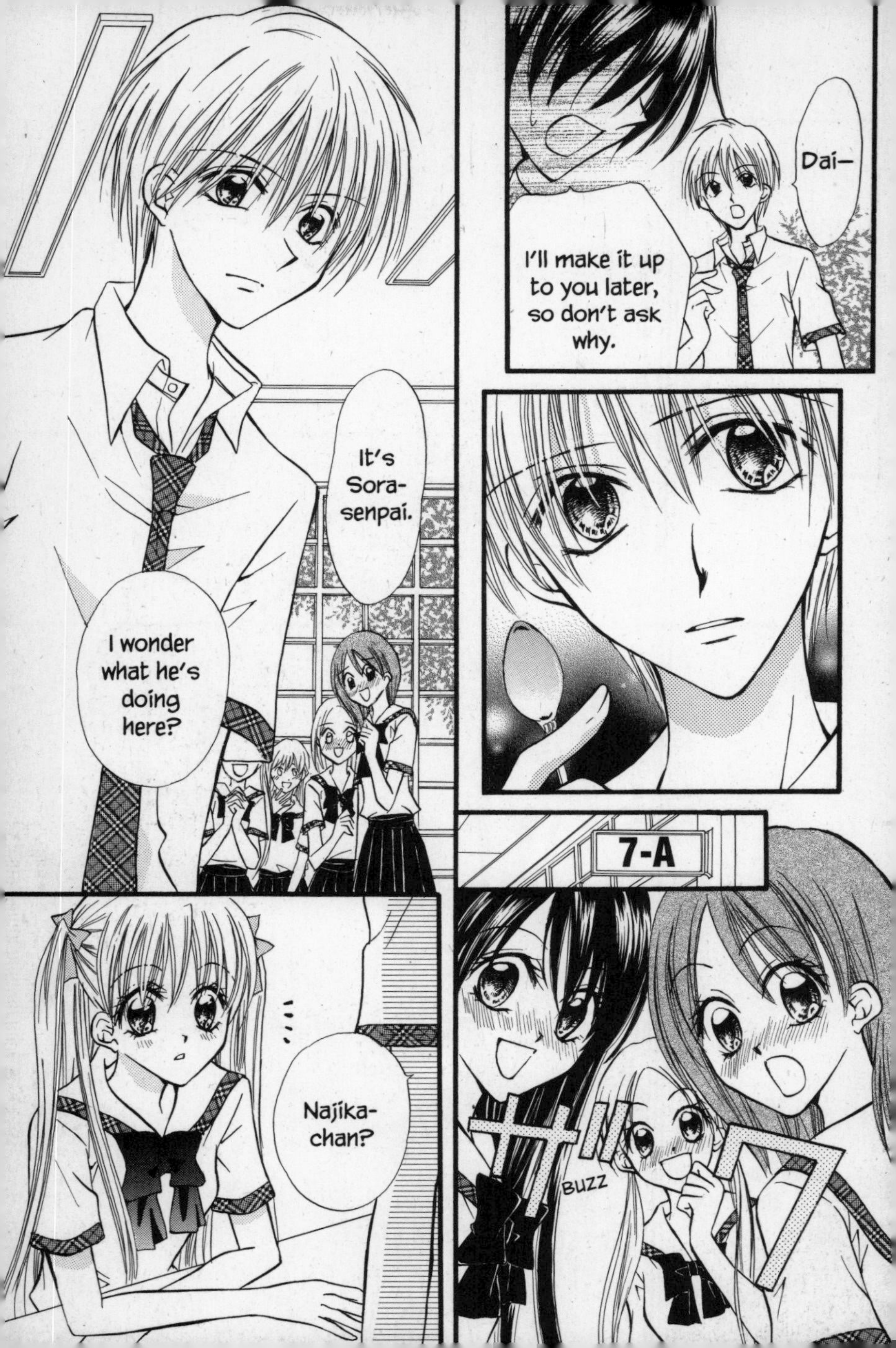

Dai—
I'll make it up to you later, so don't ask why.
It's Sora-senpai.
I wonder what he's doing here?
7-A
BUZZ
Najika-chan?

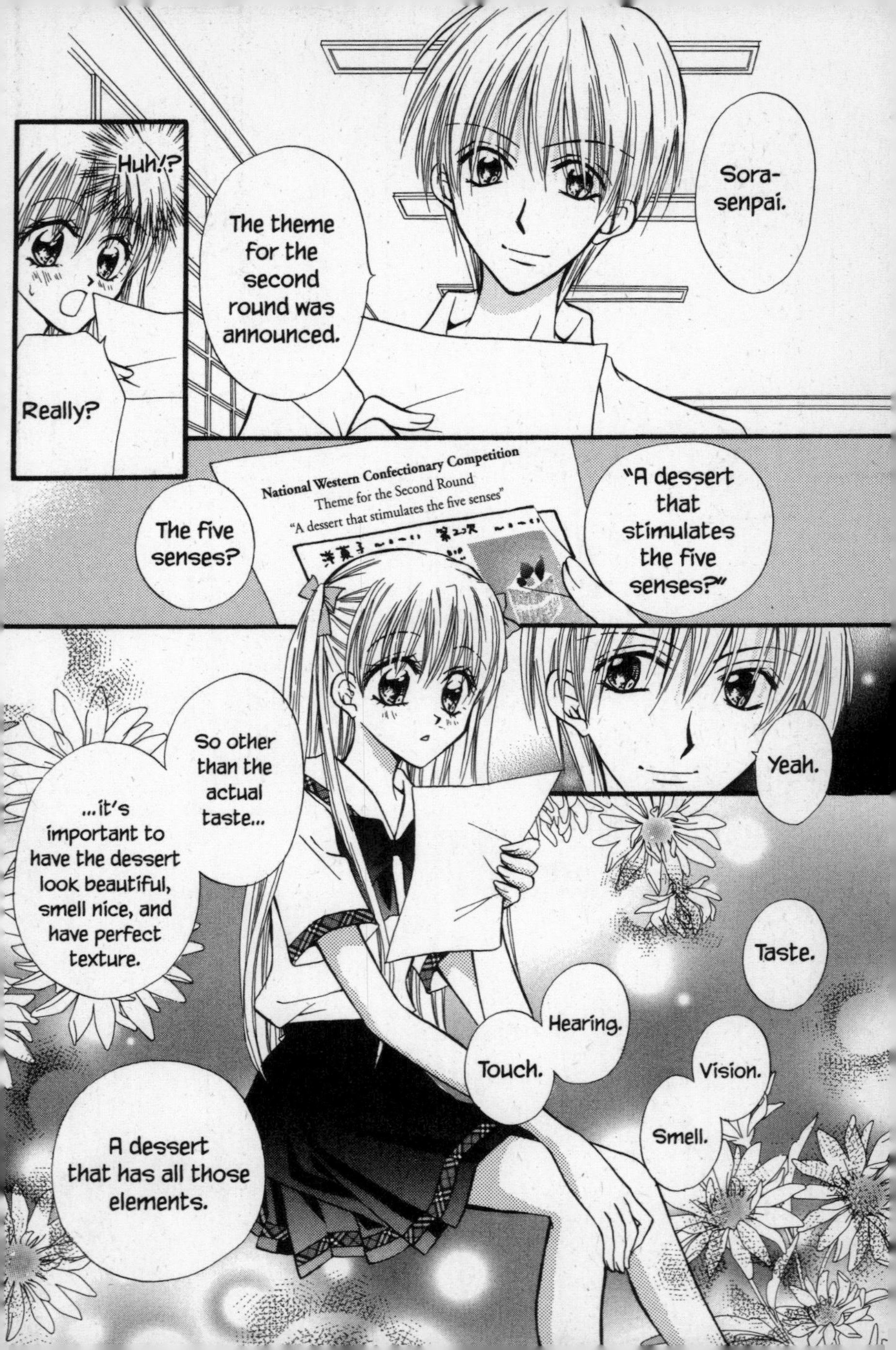

Sora-senpai.
The theme for the second round was announced.
Huh!?
Really?
"A dessert that stimulates the five senses?"
National Western Confectionary Competition
Theme for the Second Round
"A dessert that stimulates the five senses"
The five senses?
Yeah.
So other than the actual taste...
...it's important to have the dessert look beautiful, smell nice, and have perfect texture.
Taste.
Hearing.
Vision.
Touch.
Smell.
A dessert that has all those elements.

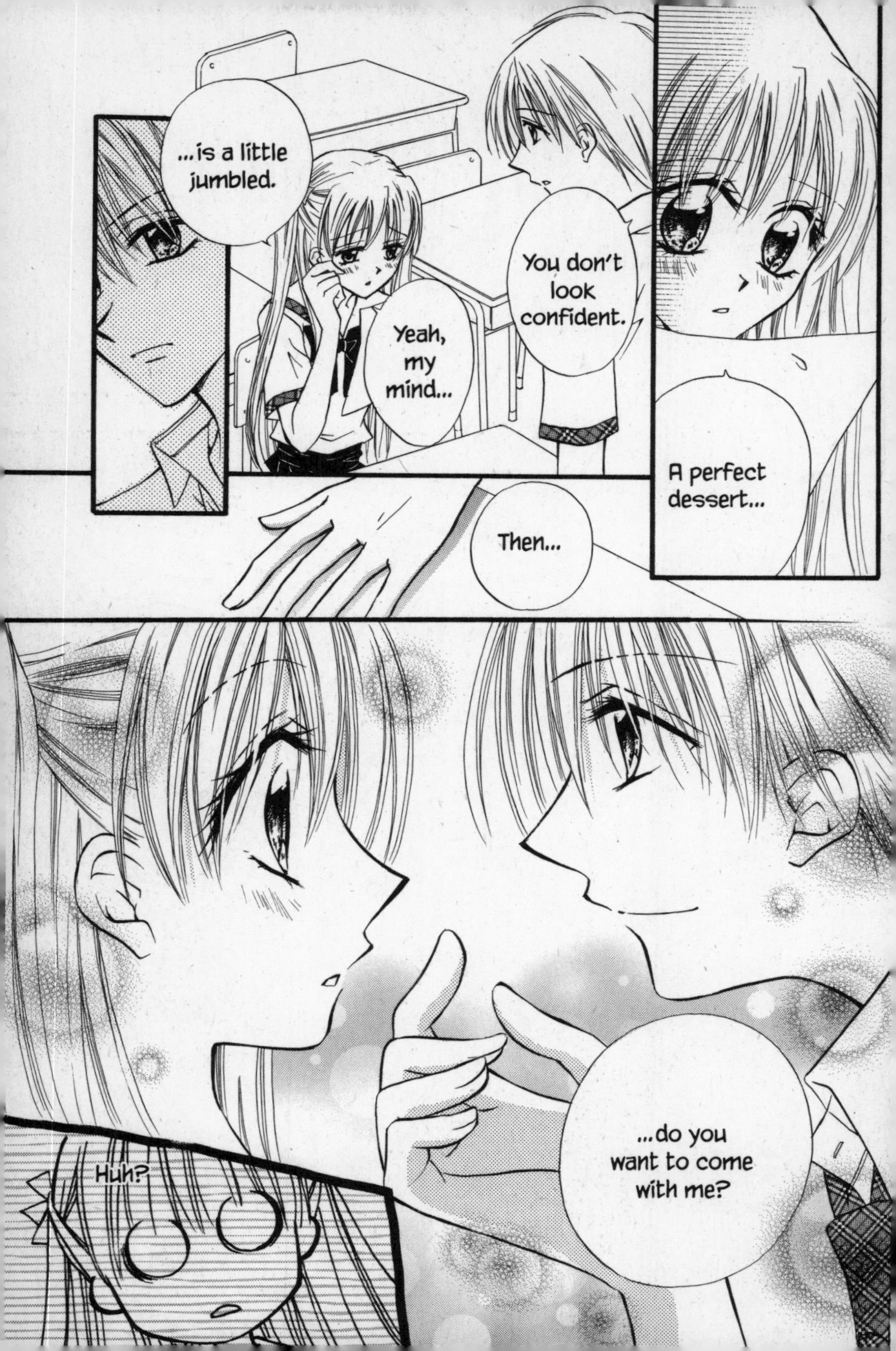

A perfect dessert...
You don't look confident.
Yeah, my mind...
...is a little jumbled.
Then...
...do you want to come with me?
Huh?

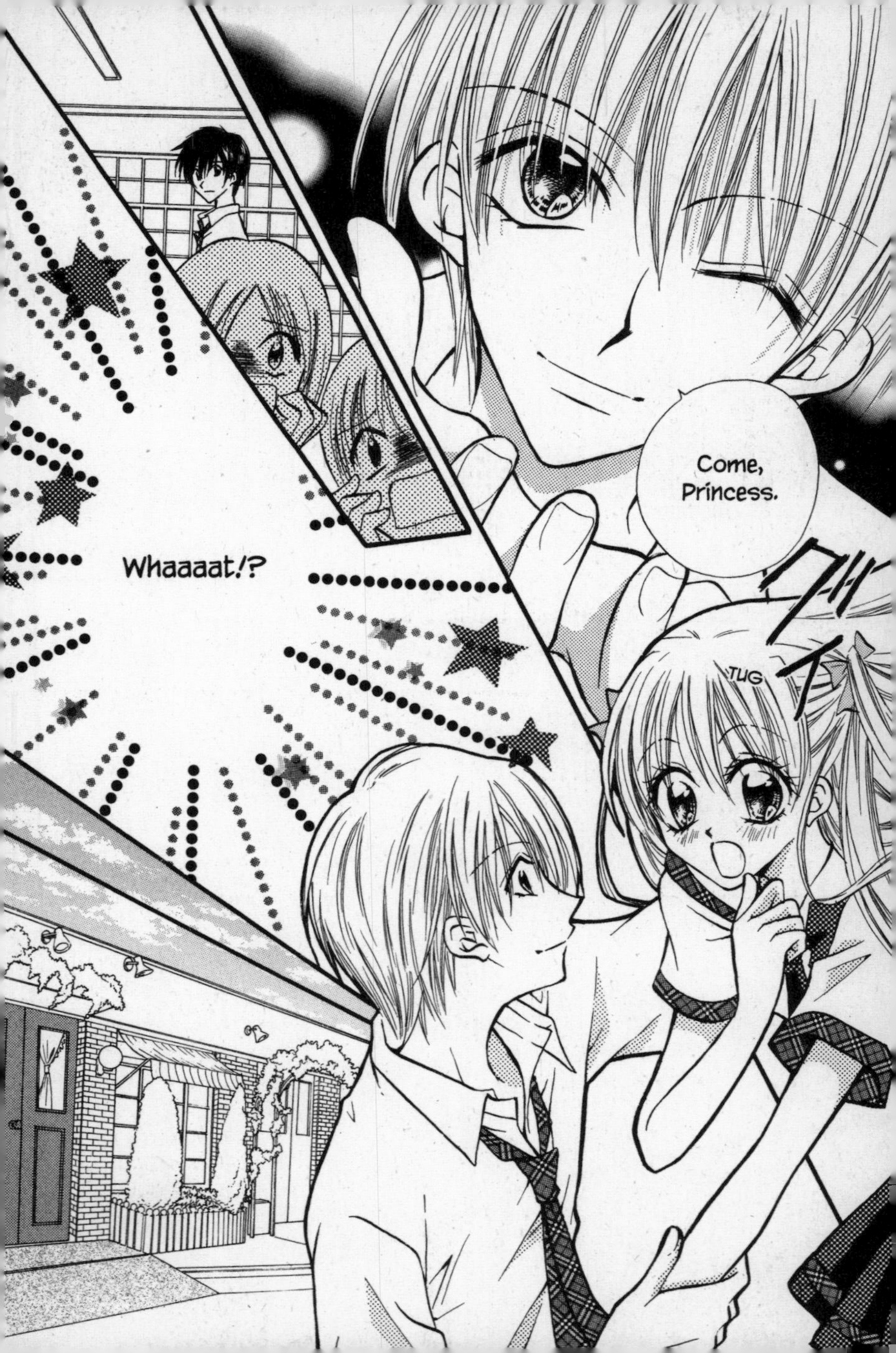
Come, Princess.
TUG
Whaaaat!?

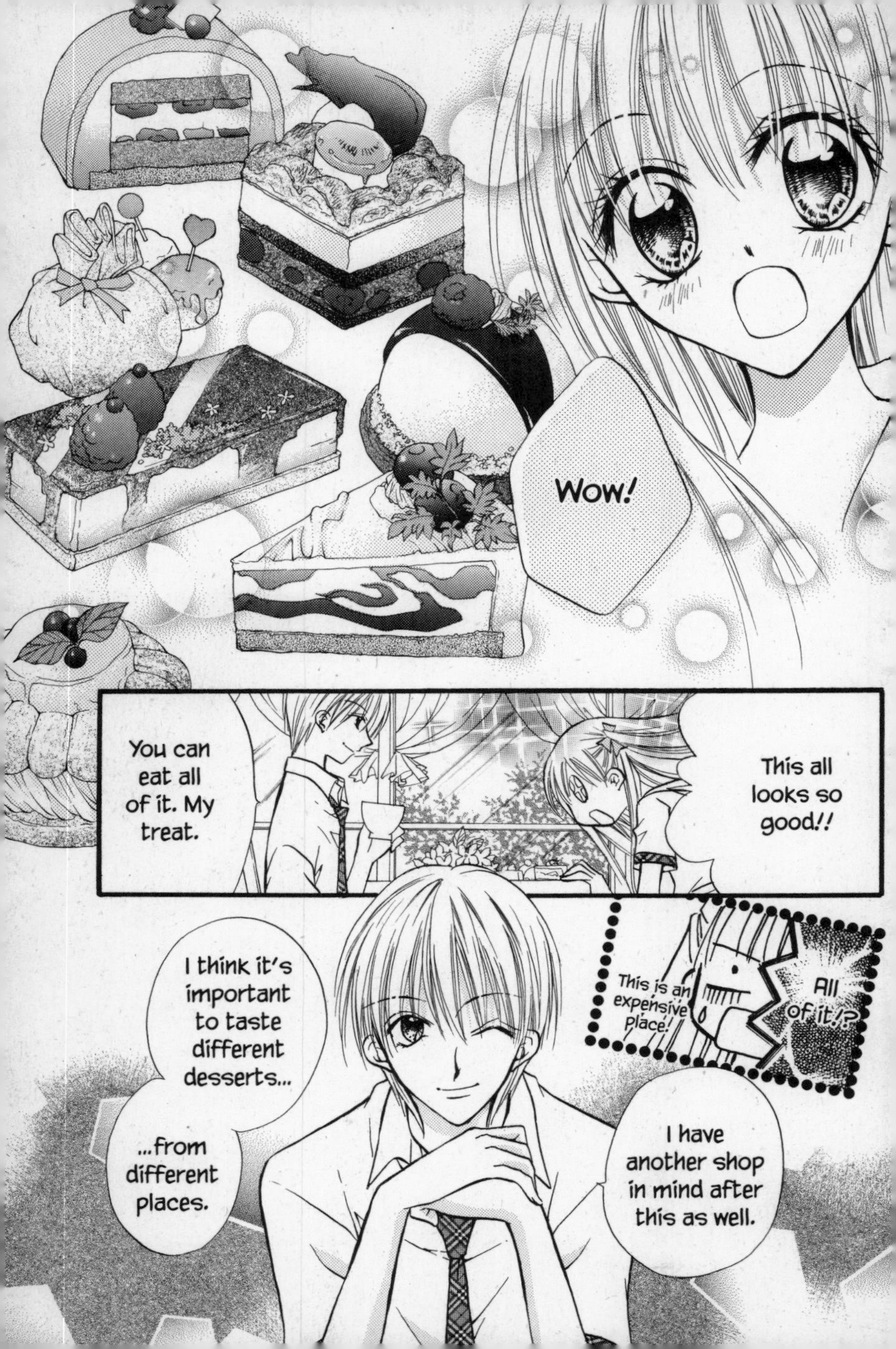
Wow!
This all looks so good!!
You can eat all of it. My treat.
All of it!?
This is an expensive place!
I think it's important to taste different desserts...
...from different places.
I have another shop in mind after this as well.

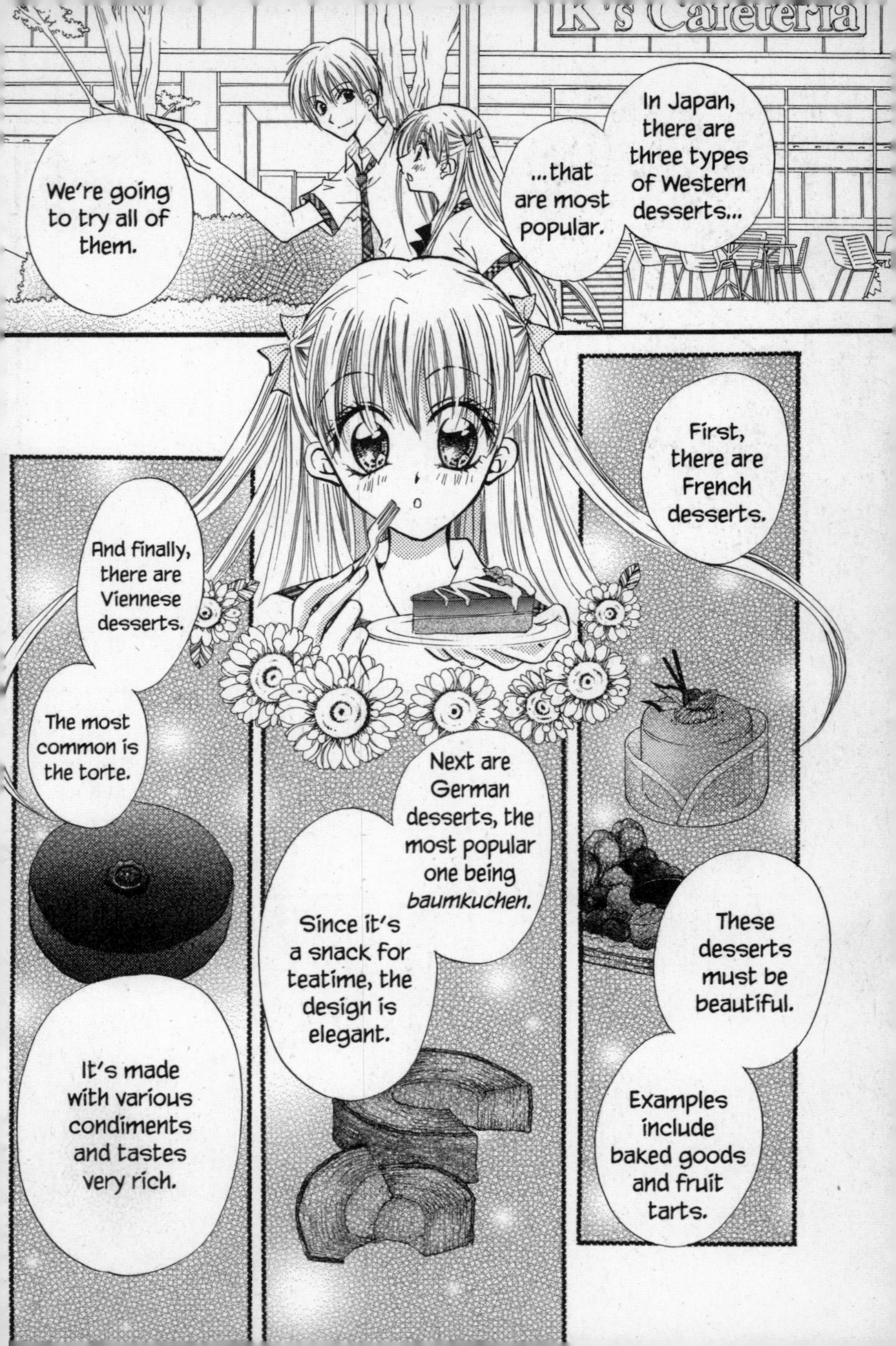
K's Cafeteria
In Japan, there are three types of Western desserts...
...that are most popular.
We're going to try all of them.
First, there are French desserts.
These desserts must be beautiful.
Examples include baked goods and fruit tarts.
Next are German desserts, the most popular one being *baumkuchen.*
Since it's a snack for teatime, the design is elegant.
And finally, there are Viennese desserts.
The most common is the torte.
It's made with various condiments and tastes very rich.

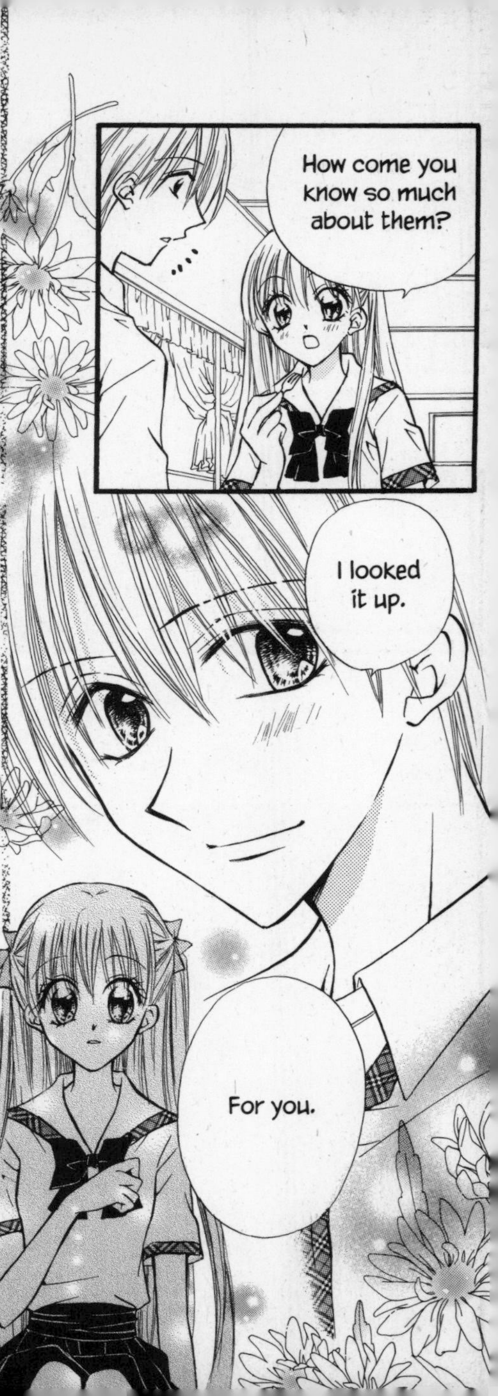
How come you know so much about them?
...
I looked it up.
For you.

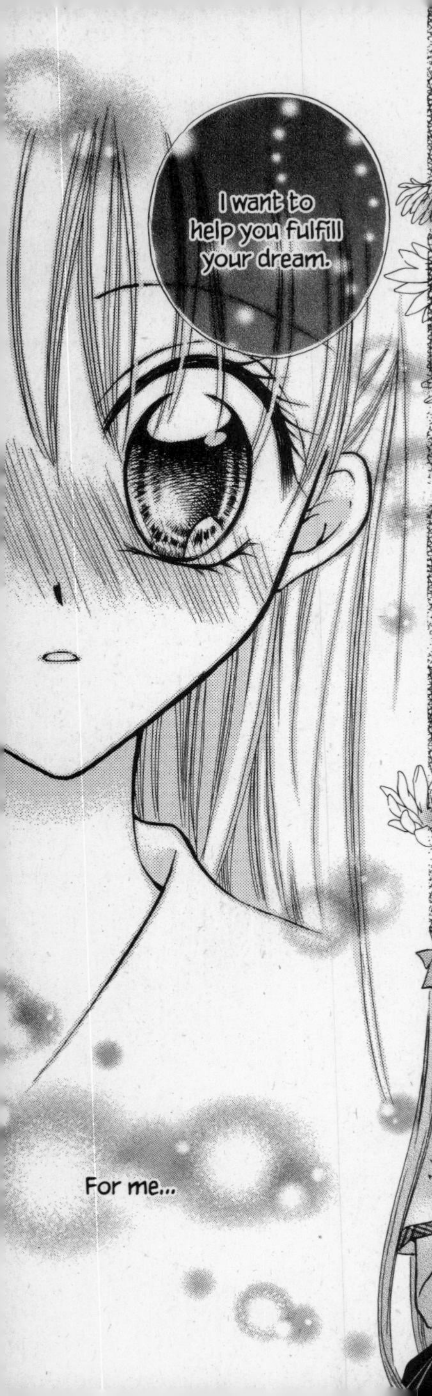
I want to help you fulfill your dream.
For me...

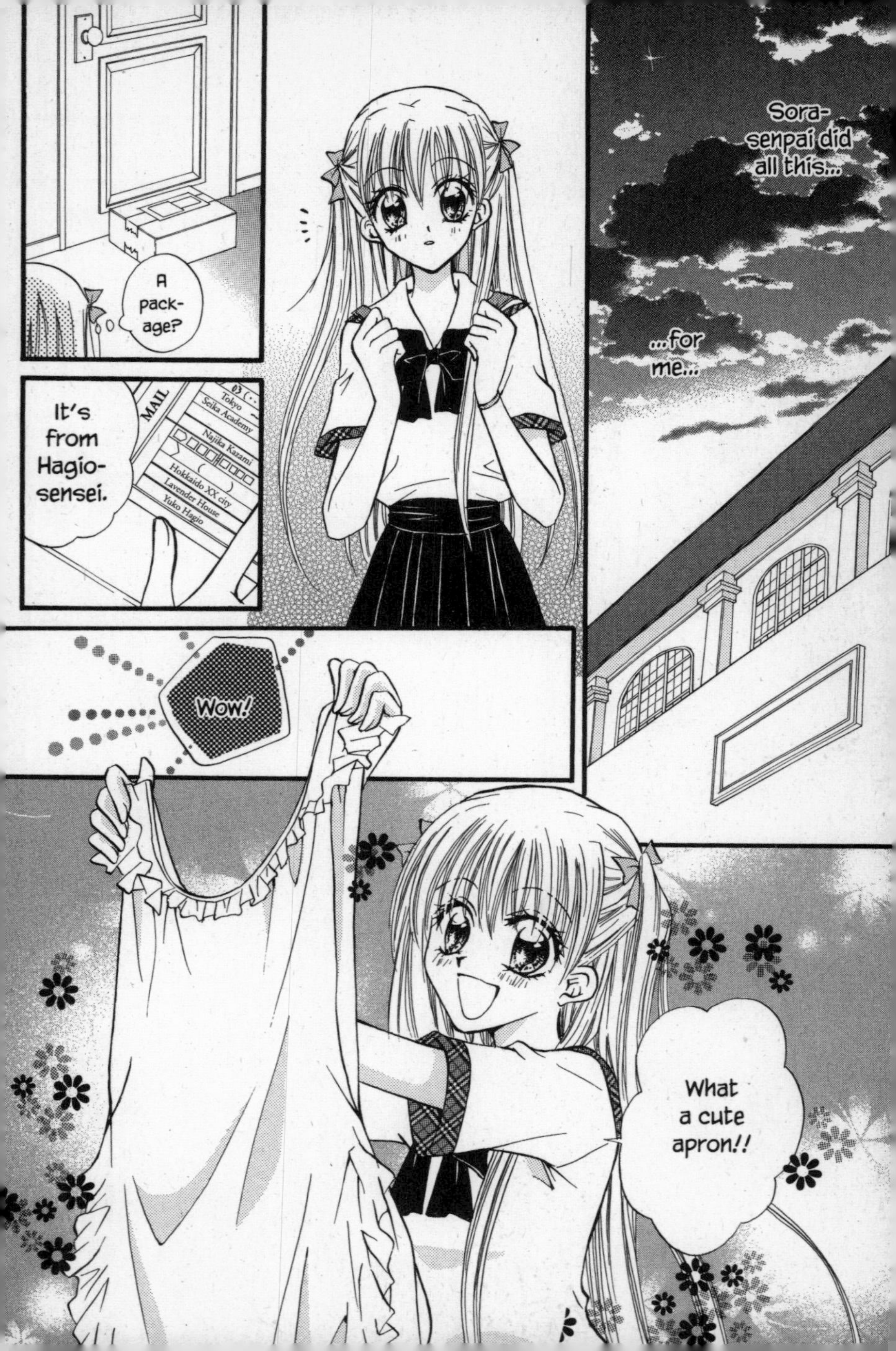
Sora-senpai did all this...
...for me...
A package?
It's from Hagio-sensei.
MAIL
Tokyo
Seika Academy
Najika Kazami
Hokkaido XX city
Lavender House
Yuko Hagio
Wow!
What a cute apron!!

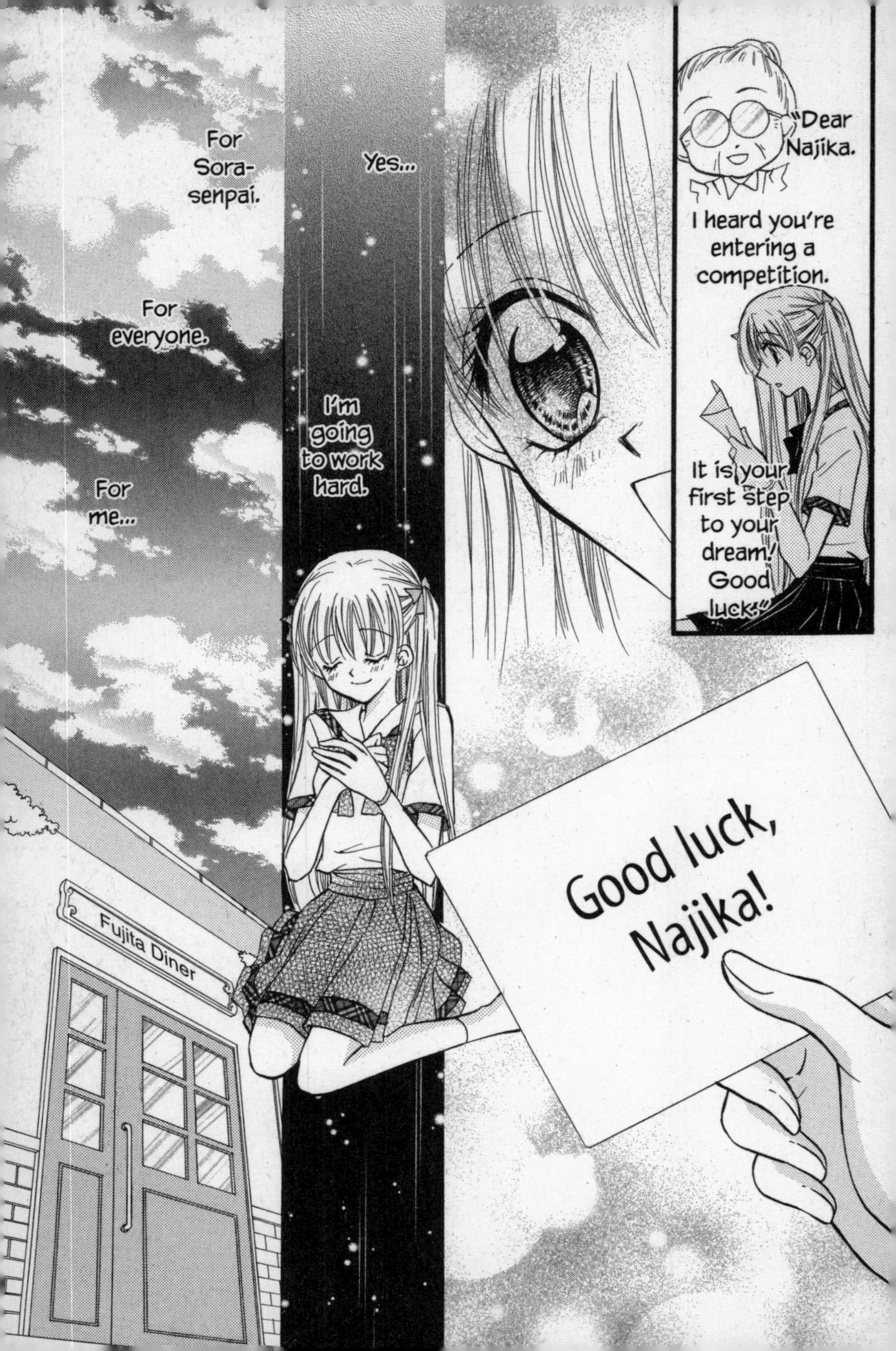
"Dear Najika.
I heard you're entering a competition.
It is your first step to your dream! Good luck."
Good luck, Najika!
Yes...
I'm going to work hard.
For Sora-senpai.
For everyone.
For me...
Fujita Diner

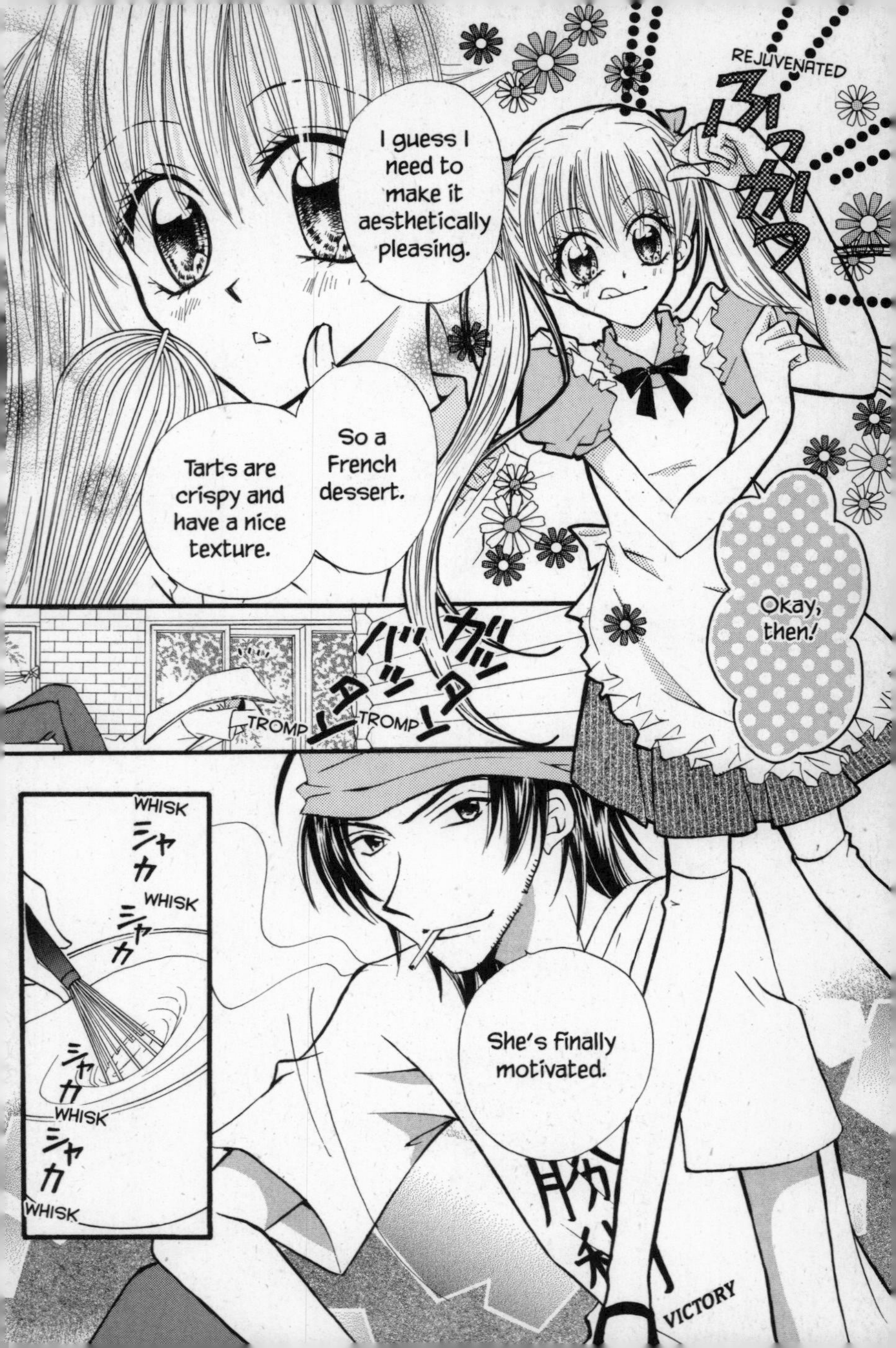

REJUVENATED
I guess I need to make it aesthetically pleasing.
So a French dessert.
Tarts are crispy and have a nice texture.
Okay, then!
TROMP
TROMP
She's finally motivated.
VICTORY
WHISK
WHISK
WHISK
WHISK

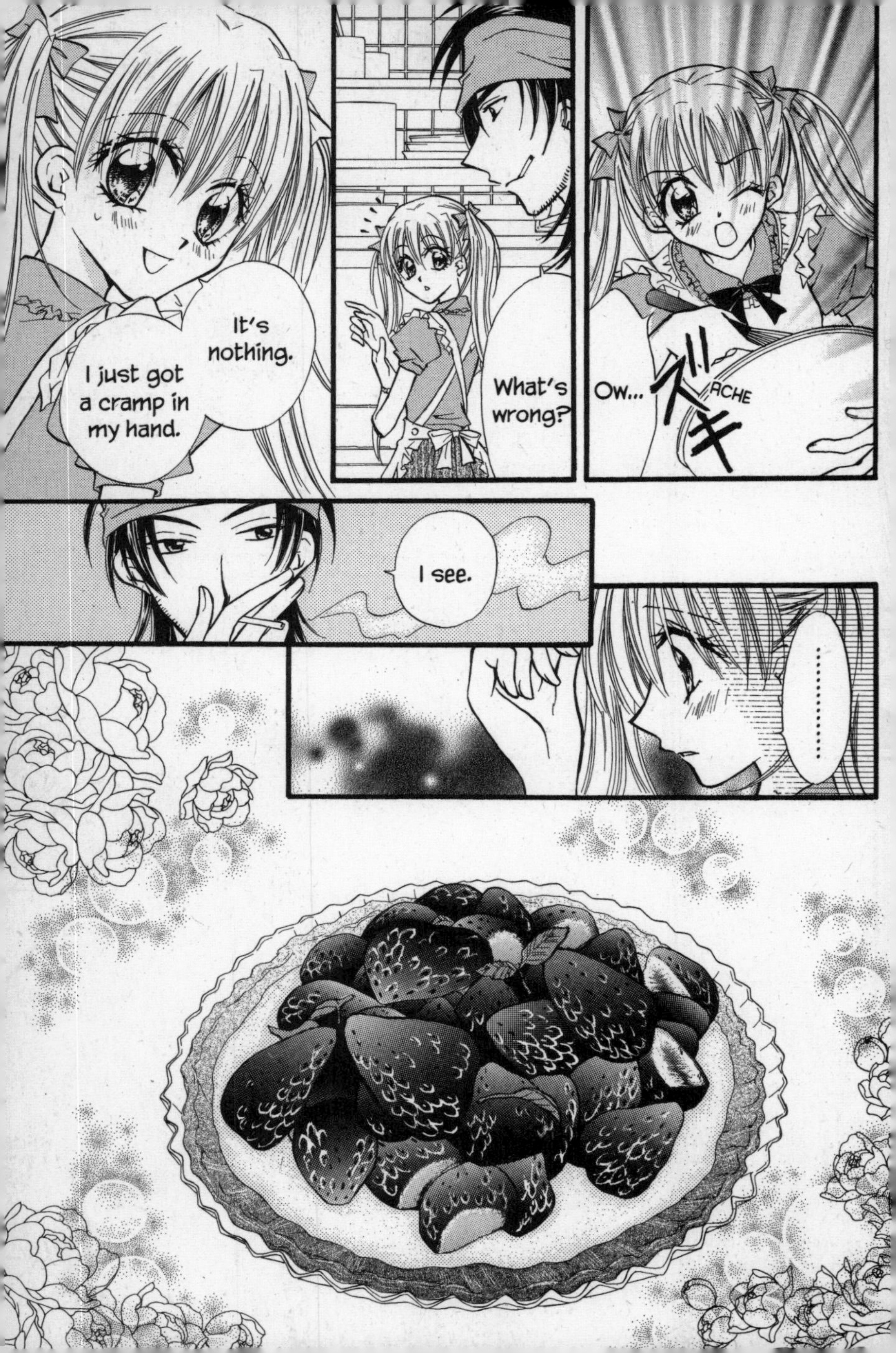

Ow...
ズキ
ACHE
What's wrong?
It's nothing.
I just got a cramp in my hand.
I see.
......

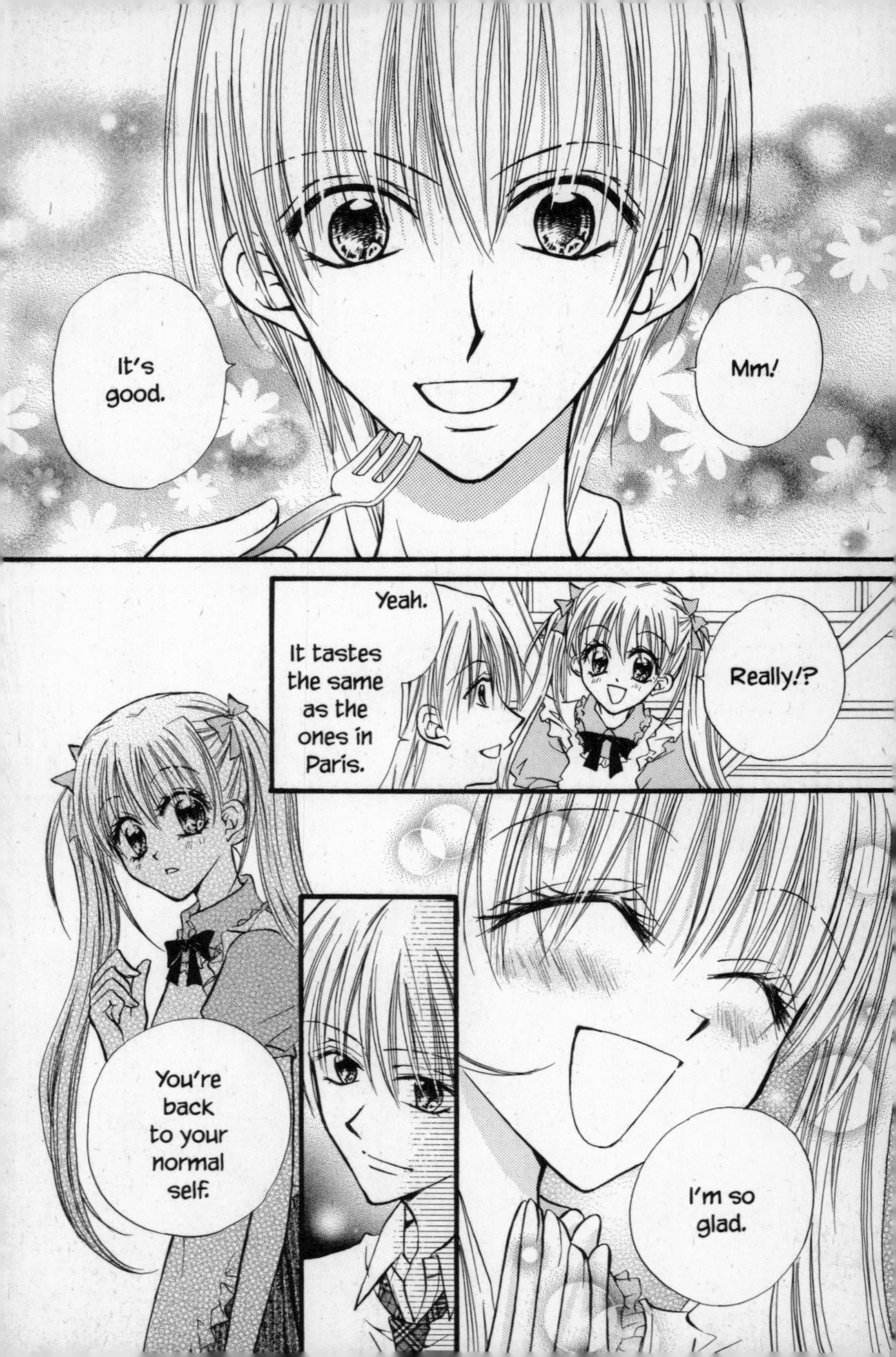
Mm!
It's good.
Really!?
Yeah.
It tastes the same as the ones in Paris.
I'm so glad.
You're back to your normal self.

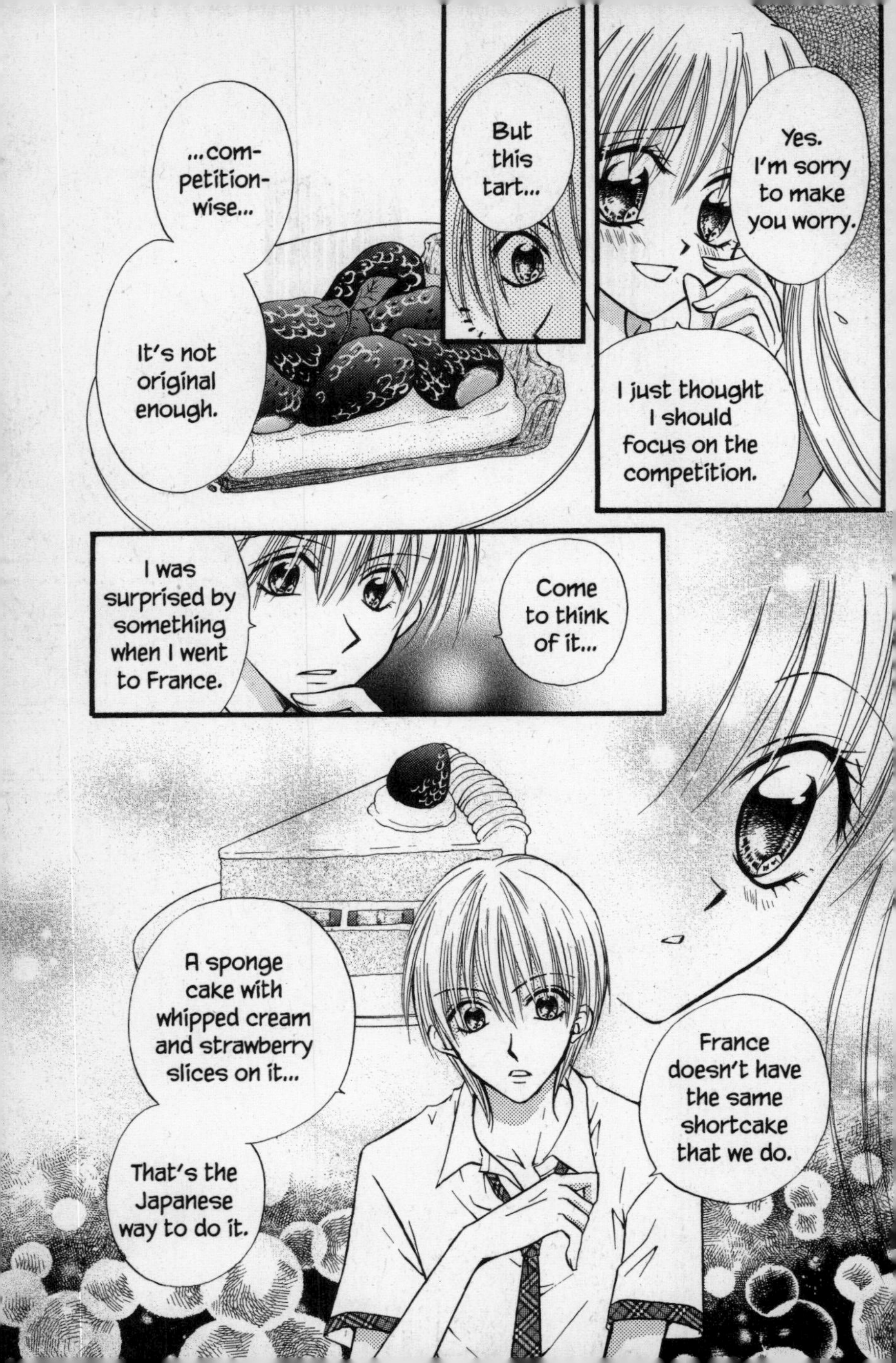

Yes. I'm sorry to make you worry.
I just thought I should focus on the competition.
But this tart...
...com- petition- wise...
It's not original enough.
Come to think of it...
I was surprised by something when I went to France.
France doesn't have the same shortcake that we do.
A sponge cake with whipped cream and strawberry slices on it...
That's the Japanese way to do it.

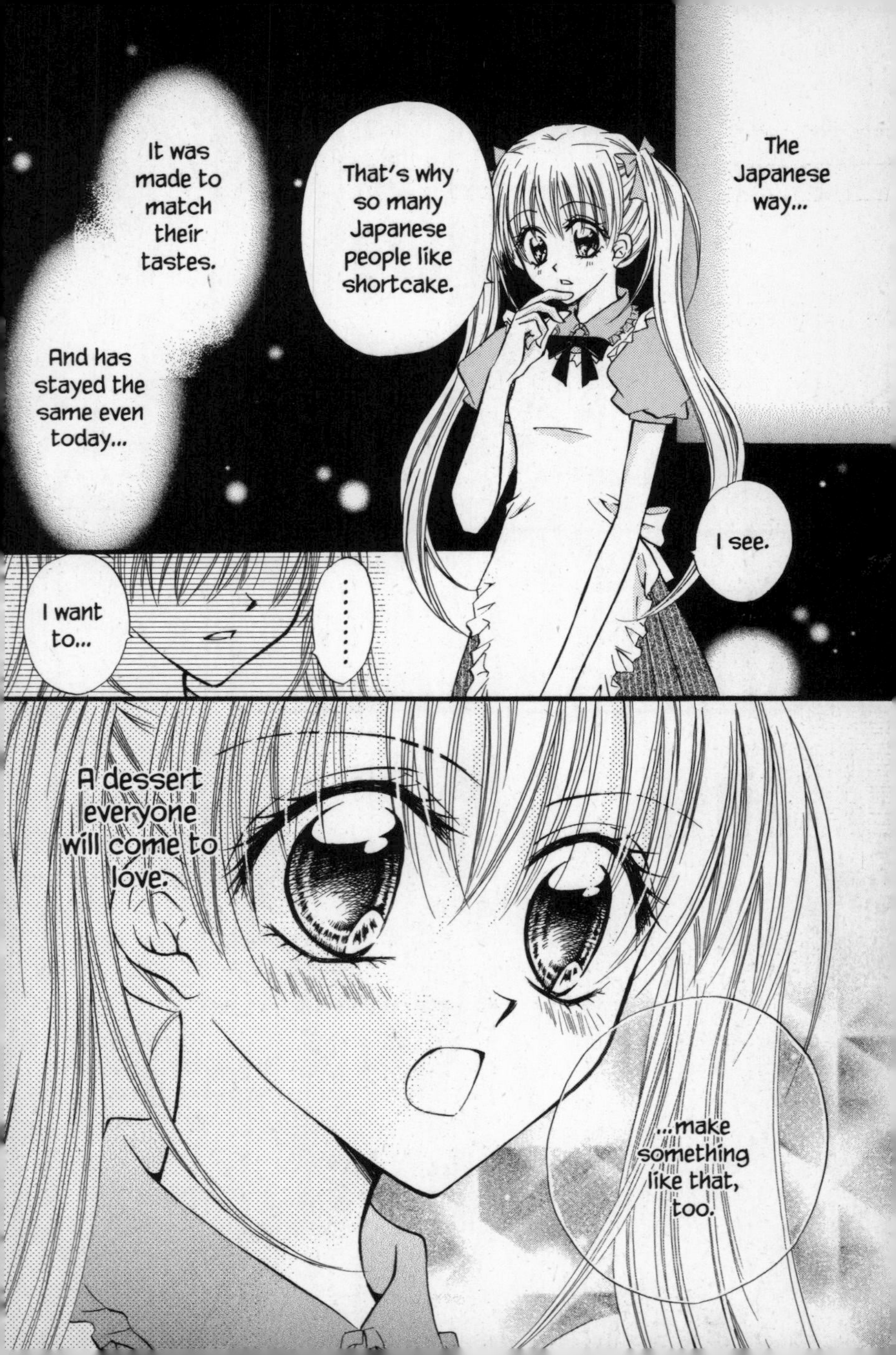

The Japanese way...
That's why so many Japanese people like shortcake.
It was made to match their tastes.
And has stayed the same even today...
I see.
......
I want to...
...make something like that, too.
A dessert everyone will come to love.

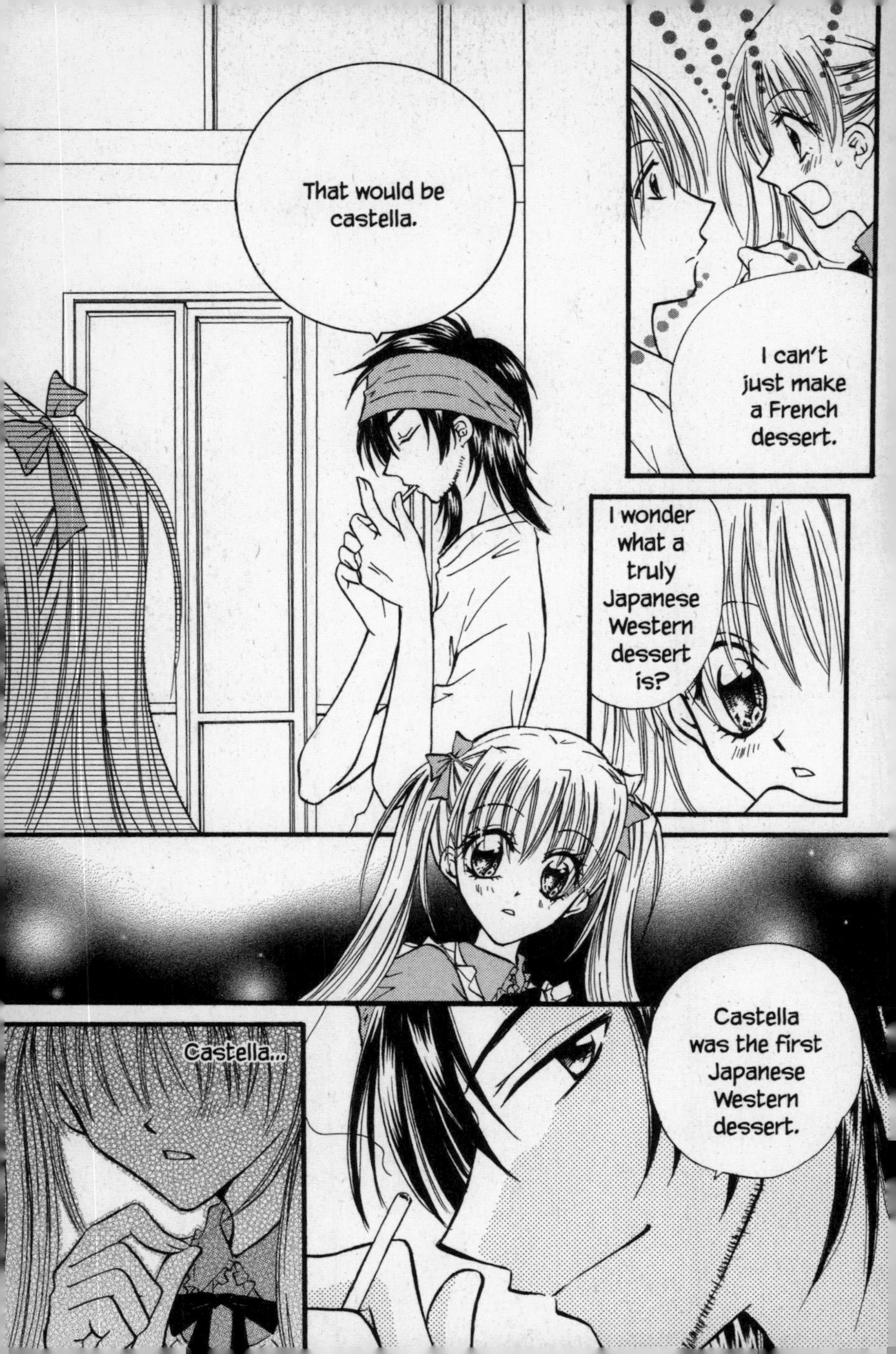
I can't just make a French dessert.
I wonder what a truly Japanese Western dessert is?
That would be castella.
Castella was the first Japanese Western dessert.
Castella...

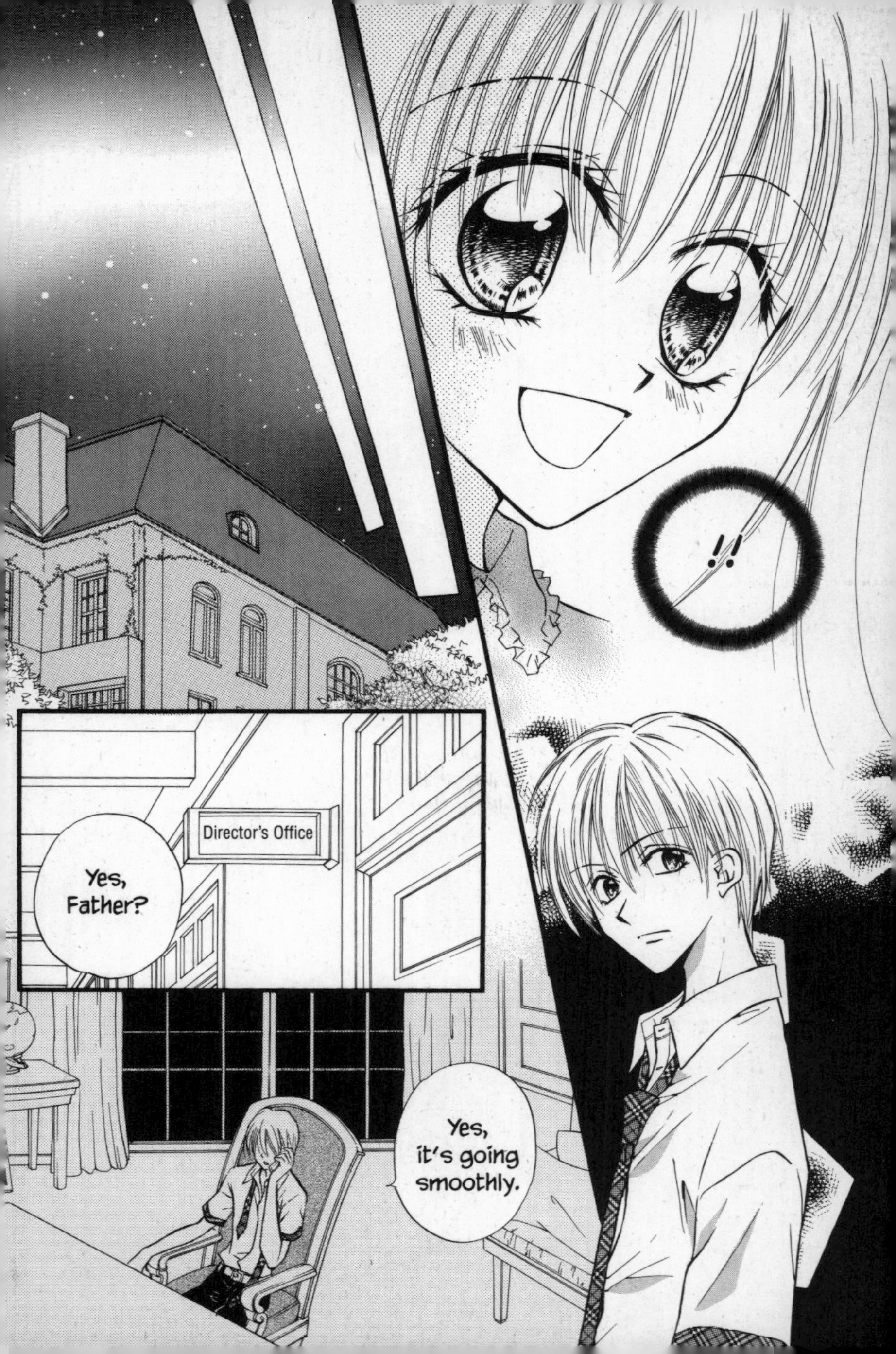
!!
Director's Office
Yes, Father?
Yes, it's going smoothly.

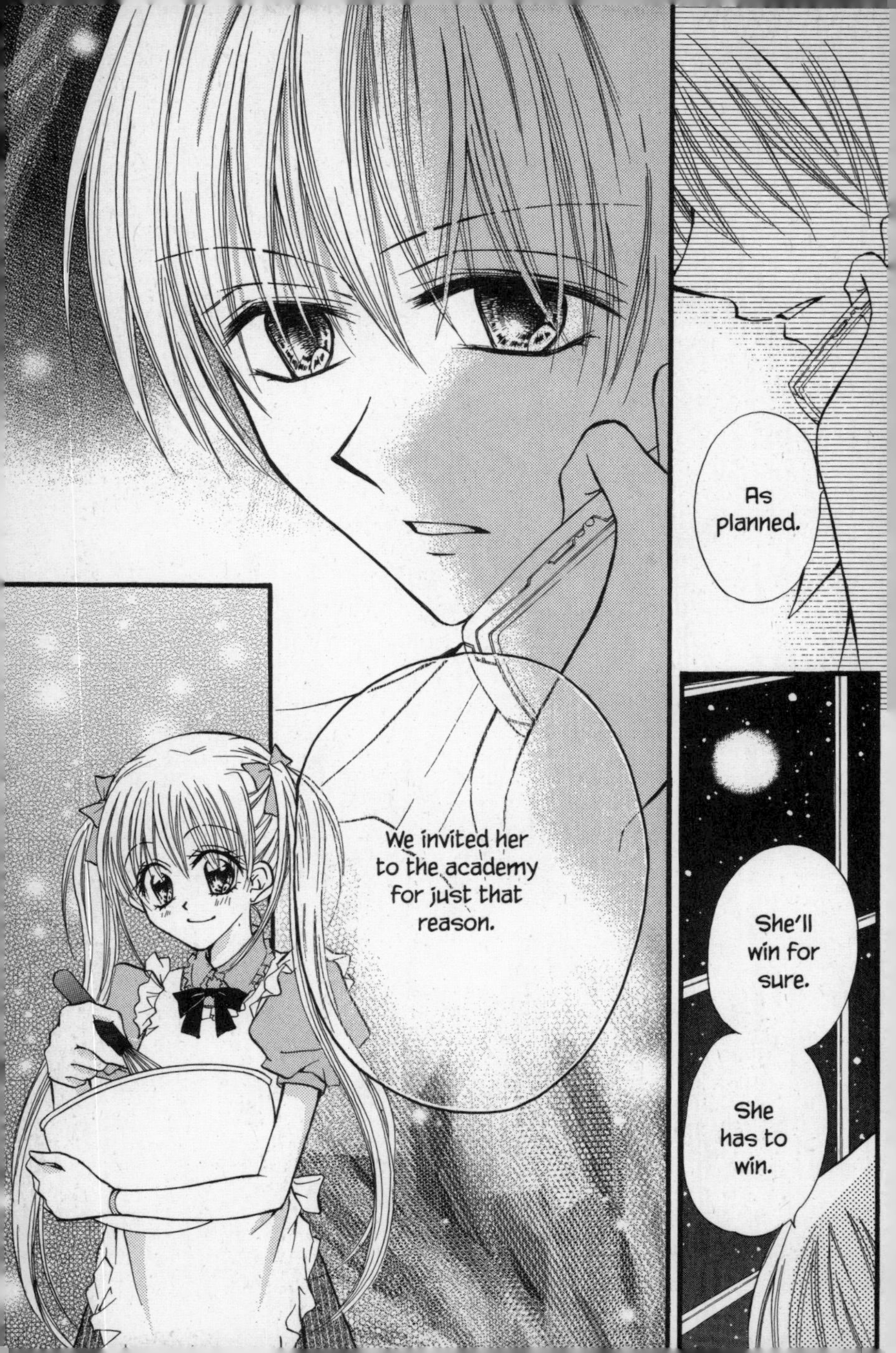
As planned.
She'll win for sure.
She has to win.
We invited her to the academy for just that reason.

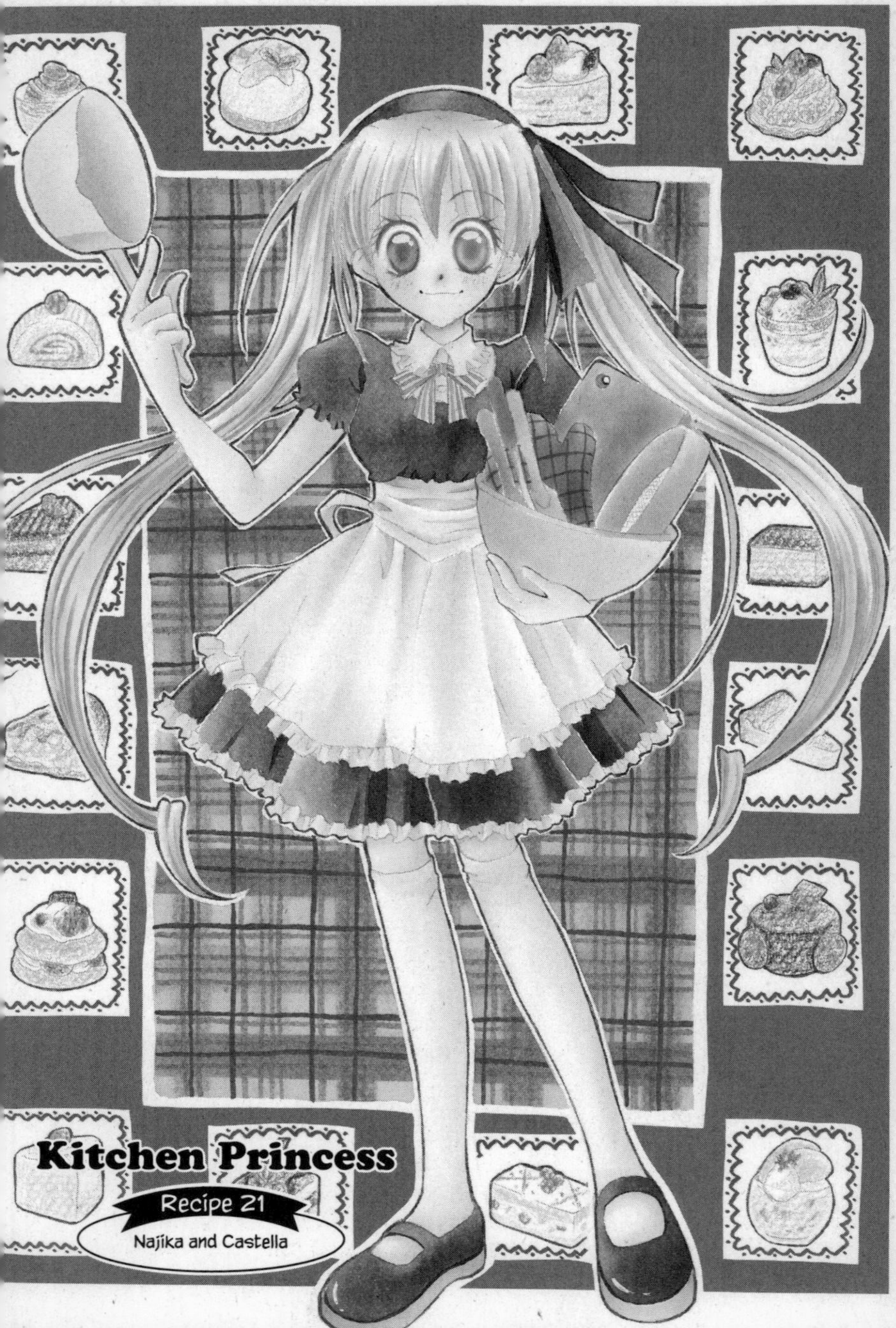
Kitchen Princess
Recipe 21
Najika and Castella

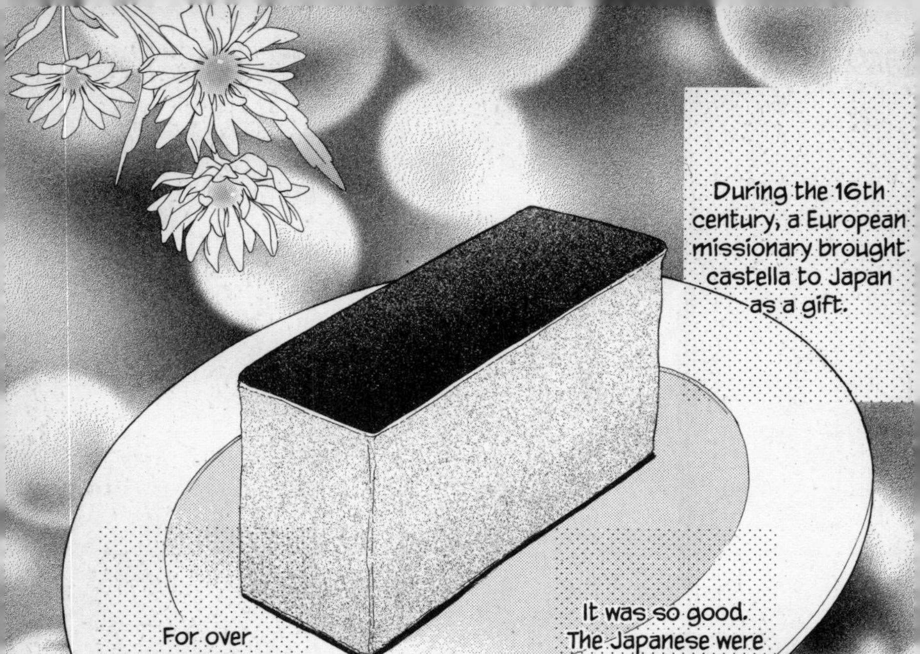
During the 16th century, a European missionary brought castella to Japan as a gift.
It was so good. The Japanese were surprised and warmly welcomed the missionary.
For over 400 years, castella has been loved by the Japanese.

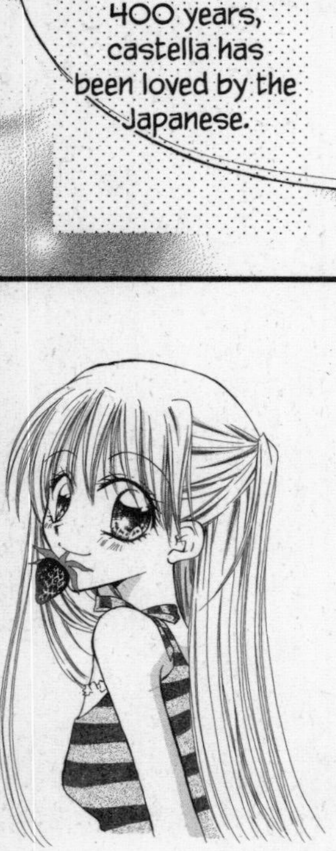

About Recipe 21's Splash Page

For this page, I didn't trace over the pencil art with a pen like I usually would. Instead, I colored over the pencils with markers. As it turned out, the pencil art blended in with the markers, and the skin color looked dull. But I actually liked it because it came out soft-looking. I would like to do it again!! I also colored the cakes on the border using colored pencils. I used pastels for the checkered pattern in the background, but it was such a hassle. I almost gave up so many times...phew.

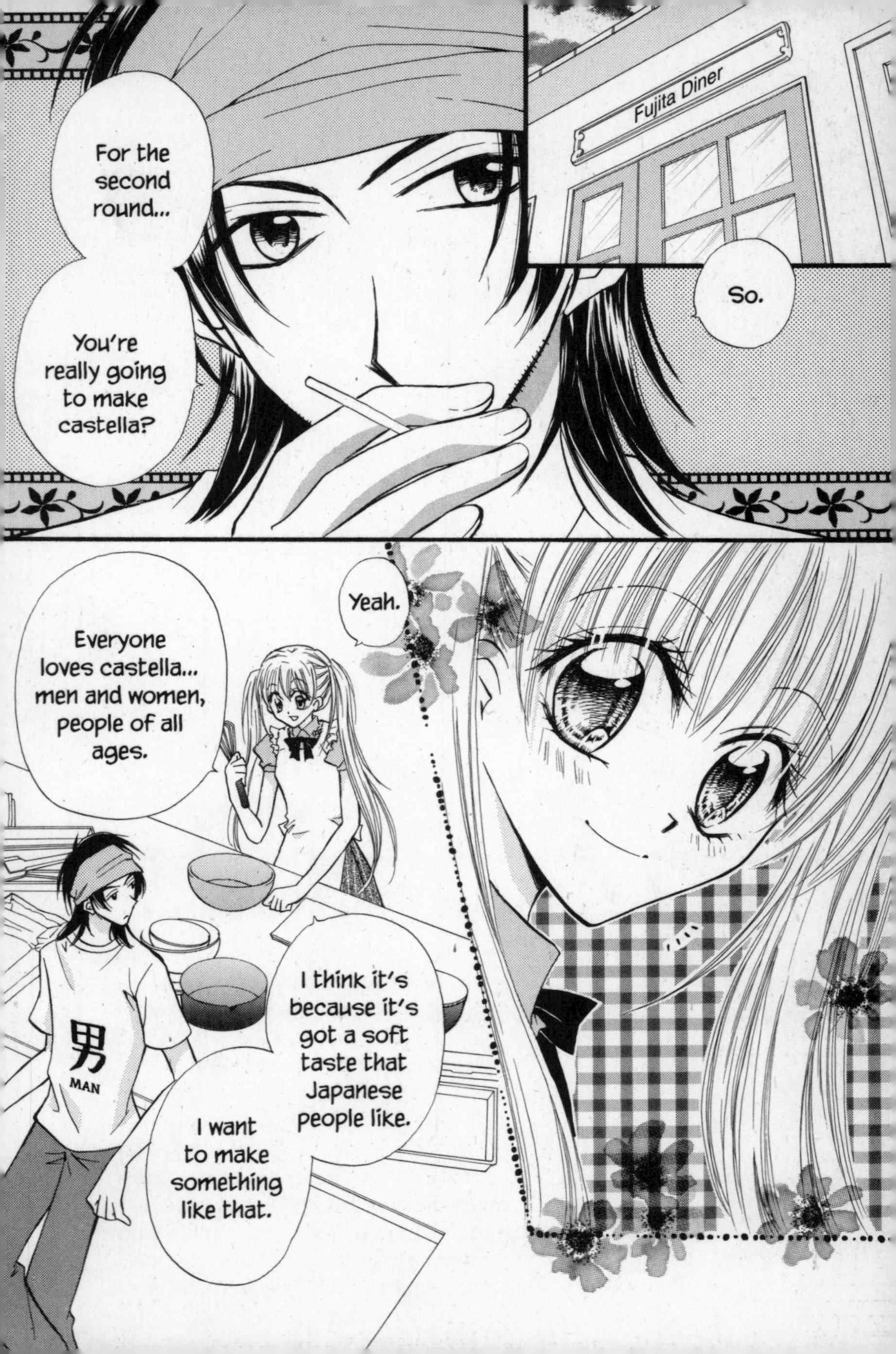

Fujita Diner
So.
For the second round...
You're really going to make castella?
Yeah.
Everyone loves castella... men and women, people of all ages.
I think it's because it's got a soft taste that Japanese people like.
I want to make something like that.
男
MAN

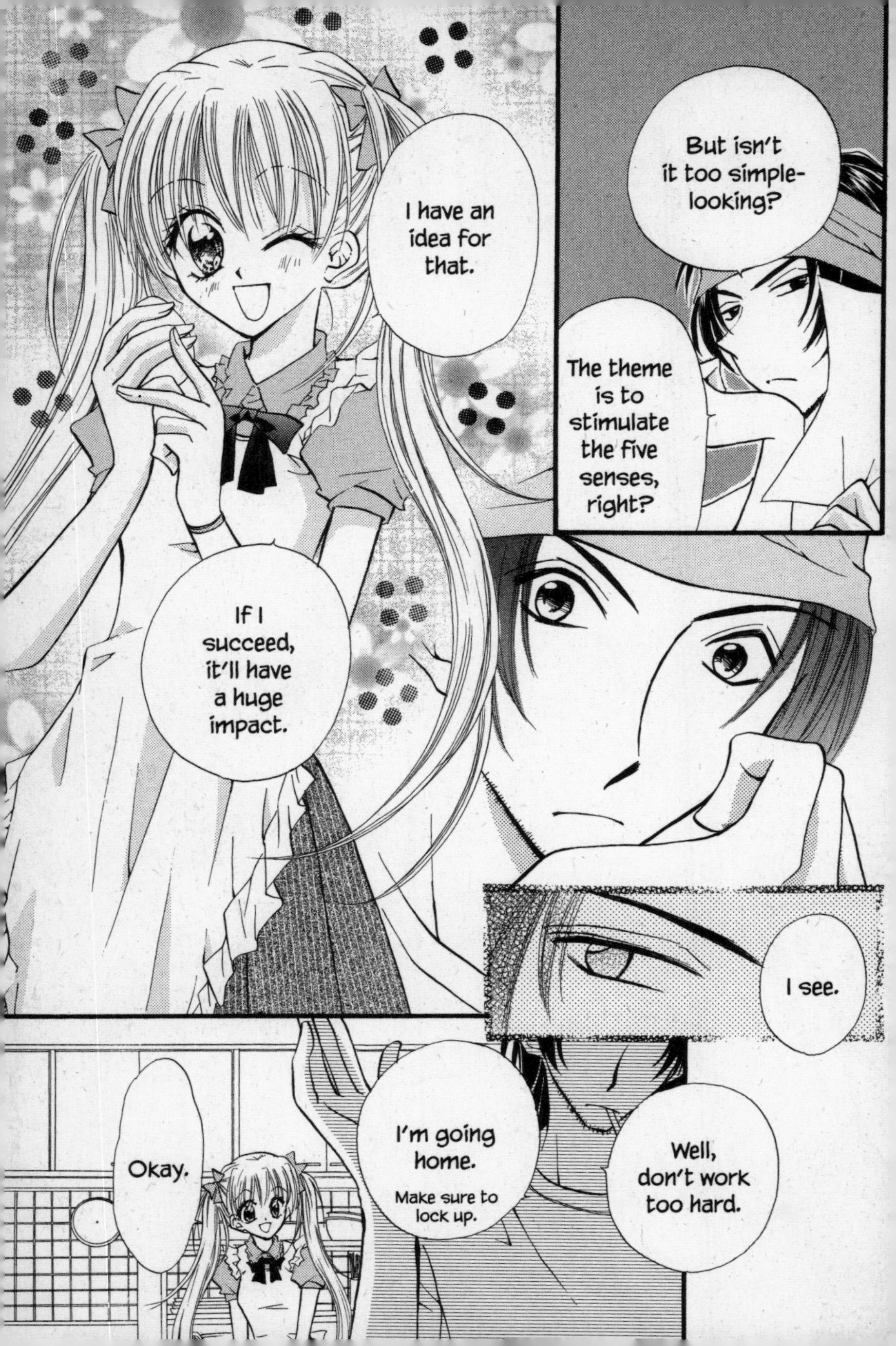

But isn't it too simple-looking?
The theme is to stimulate the five senses, right?
I have an idea for that.
If I succeed, it'll have a huge impact.
I see.
Well, don't work too hard.
I'm going home.
Make sure to lock up.
Okay.

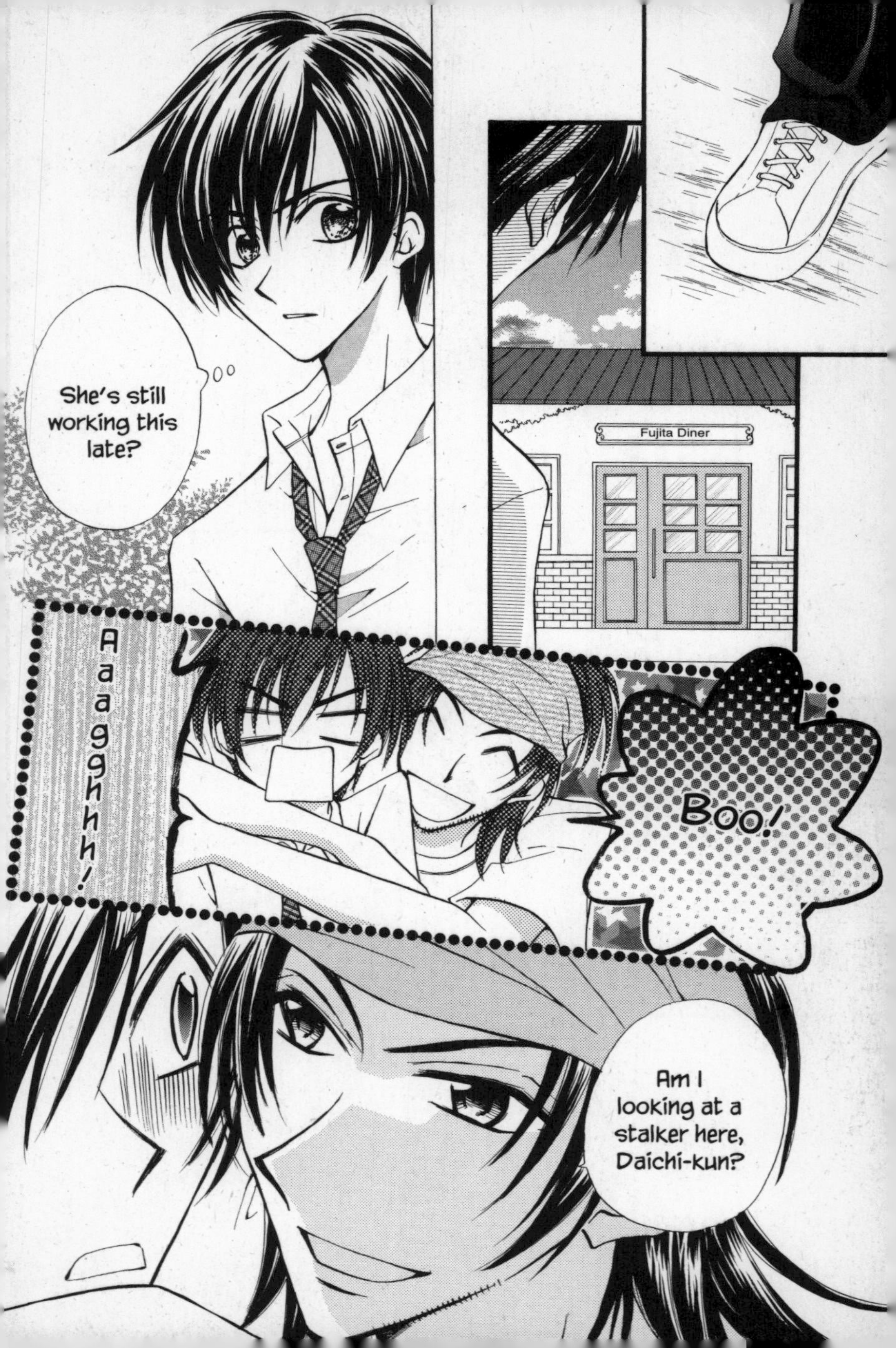
Fujita Diner
She's still working this late?
Boo!
Aaagghhh!
Am I looking at a stalker here, Daichi-kun?

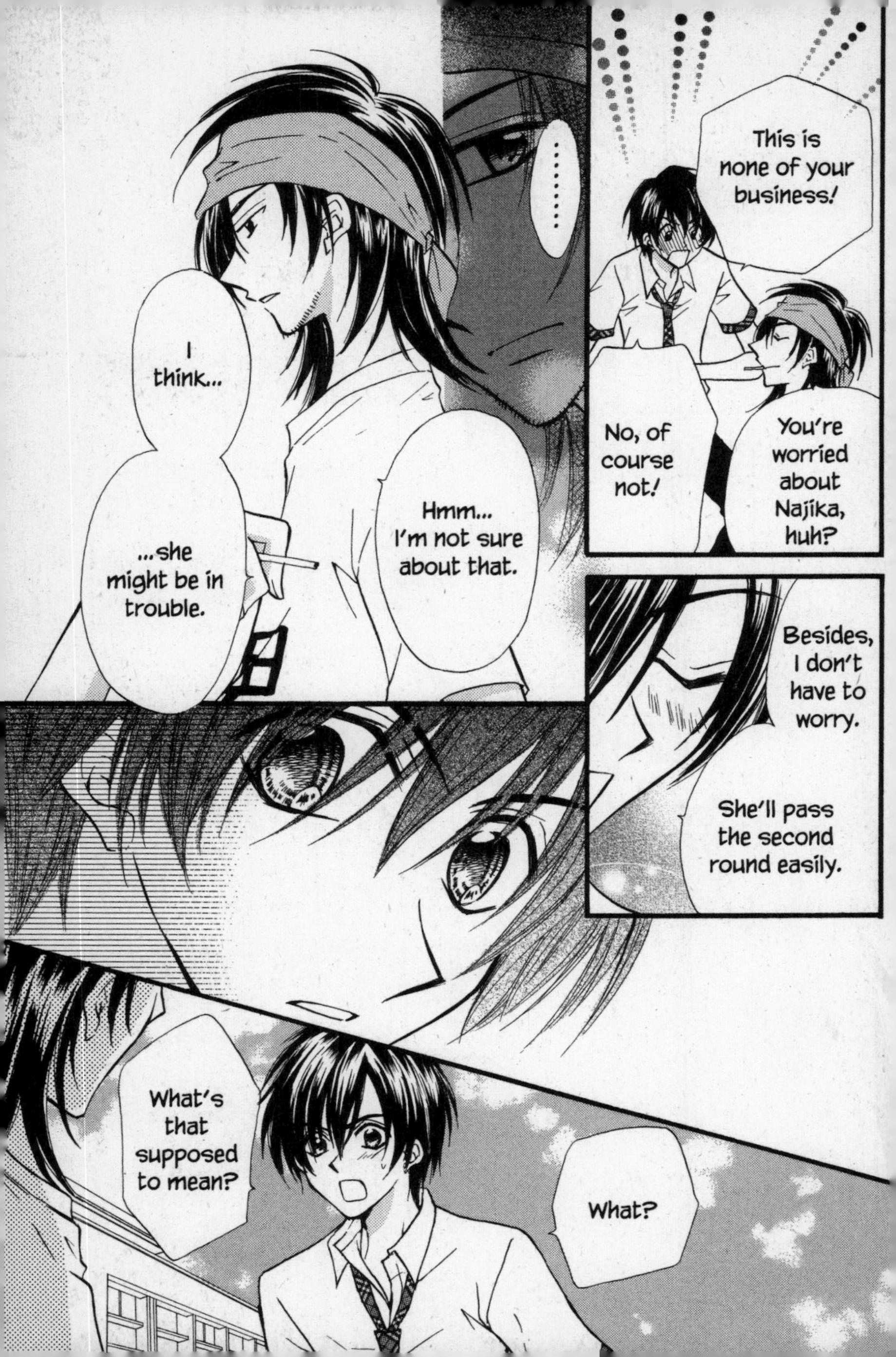
This is none of your business!
You're worried about Najika, huh?
No, of course not!
Besides, I don't have to worry.
She'll pass the second round easily.
......
Hmm... I'm not sure about that.
I think...
...she might be in trouble.
What?
What's that supposed to mean?

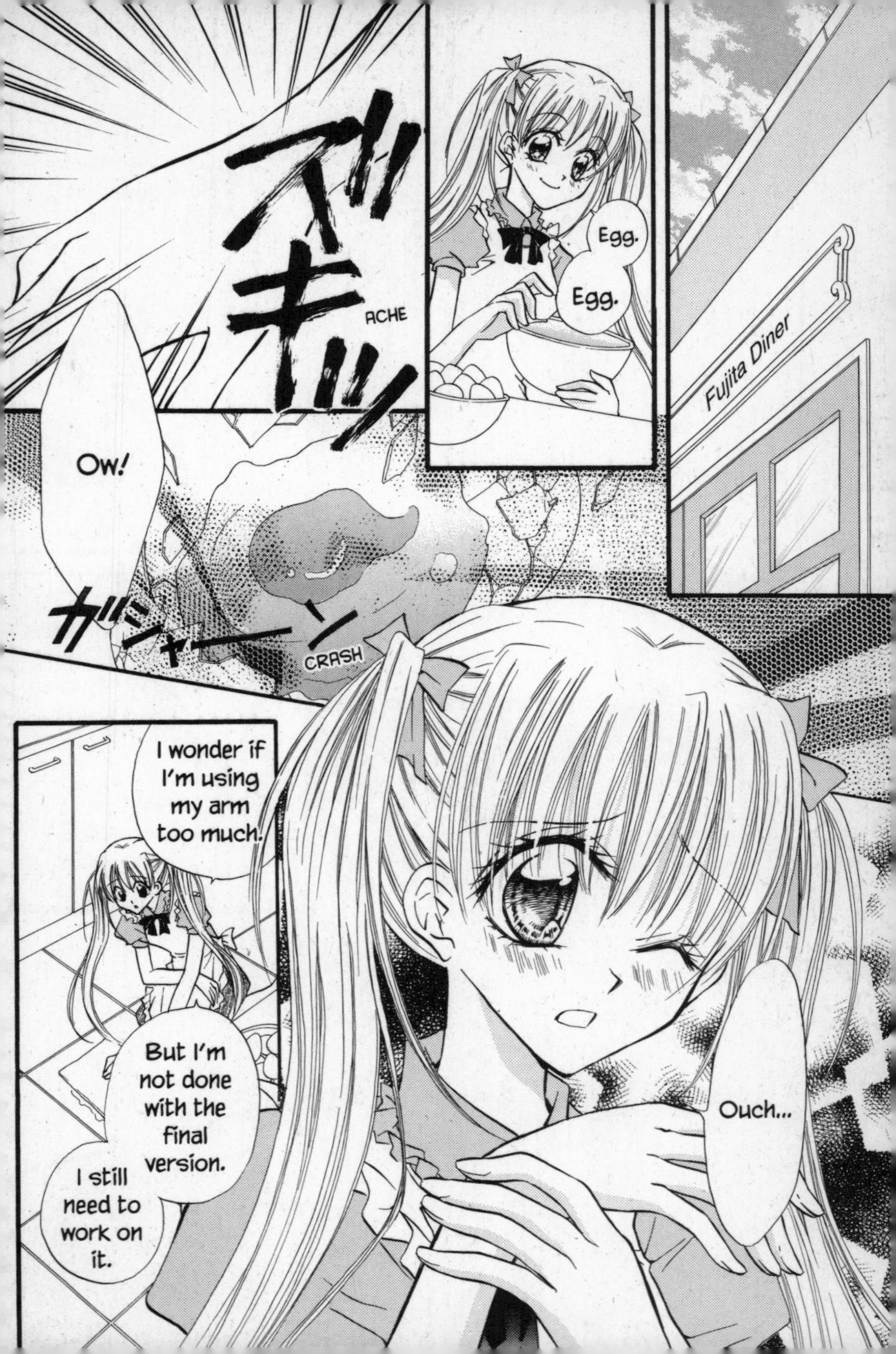
Fujita Diner
Egg.
Egg.
ACHE
Ow!
CRASH
Ouch...
I wonder if I'm using my arm too much.
But I'm not done with the final version.
I still need to work on it.

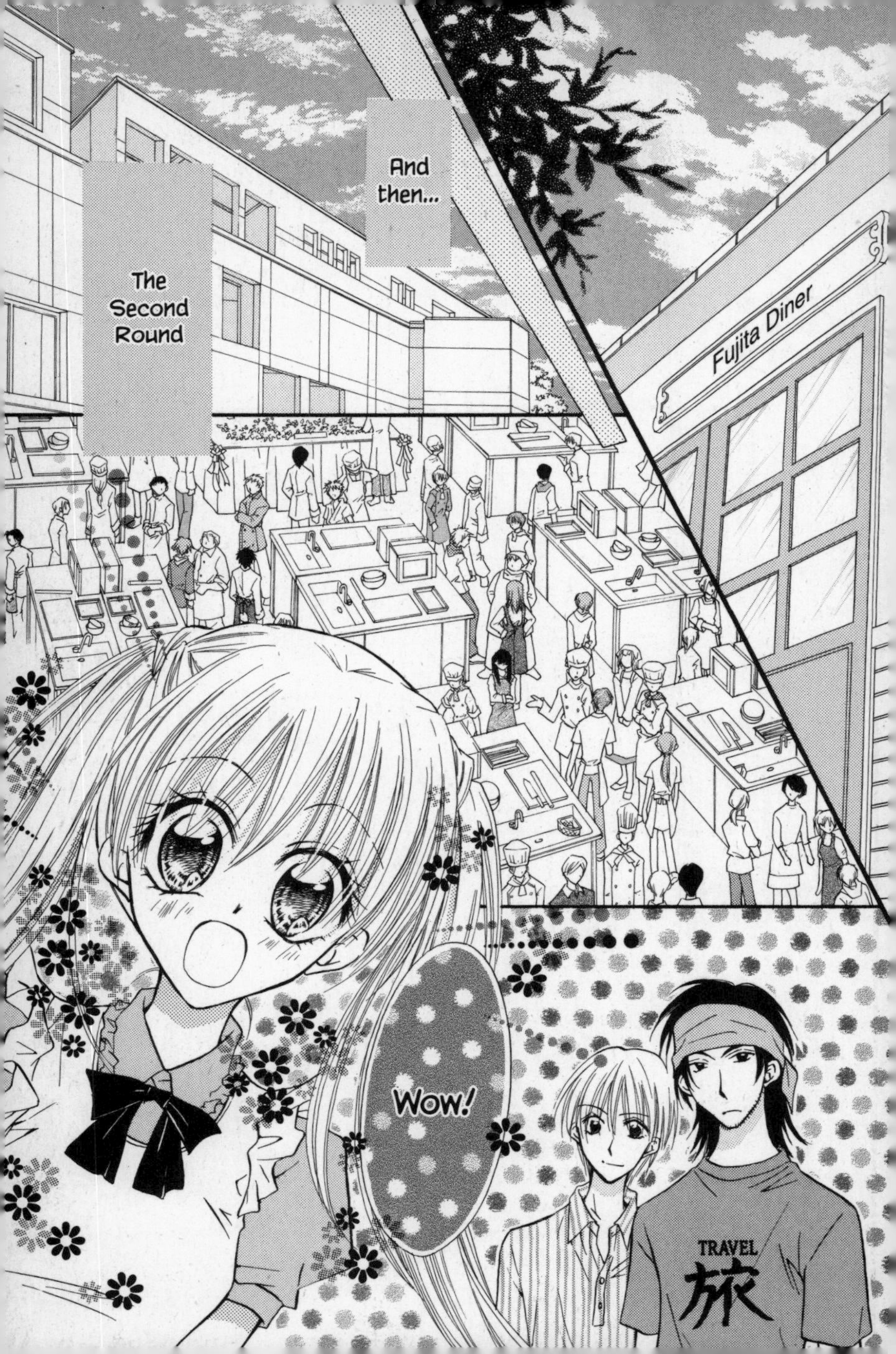
Fujita Diner
And then...
The Second Round
TRAVEL 旅
Wow!

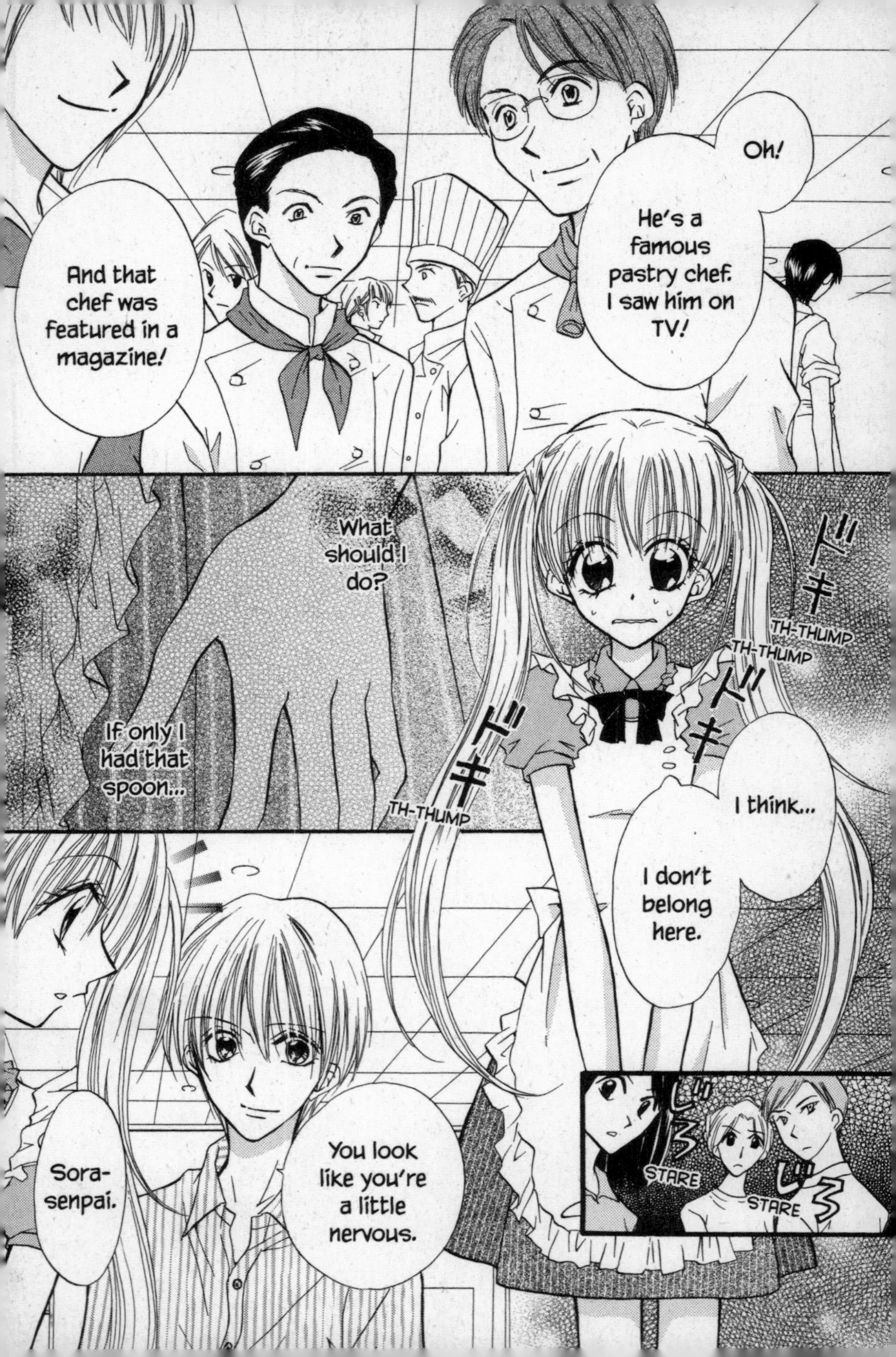
Oh!
He's a famous pastry chef. I saw him on TV!
And that chef was featured in a magazine!
TH-THUMP
TH-THUMP
TH-THUMP
I think...
I don't belong here.
STARE
STARE
What should I do?
If only I had that spoon...
You look like you're a little nervous.
Sora-senpai.

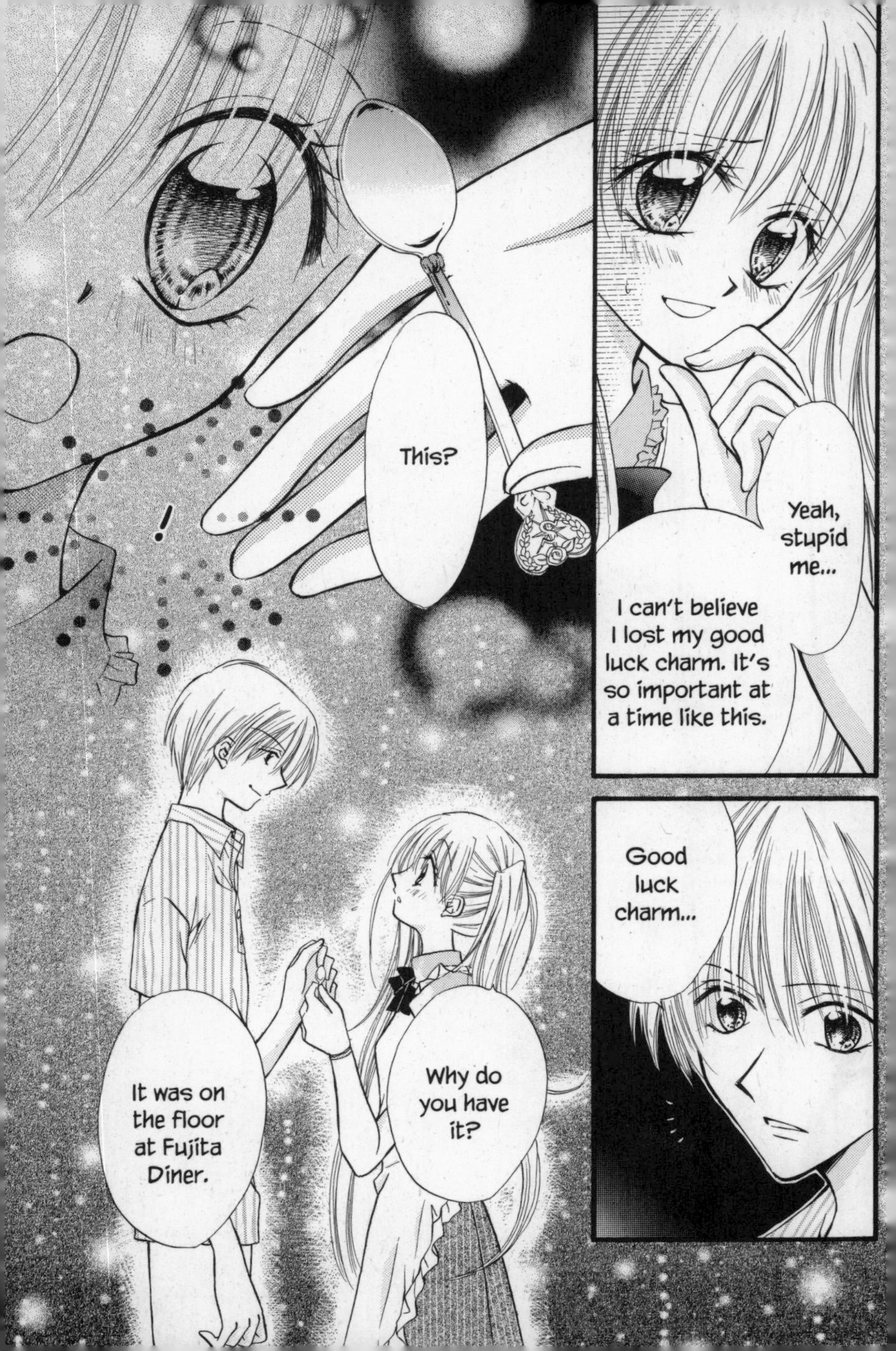

Yeah, stupid me...
I can't believe I lost my good luck charm. It's so important at a time like this.
Good luck charm...
!
This?
Why do you have it?
It was on the floor at Fujita Diner.

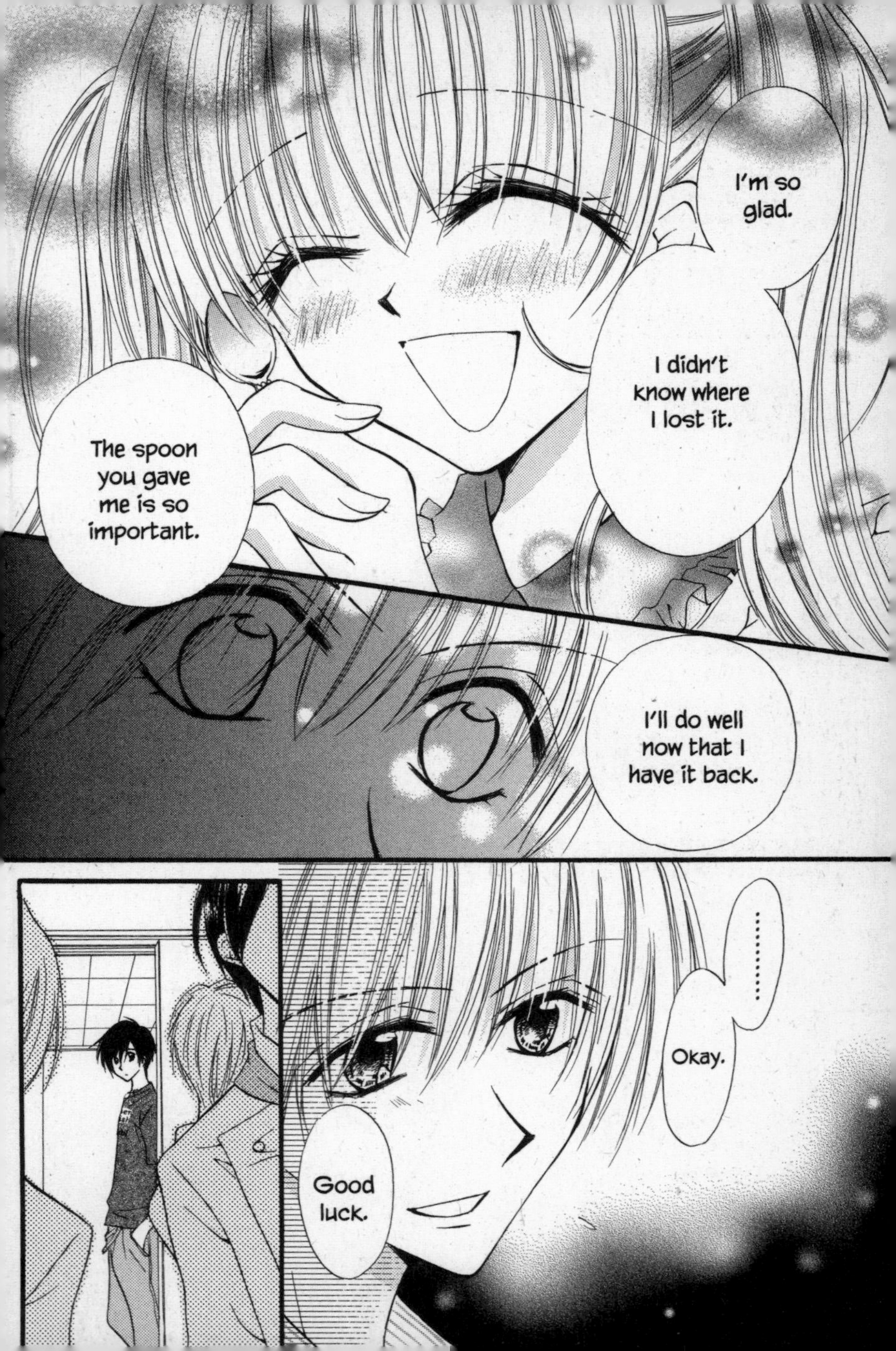
I'm so glad.
I didn't know where I lost it.
The spoon you gave me is so important.
I'll do well now that I have it back.
......
Okay.
Good luck.

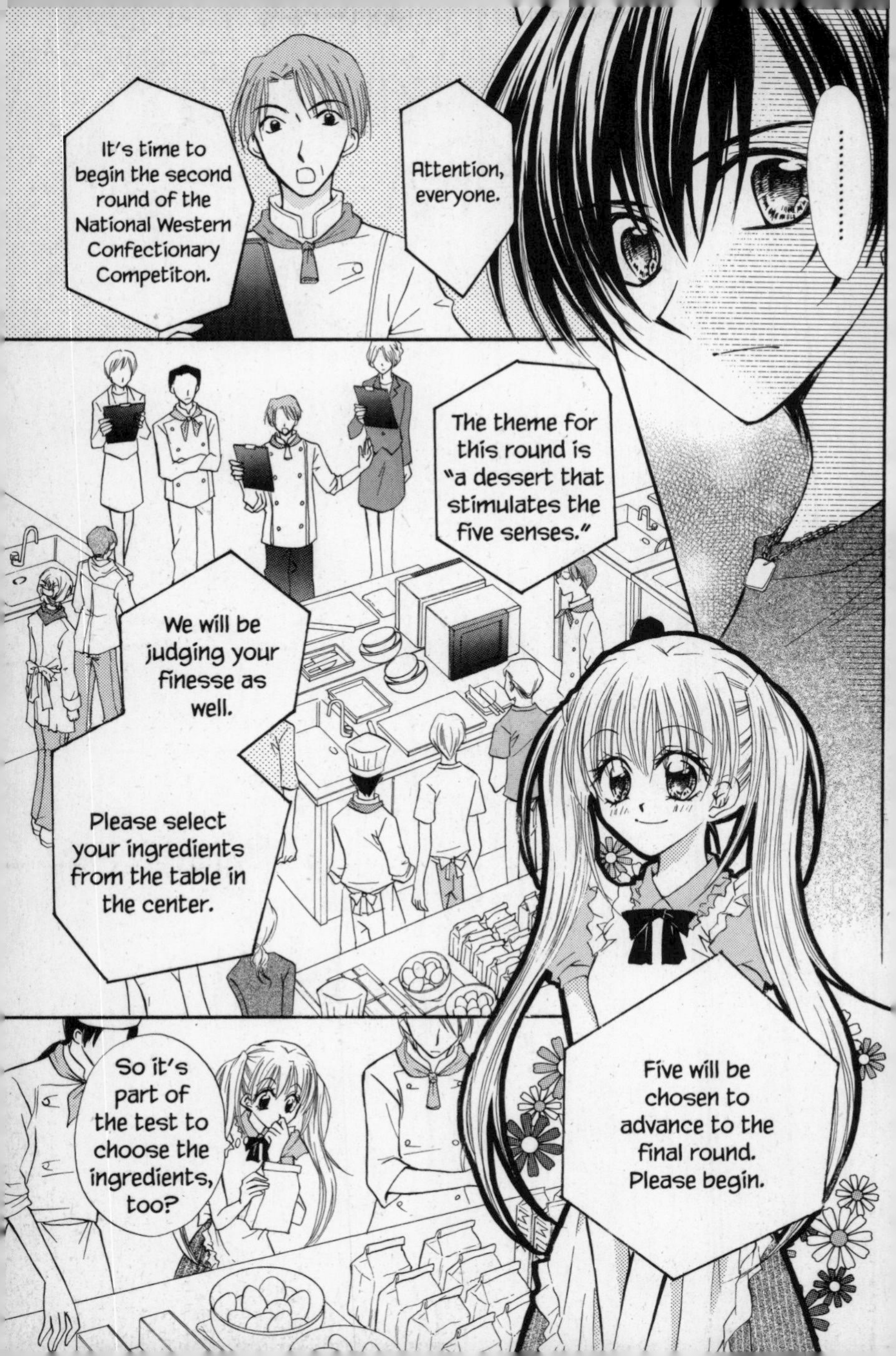
......
Attention, everyone.
It's time to begin the second round of the National Western Confectionary Competiton.
The theme for this round is "a dessert that stimulates the five senses."
We will be judging your finesse as well.
Please select your ingredients from the table in the center.
Five will be chosen to advance to the final round. Please begin.
So it's part of the test to choose the ingredients, too?

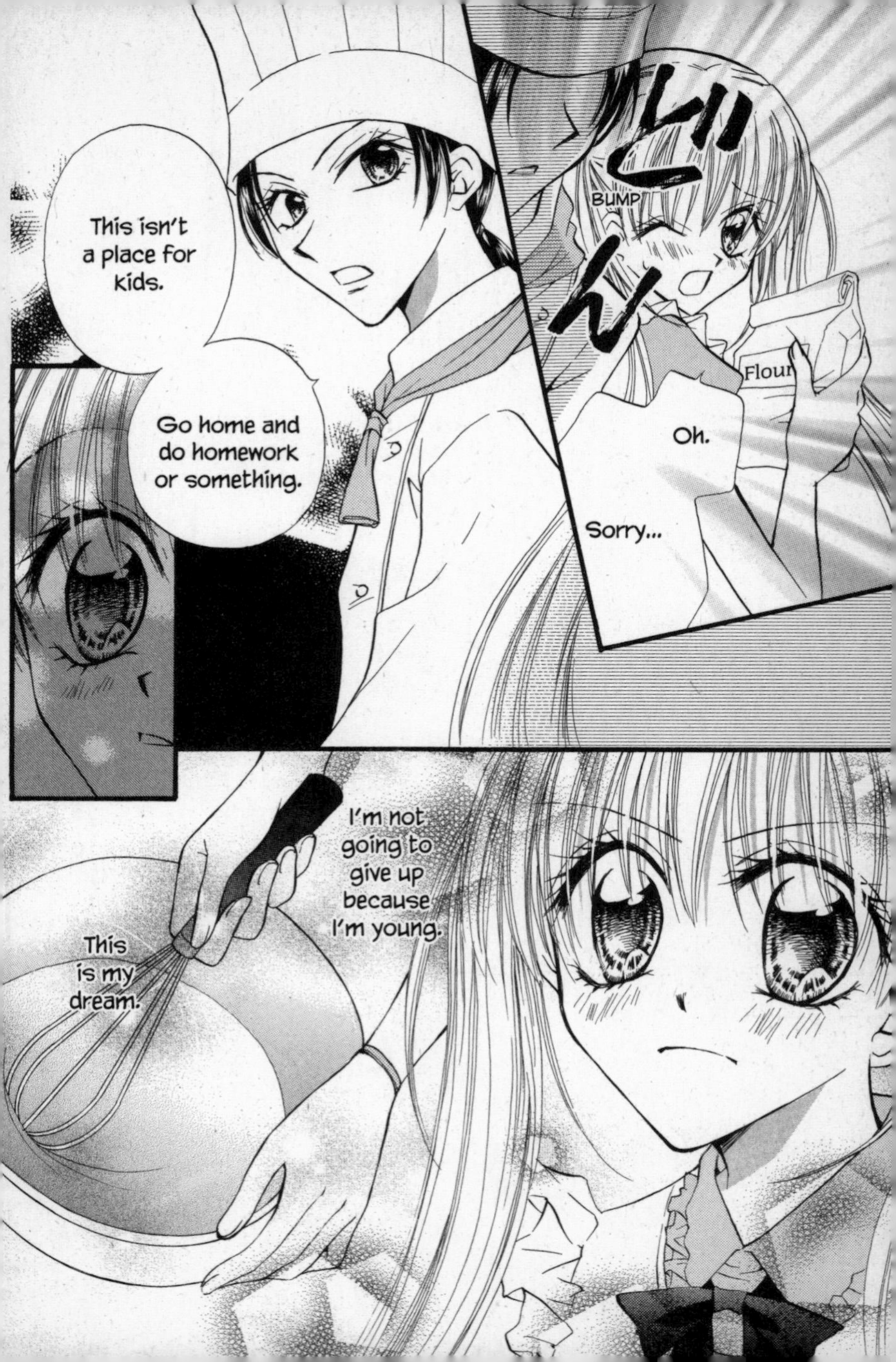
BUMP
Flour
Oh.
Sorry...
This isn't a place for kids.
Go home and do homework or something.
I'm not going to give up because I'm young.
This is my dream.

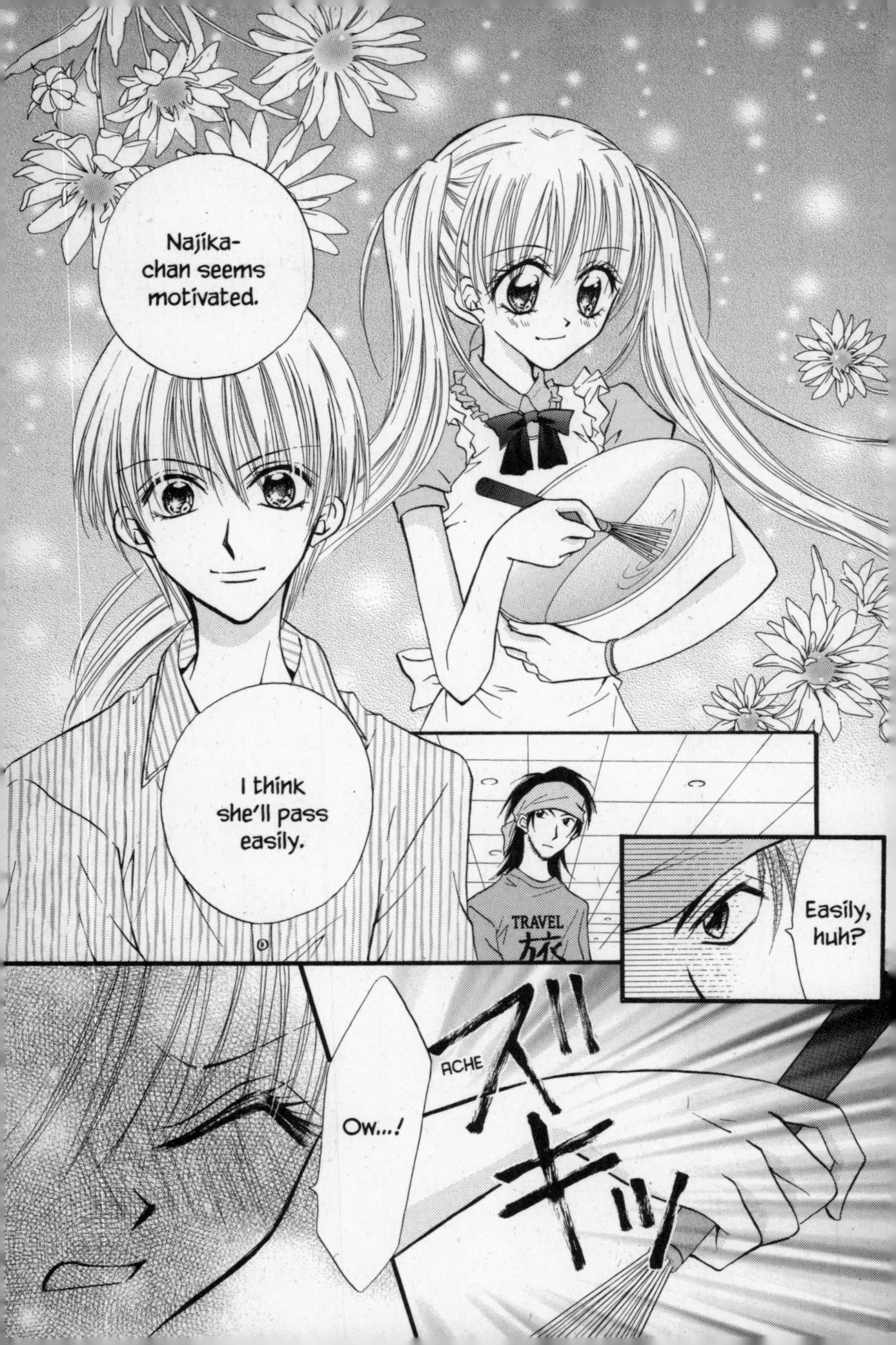
Najika-chan seems motivated.
I think she'll pass easily.
Easily, huh?
TRAVEL 旅
ズキッ
ACHE
Ow...!

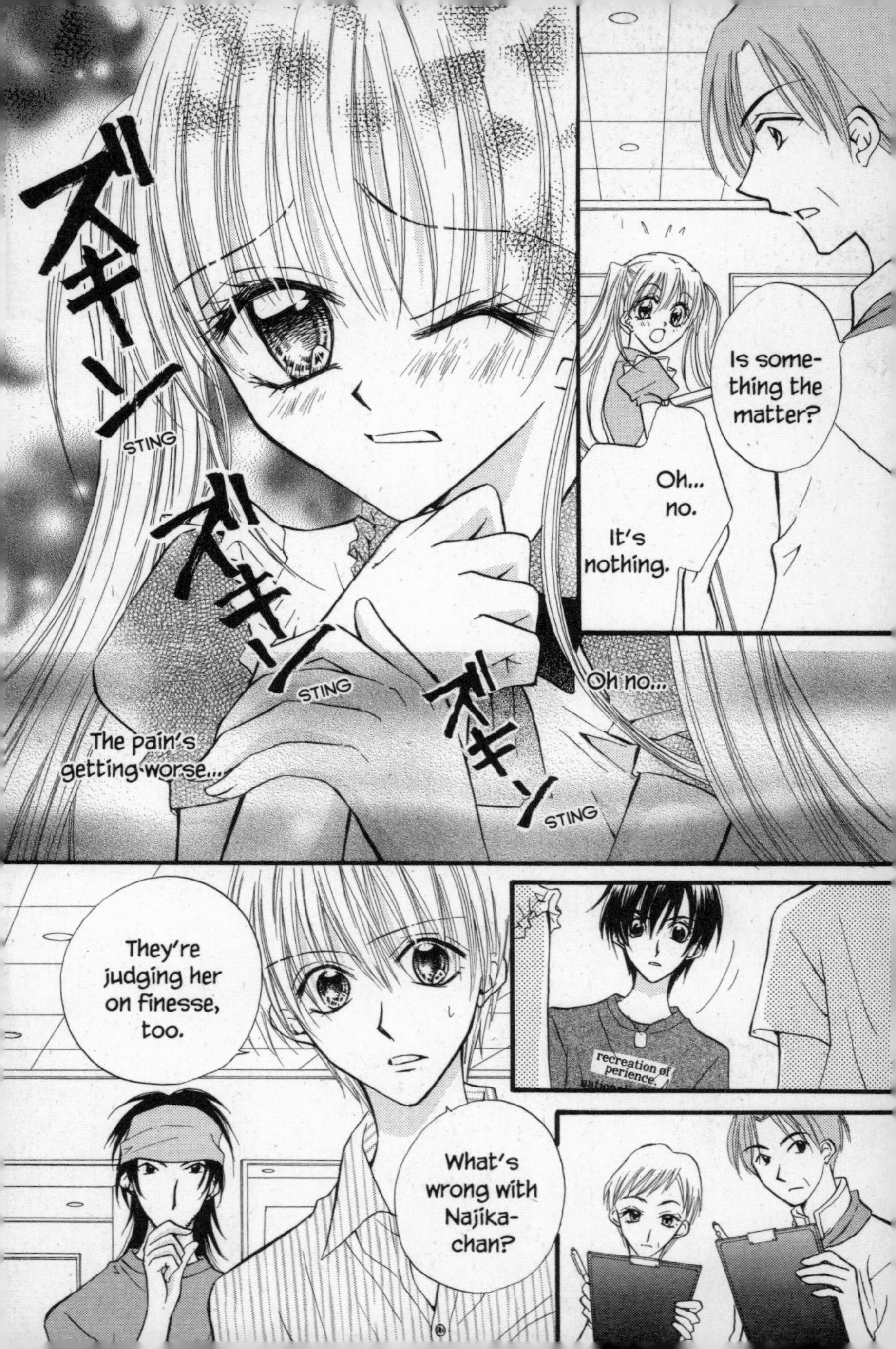

Is some-thing the matter?
Oh... no. It's nothing.
Oh no...
ズキーン
STING
ズキーン
STING
ズキーン
STING
The pain's getting worse...
recreation of perience.
They're judging her on finesse, too.
What's wrong with Najika-chan?

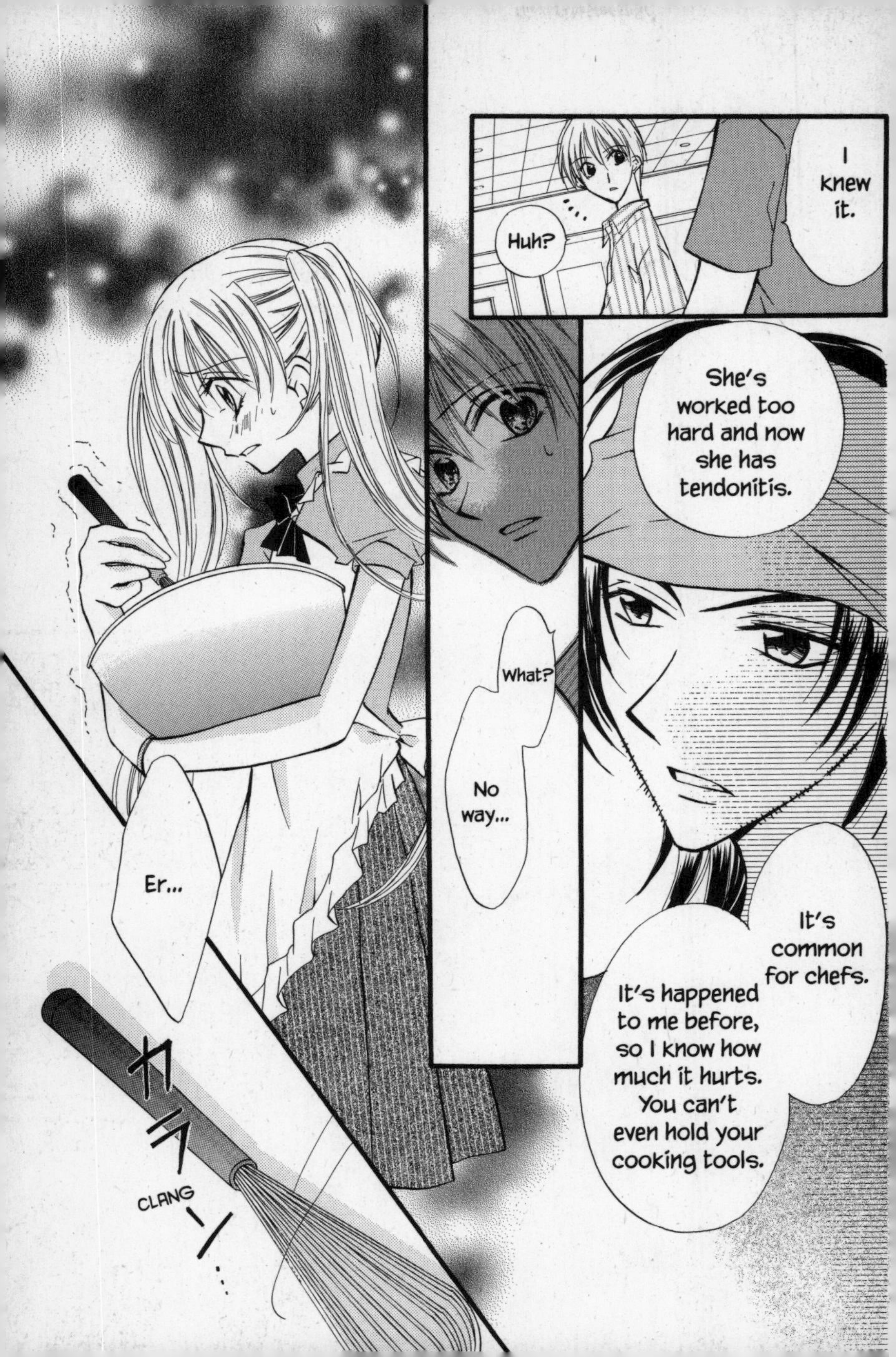
I knew it.
....
Huh?
She's worked too hard and now she has tendonitis.
What?
No way...
It's common for chefs.
It's happened to me before, so I know how much it hurts. You can't even hold your cooking tools.
Er...
CLANG

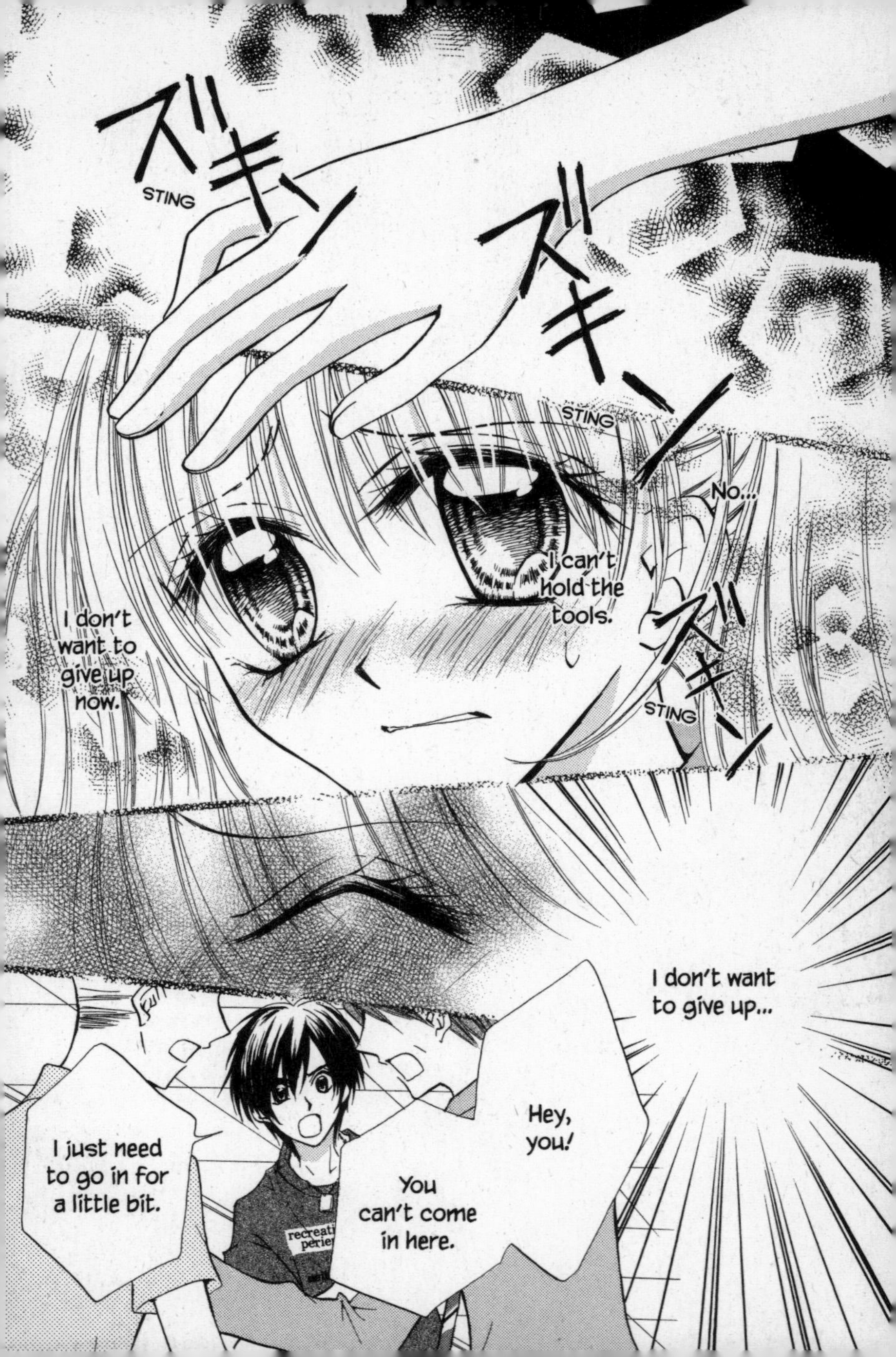

ズキーン
STING
ズキン
STING
No...
I can't hold the tools.
ズキーン
STING
I don't want to give up now.
I don't want to give up...
Hey, you!
You can't come in here.
I just need to go in for a little bit.

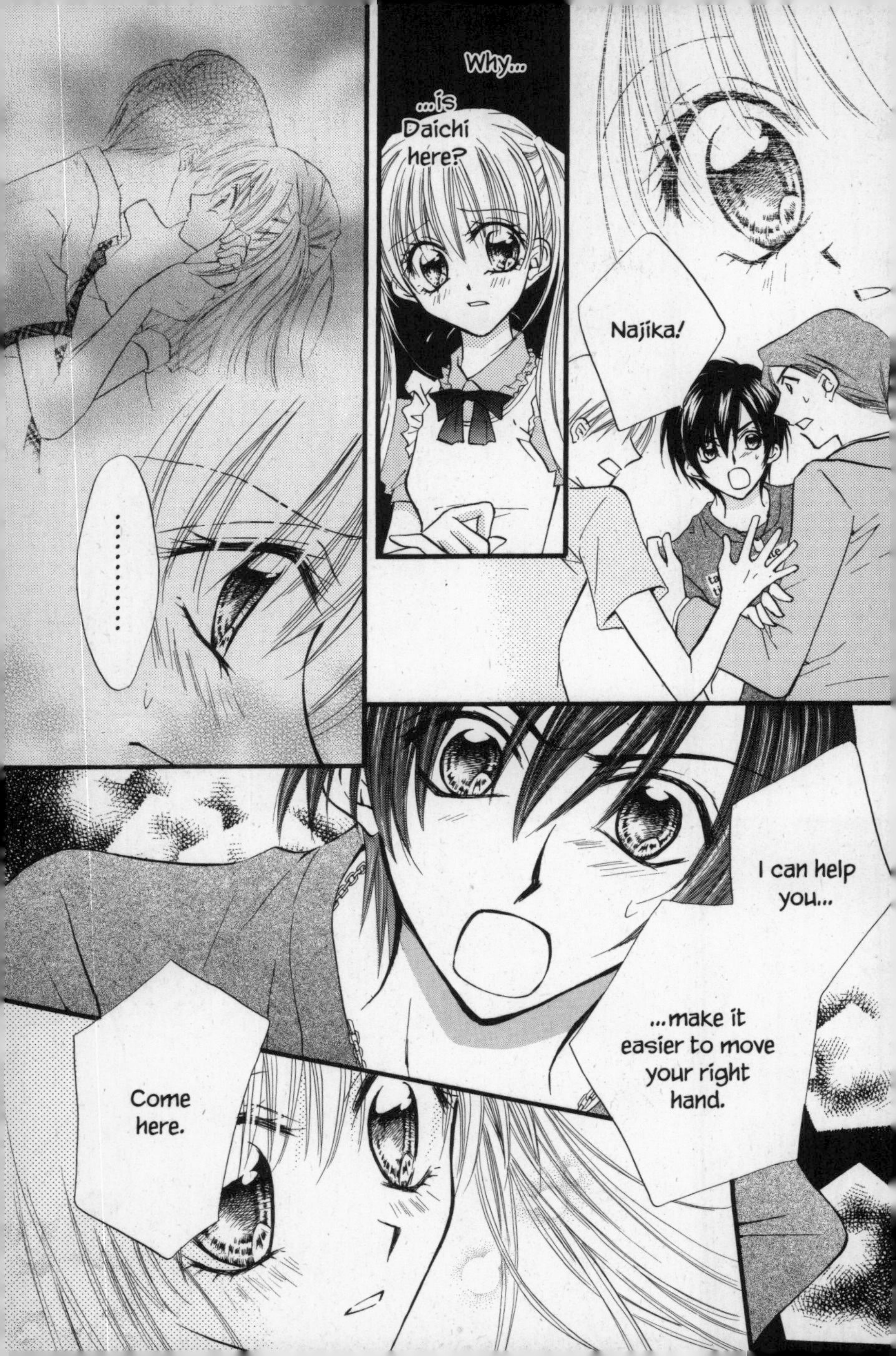
Najika!
Why...
...is Daichi here?
......
I can help you...
...make it easier to move your right hand.
Come here.

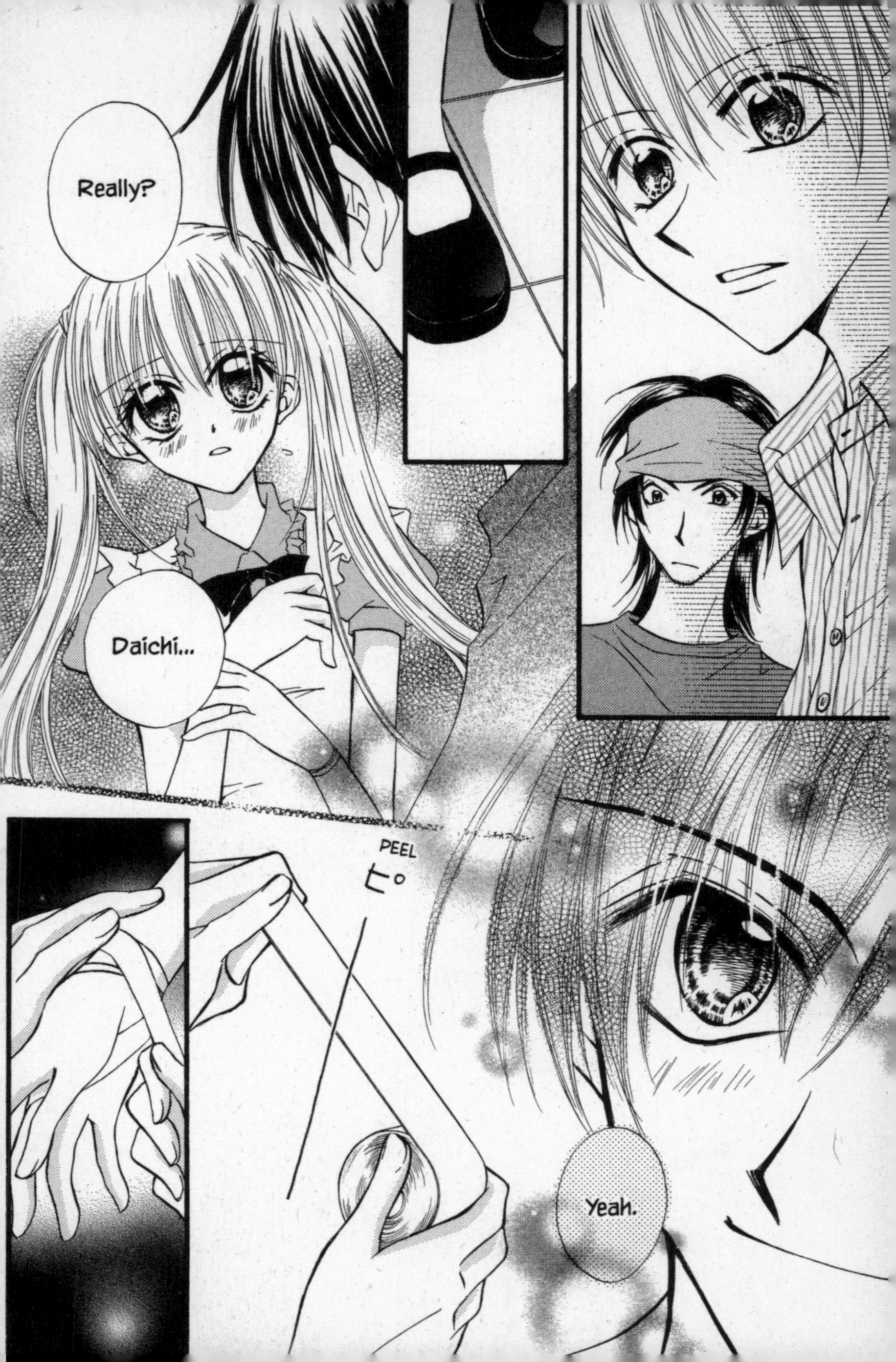
Really?
Daichi...
Yeah.
PEEL
ピ

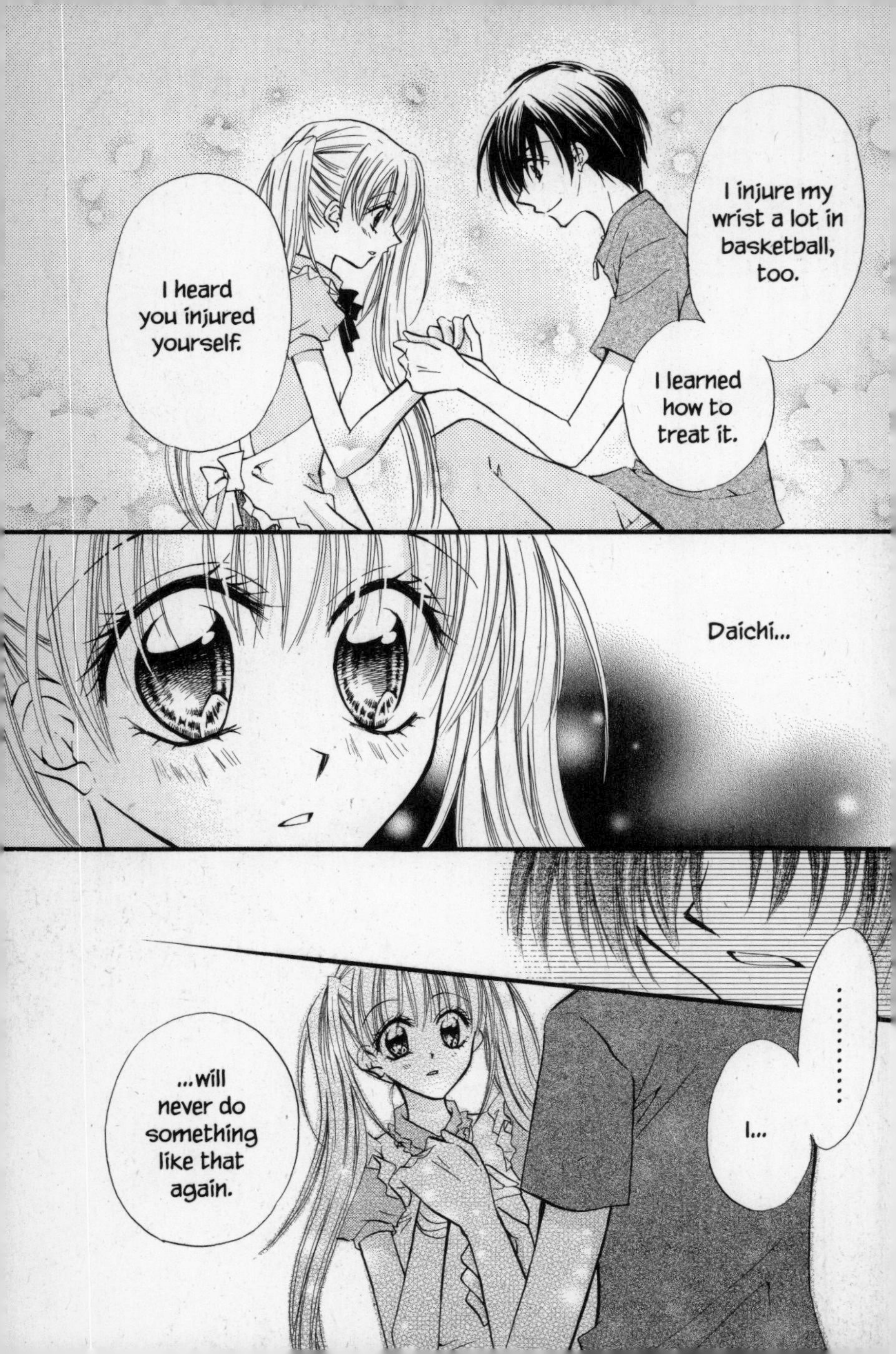
I injure my wrist a lot in basketball, too.
I learned how to treat it.
I heard you injured yourself.
Daichi...
....
I...
...will never do something like that again.

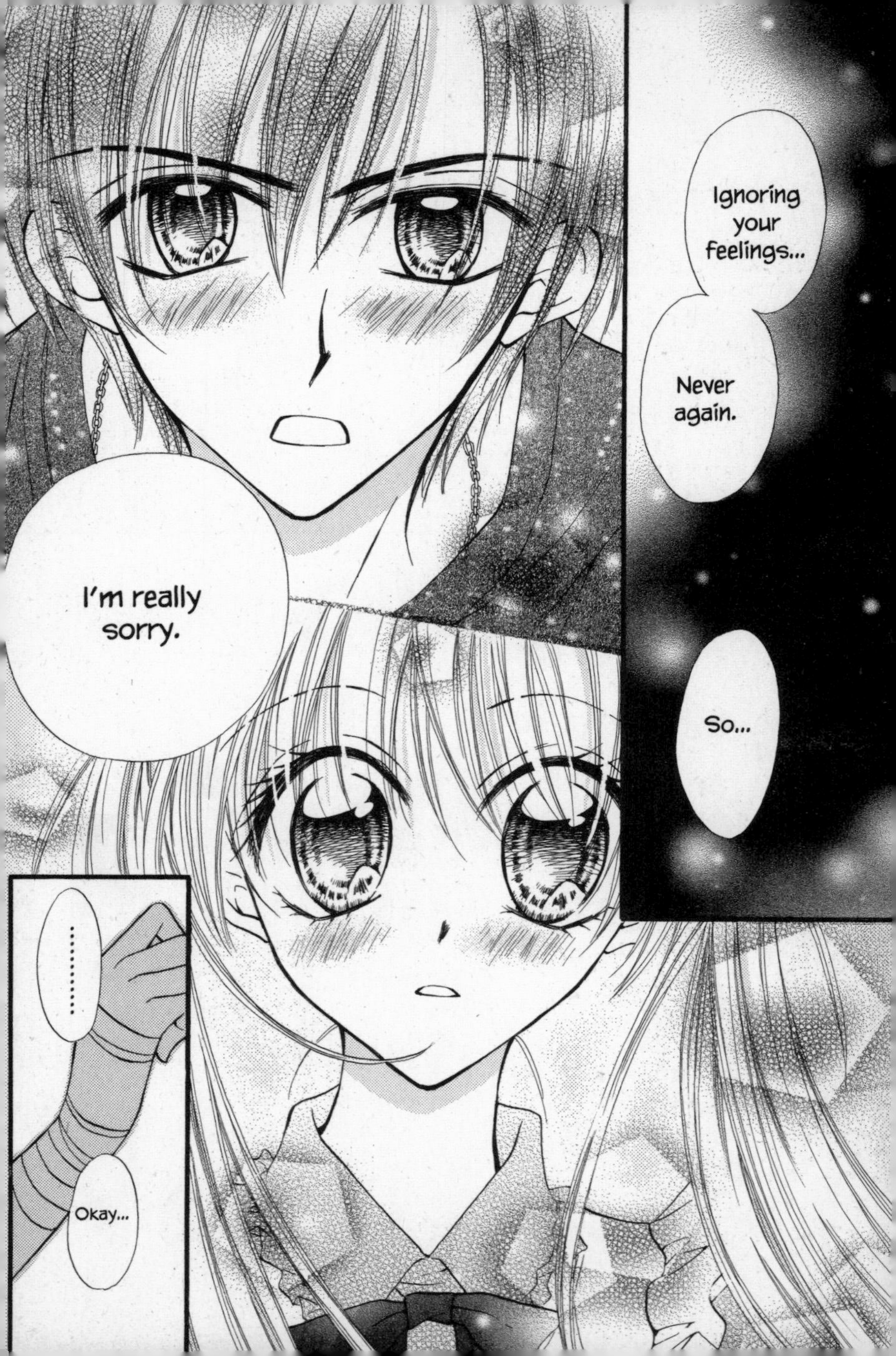
Ignoring your feelings...
Never again.
So...
I'm really sorry.
....
Okay...

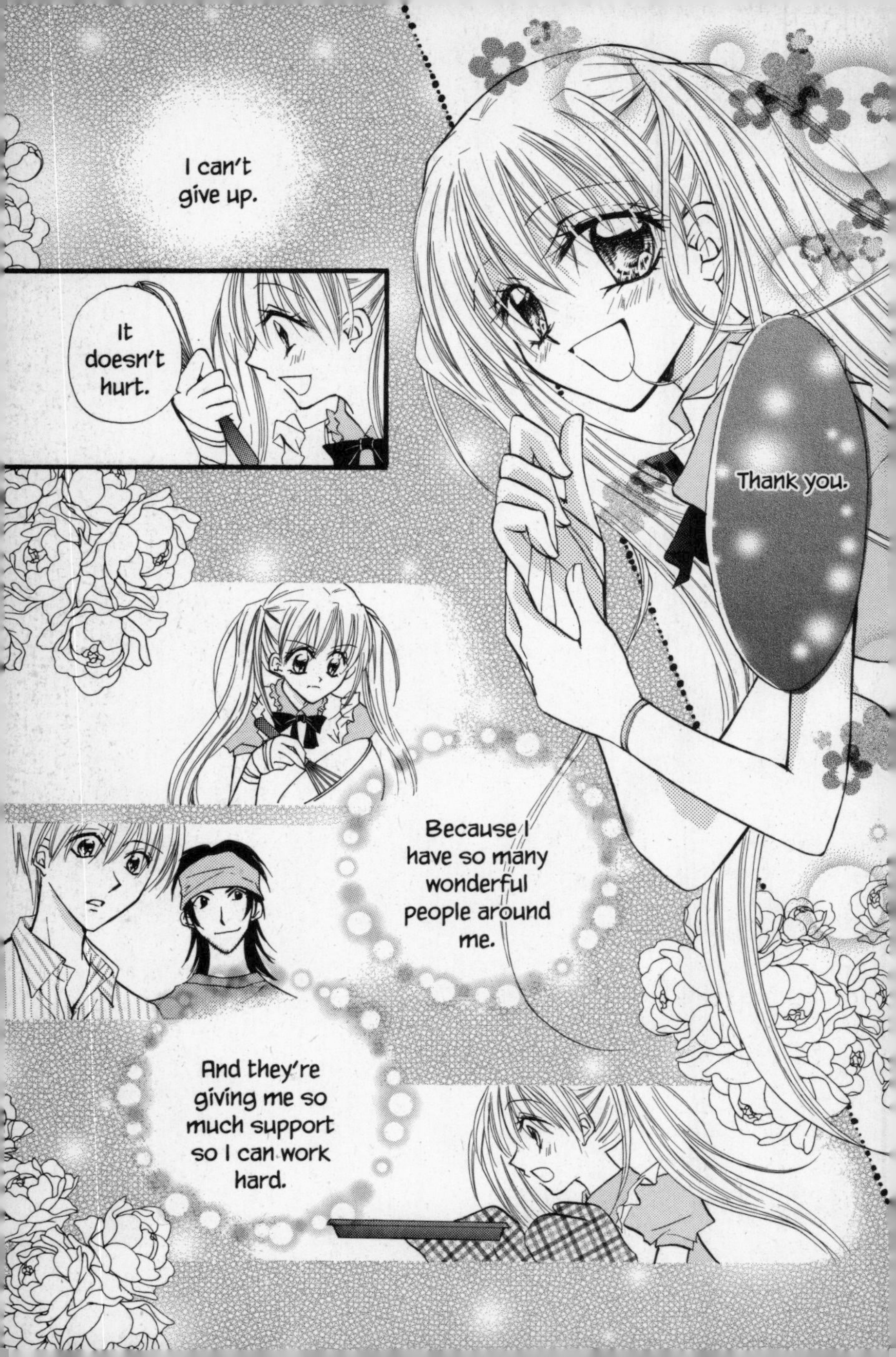
Thank you.
I can't give up.
It doesn't hurt.
Because I have so many wonderful people around me.
And they're giving me so much support so I can work hard.

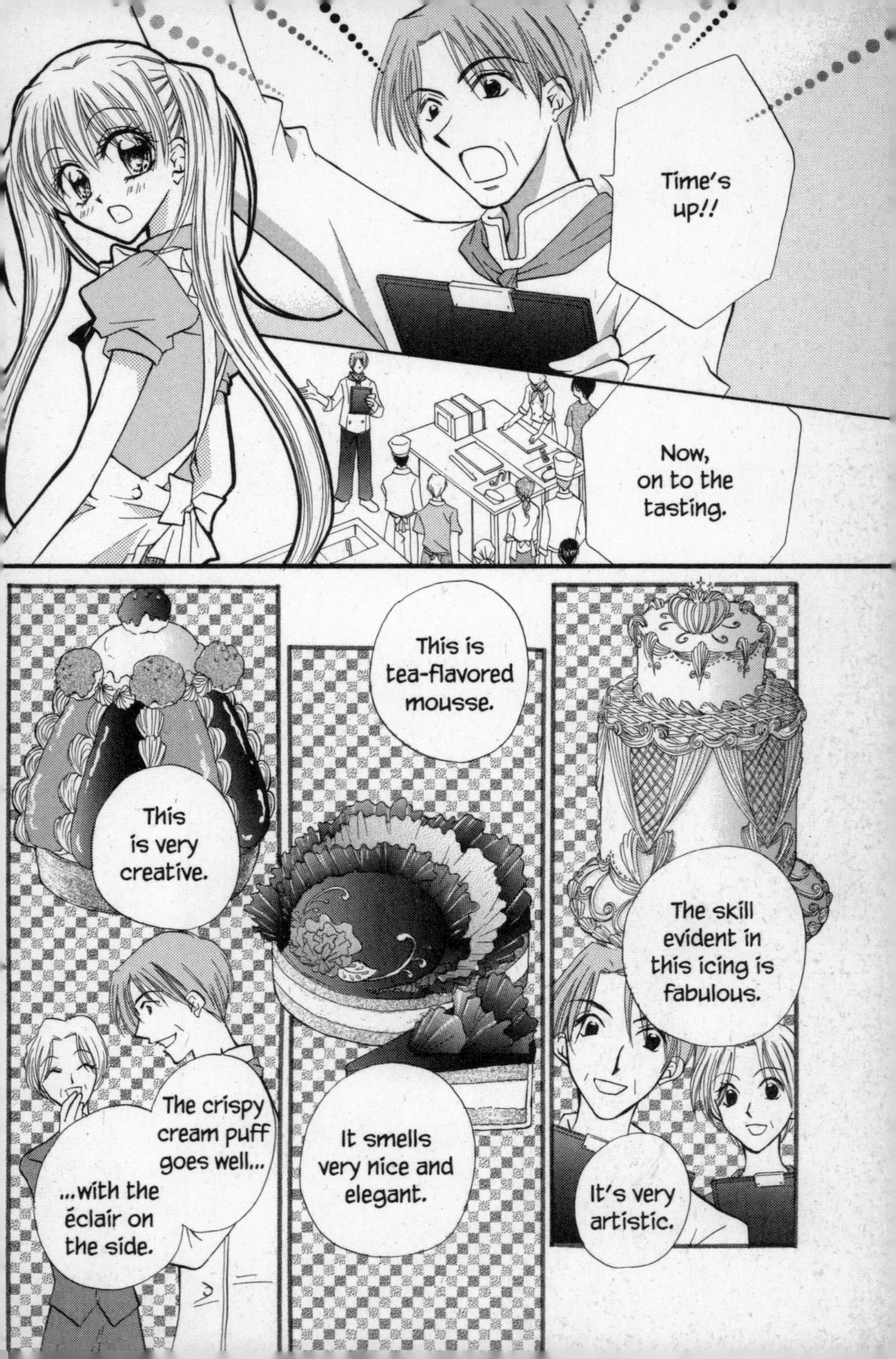
Time's up!!
Now, on to the tasting.
The skill evident in this icing is fabulous.
It's very artistic.
This is tea-flavored mousse.
It smells very nice and elegant.
This is very creative.
The crispy cream puff goes well...
...with the éclair on the side.

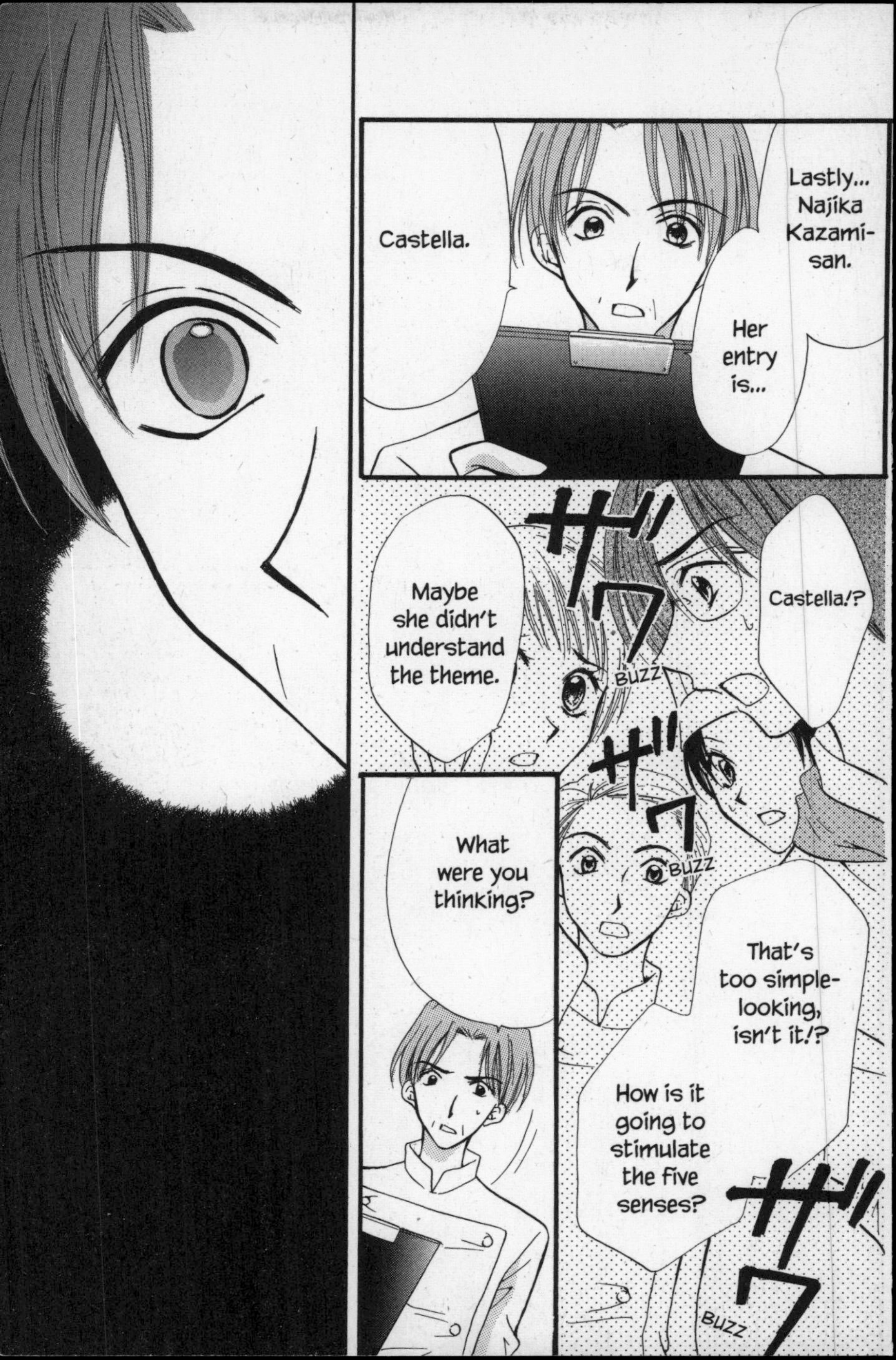
Lastly... Najika Kazami-san.
Her entry is...
Castella.
Castella!?
ザワ
BUZZ
Maybe she didn't understand the theme.
ザワ
BUZZ
That's too simple-looking, isn't it!?
How is it going to stimulate the five senses?
ザワ
BUZZ
What were you thinking?

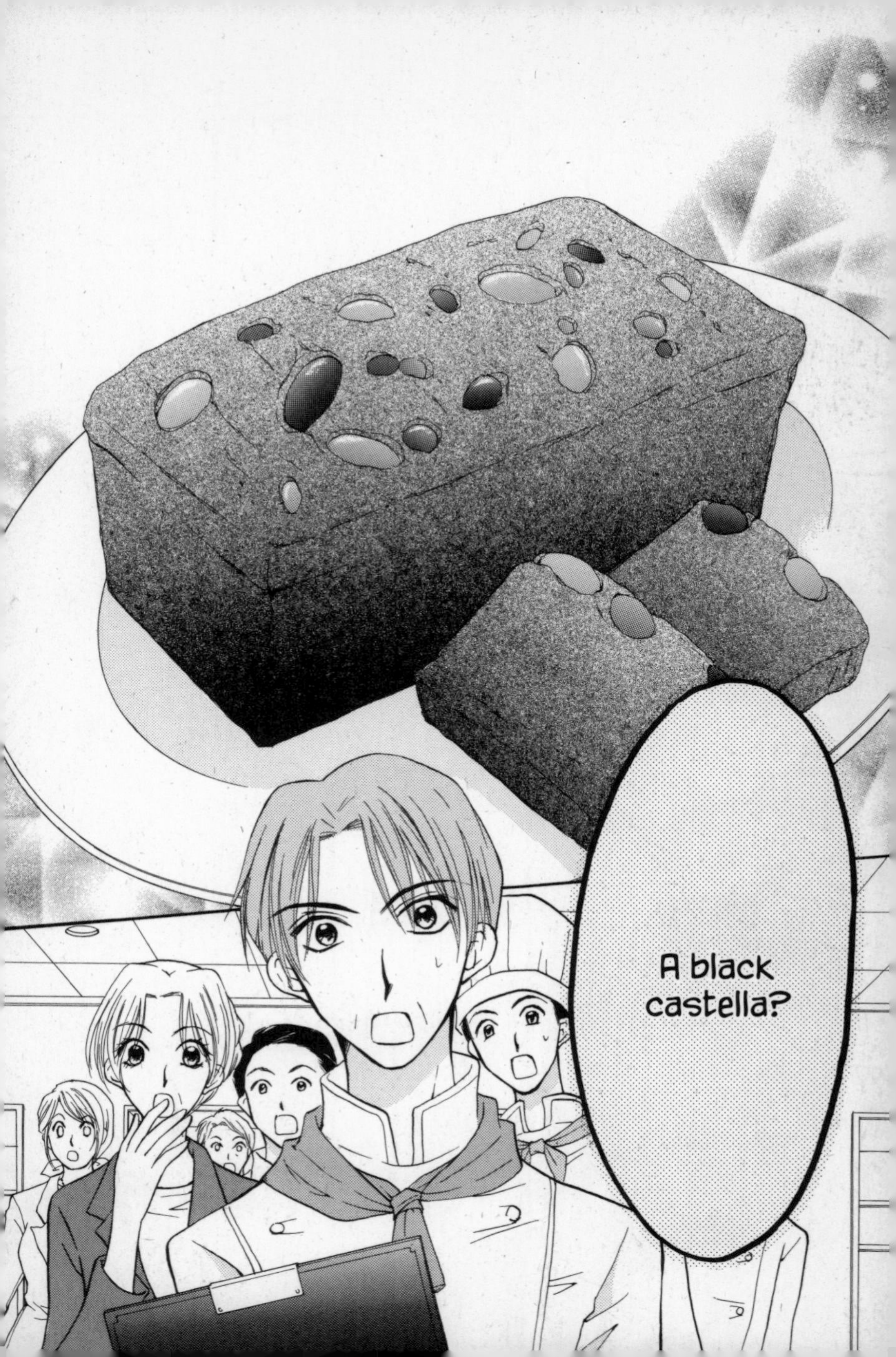
A black castella?

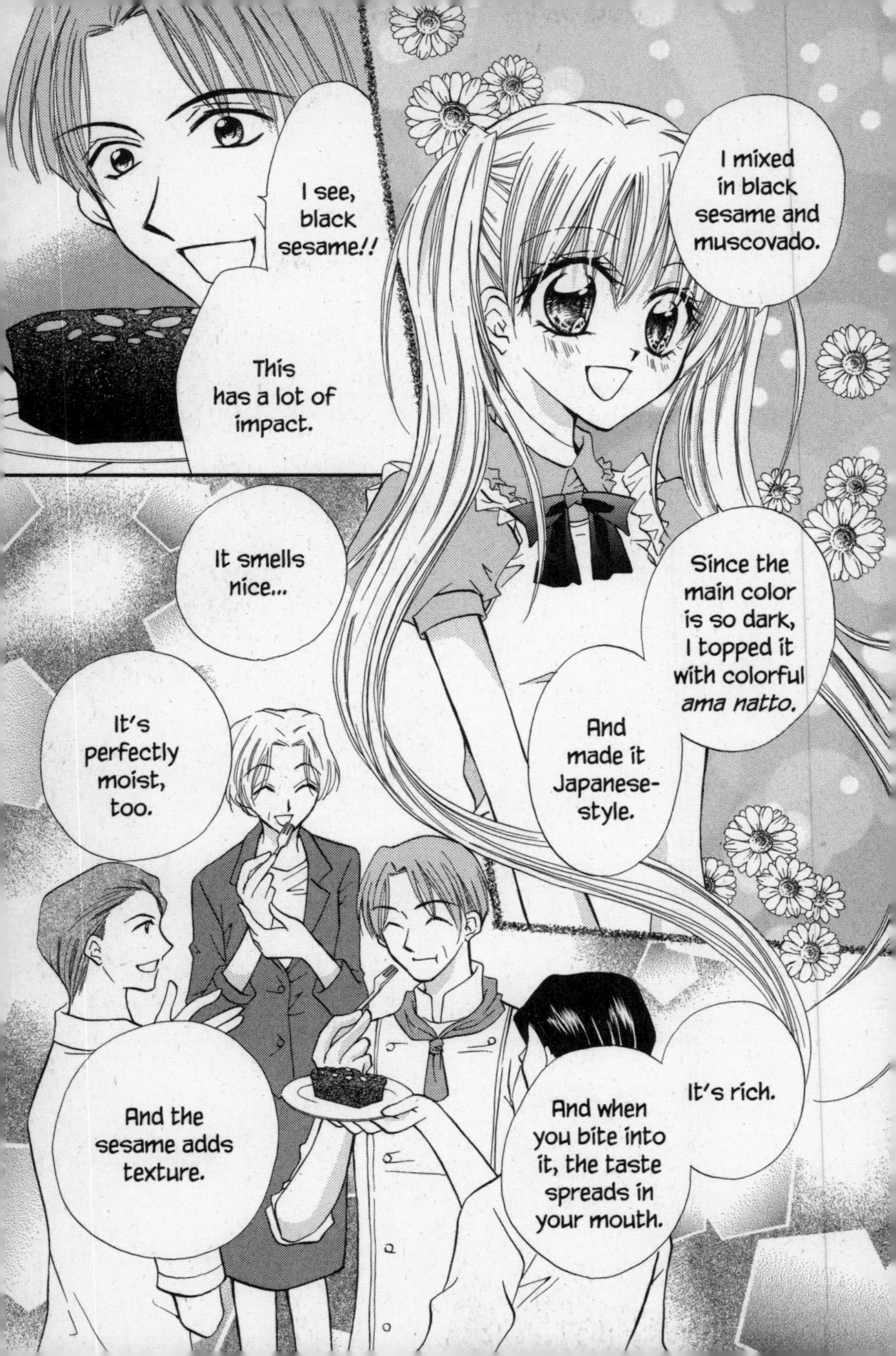

I mixed in black sesame and muscovado.
Since the main color is so dark, I topped it with colorful *ama natto.*
And made it Japanese-style.
I see, black sesame!!
This has a lot of impact.
It smells nice...
It's perfectly moist, too.
It's rich.
And when you bite into it, the taste spreads in your mouth.
And the sesame adds texture.

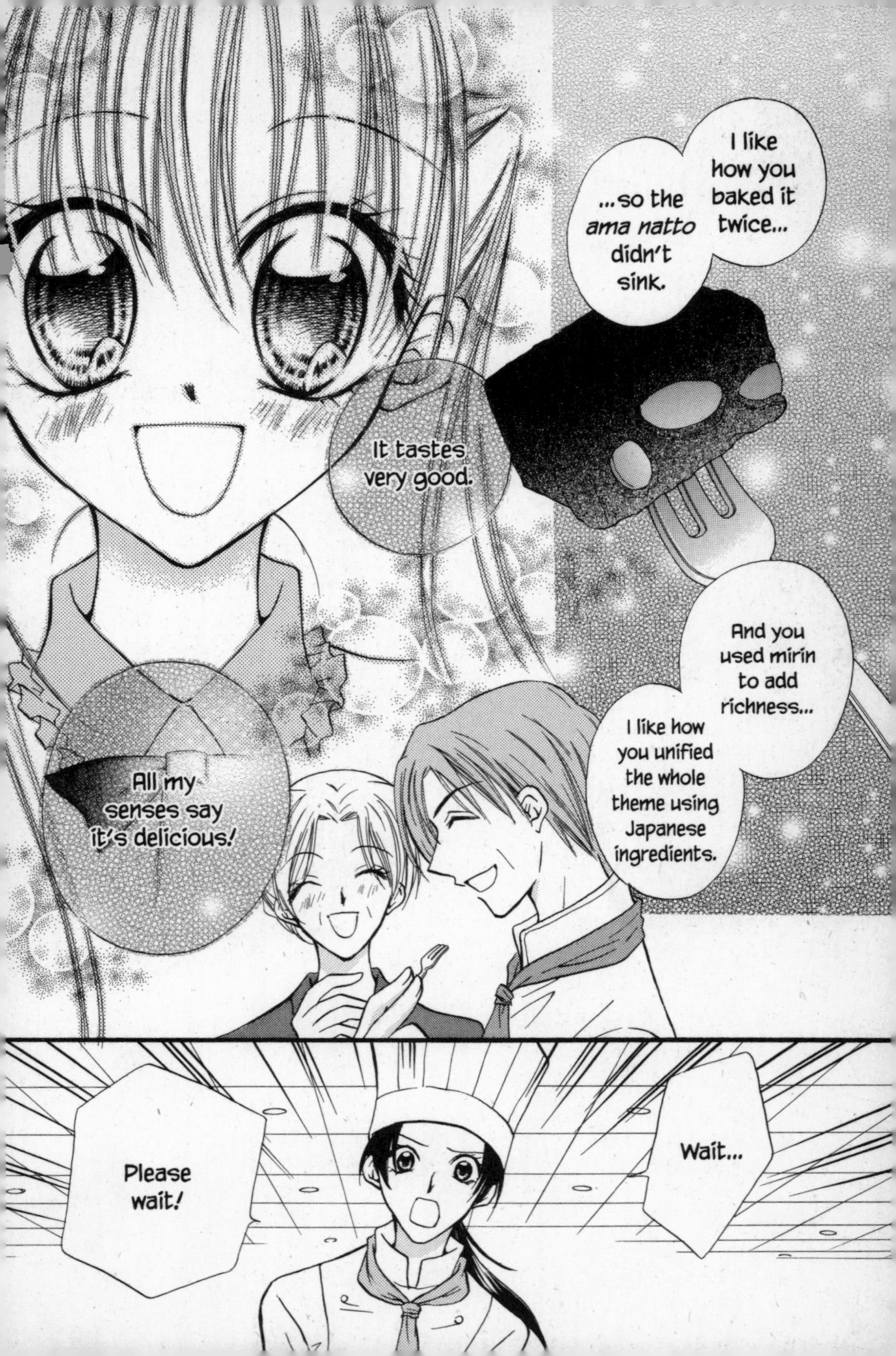
I like how you baked it twice...
...so the *ama natto* didn't sink.
It tastes very good.
And you used mirin to add richness...
I like how you unified the whole theme using Japanese ingredients.
All my senses say it's delicious!
Wait...
Please wait!

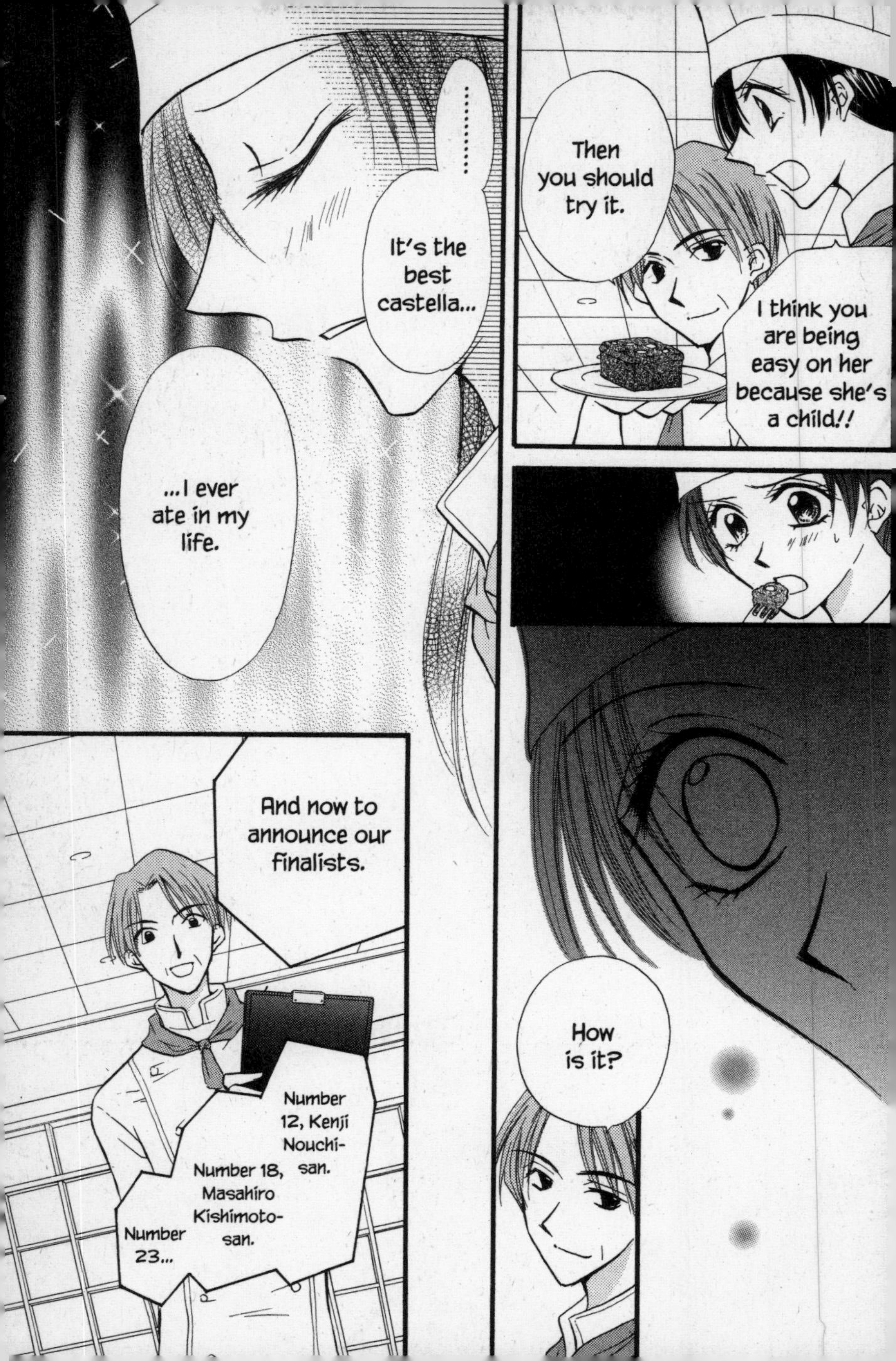
I think you are being easy on her because she's a child!!
Then you should try it.
How is it?
......
It's the best castella...
...I ever ate in my life.
And now to announce our finalists.
Number 12, Kenji Nouchi-san.
Number 18, Masahiro Kishimoto-san.
Number 23...

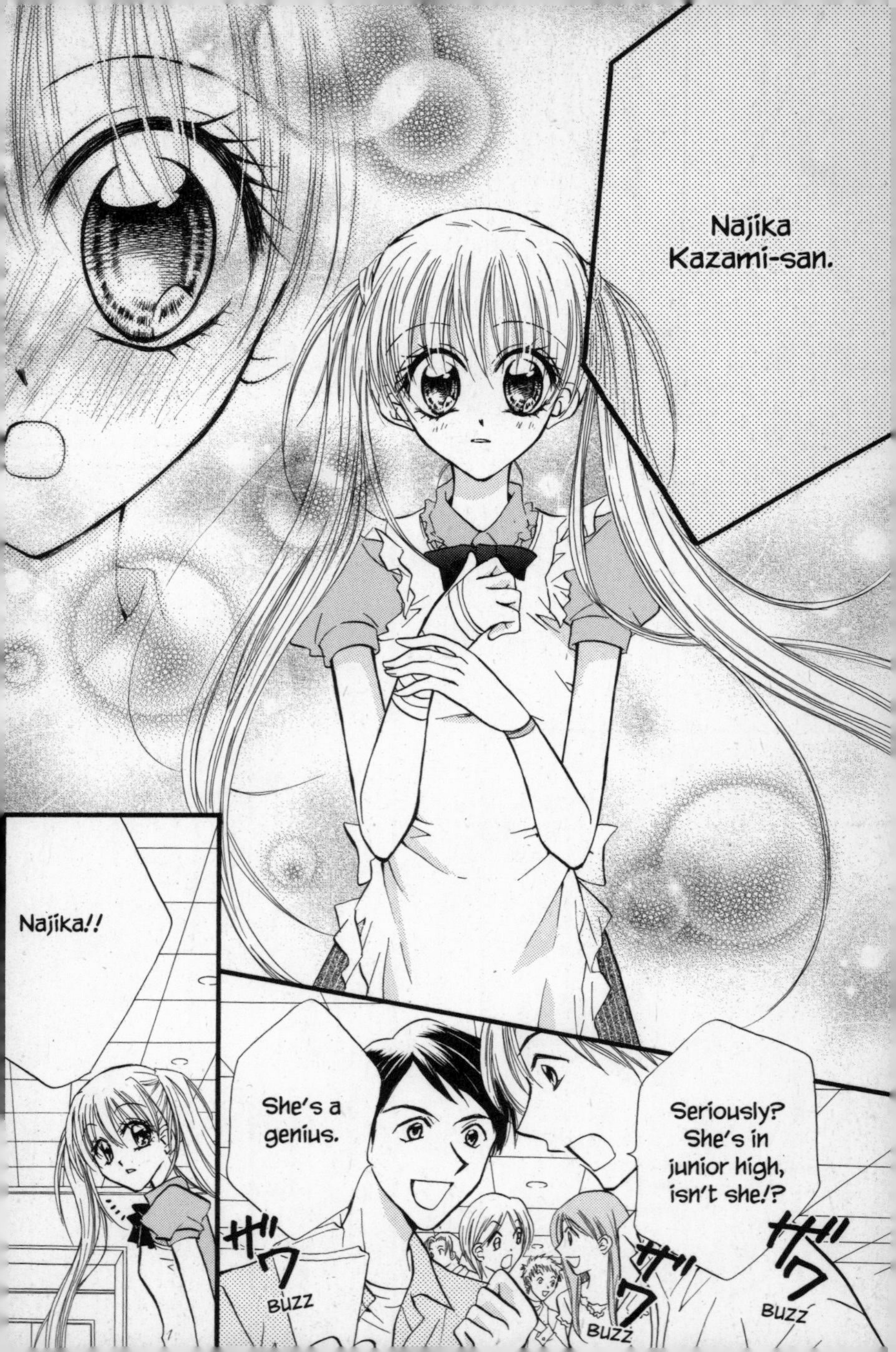
Najika
Kazami-san.
Seriously? She's in junior high, isn't she!?
She's a genius.
ザワ
BUZZ
ザワ
BUZZ
ザワ
BUZZ
Najika!!

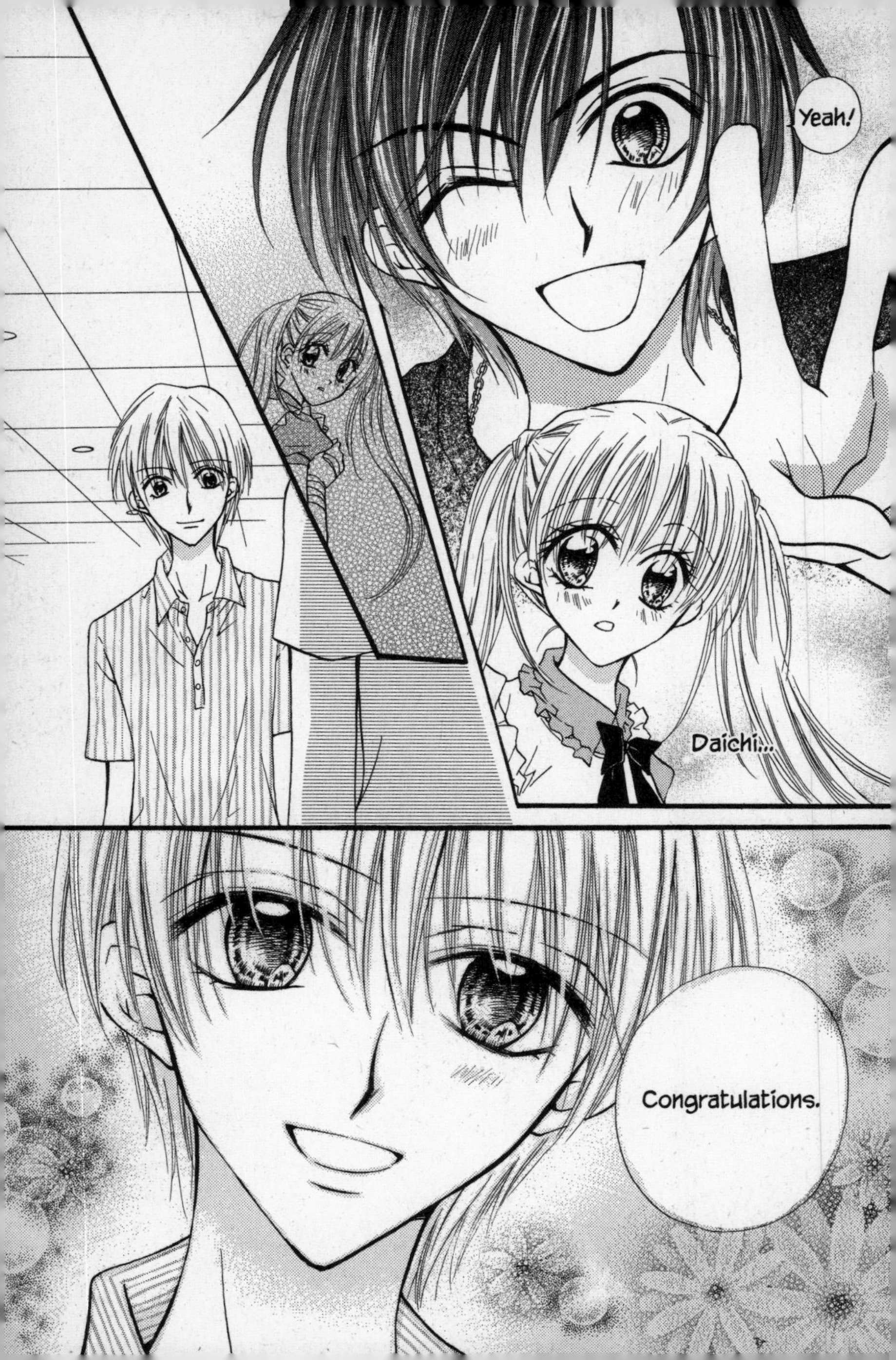
Yeah!
Daichi...
Congratulations.

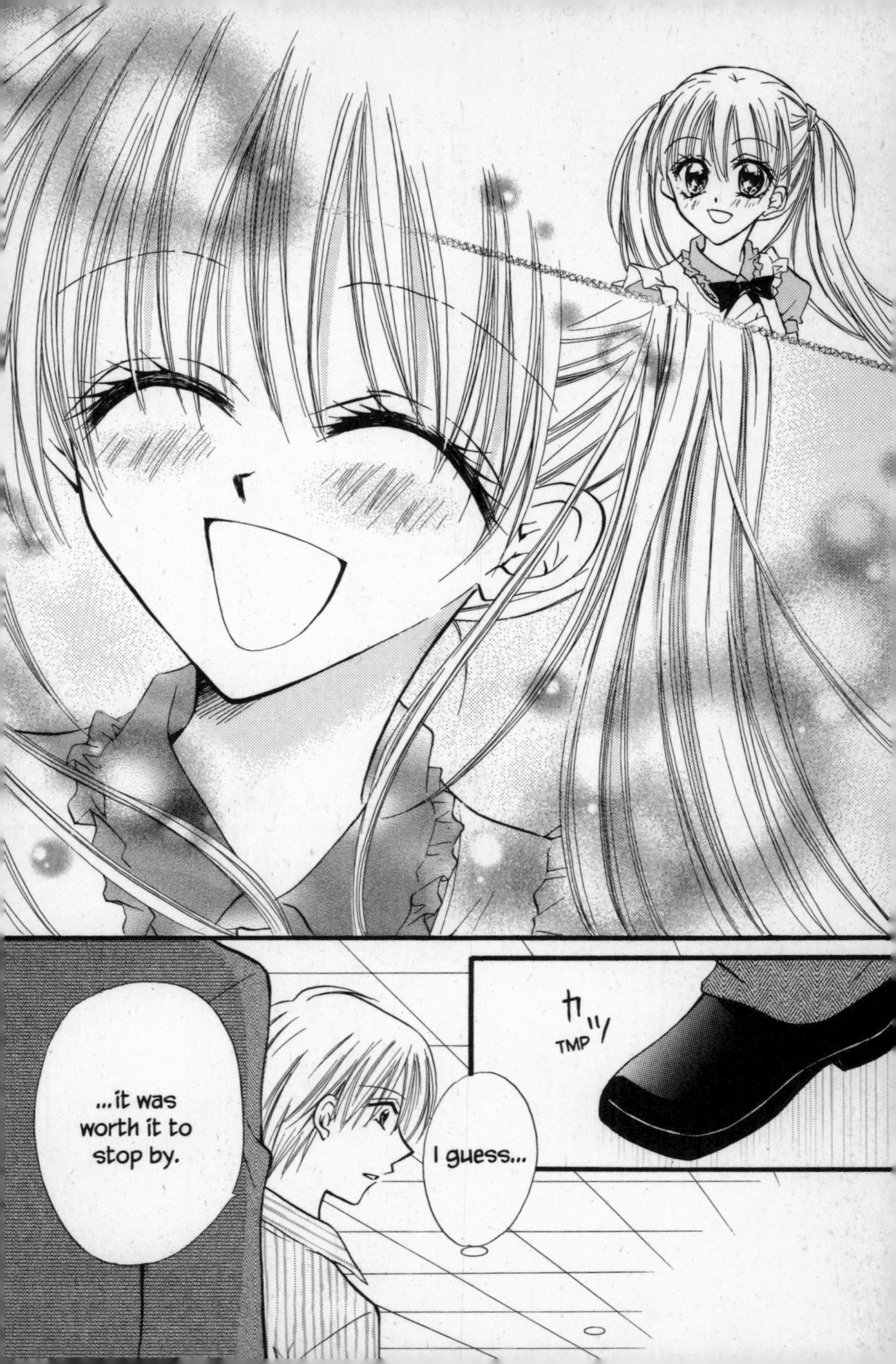

カッ
TMP
I guess...
...it was worth it to stop by.

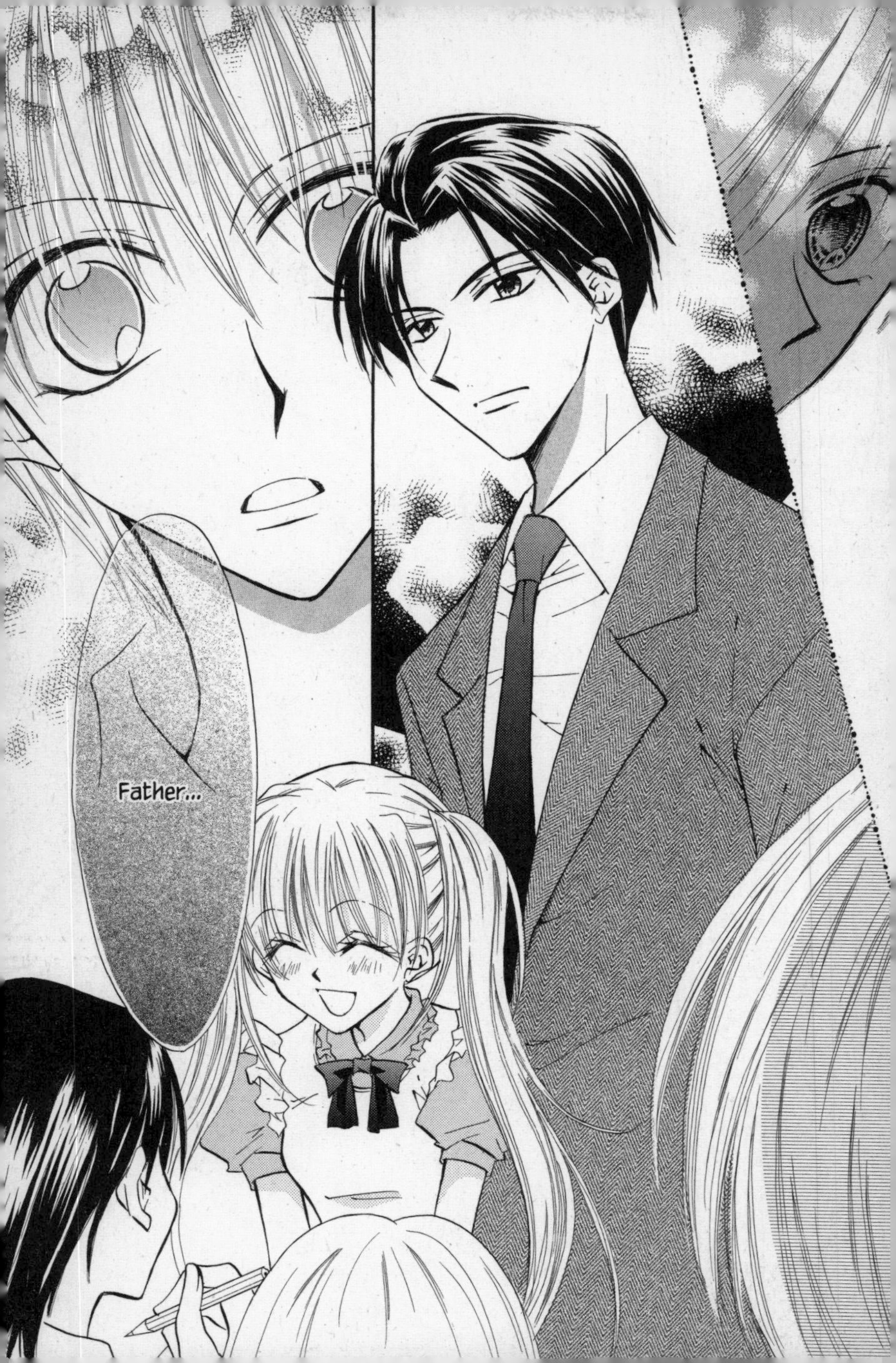
Father...

For this volume, I'll write my memories of each chapter here. I'm trying not to give spoilers... but I can't guarantee it. So it might be better to read this after you've read the manga. ♥

Recipe 20

We gave Najika a new apron!! The screen tone I was using for the old one went out of print, so it was perfect timing! It's not because the screen tone went out of print. It was really a coincidence. ^_^

But seriously, there are hardly any research materials on aprons. If there were a photograph book of aprons, I would definitely buy it!! There's a photograph book of celebrities wearing glasses, so I think there should be a book of celebrities wearing aprons. Or maybe there is one, and I just don't know about it.

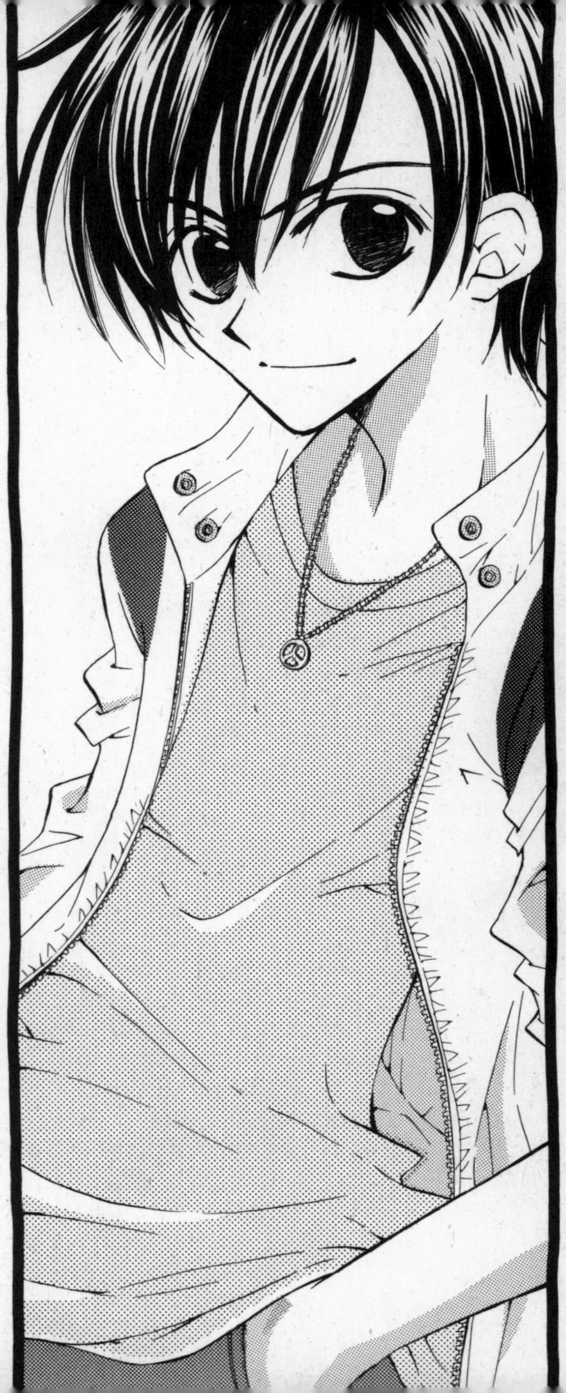

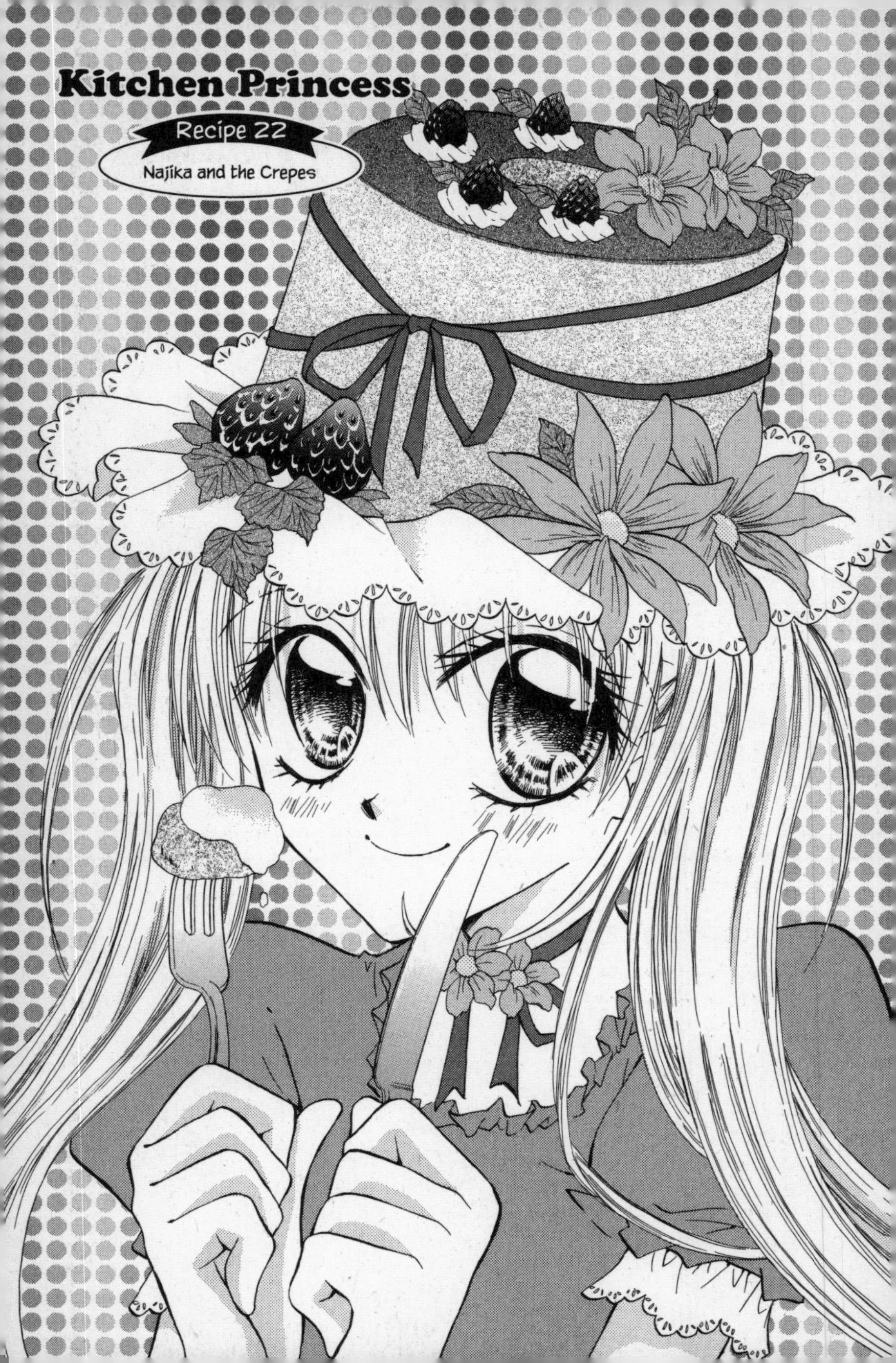
Kitchen Princess
Recipe 22
Najika and the Crepes

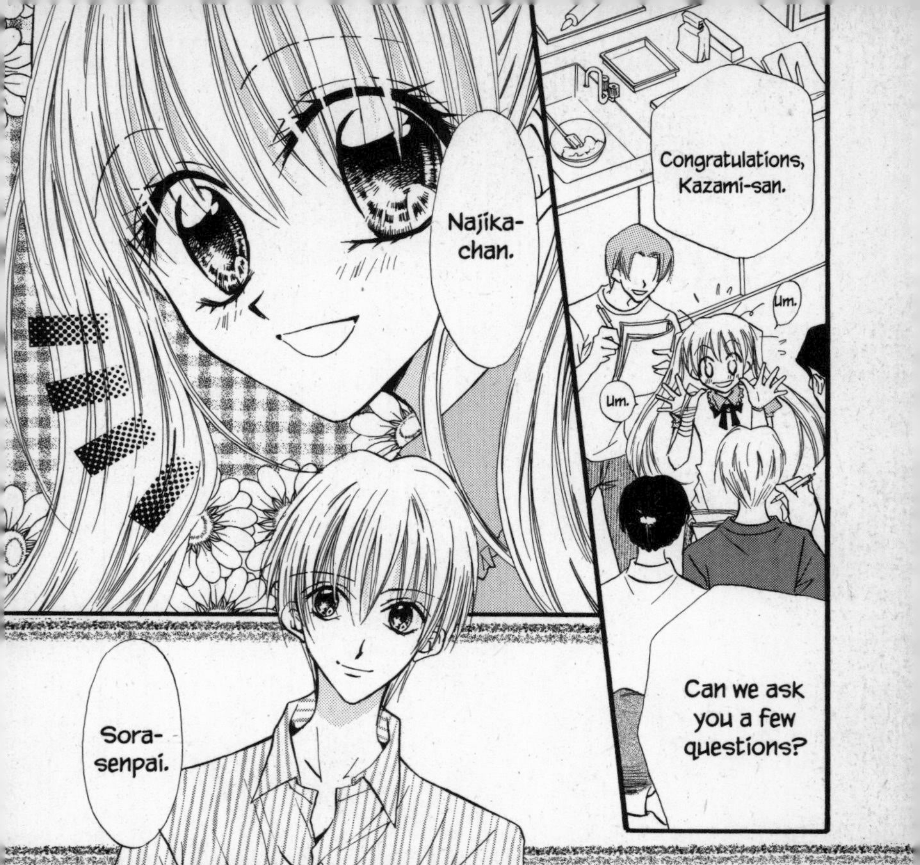
Congratulations, Kazami-san.
Um.
Um.
Can we ask you a few questions?
Najika-chan.
Sora-senpai.

About Recipe 22's Splash Page

First, I've always wanted to draw a hat in the shape of a cake.

I was wondering what cake to use, but I chose a chiffon cake because the shape was the easiest to deal with.

But I realized later that it must be heavy.

The chiffon cake is something my little sister buys me every year for my birthday, and it is very special to me. ♡

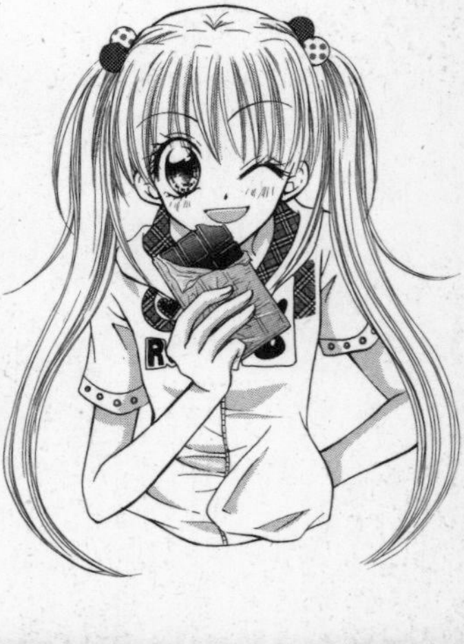

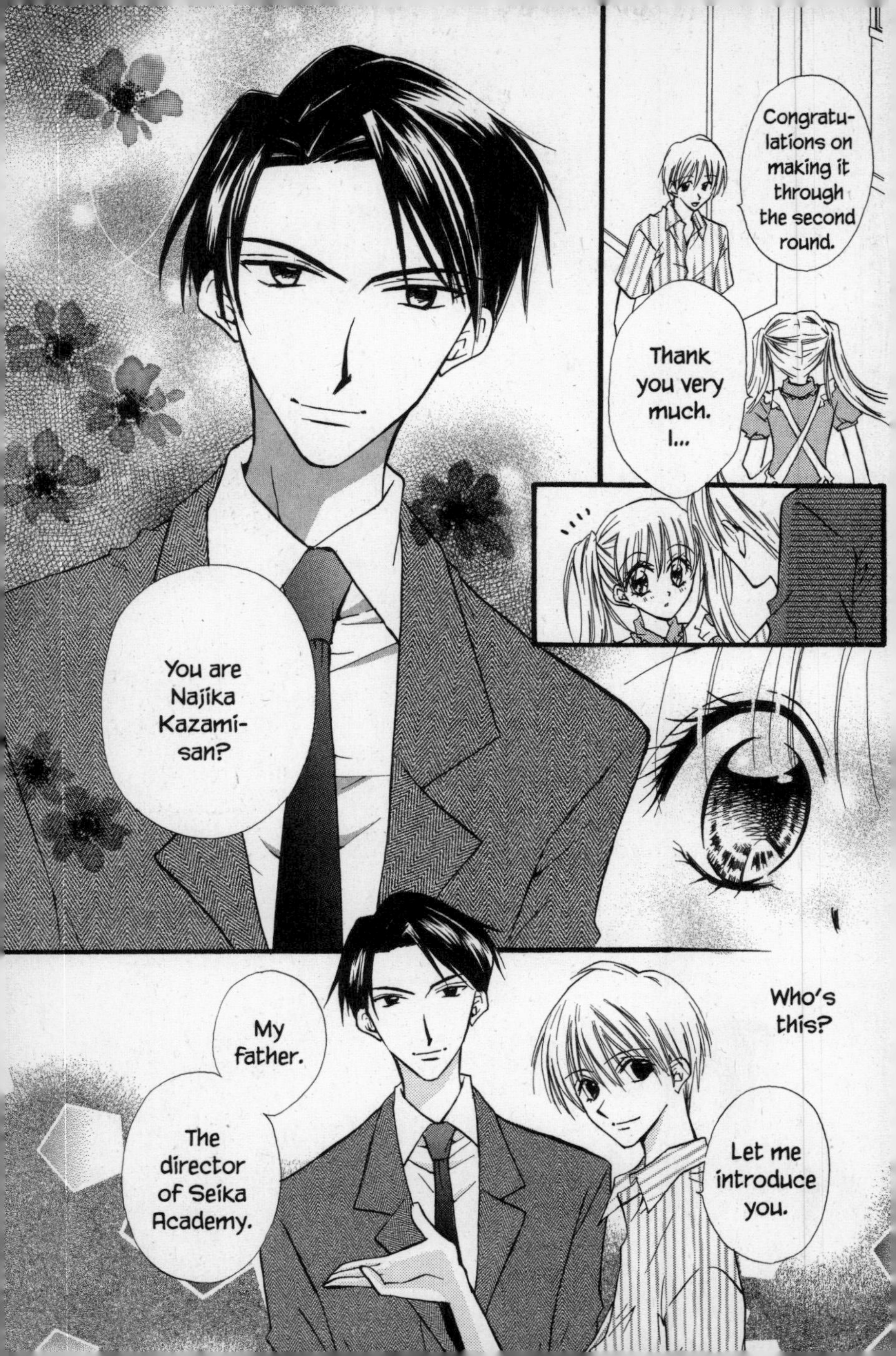

Congratulations on making it through the second round.
Thank you very much. I...
You are Najika Kazami-san?
Who's this?
Let me introduce you.
My father.
The director of Seika Academy.

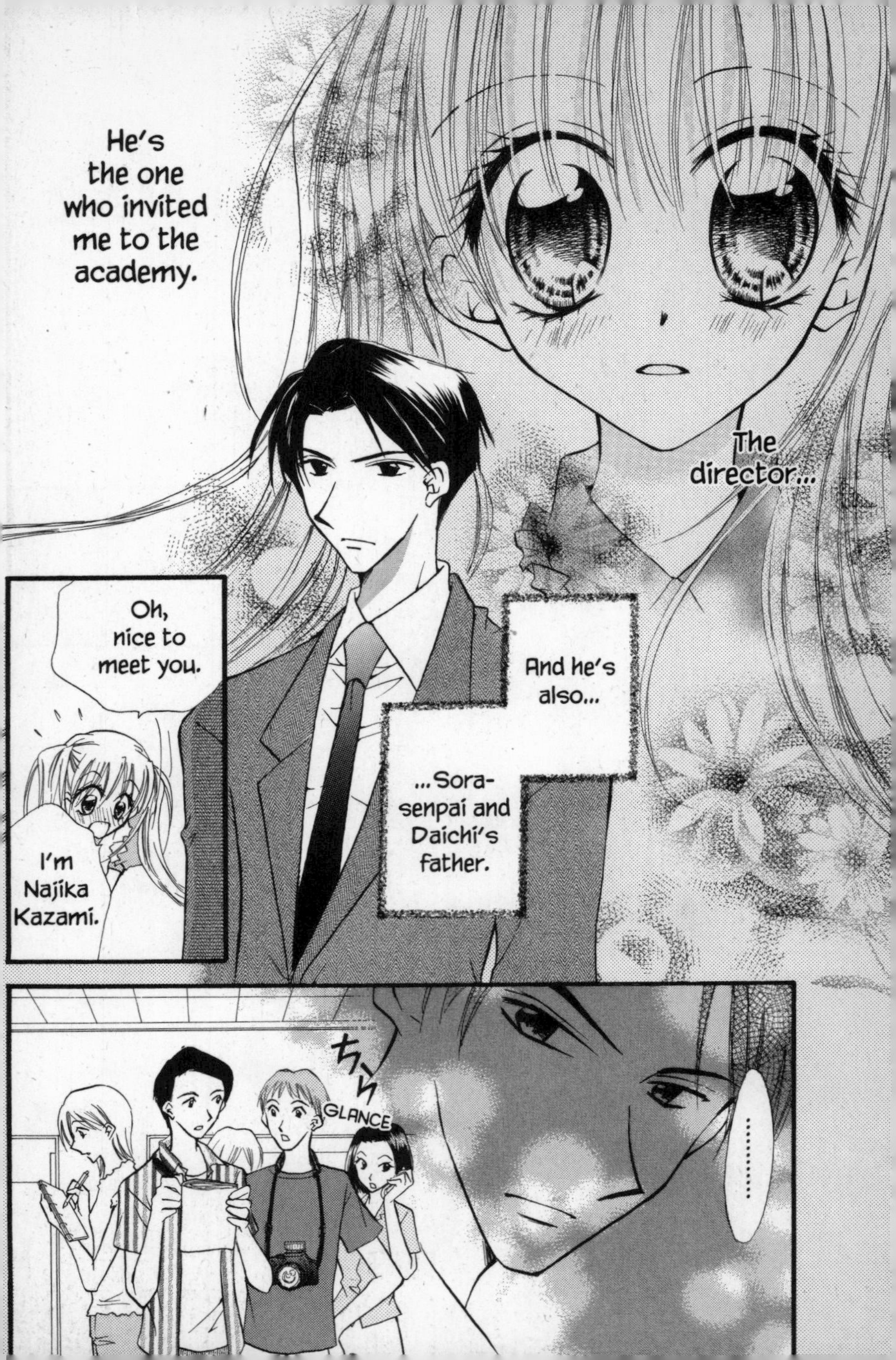
He's the one who invited me to the academy.
The director...
And he's also...
...Sora-senpai and Daichi's father.
Oh, nice to meet you.
I'm Najika Kazami.
......
ちら
GLANCE

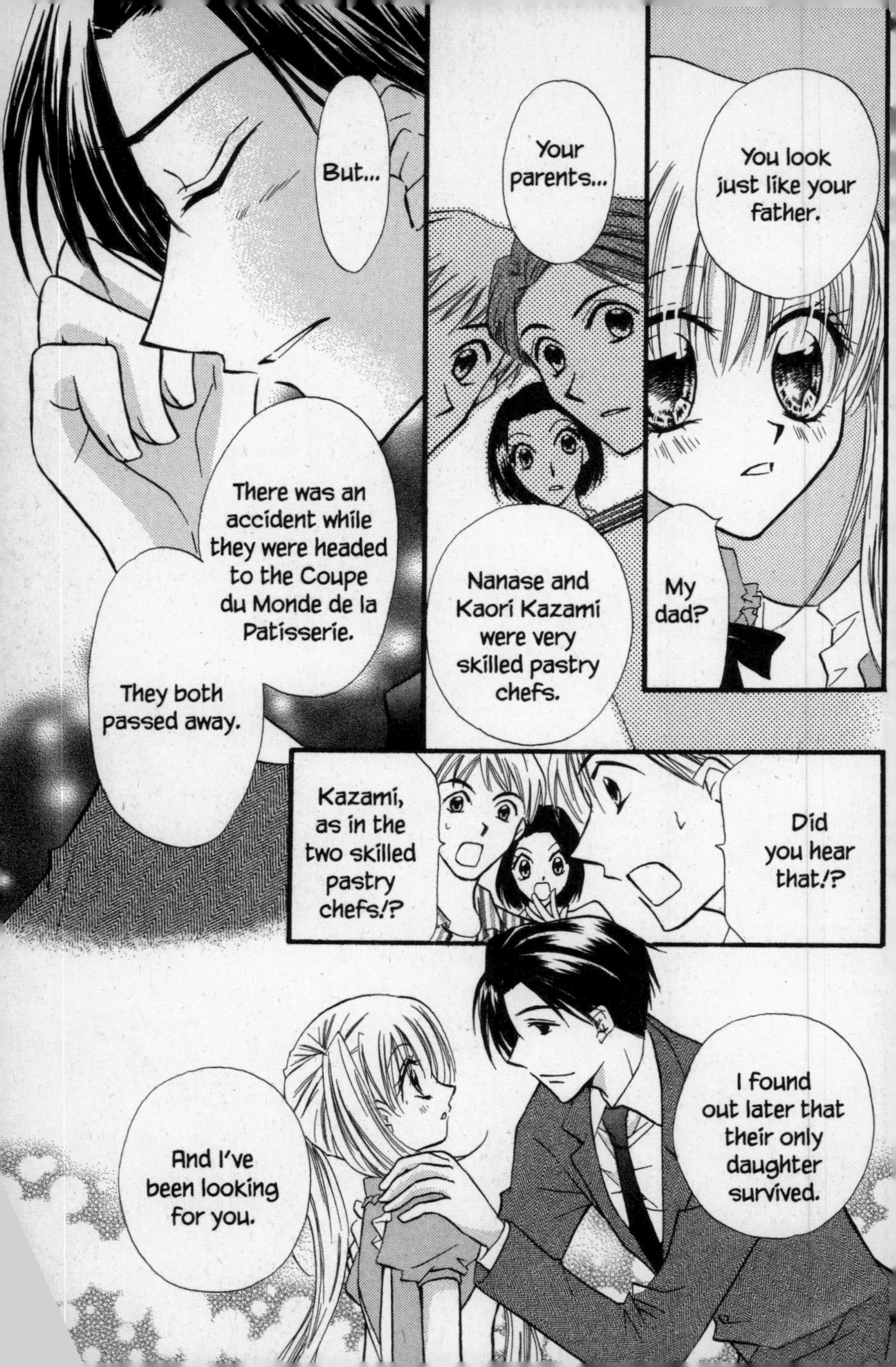
You look just like your father.
My dad?
Your parents...
Nanase and Kaori Kazami were very skilled pastry chefs.
But...
There was an accident while they were headed to the Coupe du Monde de la Patisserie.
They both passed away.
Did you hear that!?
Kazami, as in the two skilled pastry chefs!?
I found out later that their only daughter survived.
And I've been looking for you.

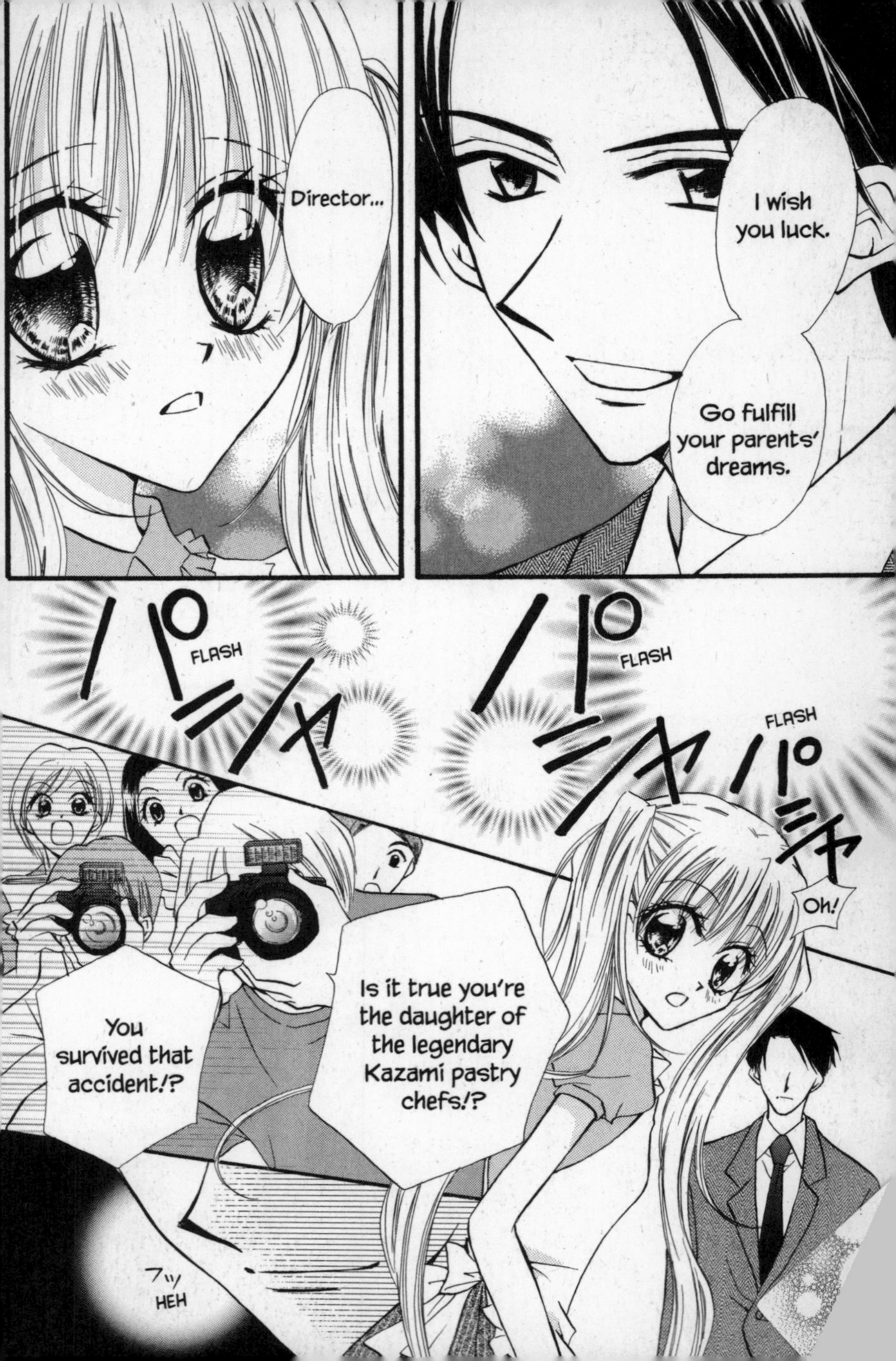
I wish you luck.
Go fulfill your parents' dreams.
Director...
パシャ
FLASH
パシャ
FLASH
パシャ
FLASH
Oh!
Is it true you're the daughter of the legendary Kazami pastry chefs!?
You survived that accident!?
フッ
HEH

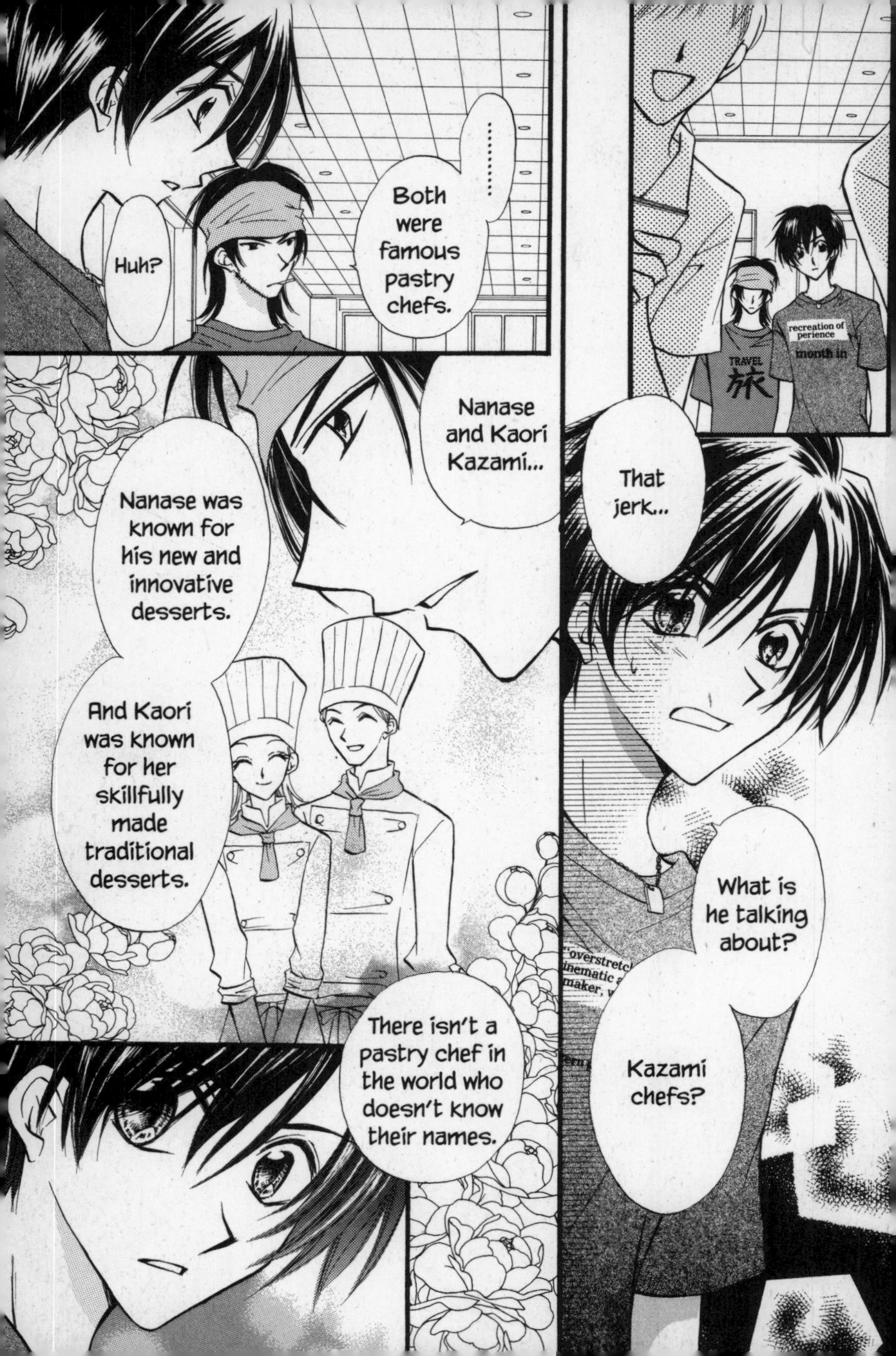

recreation of
perience
month in
TRAVEL
旅
......
Both were famous pastry chefs.
Huh?
That jerk...
What is he talking about?
Kazami chefs?
Nanase and Kaori Kazami...
Nanase was known for his new and innovative desserts.
And Kaori was known for her skillfully made traditional desserts.
There isn't a pastry chef in the world who doesn't know their names.

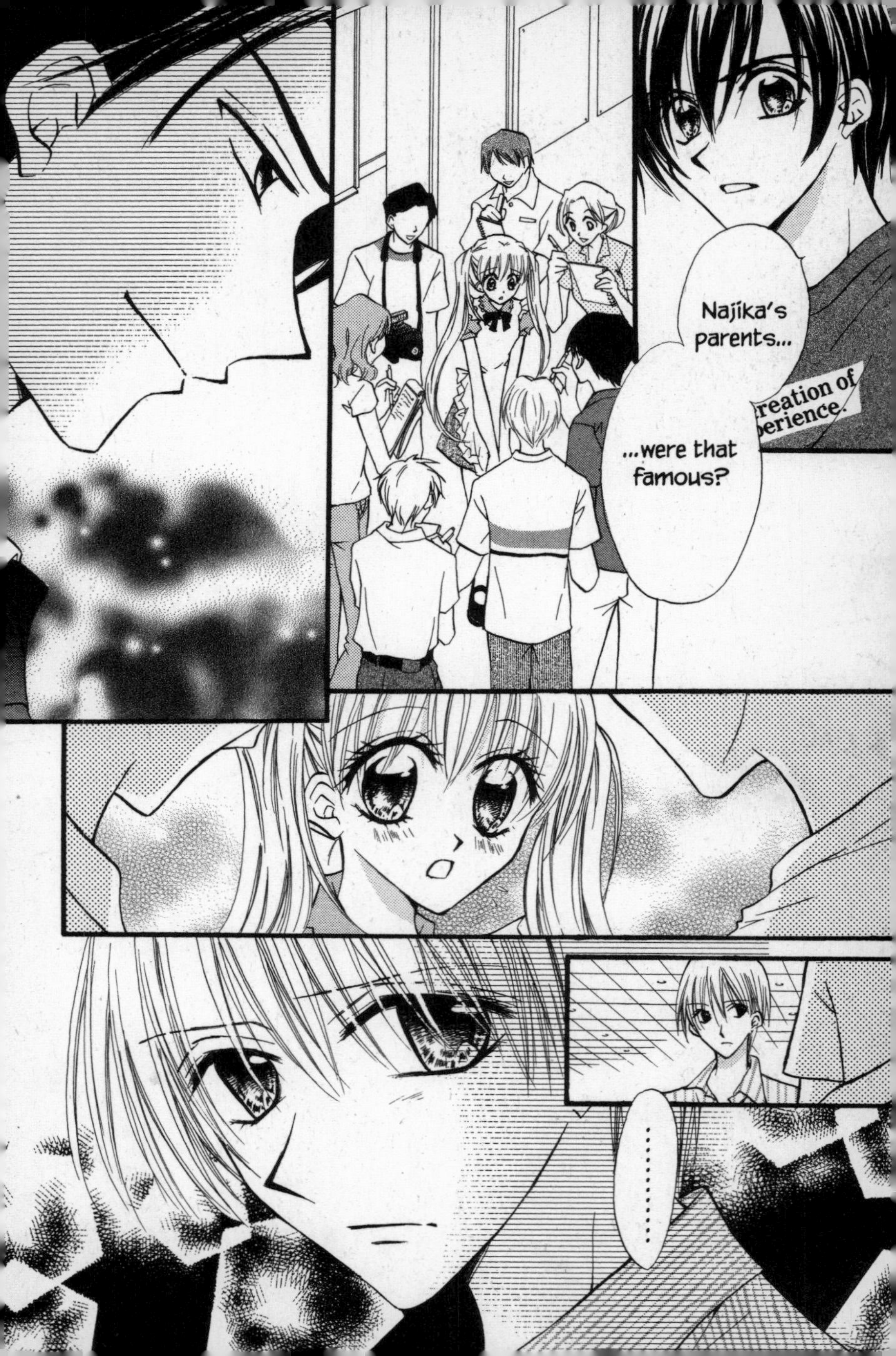
Najika's parents...
...were that famous?
reation of perience.
......

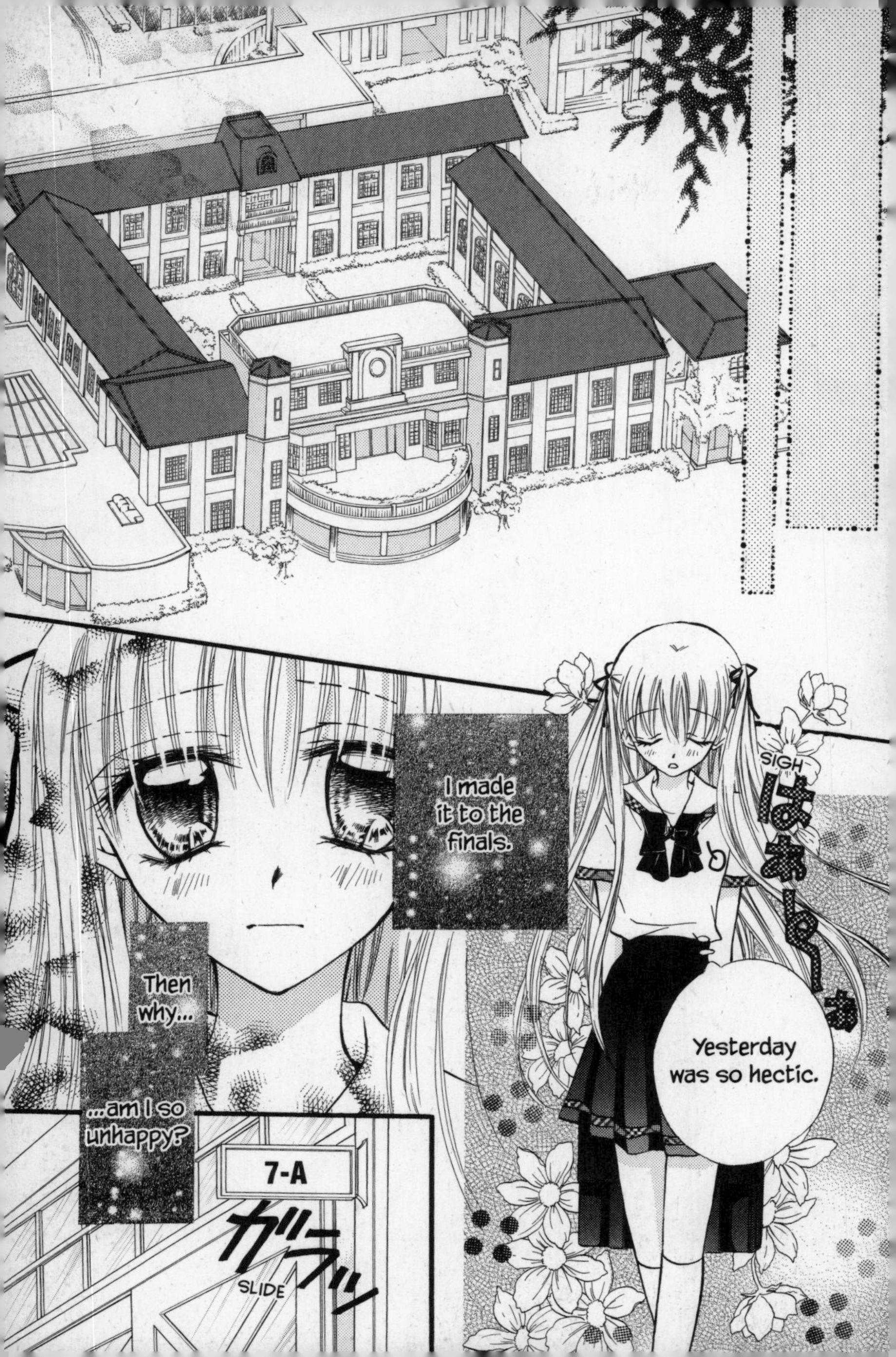
SIGH
Yesterday was so hectic.
I made it to the finals.
Then why...
...am I so unhappy?
7-A
SLIDE

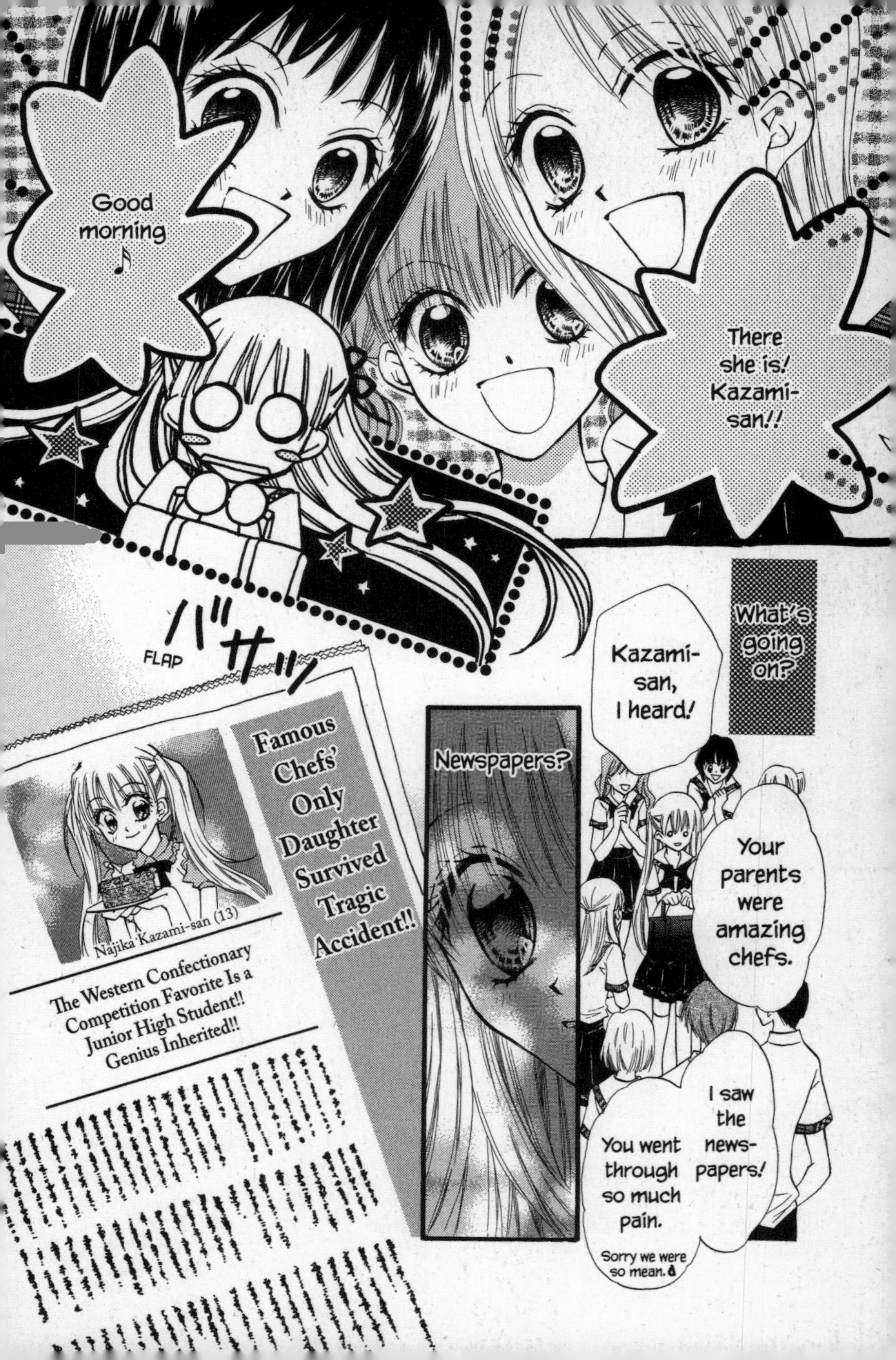
There she is! Kazami-san!!
Good morning ♪
What's going on?
Kazami-san, I heard!
Your parents were amazing chefs.
I saw the news-papers!
You went through so much pain.
Sorry we were so mean.
Newspapers?
バサッ
FLAP
Famous Chefs' Only Daughter Survived Tragic Accident!!
Najika Kazami-san (13)
The Western Confectionary Competition Favorite Is a Junior High Student!! Genius Inherited!!

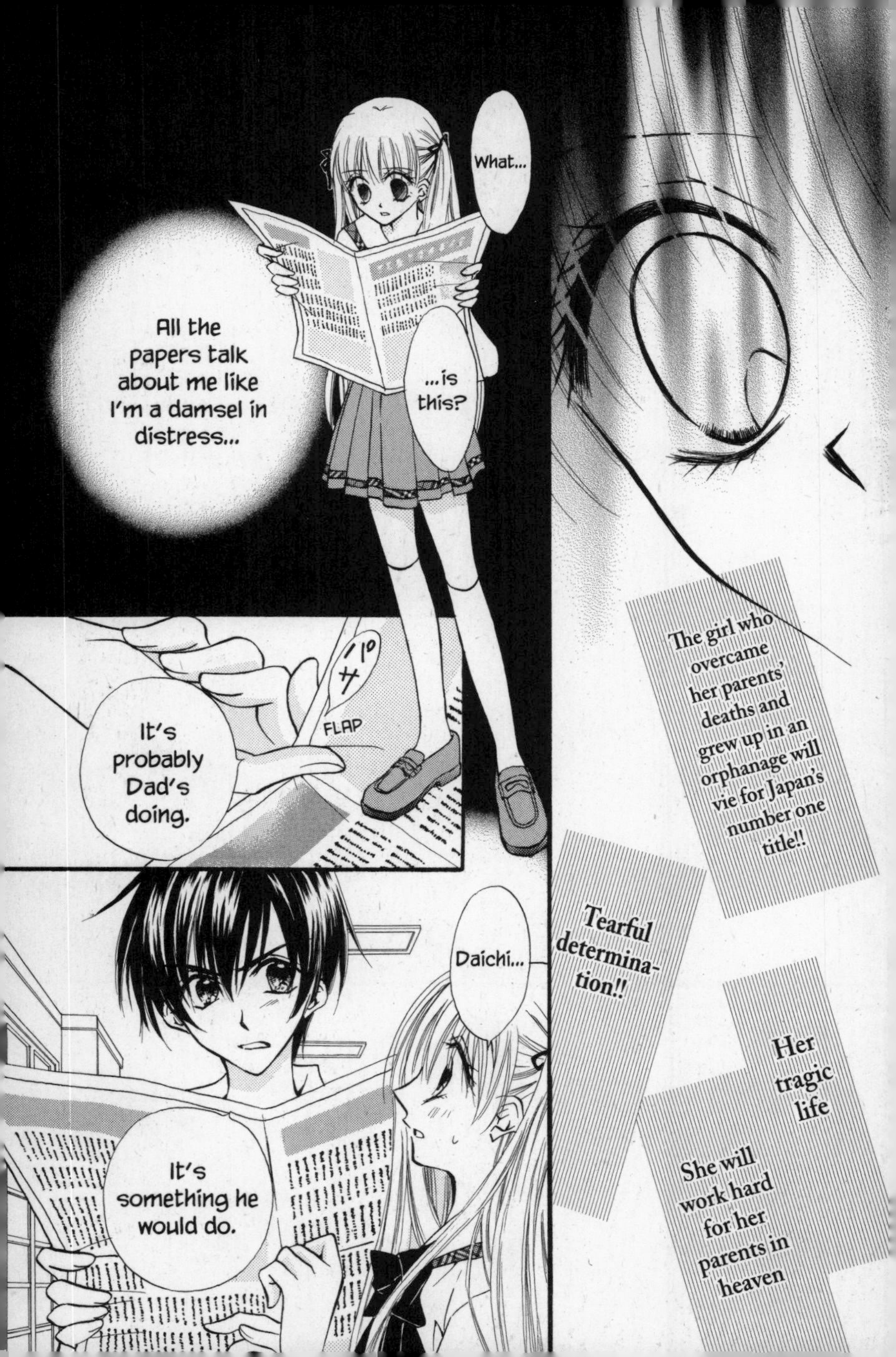

The girl who overcame her parents' deaths and grew up in an orphanage will vie for Japan's number one title!!
Tearful determina-tion!!
Her tragic life
She will work hard for her parents in heaven
What...
...is this?
All the papers talk about me like I'm a damsel in distress...
パサ
FLAP
It's probably Dad's doing.
Daichi...
It's something he would do.

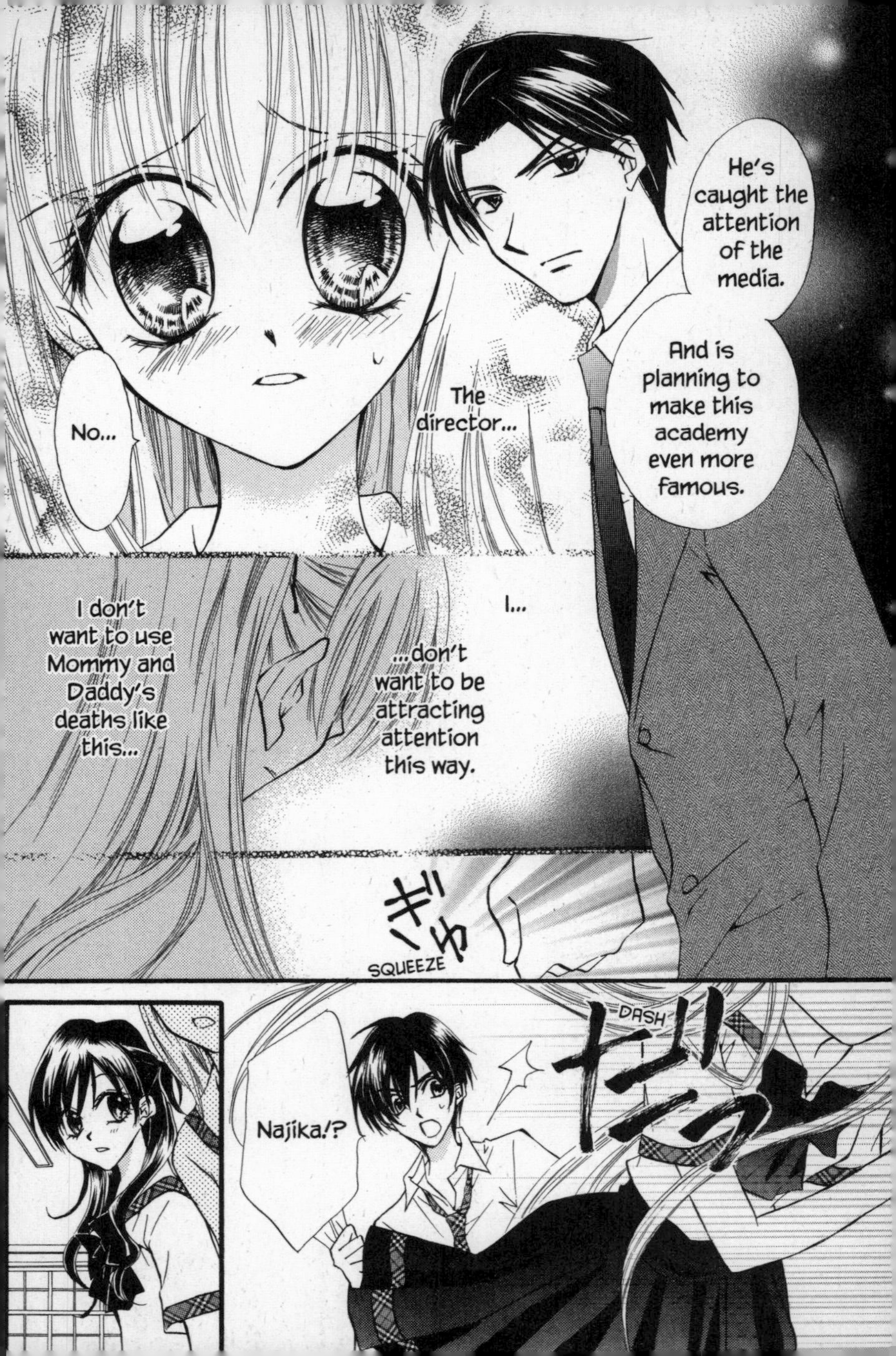
He's caught the attention of the media.
And is planning to make this academy even more famous.
The director...
No...
I...
...don't want to be attracting attention this way.
I don't want to use Mommy and Daddy's deaths like this...
SQUEEZE
DASH
Najika!?

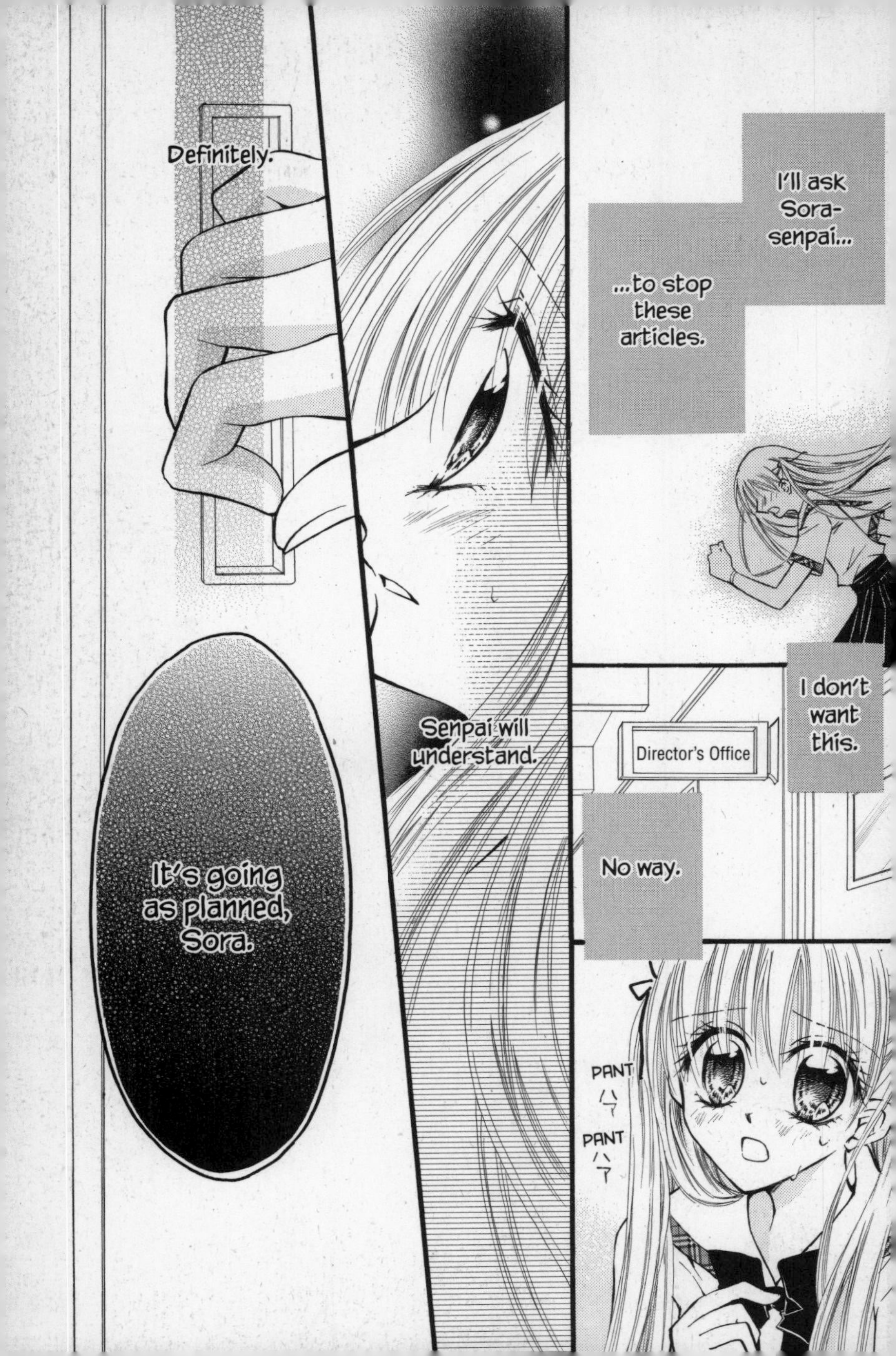
I'll ask Sora-senpai...
...to stop these articles.
I don't want this.
Director's Office
No way.
PANT
PANT
Senpai will understand.
Definitely.
It's going as planned, Sora.

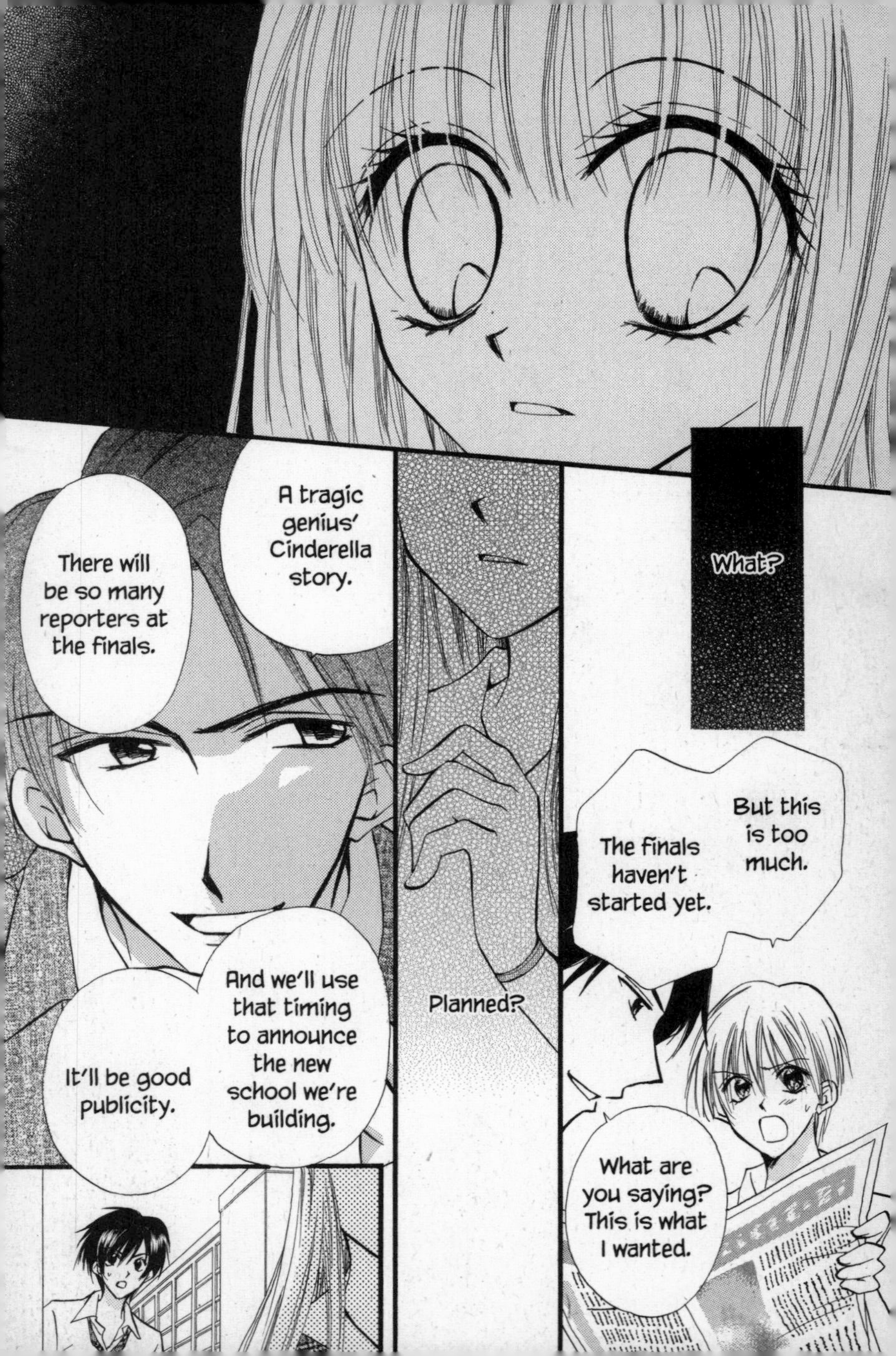
What?
But this is too much.
The finals haven't started yet.
What are you saying? This is what I wanted.
Planned?
A tragic genius' Cinderella story.
There will be so many reporters at the finals.
And we'll use that timing to announce the new school we're building.
It'll be good publicity.

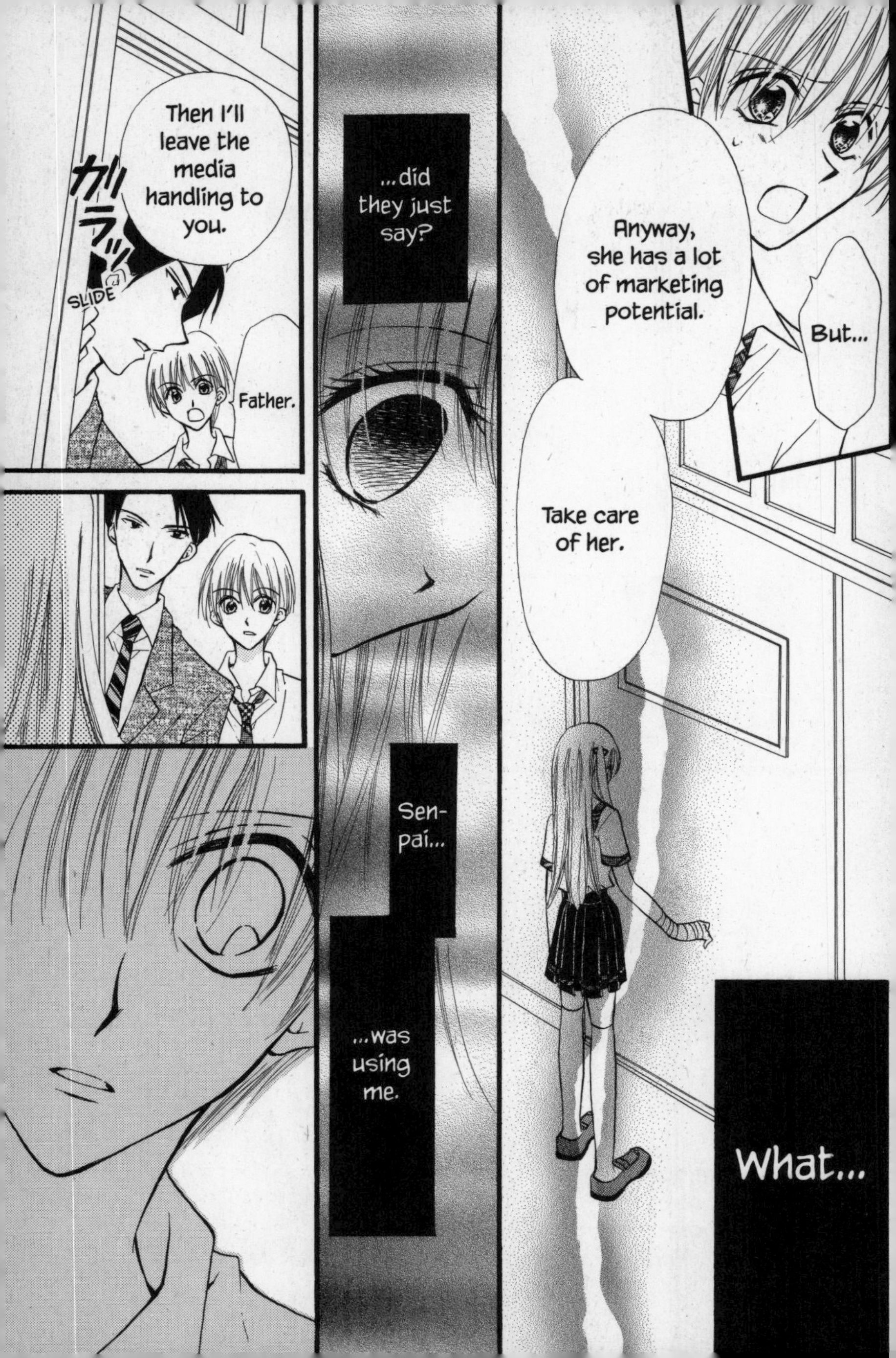
Anyway, she has a lot of marketing potential.
Take care of her.
But...
What...
...did they just say?
Sen-pai...
...was using me.
Then I'll leave the media handling to you.
ガラッ
SLIDE
Father.

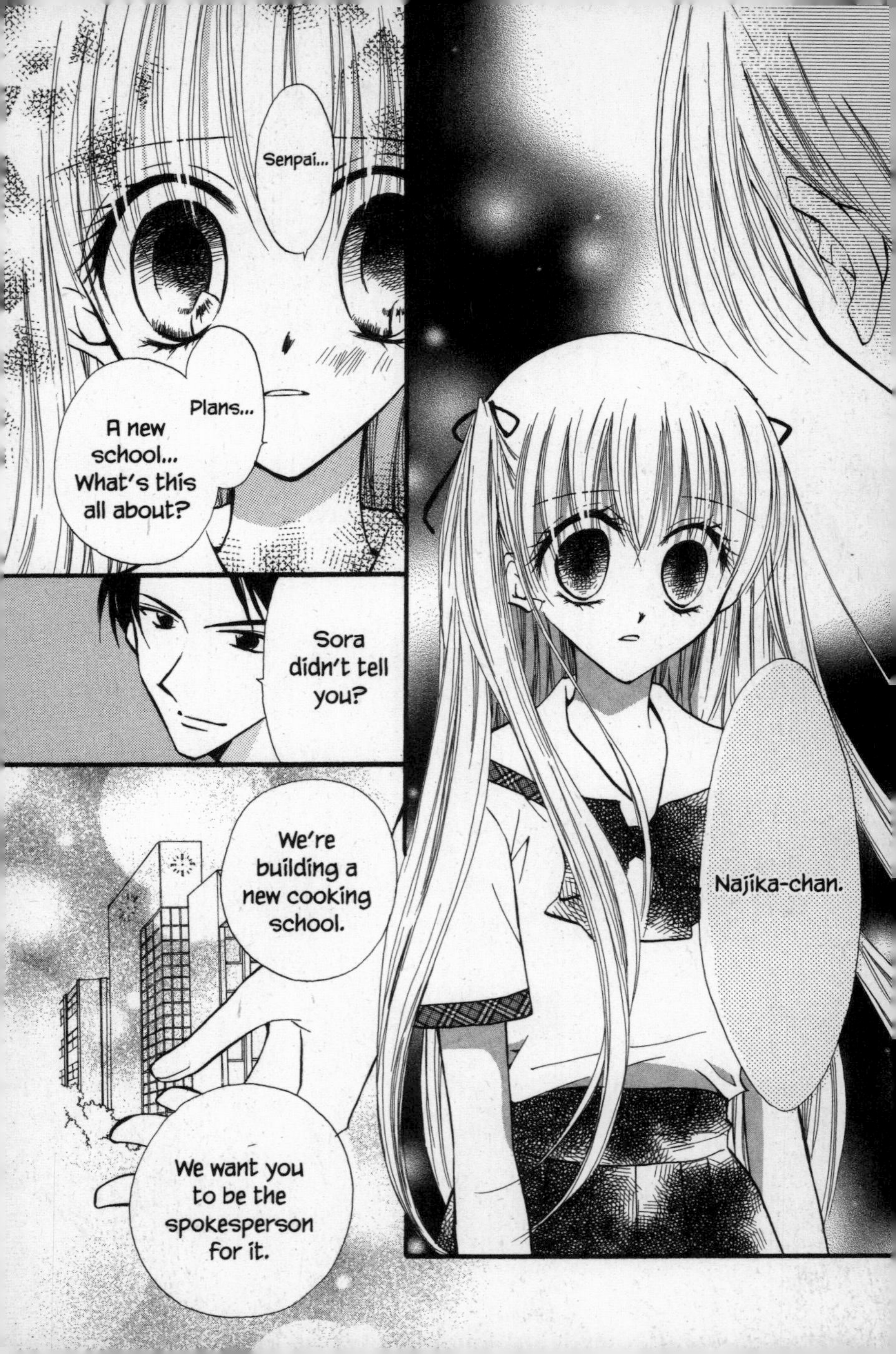
Najika-chan.
Senpai...
Plans... A new school... What's this all about?
Sora didn't tell you?
We're building a new cooking school.
We want you to be the spokesperson for it.

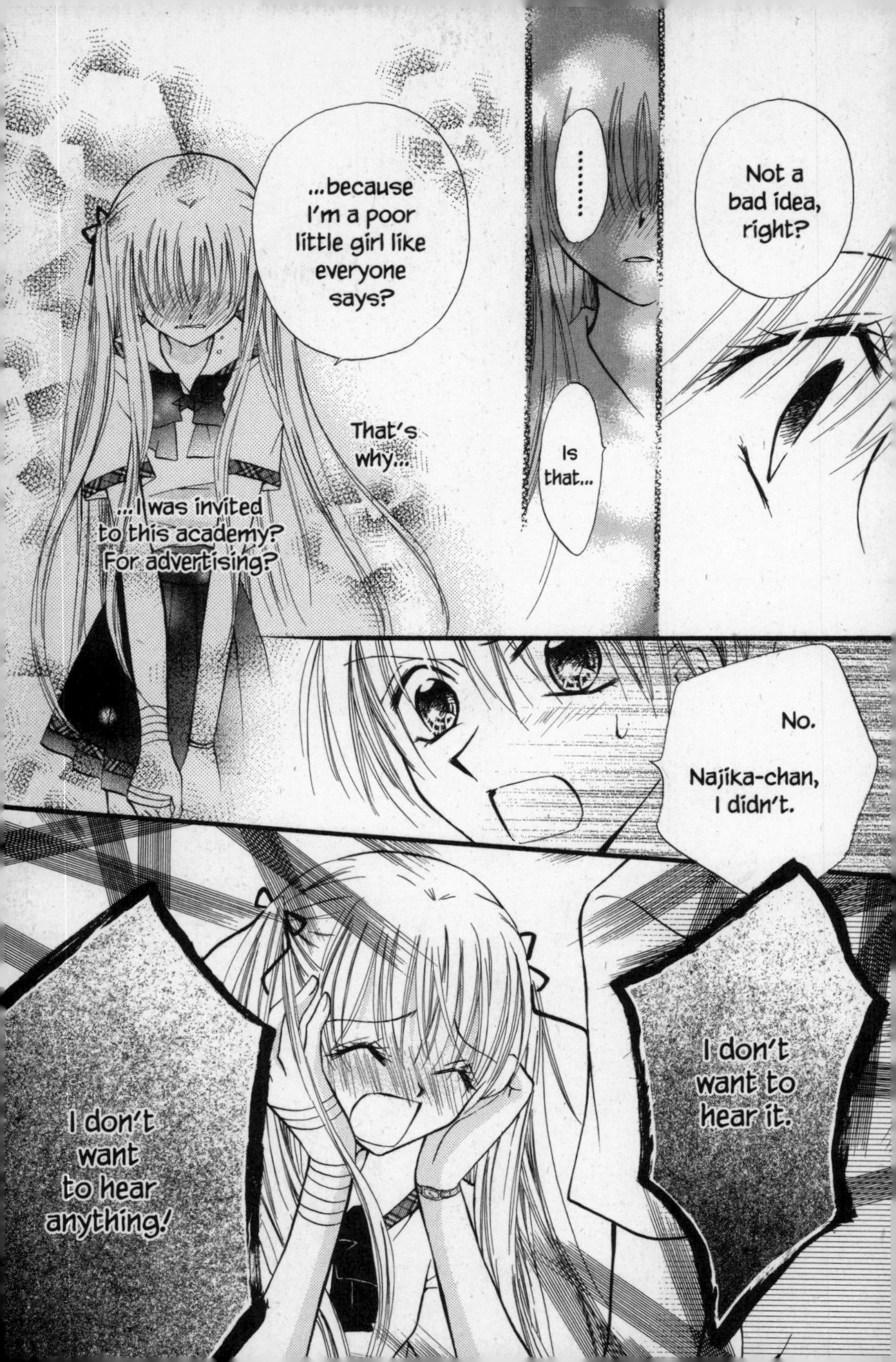

Not a bad idea, right?
......
Is that...
No.
Najika-chan, I didn't.
...because I'm a poor little girl like everyone says?
That's why...
...I was invited to this academy? For advertising?
I don't want to hear it.
I don't want to hear anything!

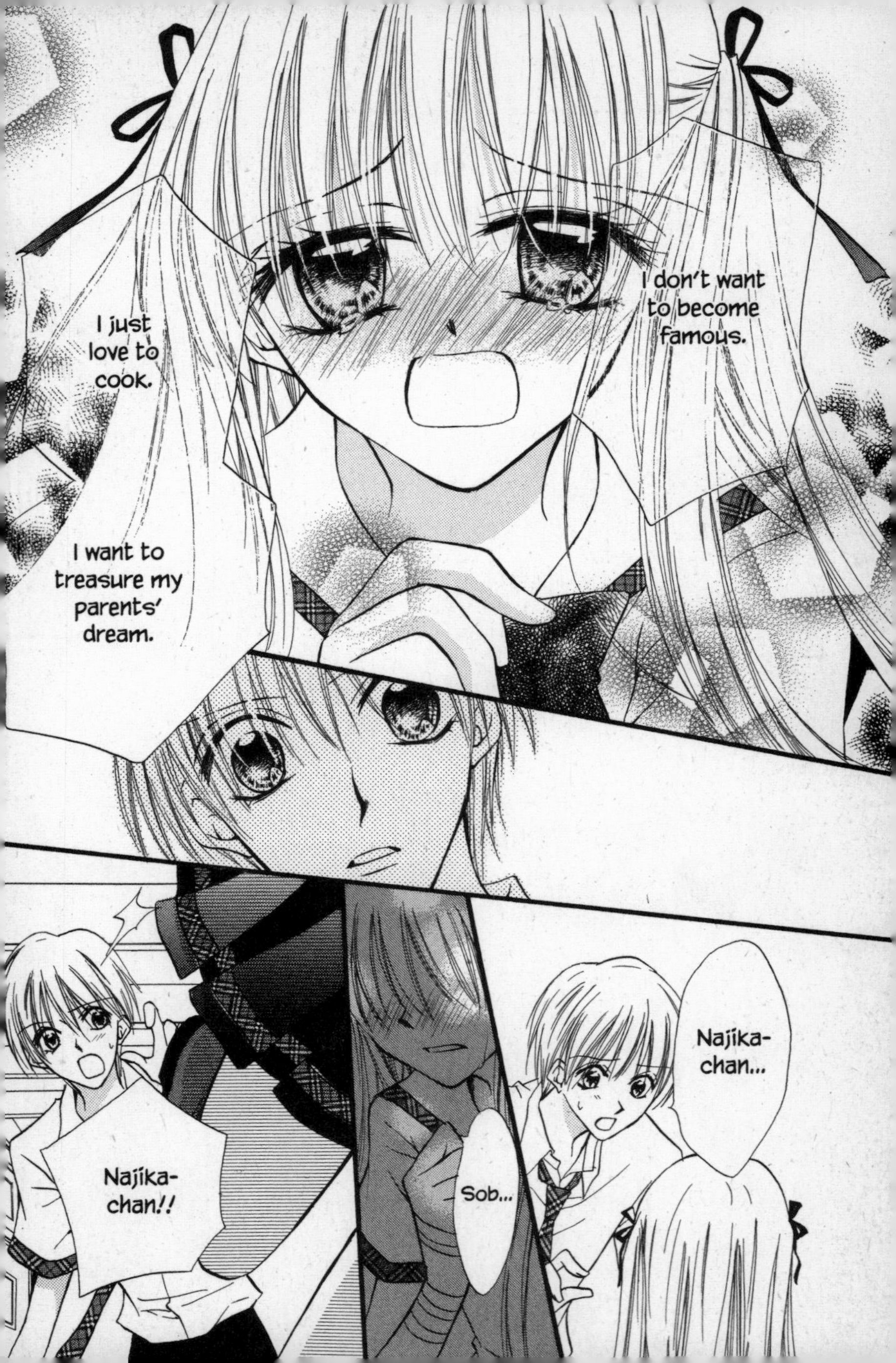
I don't want to become famous.
I just love to cook.
I want to treasure my parents' dream.
Najika-chan...
Sob...
Najika-chan!!

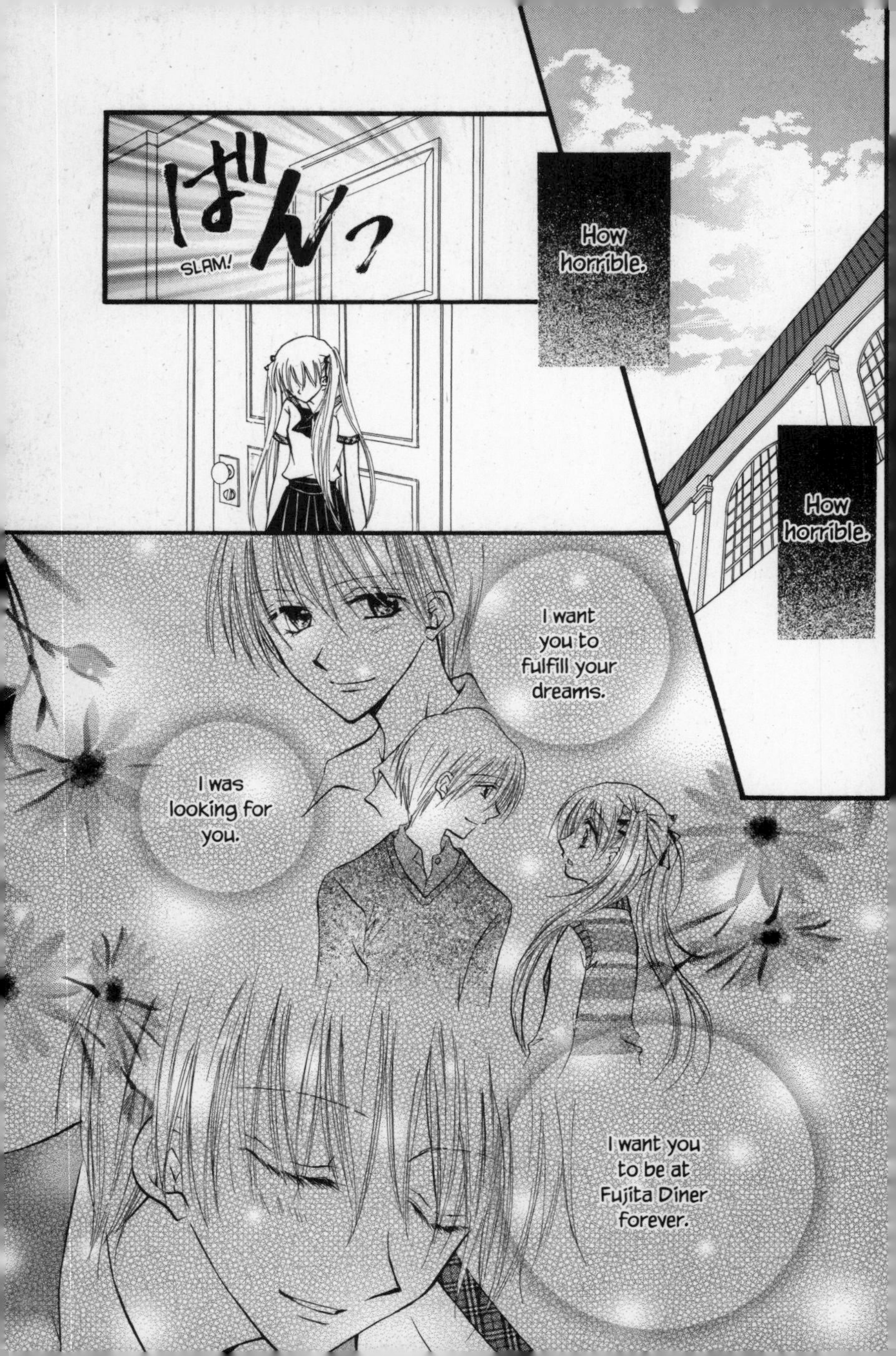
How horrible.
How horrible.
ばんっ
SLAM!
I want you to fulfill your dreams.
I was looking for you.
I want you to be at Fujita Diner forever.

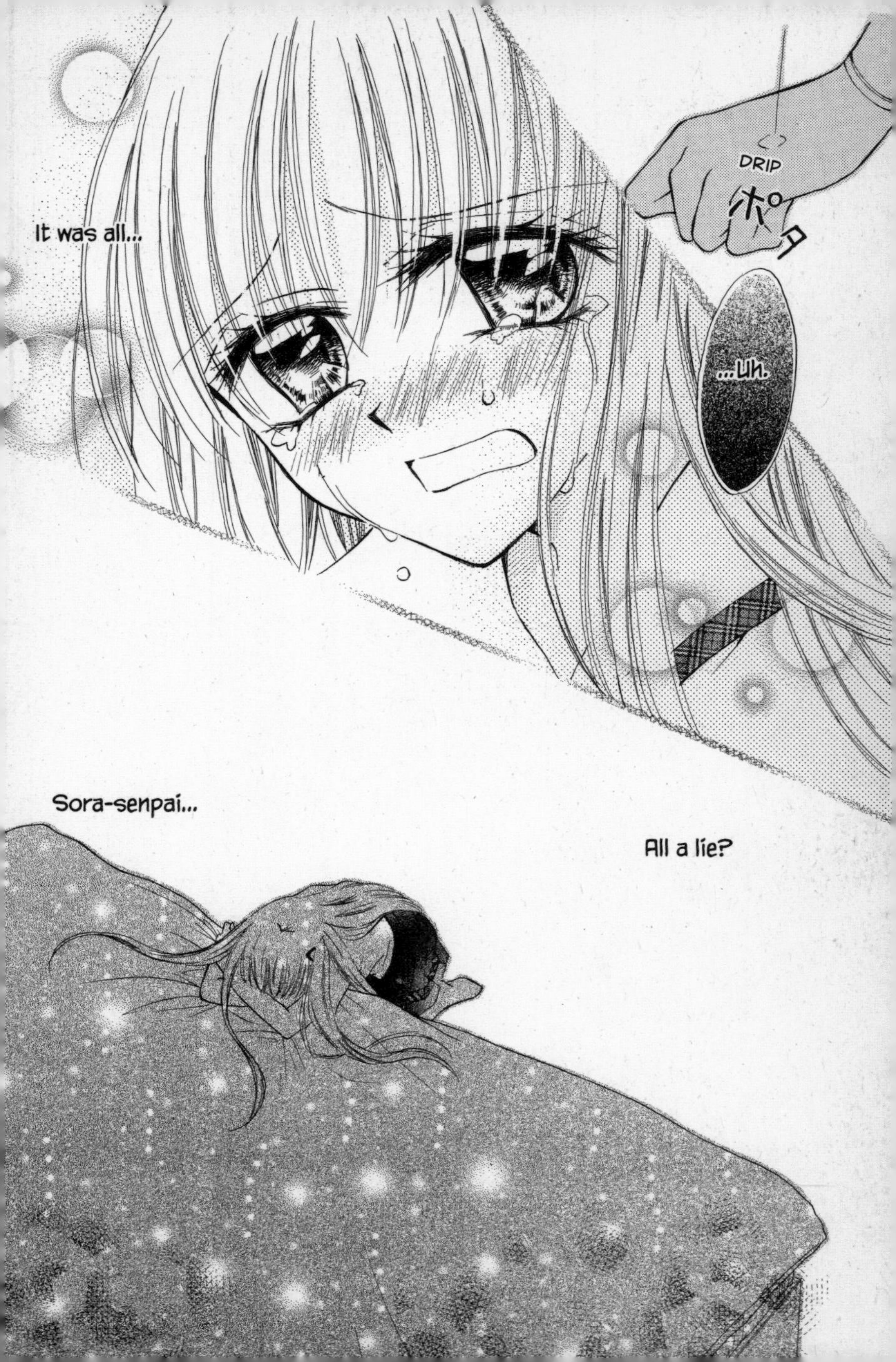
DRIP
ポタ
...Uh.
It was all...
Sora-senpai...
All a lie?

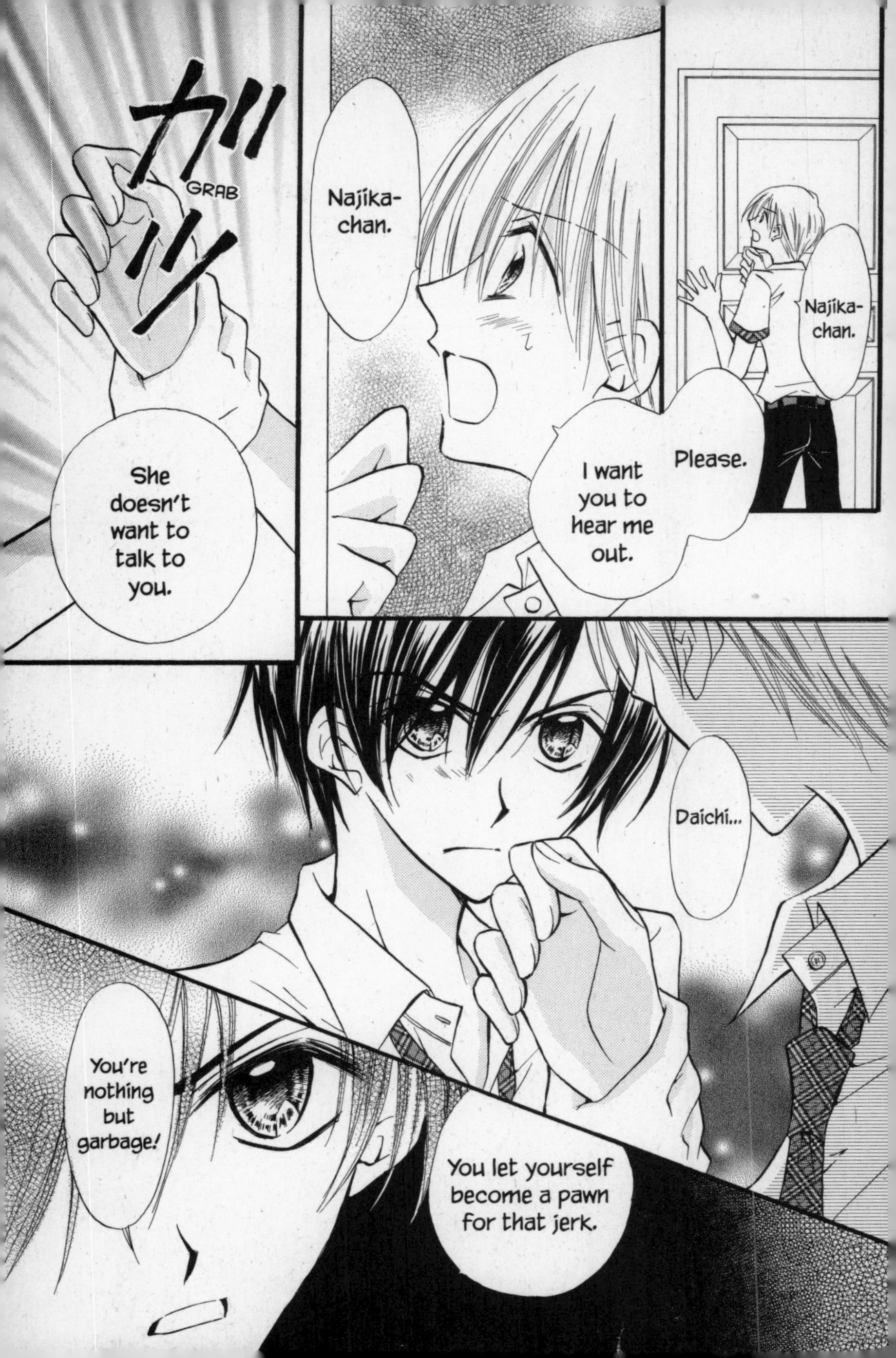
Najika-chan.
Please.
I want you to hear me out.
Najika-chan.
GRAB
She doesn't want to talk to you.
Daichi...
You're nothing but garbage!
You let yourself become a pawn for that jerk.

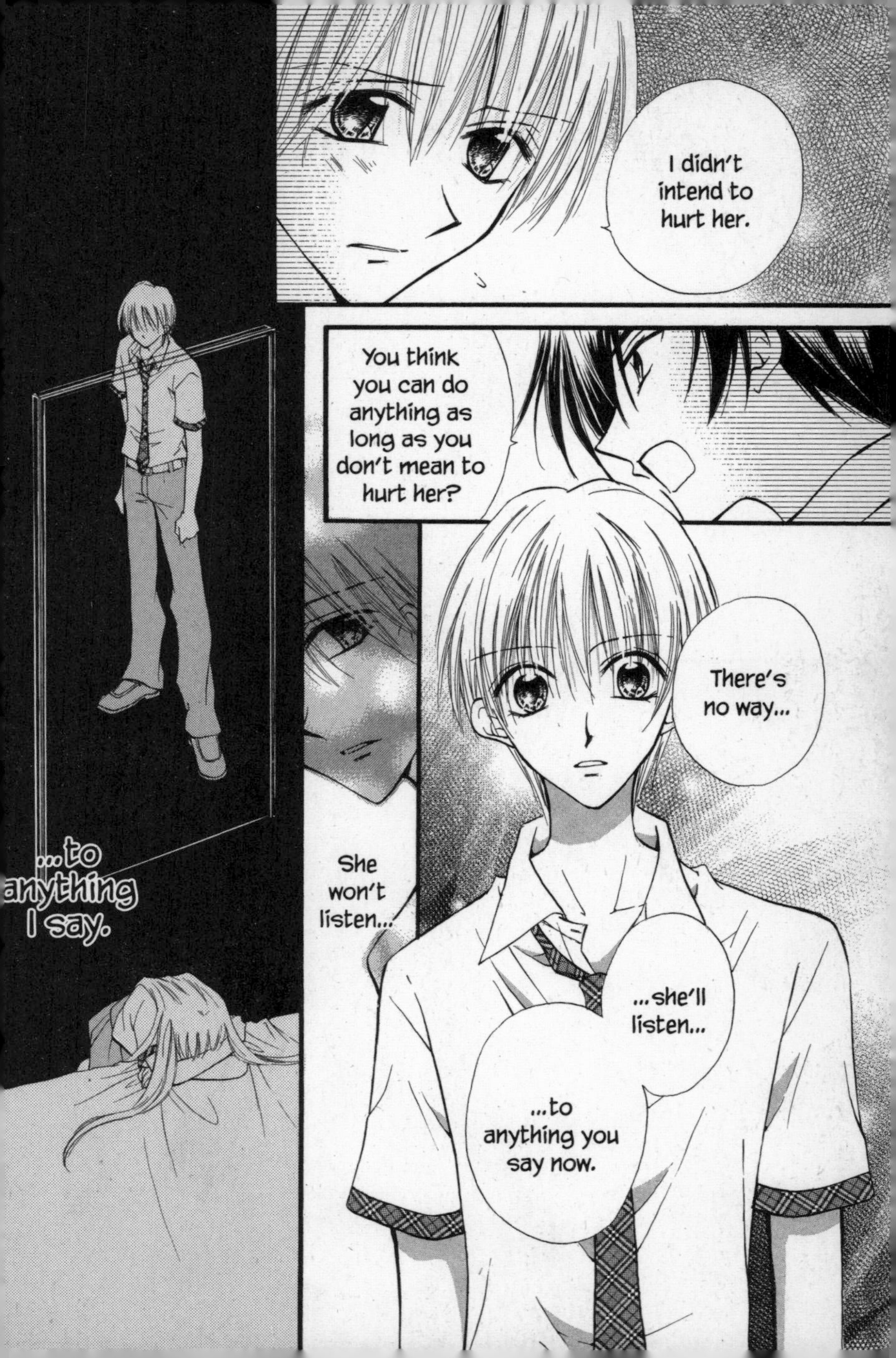
I didn't intend to hurt her.
You think you can do anything as long as you don't mean to hurt her?
There's no way...
...she'll listen...
...to anything you say now.
She won't listen...
...to anything I say.

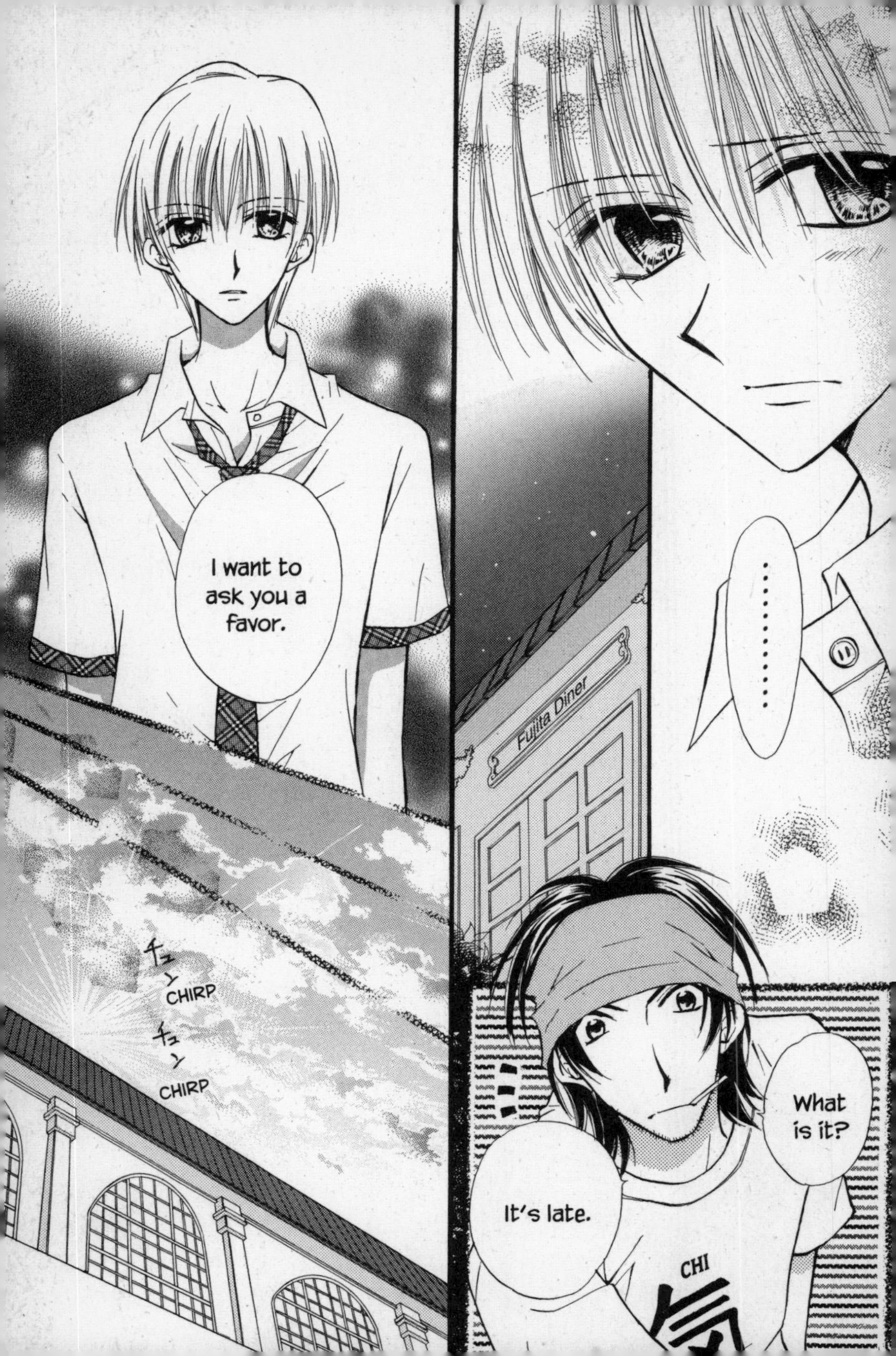
......
Fujita Diner
What is it?
It's late.
CHI
I want to ask you a favor.
チュン
CHIRP
チュン
CHIRP

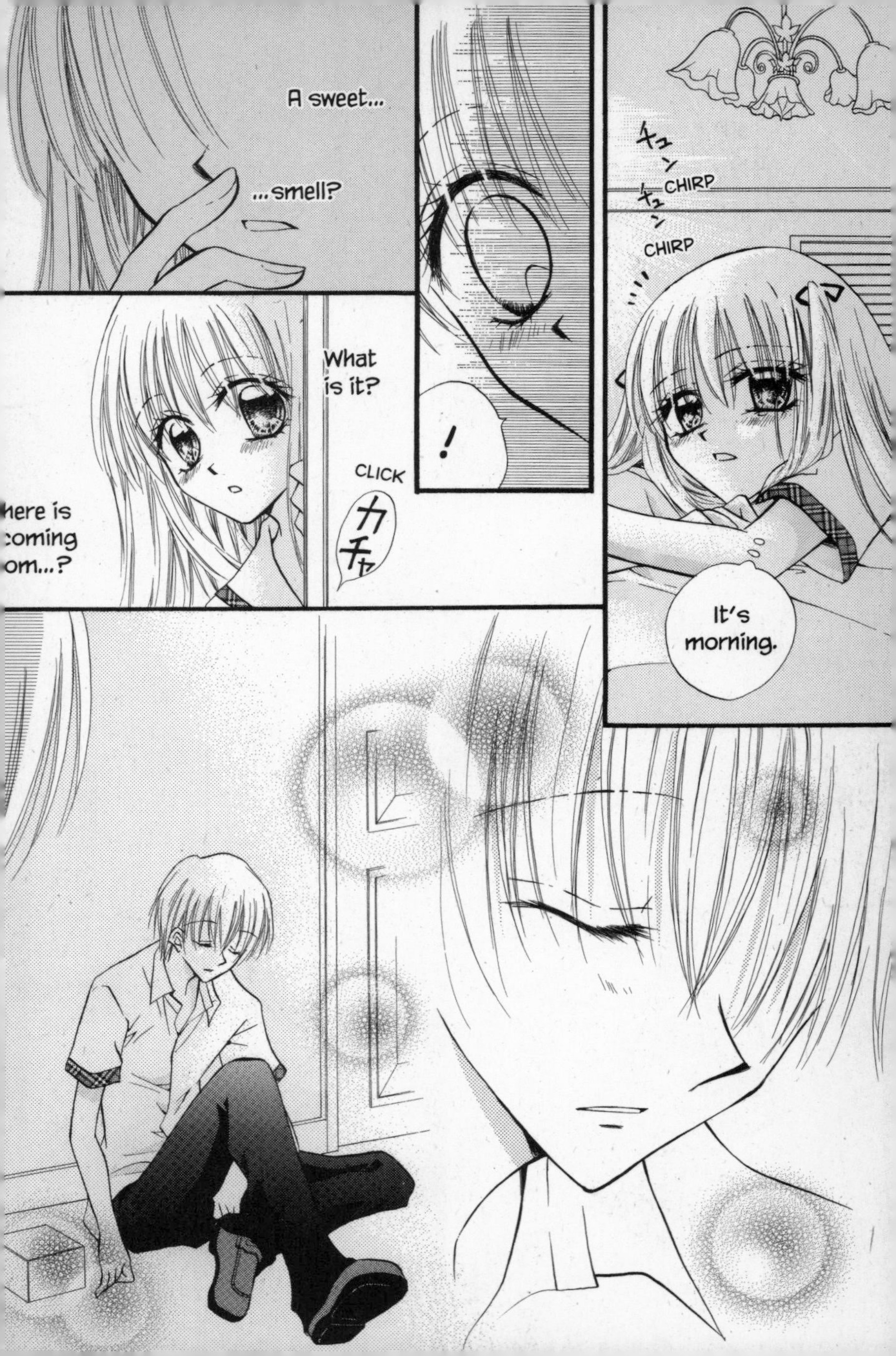
チュン
CHIRP
チュン
CHIRP
It's morning.
!
A sweet...
...smell?
What is it?
CLICK
カチャ
here is
coming
om...?

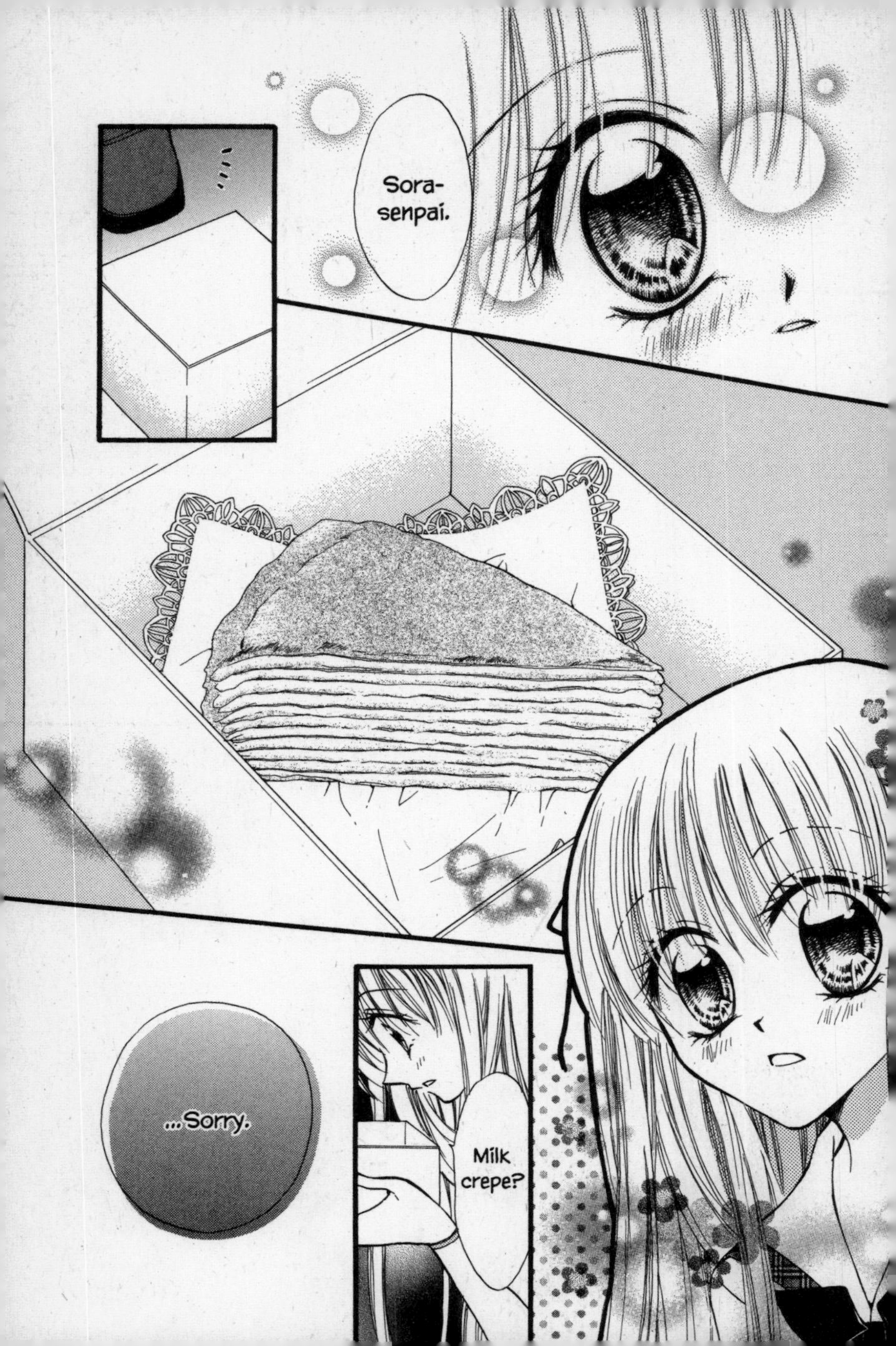
Sora-senpai.
Milk crepe?
...Sorry.

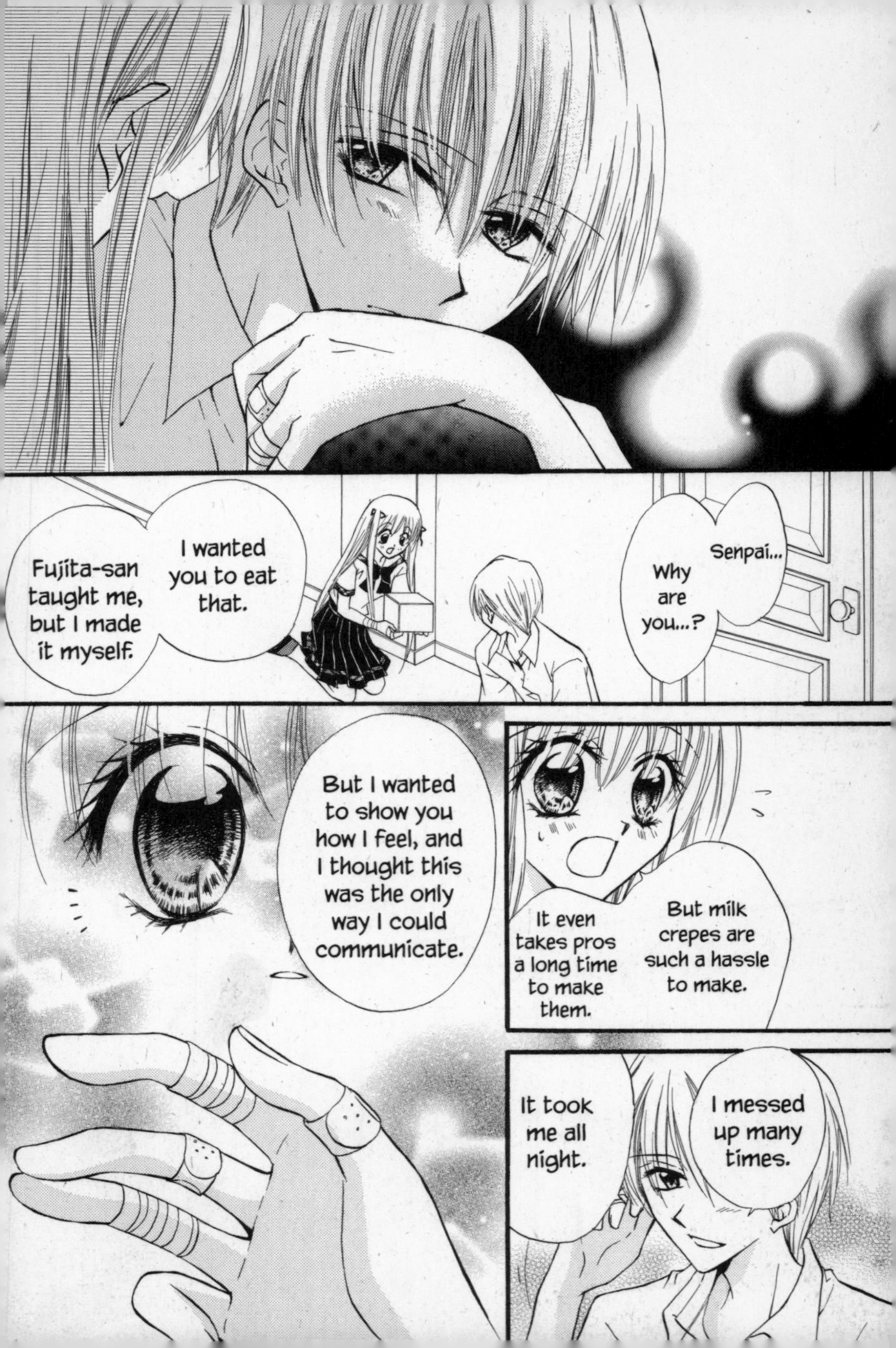

Senpai... Why are you...?
I wanted you to eat that.
Fujita-san taught me, but I made it myself.
But milk crepes are such a hassle to make.
It even takes pros a long time to make them.
I messed up many times.
It took me all night.
But I wanted to show you how I feel, and I thought this was the only way I could communicate.

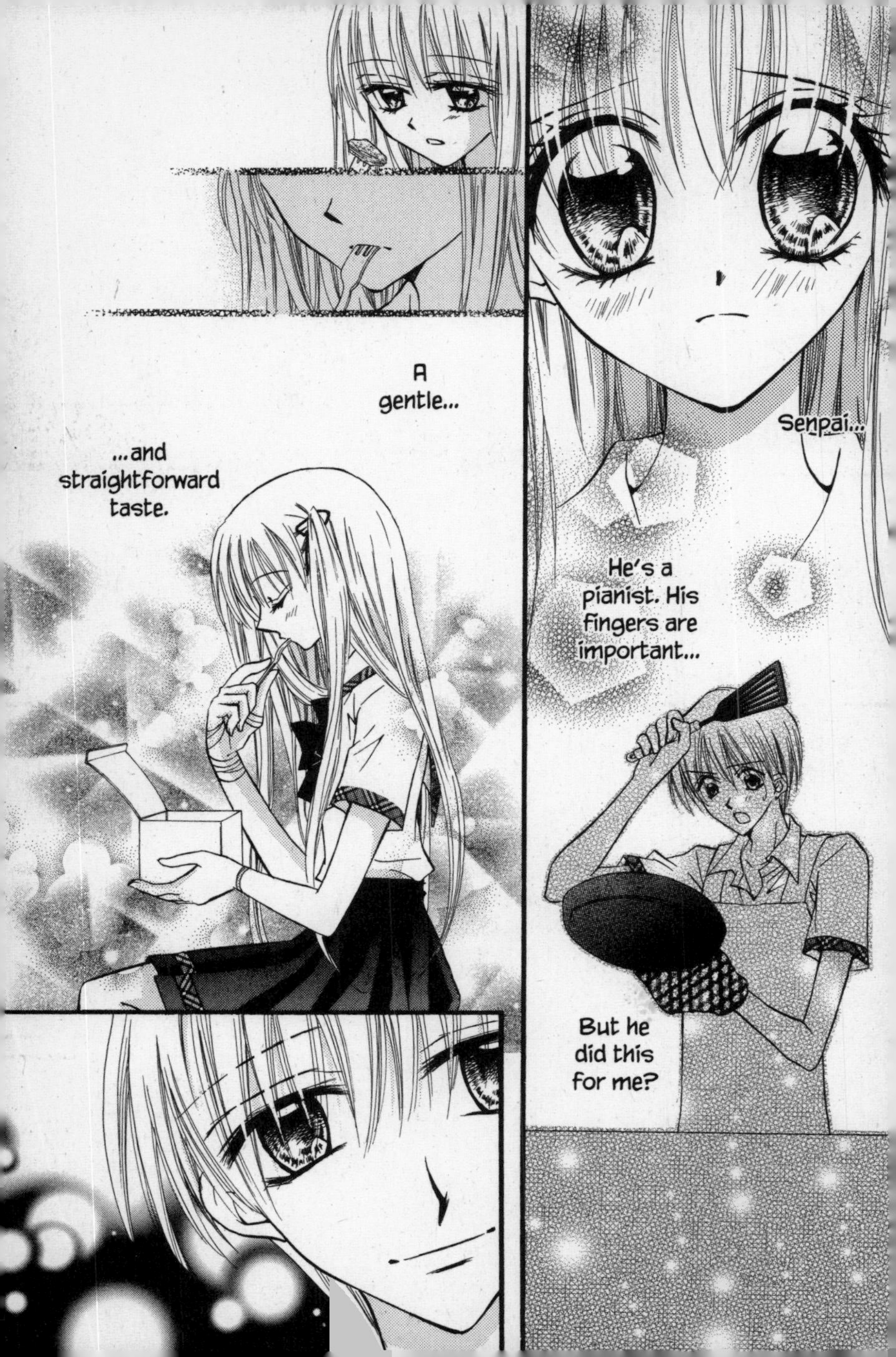
Senpai...
He's a pianist. His fingers are important...
But he did this for me?
A gentle...
...and straightforward taste.

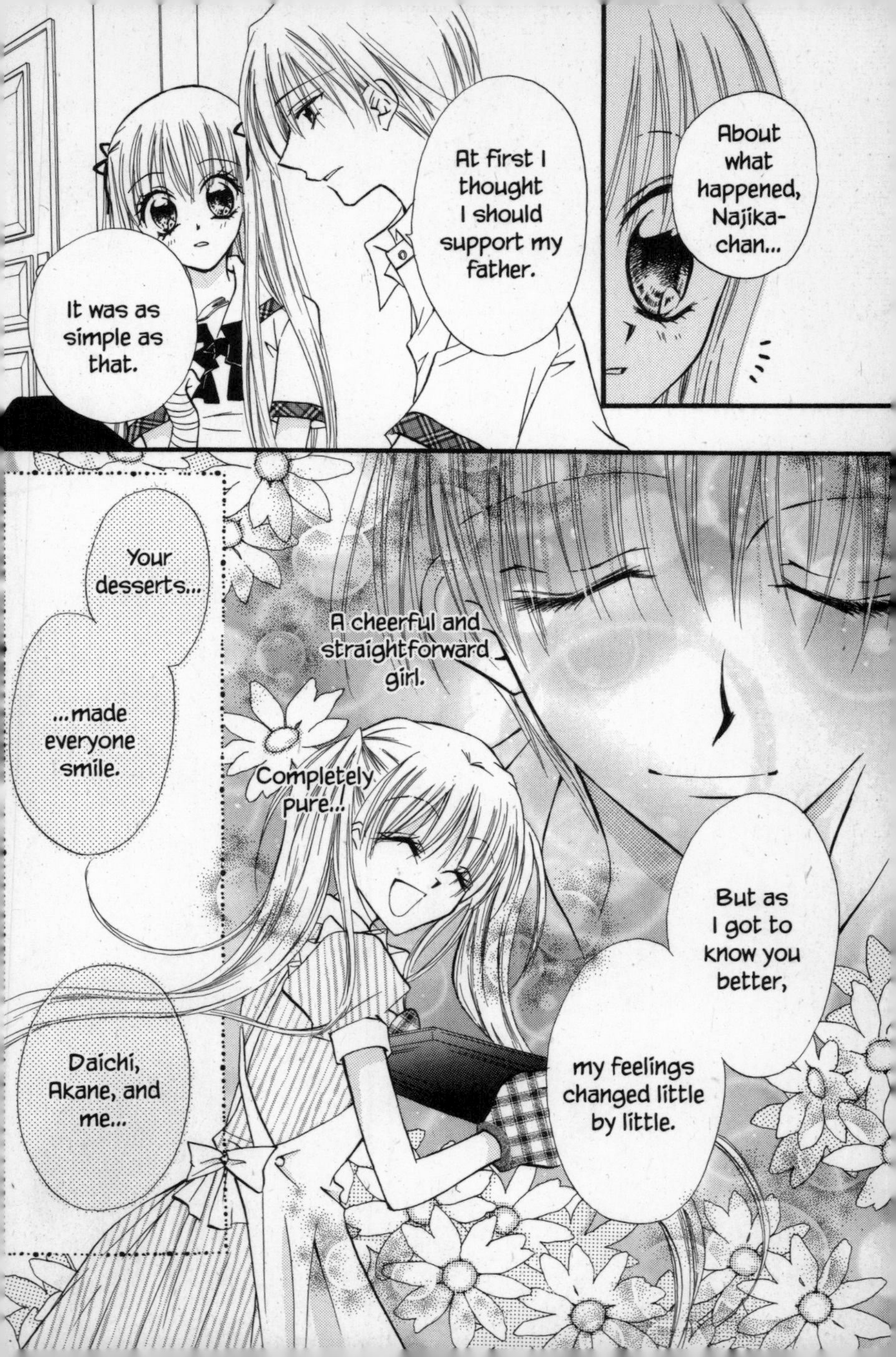
About what happened, Najika-chan...
At first I thought I should support my father.
It was as simple as that.
But as I got to know you better,
my feelings changed little by little.
A cheerful and straightforward girl.
Completely pure...!
Your desserts...
...made everyone smile.
Daichi, Akane, and me...

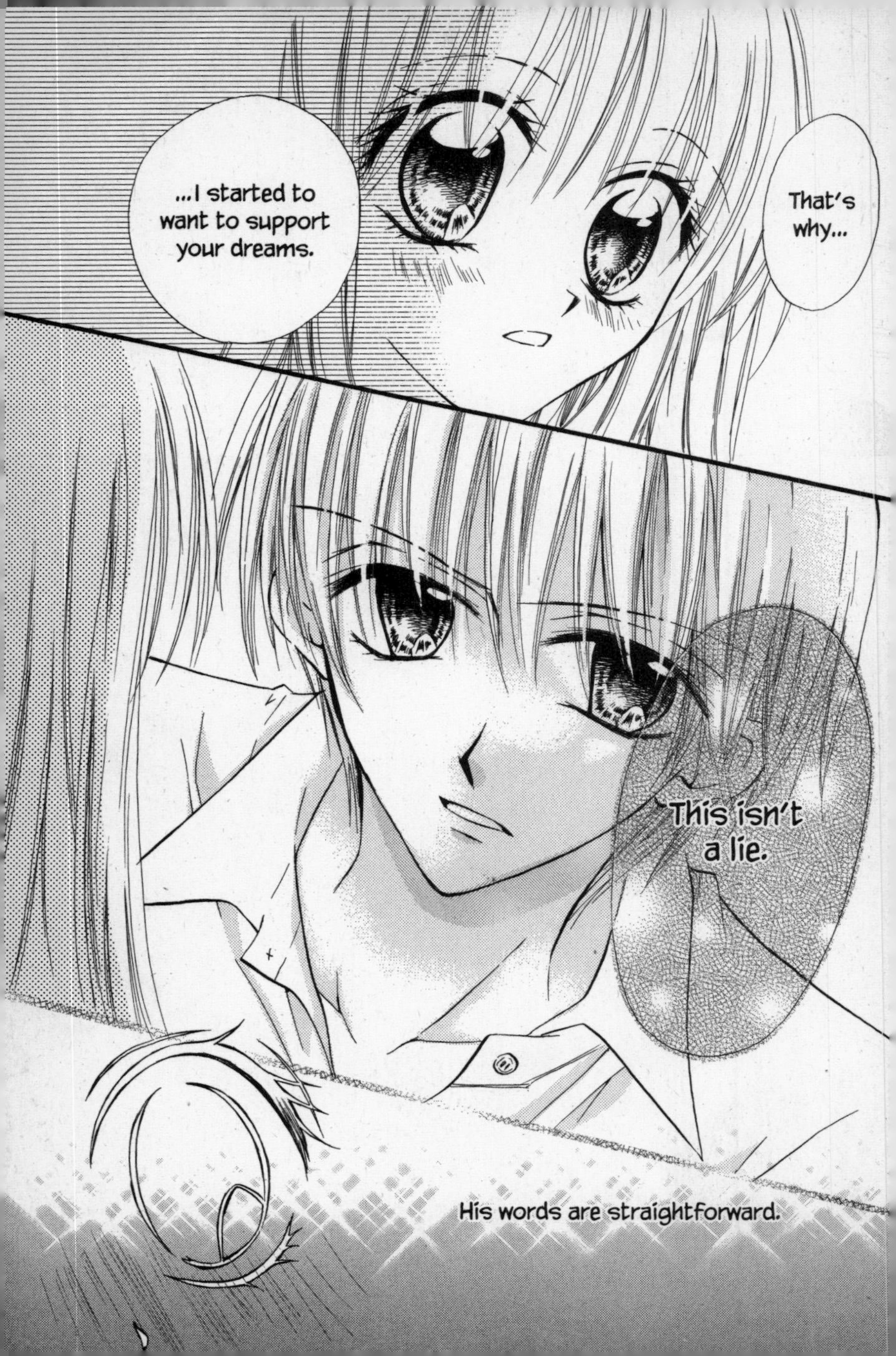
That's why...
...I started to want to support your dreams.
This isn't a lie.
His words are straightforward.

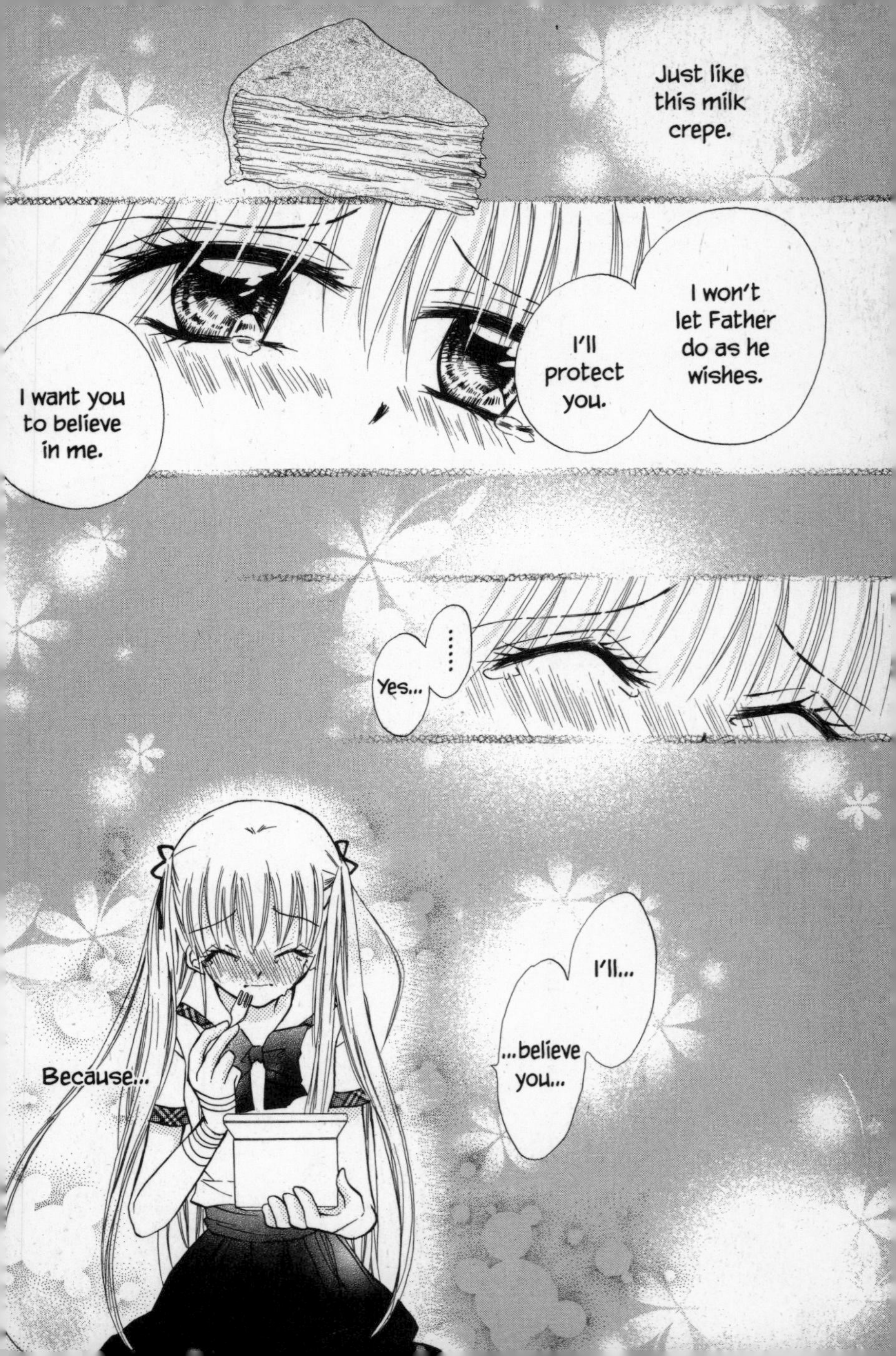
Just like this milk crepe.
I won't let Father do as he wishes.
I'll protect you.
I want you to believe in me.
......
Yes...
I'll...
...believe you...
Because...

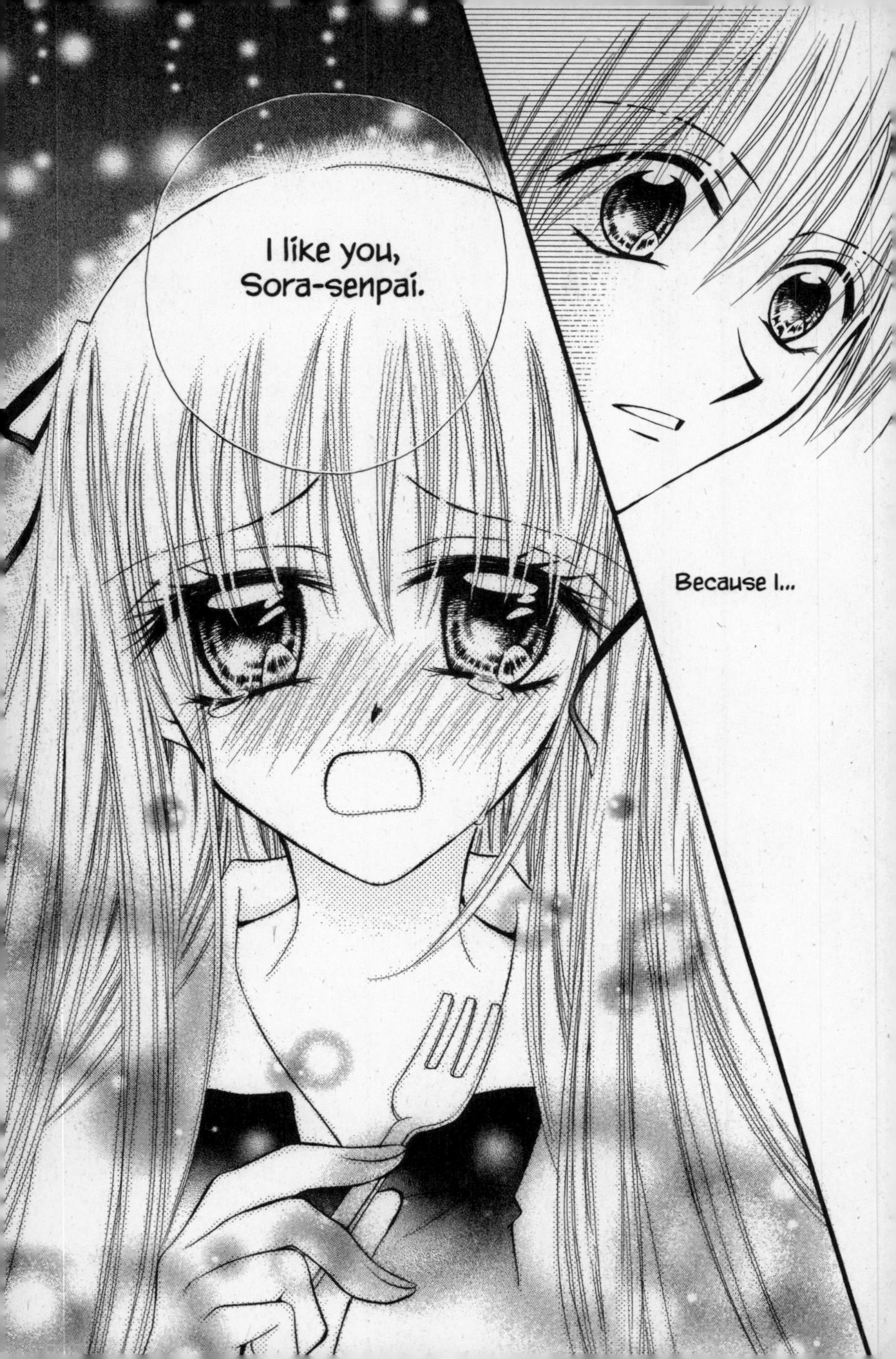
Because I...
I like you, Sora-senpai.

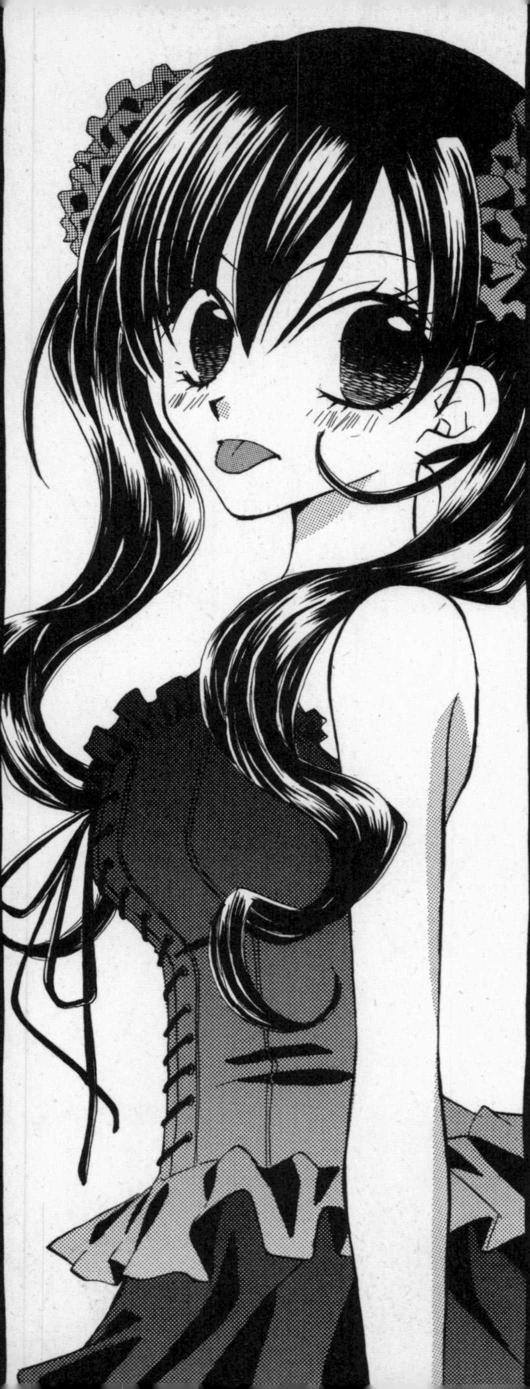

Recipe 21

I had asked in previous volumes to let me know if you had any good ideas for Fujita-san's t-shirt. ♡ Since then, I received many ideas, so I used them. ♡

I'm still looking for suggestions, so please send me letters if you think of something!!

The castella in this chapter is something Miyuki-sensei made, and I got to taste it.

The black sesame went so well with the castella. The judges' words summed up exactly how I felt about the castella.

Recipe 22

This is the chapter in which the director makes his entrance.

While I was still planning the chapter, the director had a completely different look. His hair was white. But I thought the father should look like Daichi, so I changed his hair color to black.

While working on this chapter, there was a bad virus going around and I had a hard time.

I got through it with mental fortitude!!

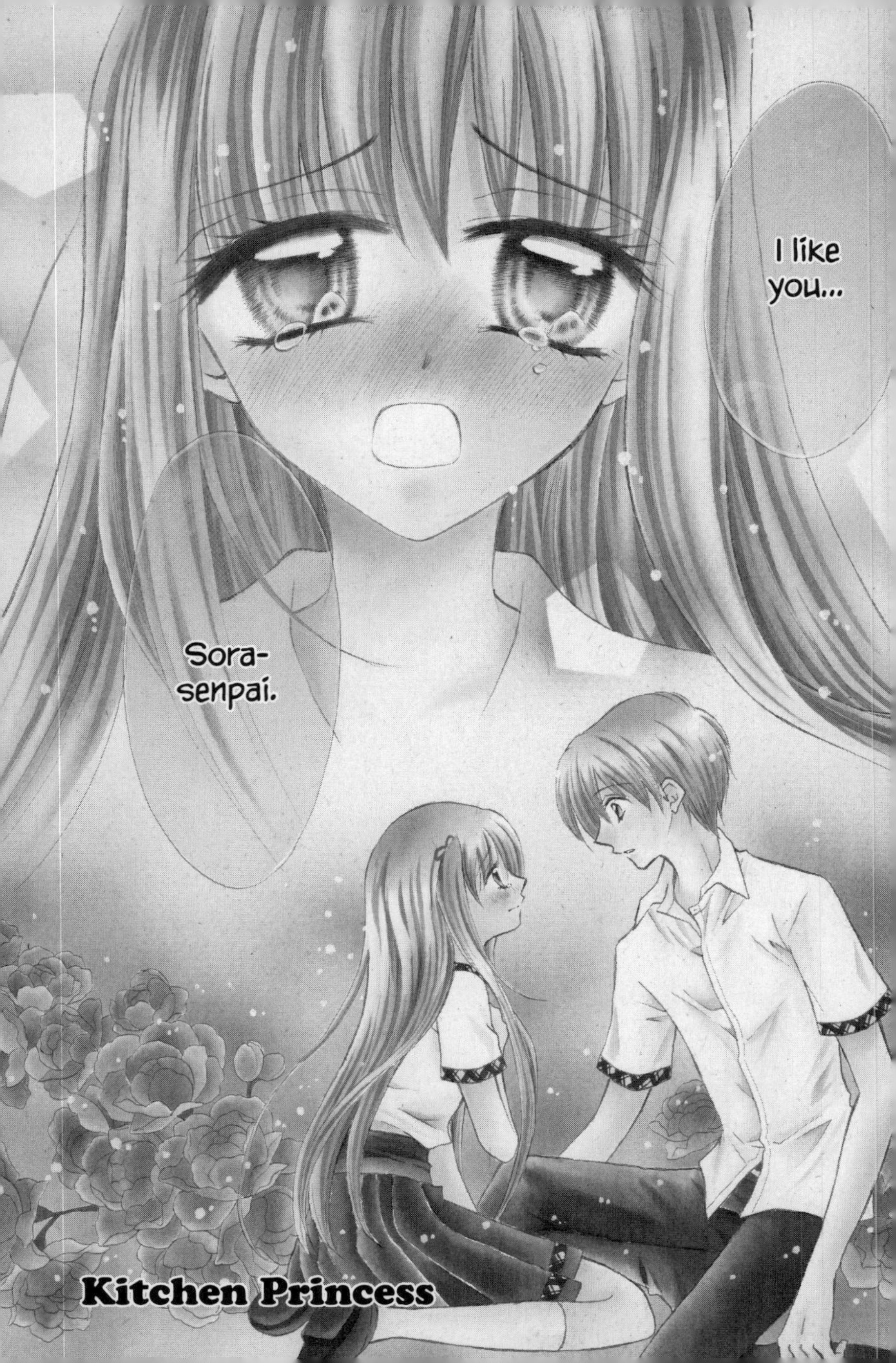
I like you...
Sora-senpai.
Kitchen Princess

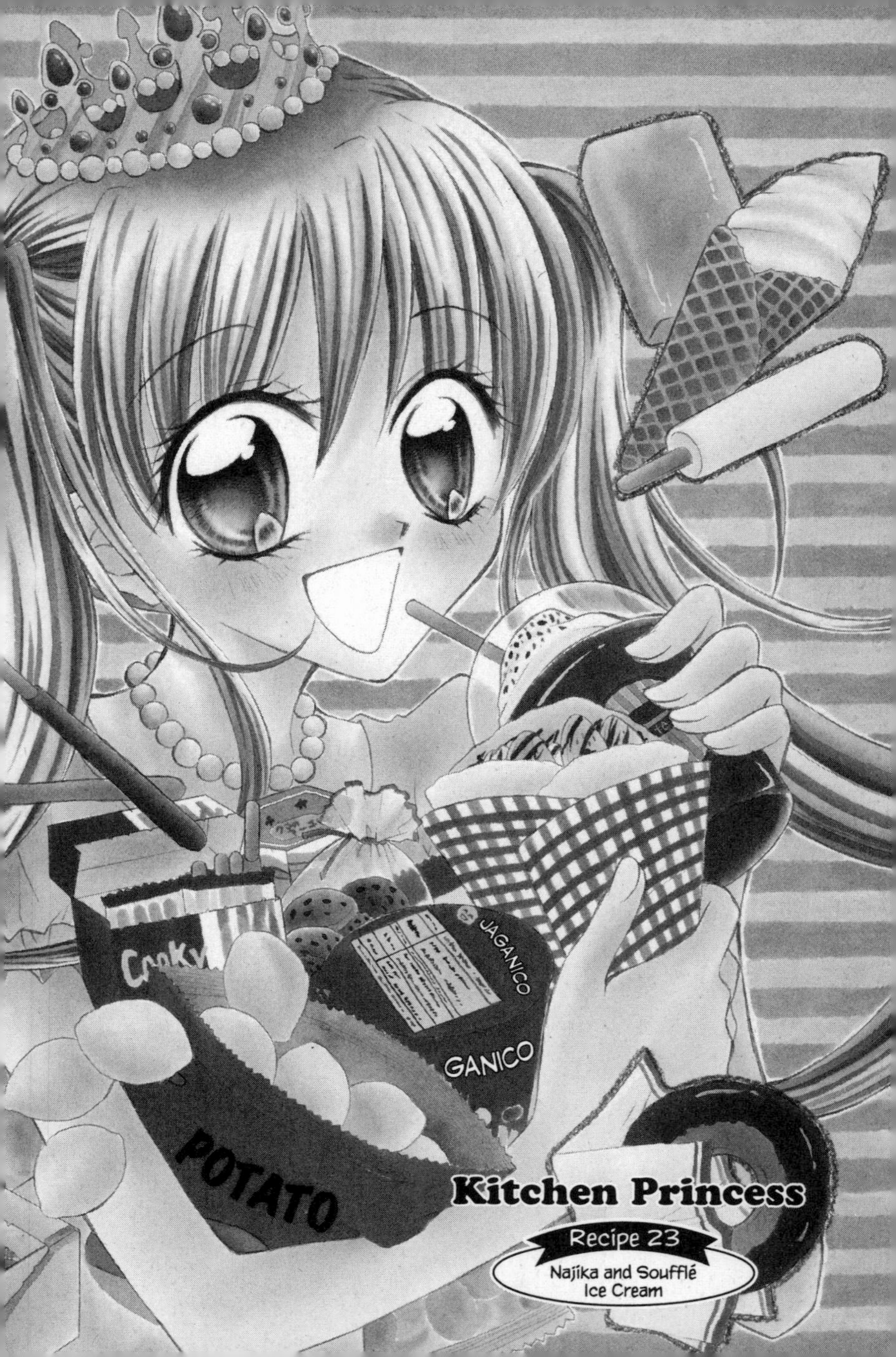
JAGANICO
GANICO
POTATO
Kitchen Princess
Recipe 23
Najika and Soufflé
Ice Cream

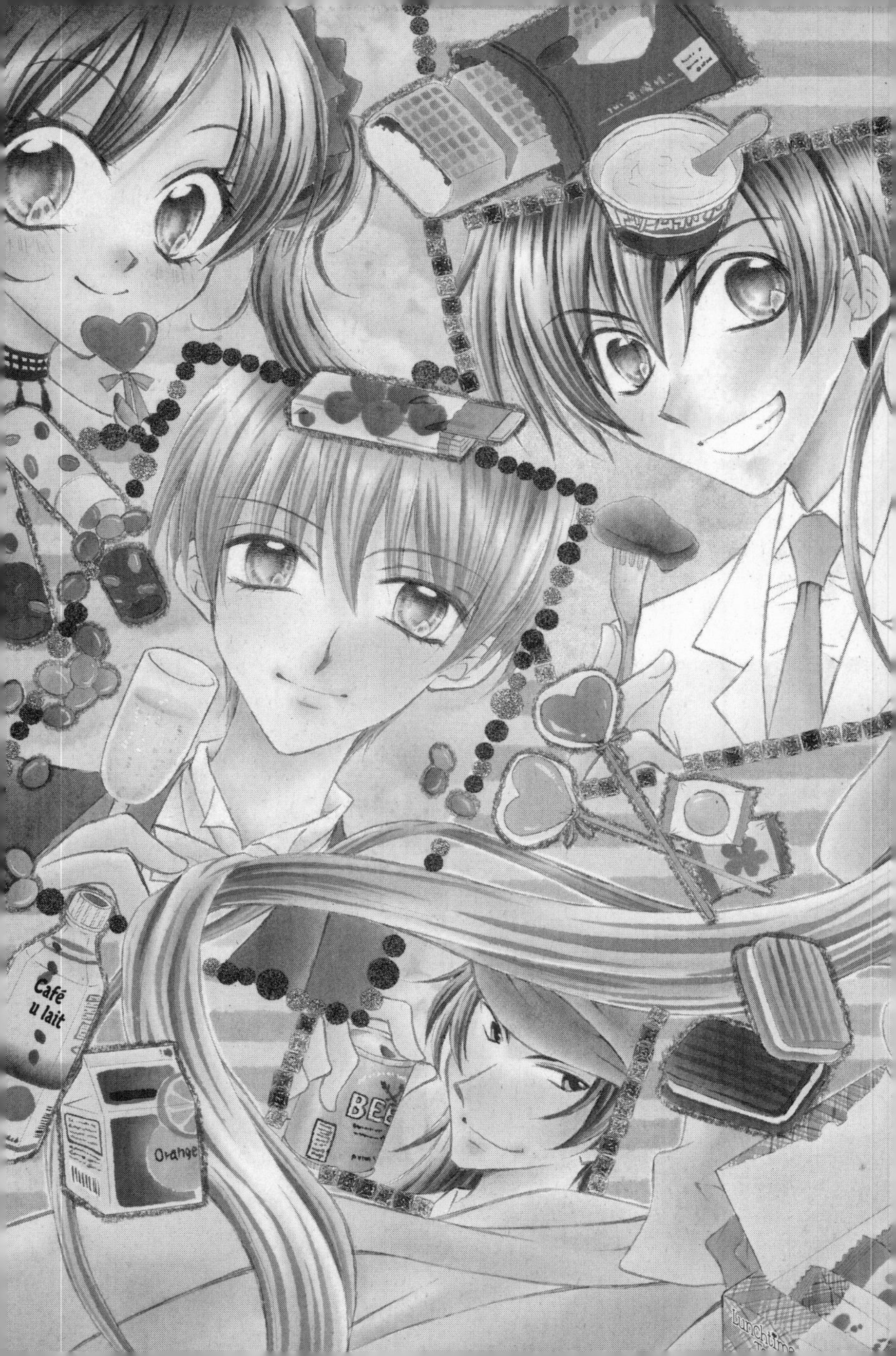
Café
u lait
Orange

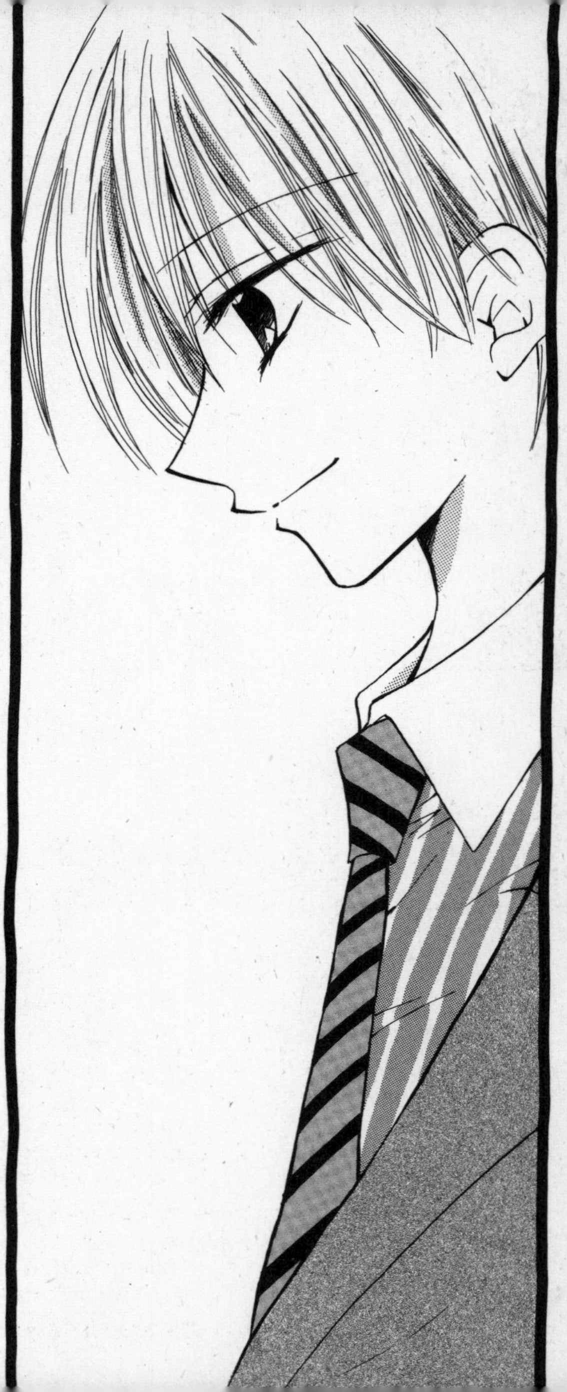

Recipe 23

This chapter was written during a busy time, and I couldn't go to Disney Resort. (It's not like I *have* to go!) Fujita-san was still young and naïve...it's very refreshing. I was shocked to find out the original form of vanilla beans look like grass. Anyway, I needed to do a lot of research on it, so my computer was very helpful!! We're living in good times!!

Side Story

So Fujita-san's home was a bakery! That was surprising. (laugh) No matter what Fujita's dad is like personally, he makes cute cakes. ♡ There was a time when I wanted to work at a bakery, too. I wanted to wear a cute uniform and stuff. ♡ Yes, I was a dreamy girl...

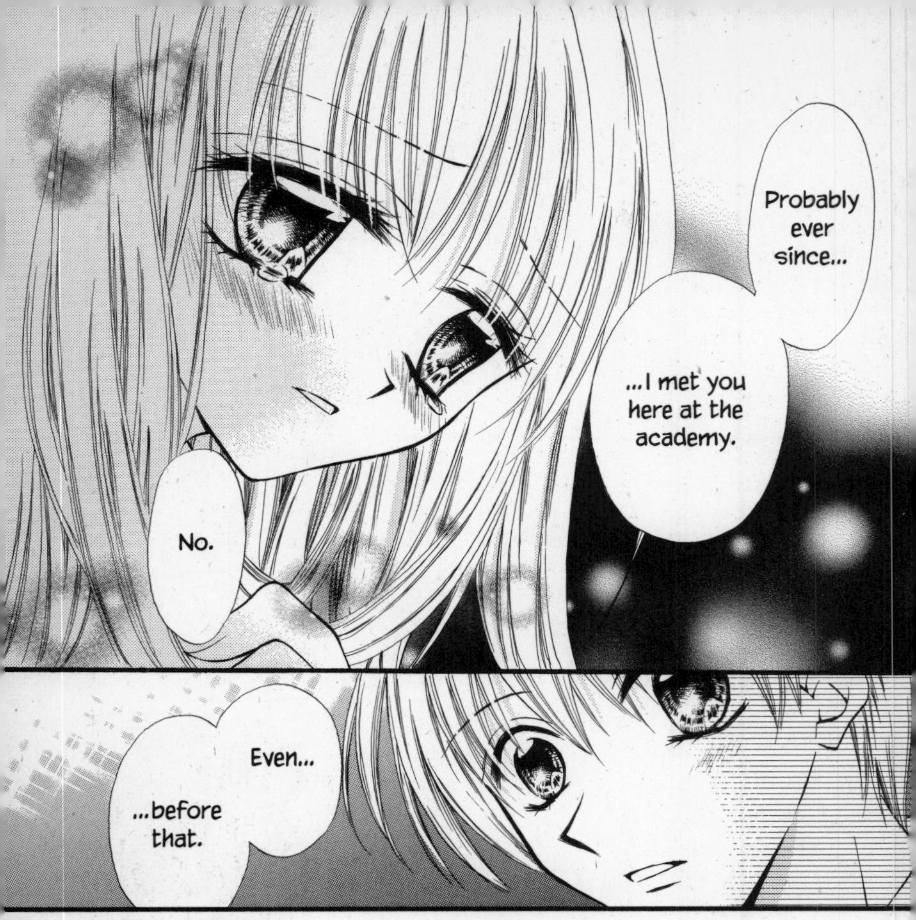
Probably ever since...
...I met you here at the academy.
No.
Even...
...before that.

About Recipe 23's Splash Page

This chapter was drawn right after we received the Kodansha Manga Award, and *Nakayoshi* allowed us to feature Kitchen Princess first in the magazine. While I was coloring these pages, reporters came to shoot the video that would play during the award ceremony. I was very nervous.

I used trendy (?) shiny stickers for the borders around Sora and Daichi. ♪ I am so anxious to see if it will come out when it prints!!

Oh, and Fujita makes his debut in color. (laugh)

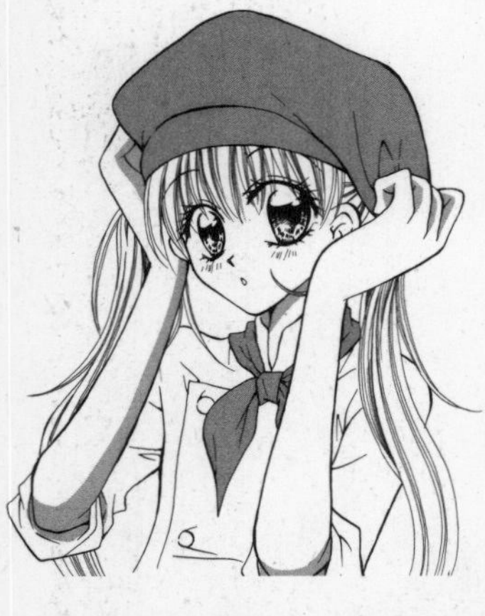

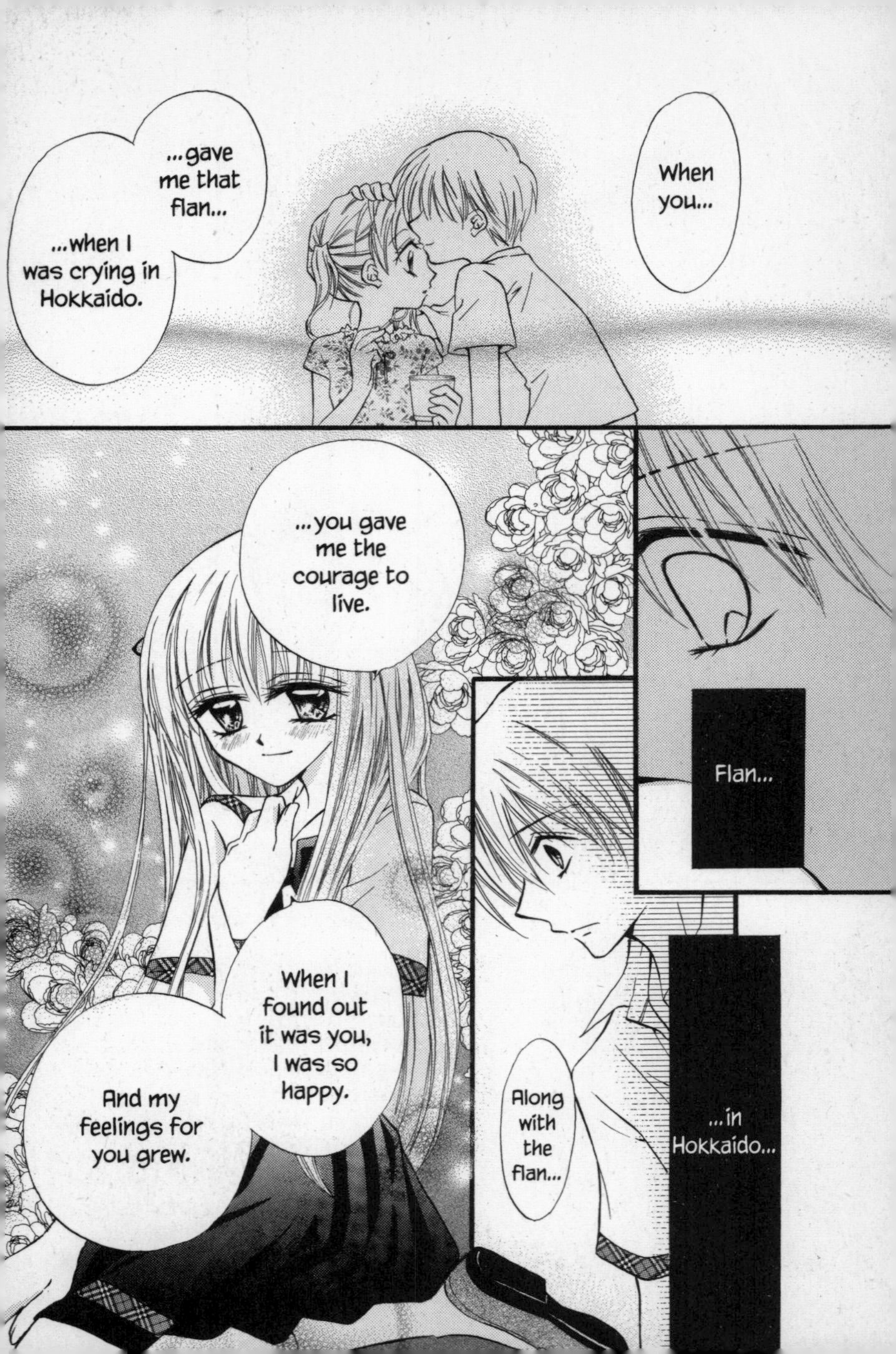
When you...
...gave me that flan...
...when I was crying in Hokkaido.
Flan...
...in Hokkaido...
Along with the flan...
...you gave me the courage to live.
When I found out it was you, I was so happy.
And my feelings for you grew.

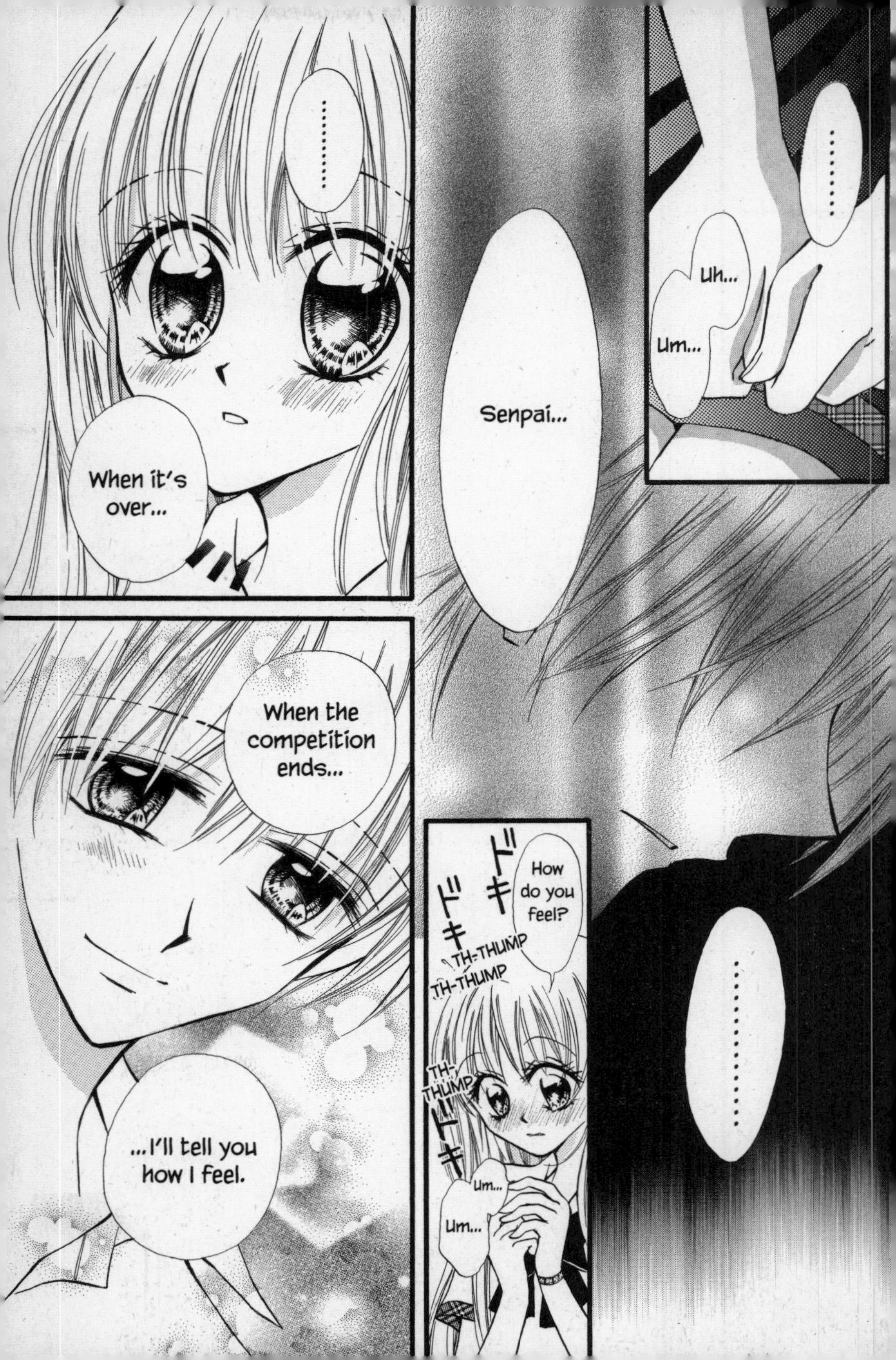
......
Uh...
Um...
Senpai...
How do you feel?
ドキ
ドキ
TH-THUMP
TH-THUMP
TH-THUMP
ドキ
ドキ
Um...
Um...
....
......
When it's over...
When the competition ends...
...I'll tell you how I feel.

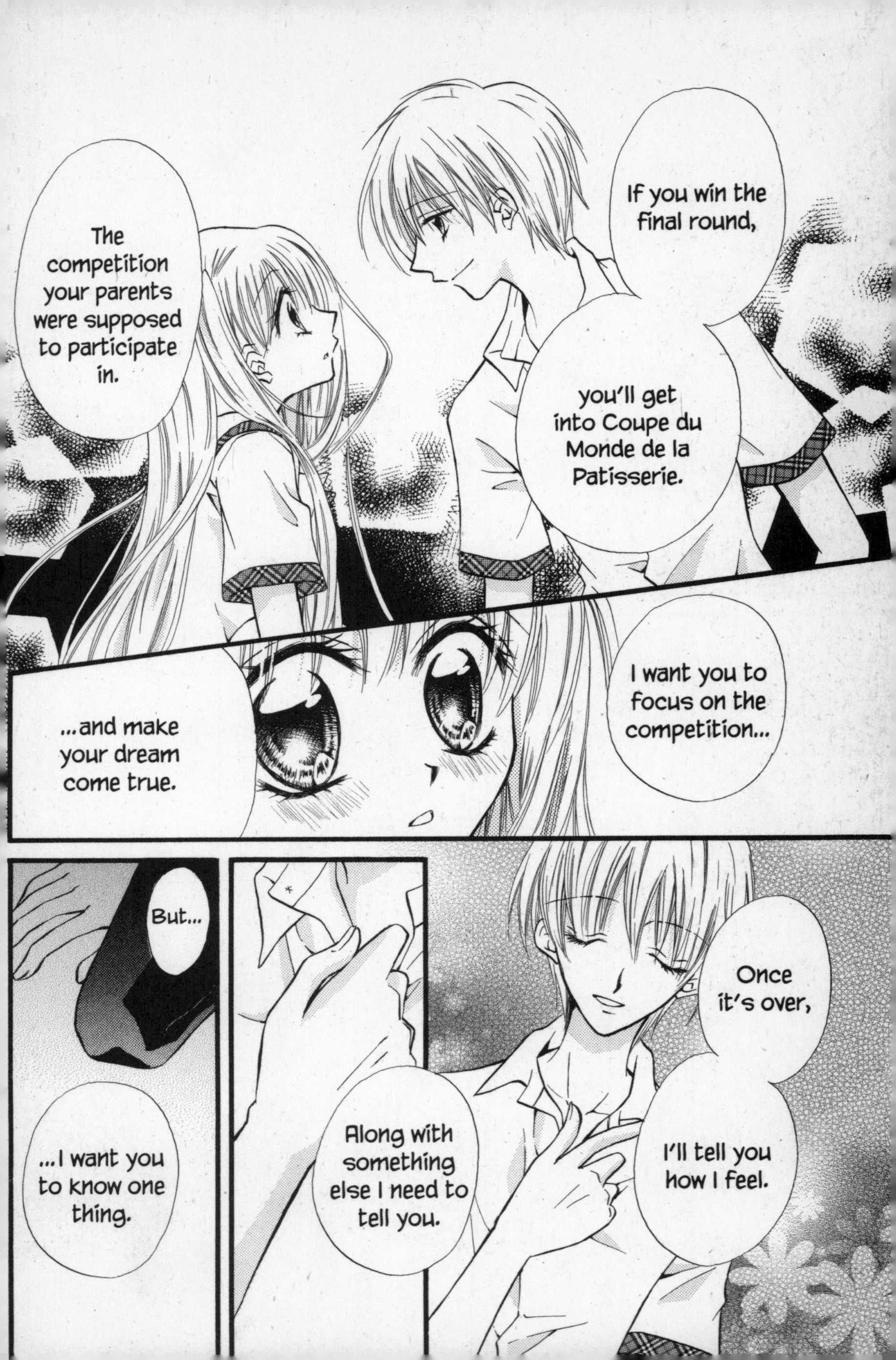
If you win the final round,
you'll get into Coupe du Monde de la Patisserie.
The competition your parents were supposed to participate in.
I want you to focus on the competition...
...and make your dream come true.
Once it's over,
I'll tell you how I feel.
Along with something else I need to tell you.
But...
...I want you to know one thing.

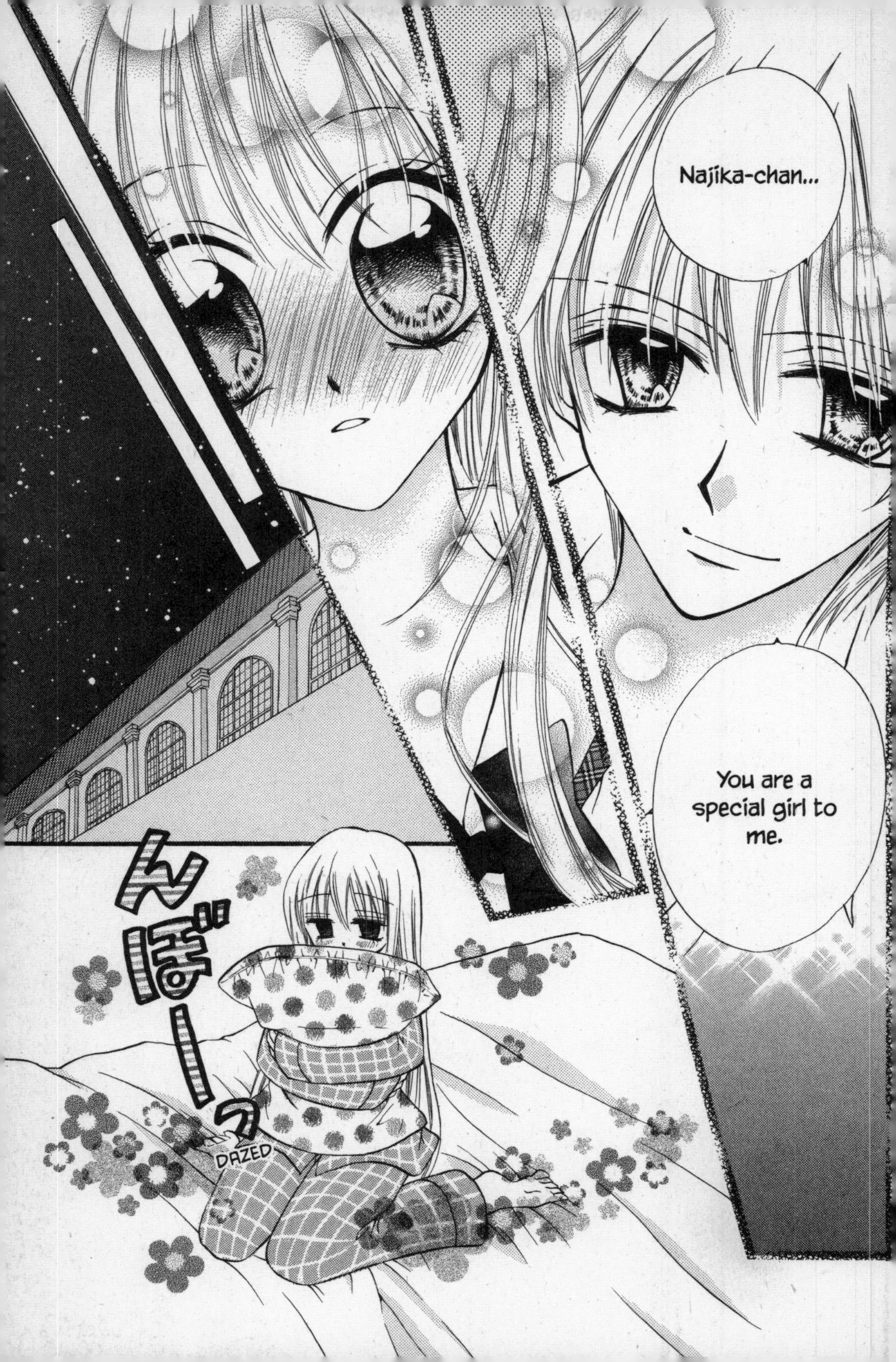

Najika-chan...
You are a special girl to me.
んぼーっ
DAZED

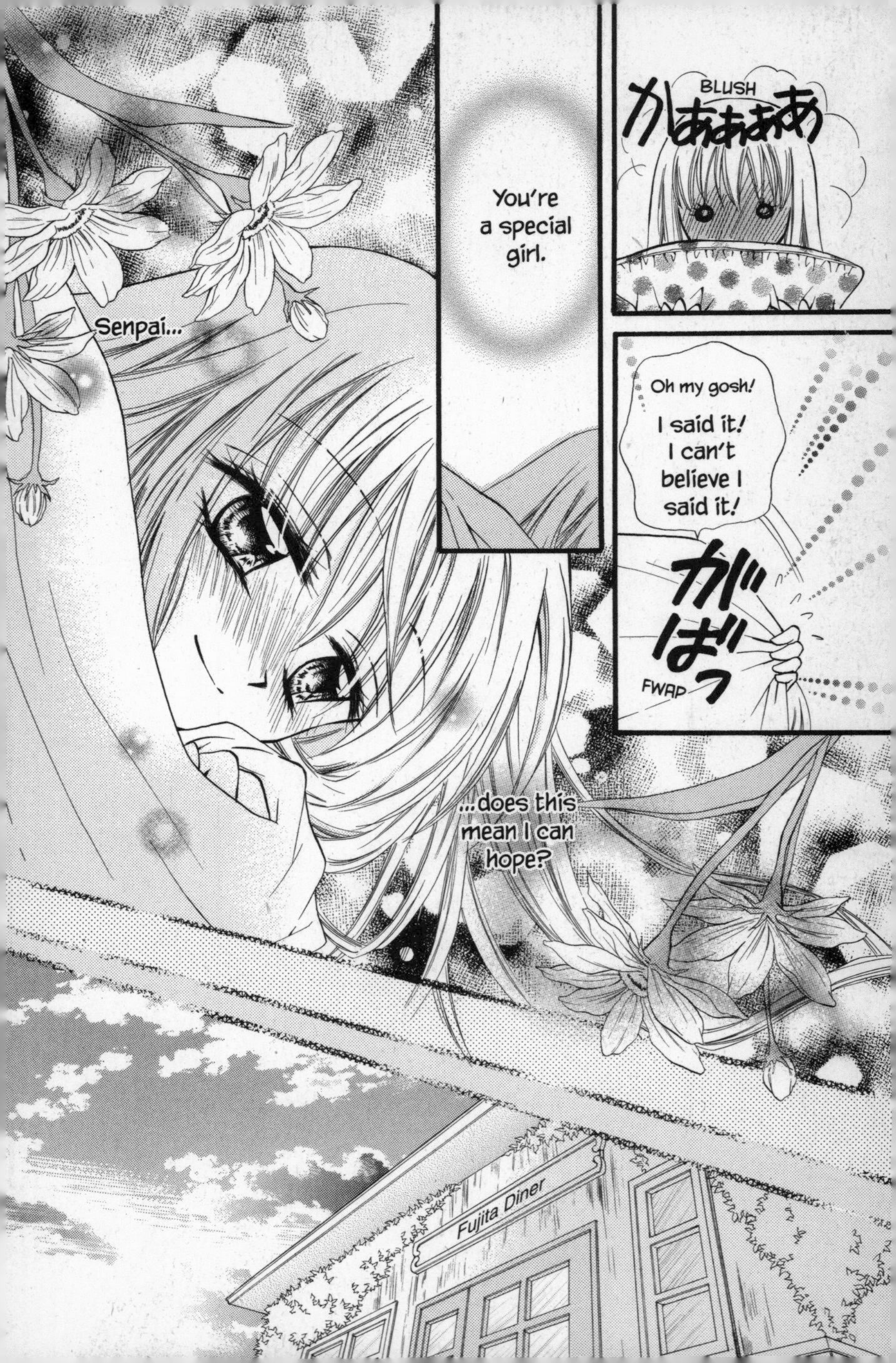
かああああ
BLUSH
Oh my gosh!
I said it! I can't believe I said it!
がばっ
FWAP
You're a special girl.
Senpai...
...does this mean I can hope?
Fujita Diner

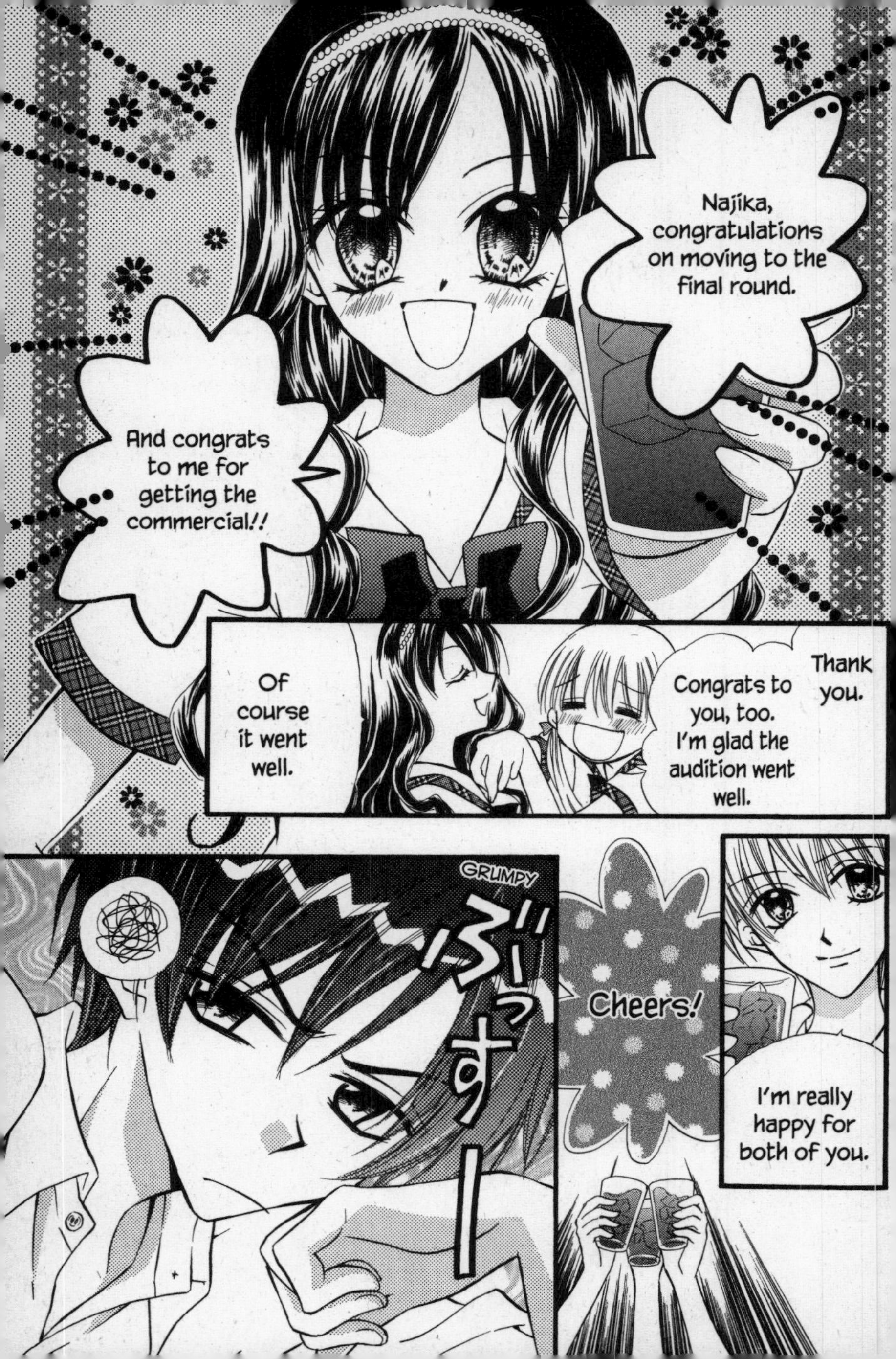
Najika, congratulations on moving to the final round.
And congrats to me for getting the commercial!!
Thank you.
Congrats to you, too. I'm glad the audition went well.
Of course it went well.
I'm really happy for both of you.
Cheers!
GRUMPY
ぶーっすー

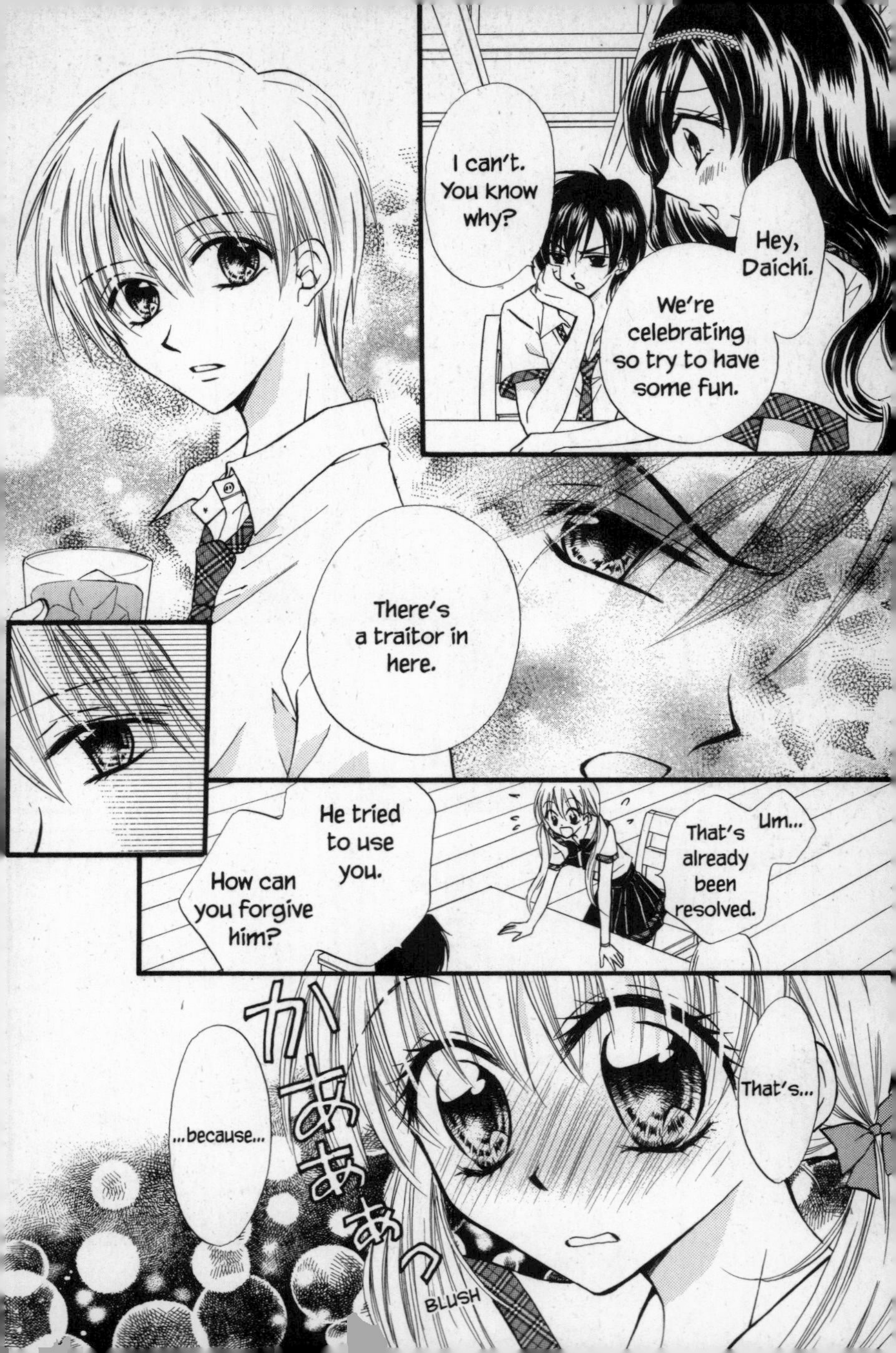

Hey, Daichi.
We're celebrating so try to have some fun.
I can't. You know why?
There's a traitor in here.
Um...
That's already been resolved.
He tried to use you.
How can you forgive him?
That's...
かあああっ
BLUSH
...because...

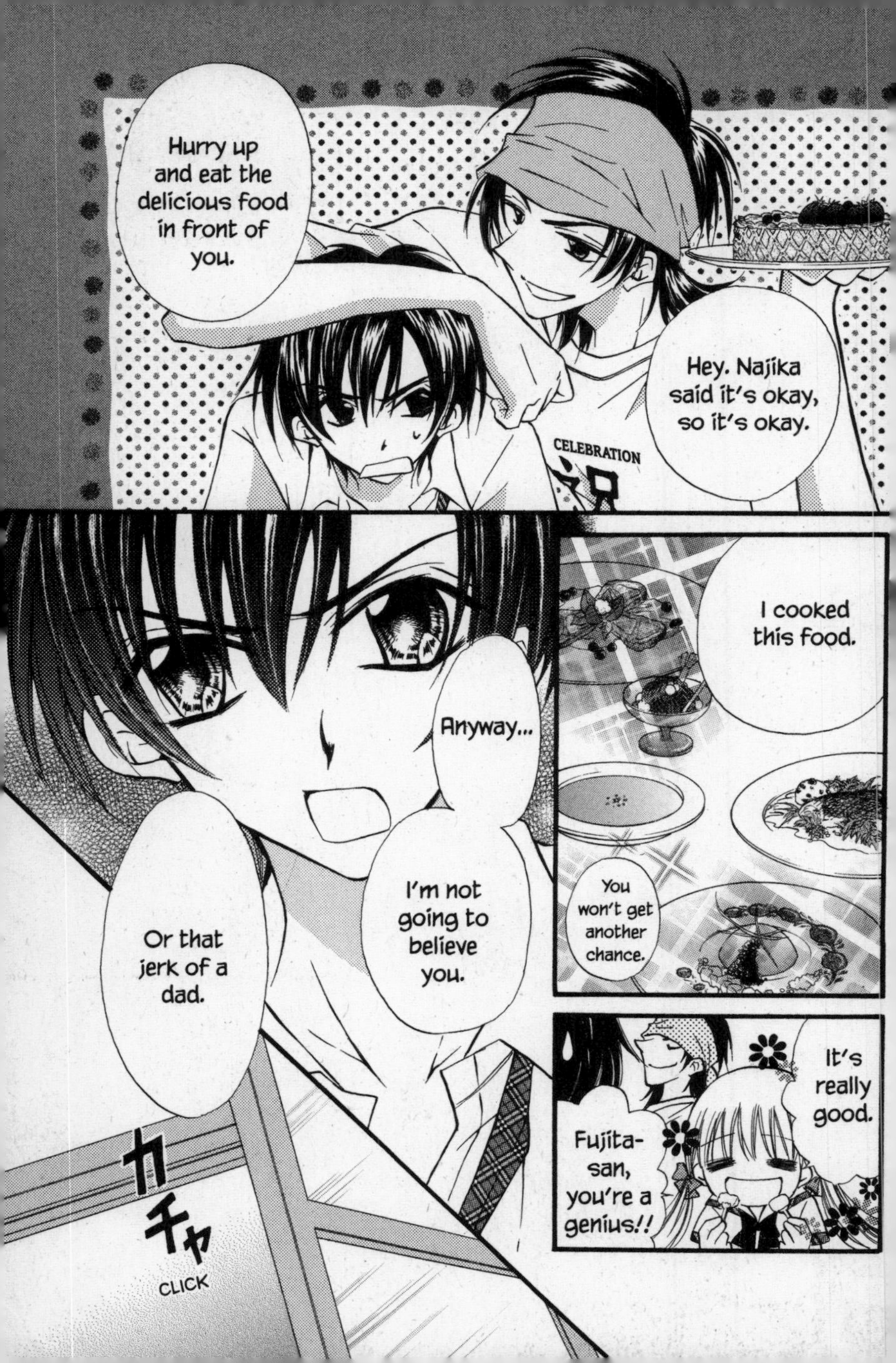
Hurry up and eat the delicious food in front of you.
Hey. Najika said it's okay, so it's okay.
CELEBRATION
I cooked this food.
You won't get another chance.
It's really good.
Fujita-san, you're a genius!!
Anyway...
I'm not going to believe you.
Or that jerk of a dad.
カチャ
CLICK

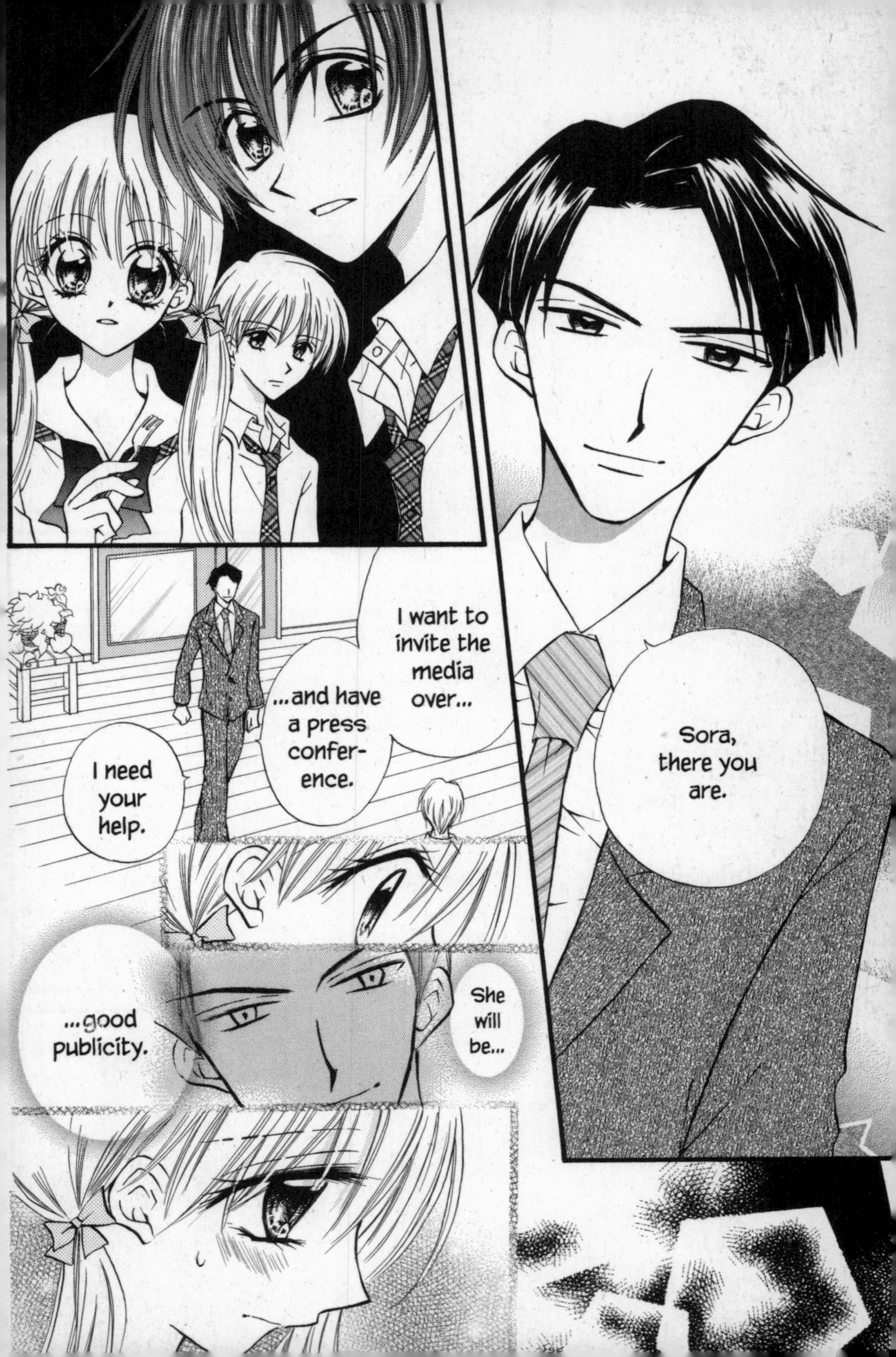
Sora, there you are.
I want to invite the media over...
...and have a press conference.
I need your help.
She will be...
...good publicity.

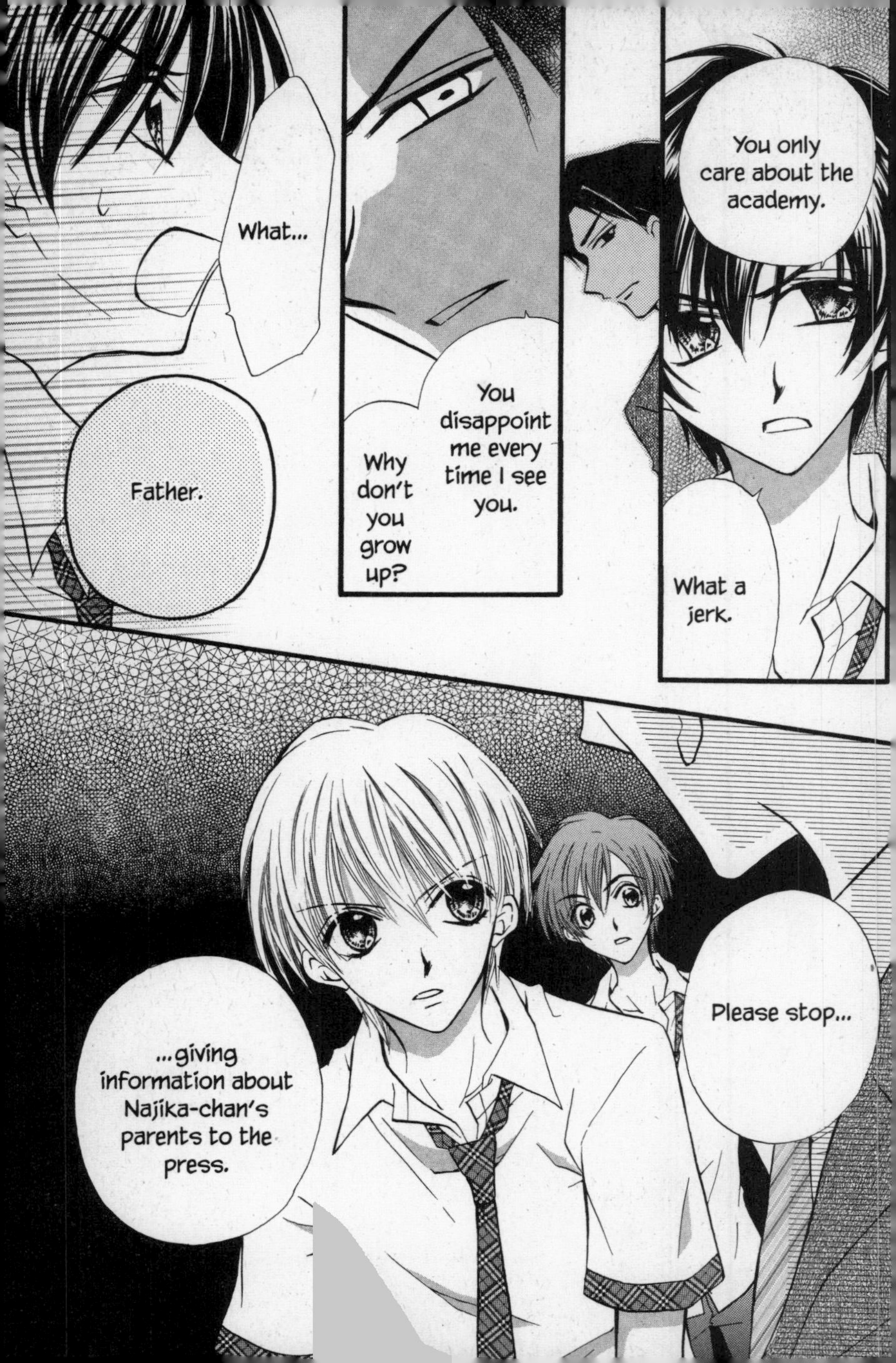

You only care about the academy.
What a jerk.
You disappoint me every time I see you.
Why don't you grow up?
What...
Father.
Please stop...
...giving information about Najika-chan's parents to the press.

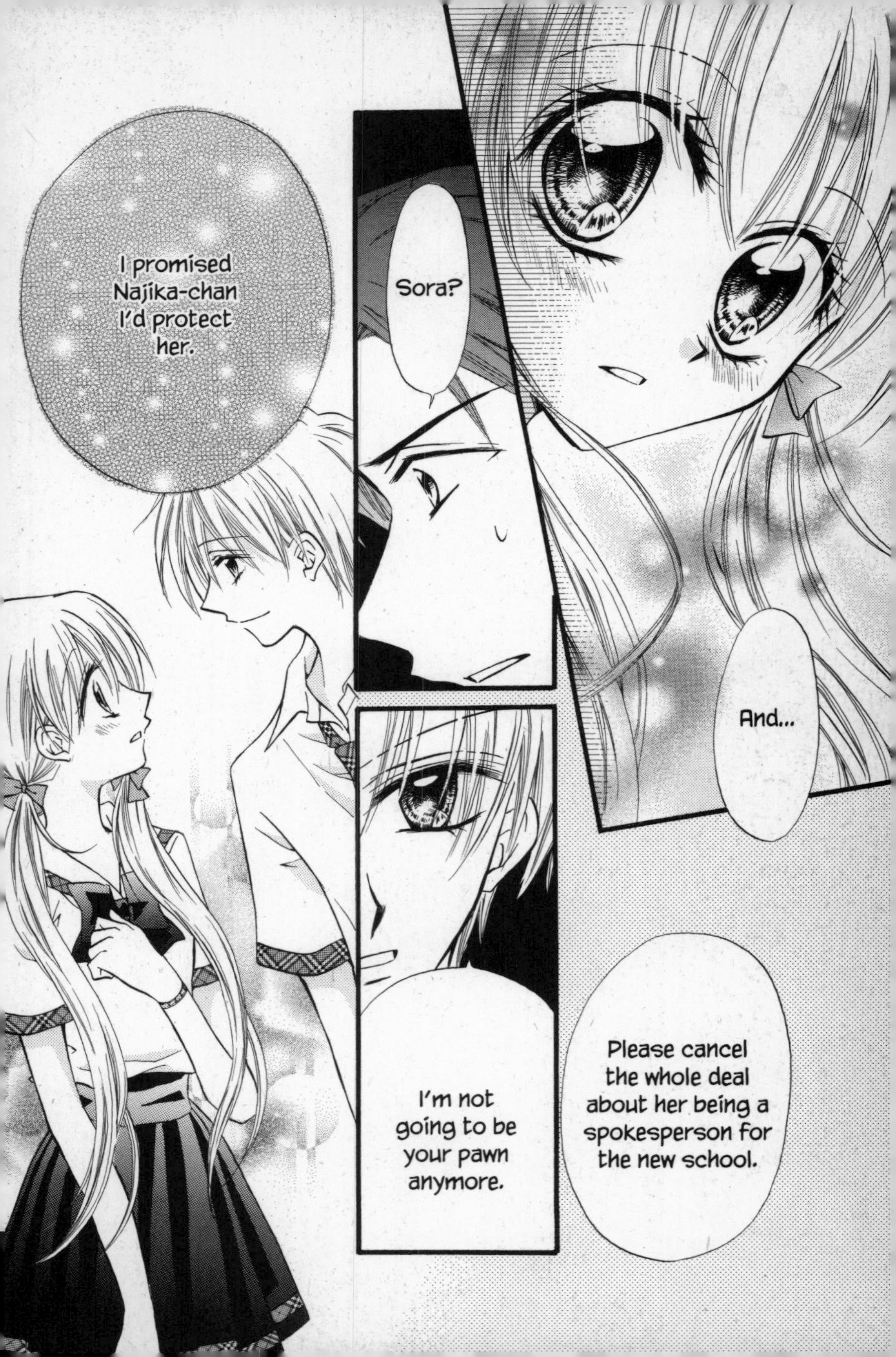
And...
Please cancel the whole deal about her being a spokesperson for the new school.
Sora?
I'm not going to be your pawn anymore.
I promised Najika-chan I'd protect her.

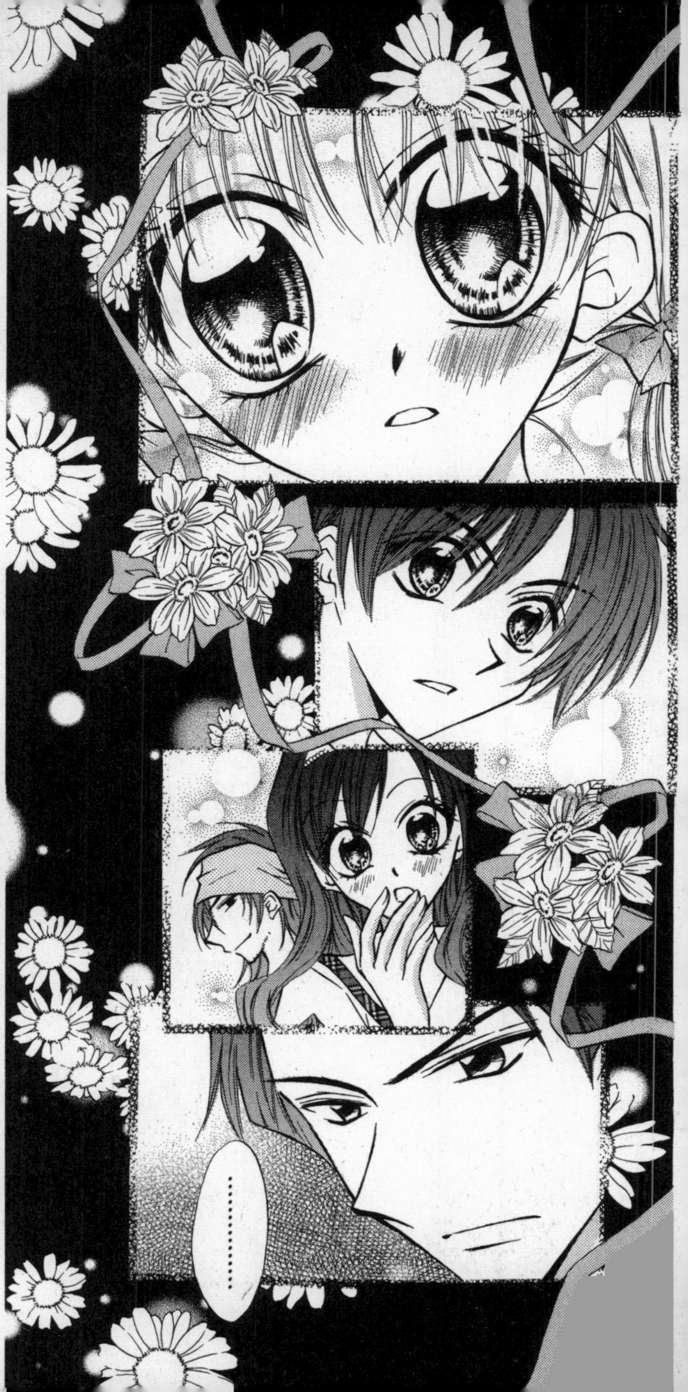
……

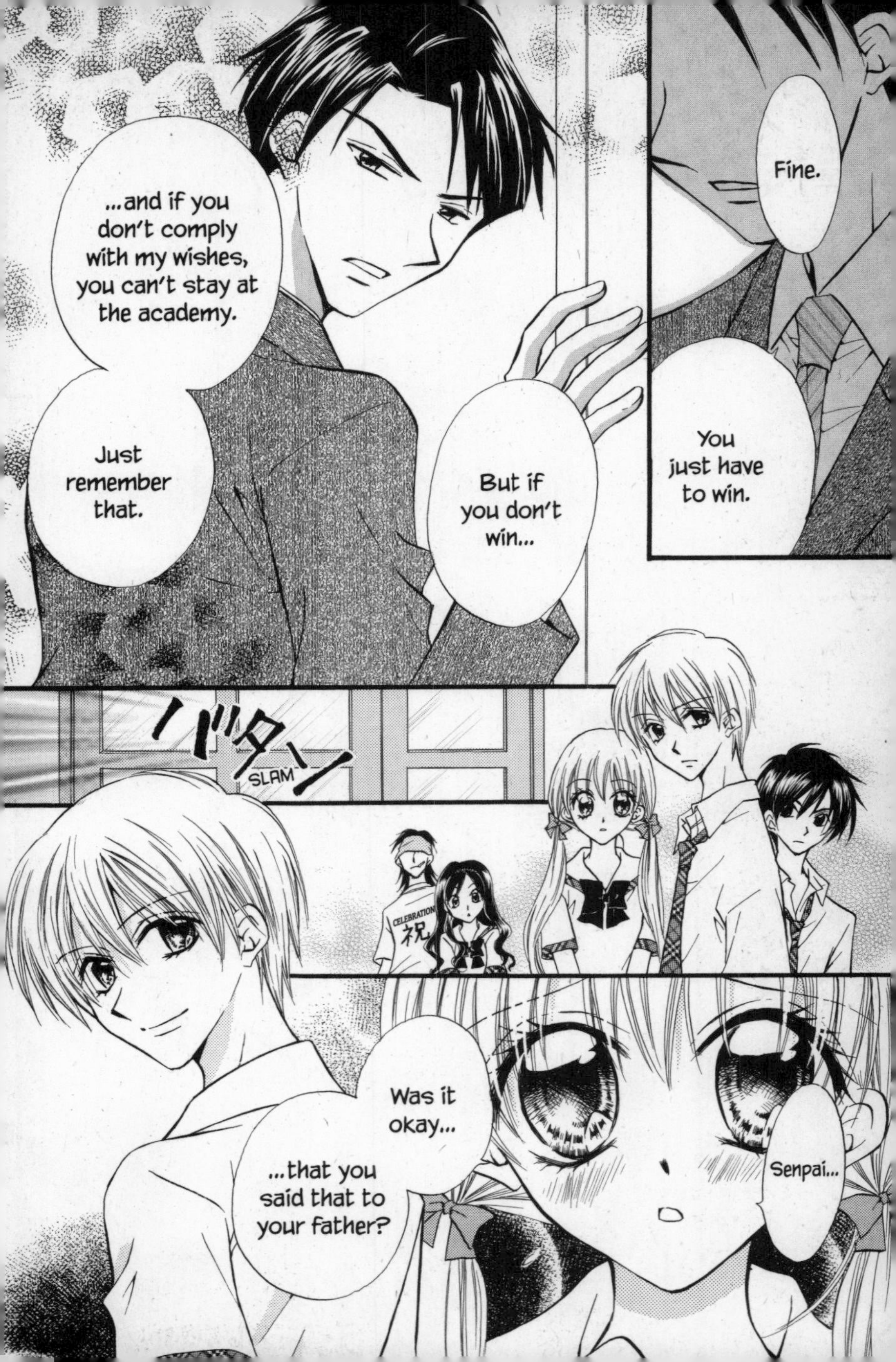
Fine.
You just have to win.
But if you don't win...
...and if you don't comply with my wishes, you can't stay at the academy.
Just remember that.
SLAM
CELEBRATION
Senpai...
Was it okay...
...that you said that to your father?

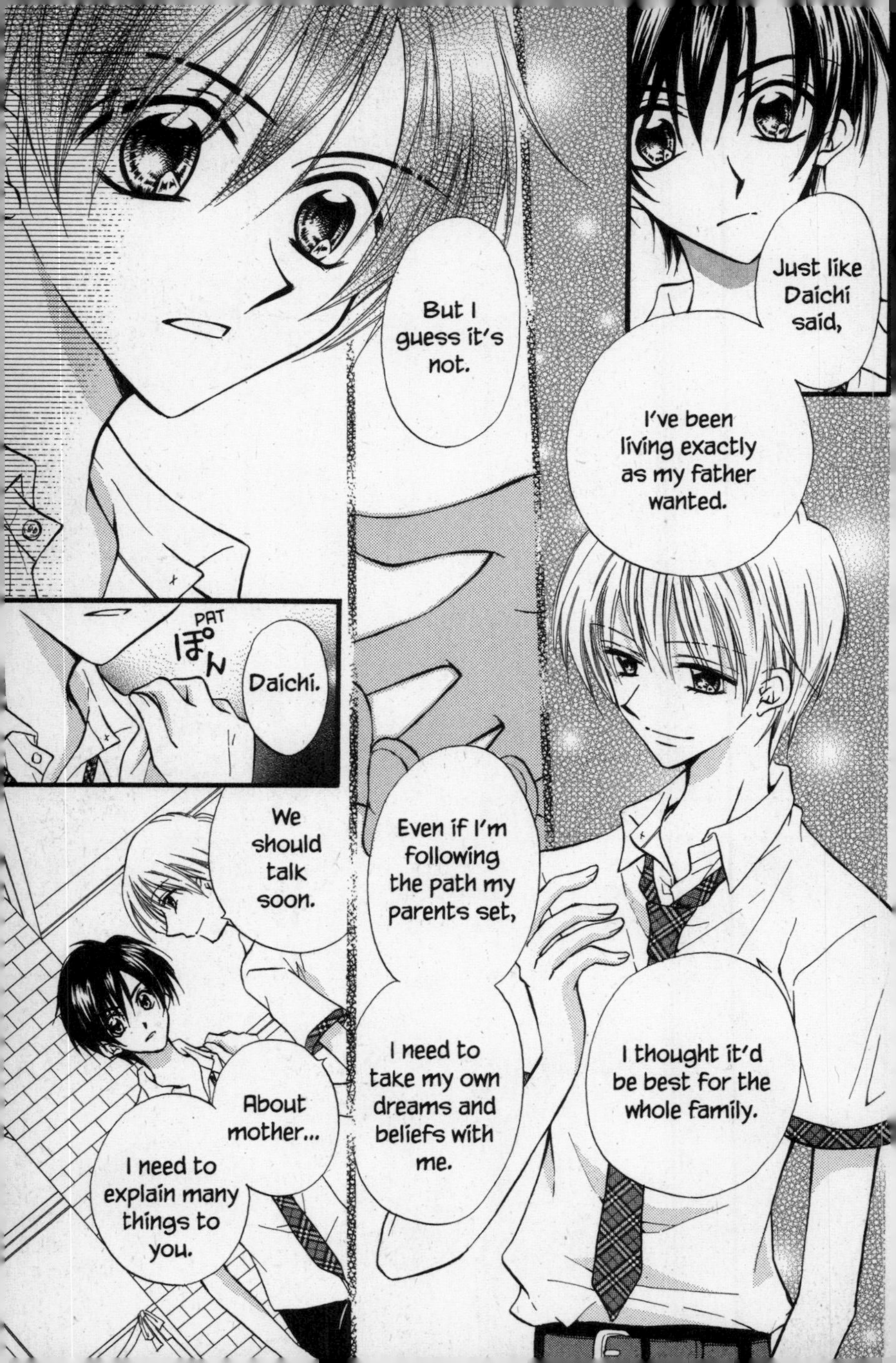
Just like Daichi said,
I've been living exactly as my father wanted.
I thought it'd be best for the whole family.
But I guess it's not.
Even if I'm following the path my parents set,
I need to take my own dreams and beliefs with me.
PAT
ぽん
Daichi.
We should talk soon.
About mother...
I need to explain many things to you.

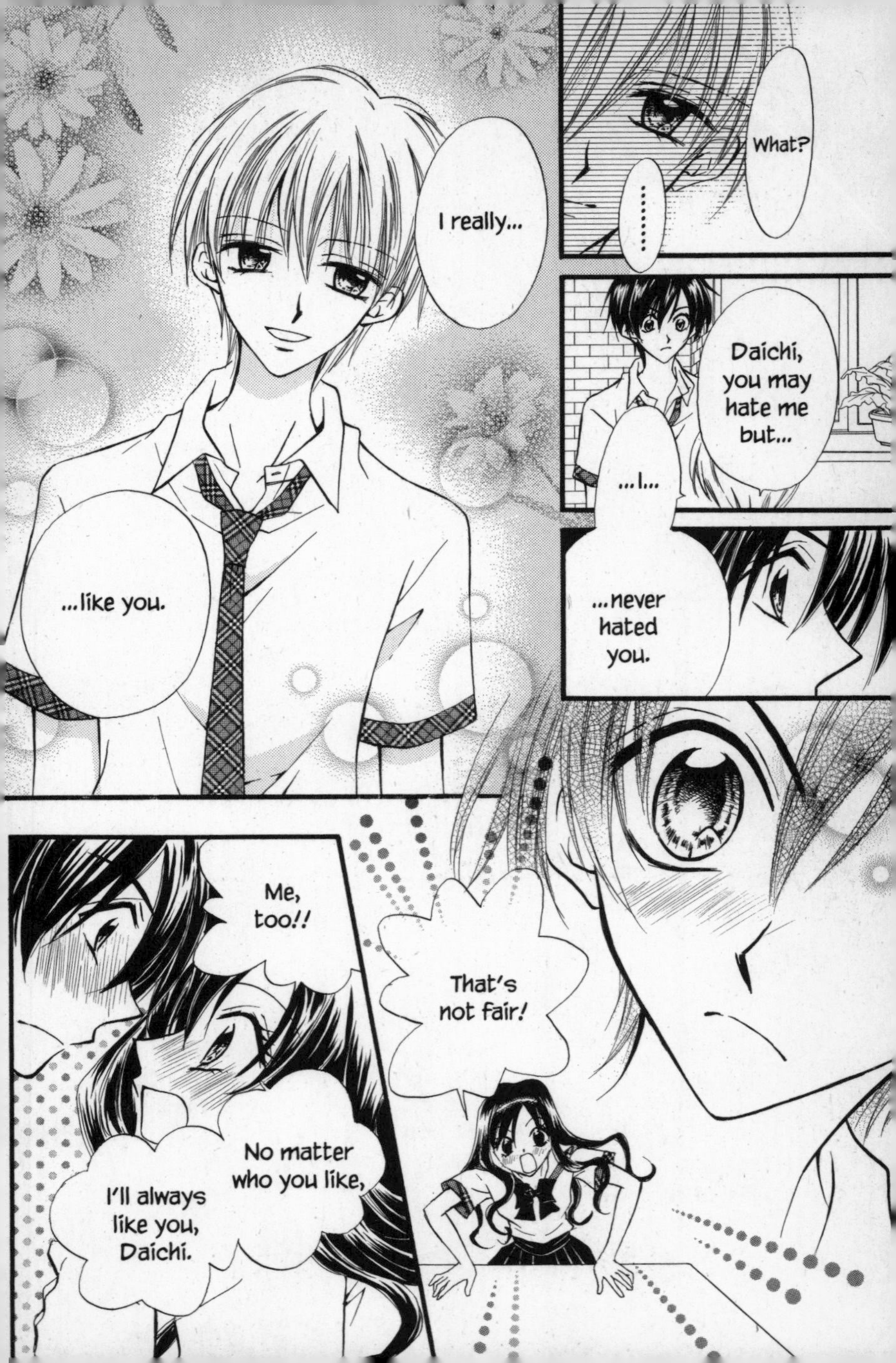
What?
......
Daichi, you may hate me but...
...I...
...never hated you.
I really...
...like you.
That's not fair!
Me, too!!
No matter who you like,
I'll always like you, Daichi.

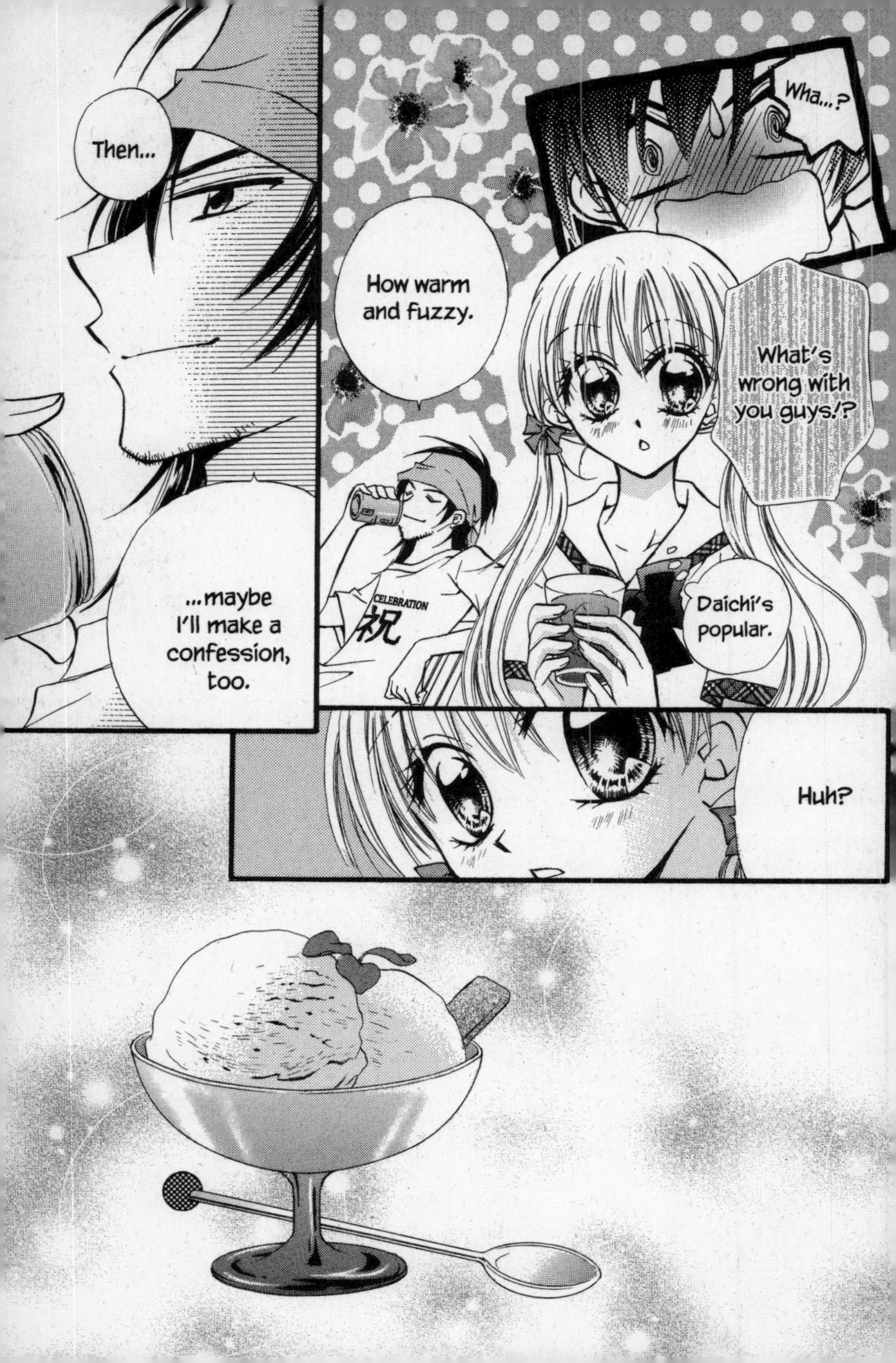
Wha...?
What's wrong with you guys!?
How warm and fuzzy.
CELEBRATION 祝
Daichi's popular.
Then...
...maybe I'll make a confession, too.
Huh?

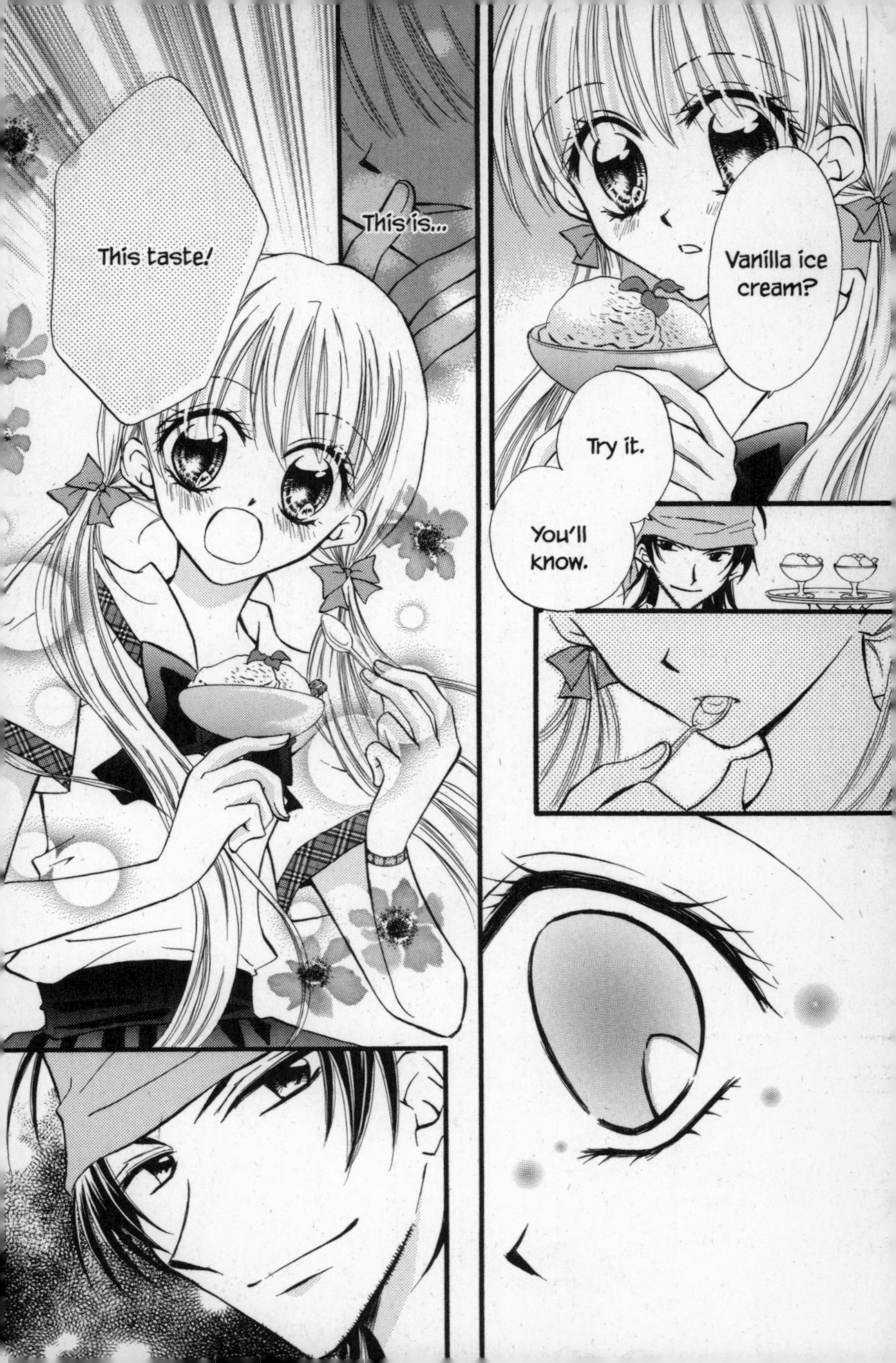
Vanilla ice cream?
Try it.
You'll know.
This is...
This taste!

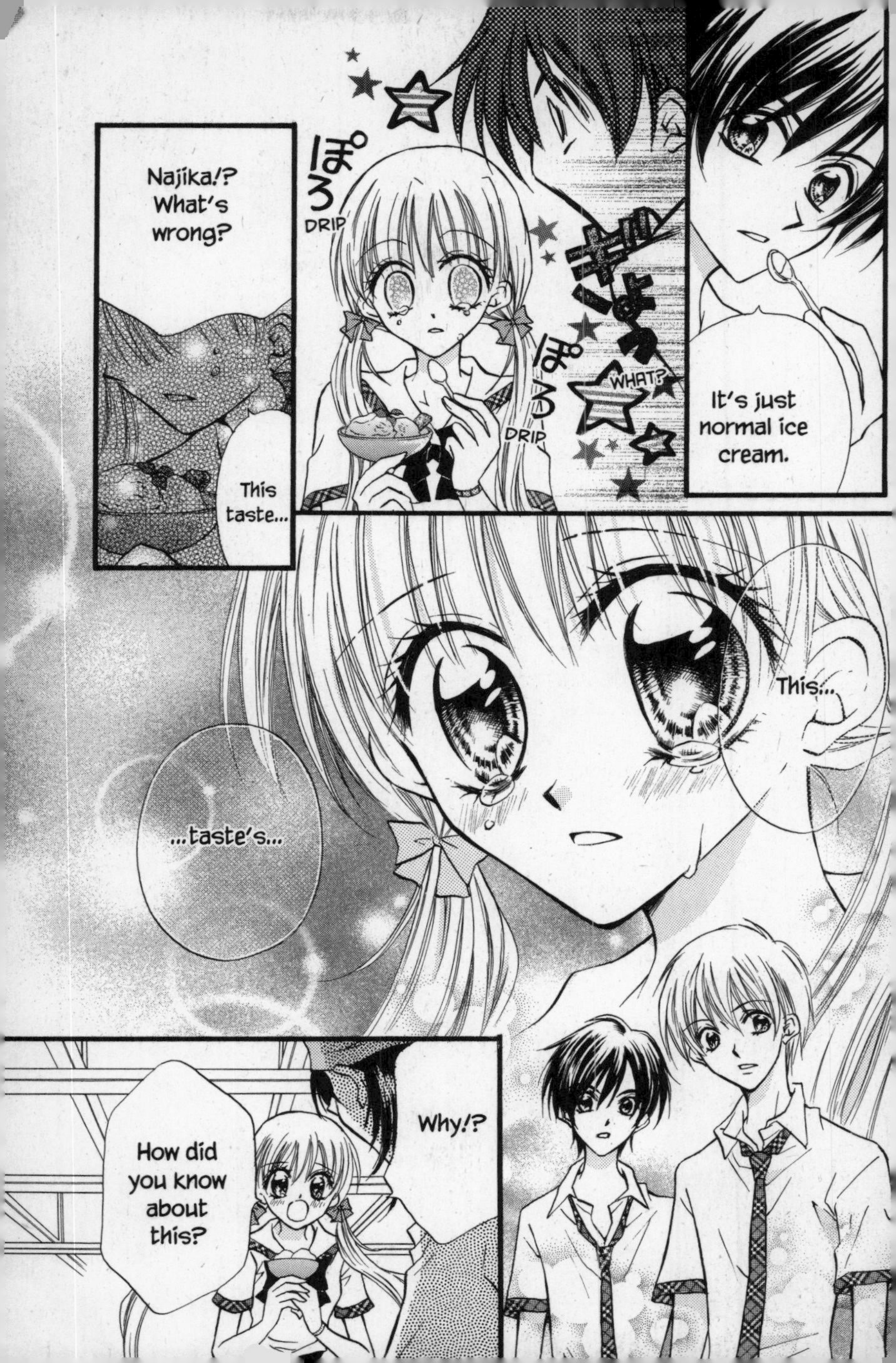
It's just normal ice cream.
ぽろ
DRIP
ぎょっ
WHAT?
ぽろ
DRIP
Najika!? What's wrong?
This taste...
This...
...taste's...
Why!?
How did you know about this?

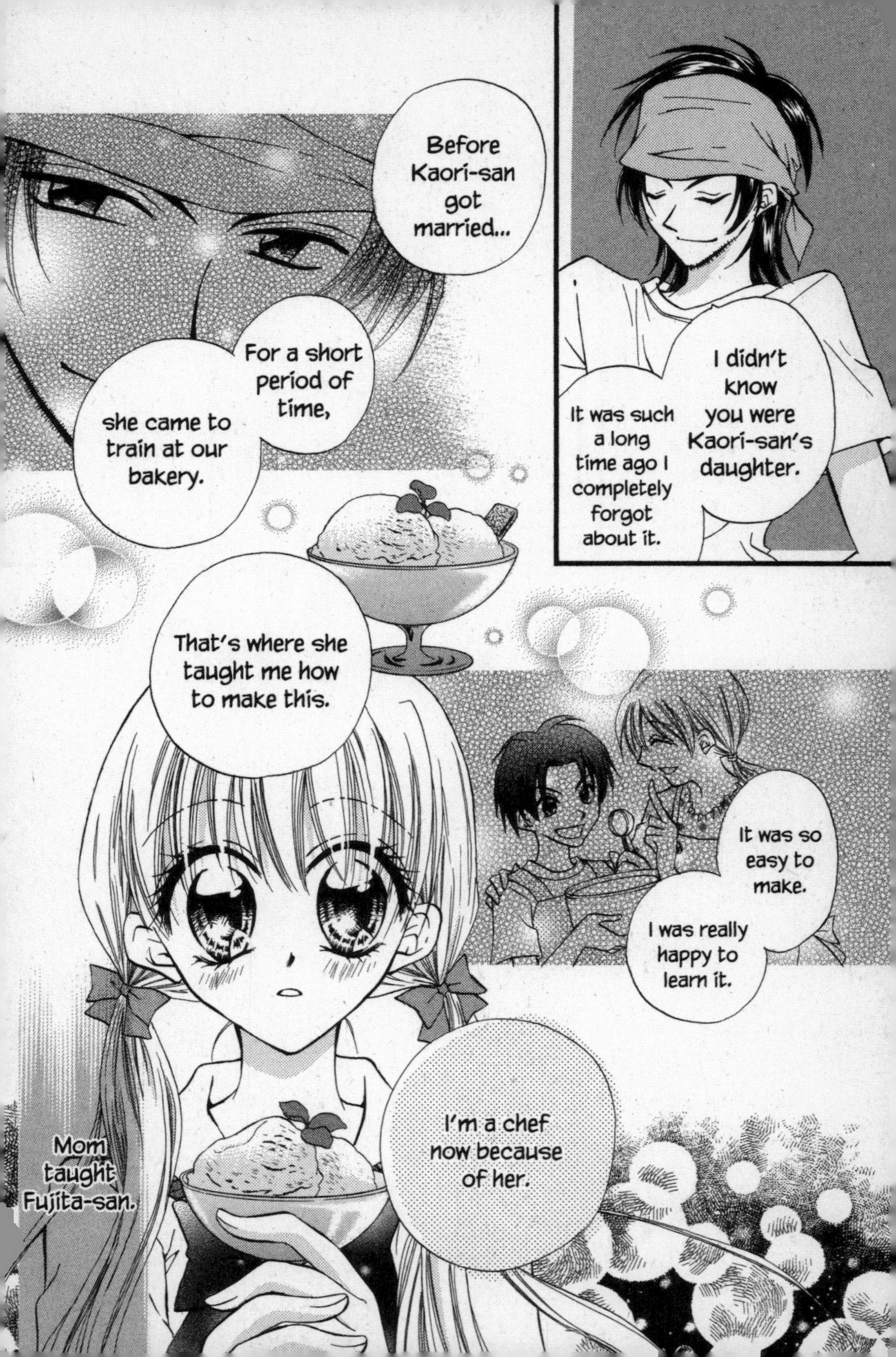
I didn't know you were Kaori-san's daughter.
It was such a long time ago I completely forgot about it.
Before Kaori-san got married...
For a short period of time,
she came to train at our bakery.
That's where she taught me how to make this.
It was so easy to make.
I was really happy to learn it.
I'm a chef now because of her.
Mom taught Fujita-san.

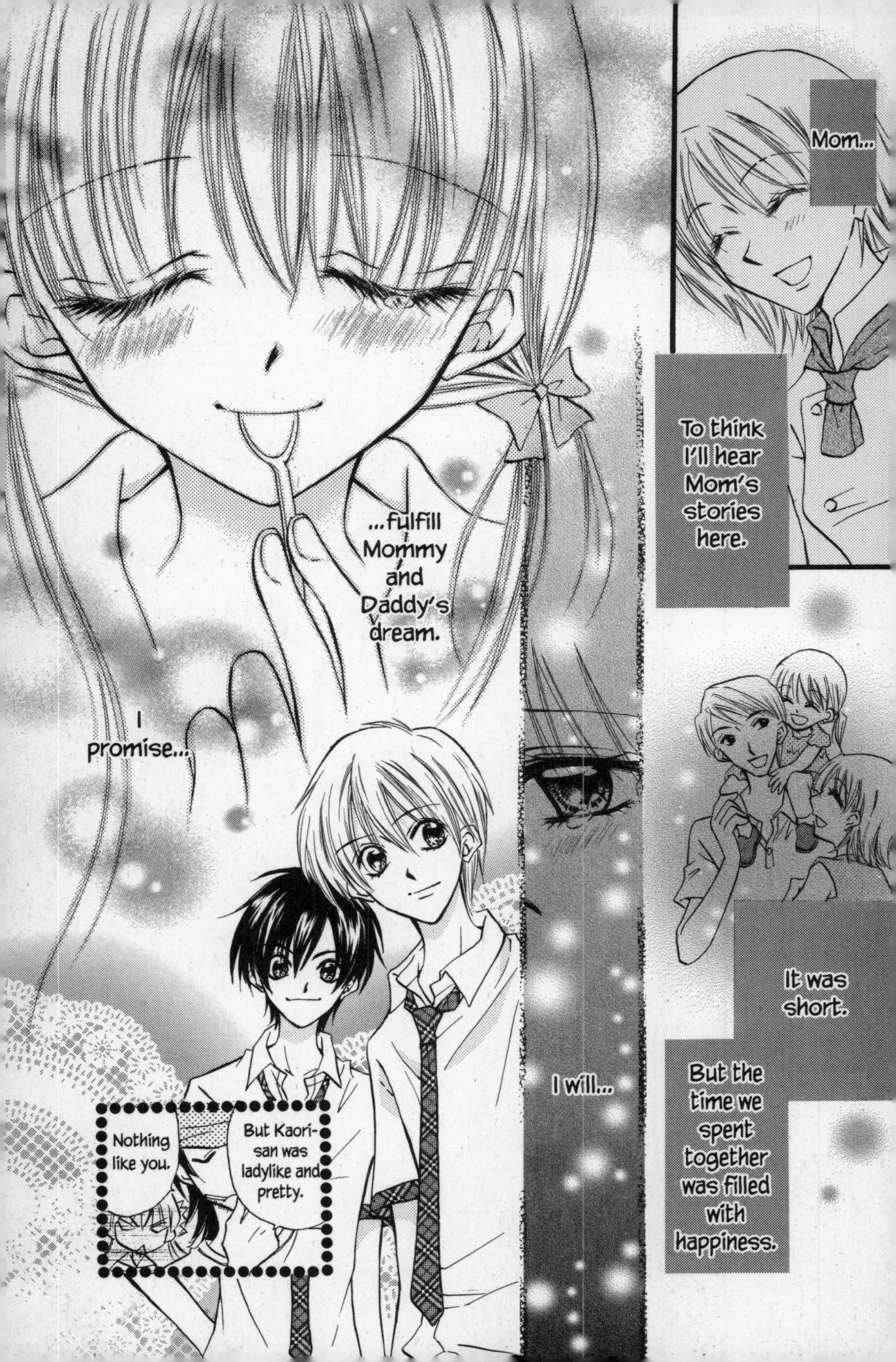

Mom...
To think I'll hear Mom's stories here.
It was short.
But the time we spent together was filled with happiness.
I will...
...fulfill Mommy and Daddy's dream.
I promise...
But Kaori-san was ladylike and pretty.
Nothing like you.

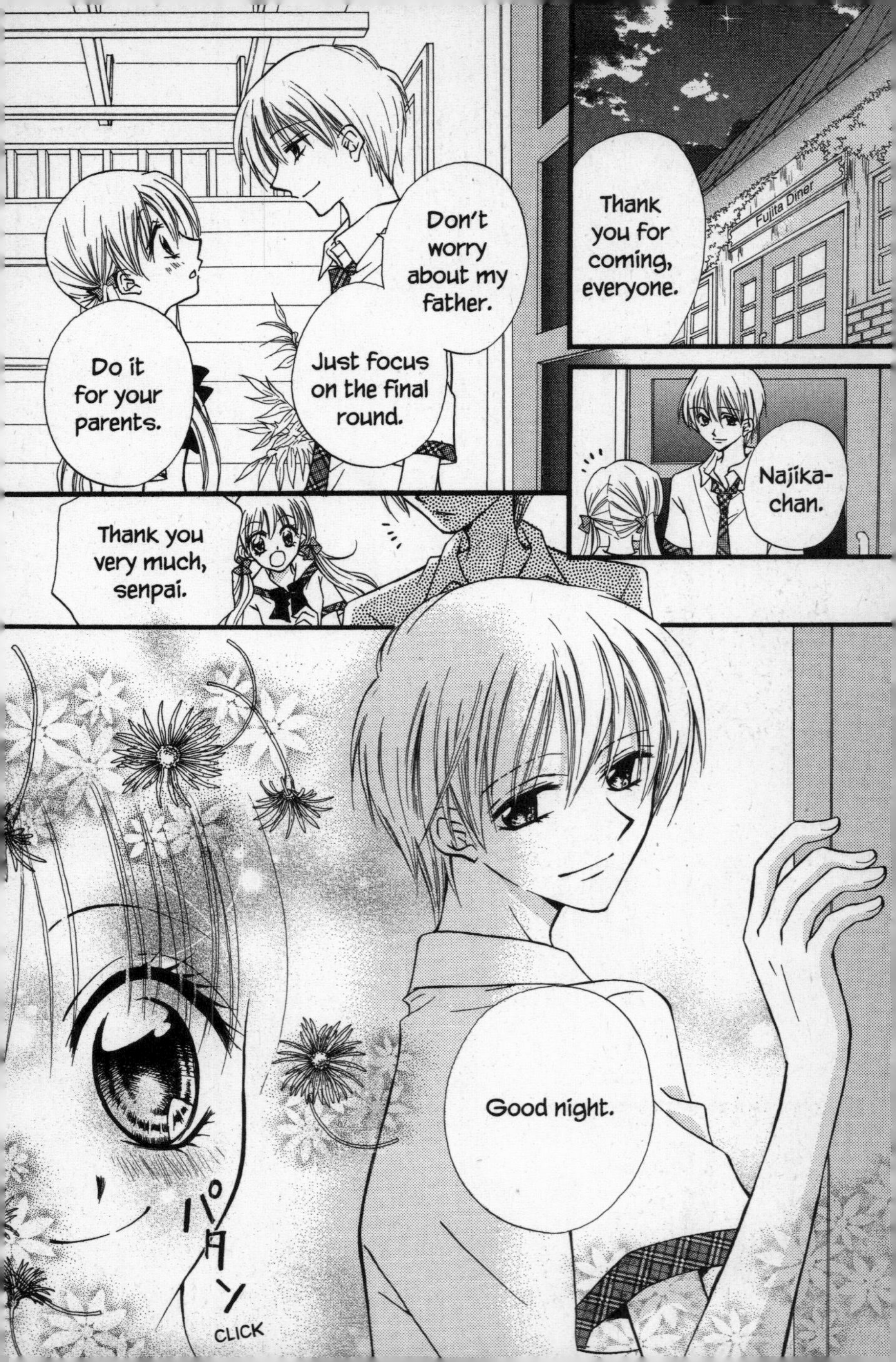
Fujita Diner
Thank you for coming, everyone.
Don't worry about my father.
Just focus on the final round.
Do it for your parents.
Najika-chan.
Thank you very much, senpai.
Good night.
パタン
CLICK

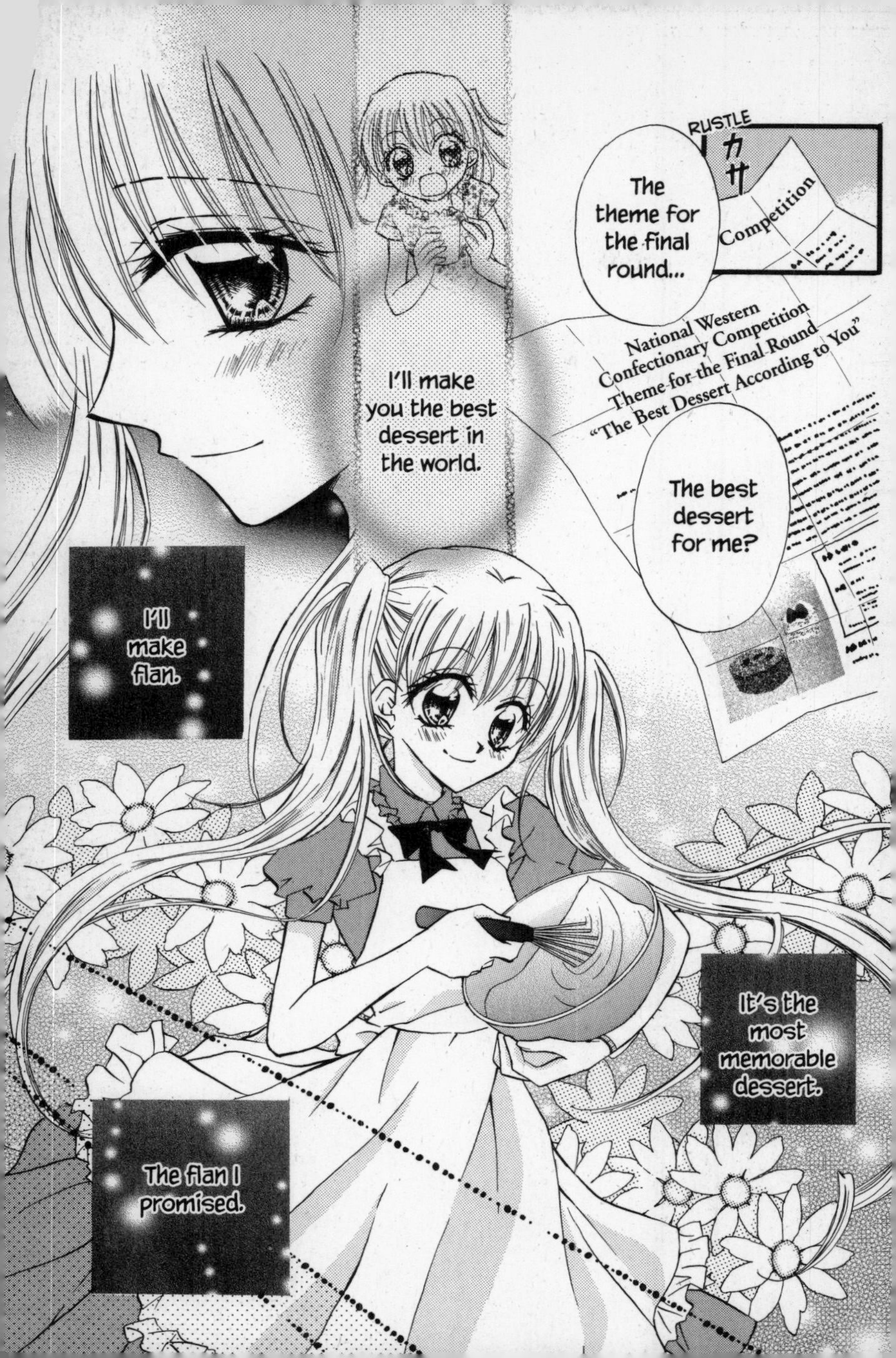
RUSTLE
カサ
Competition
The theme for the final round...
National Western Confectionary Competition
Theme for the Final Round
"The Best Dessert According to You"
The best dessert for me?
I'll make you the best dessert in the world.
I'll make flan.
It's the most memorable dessert.
The flan I promised.

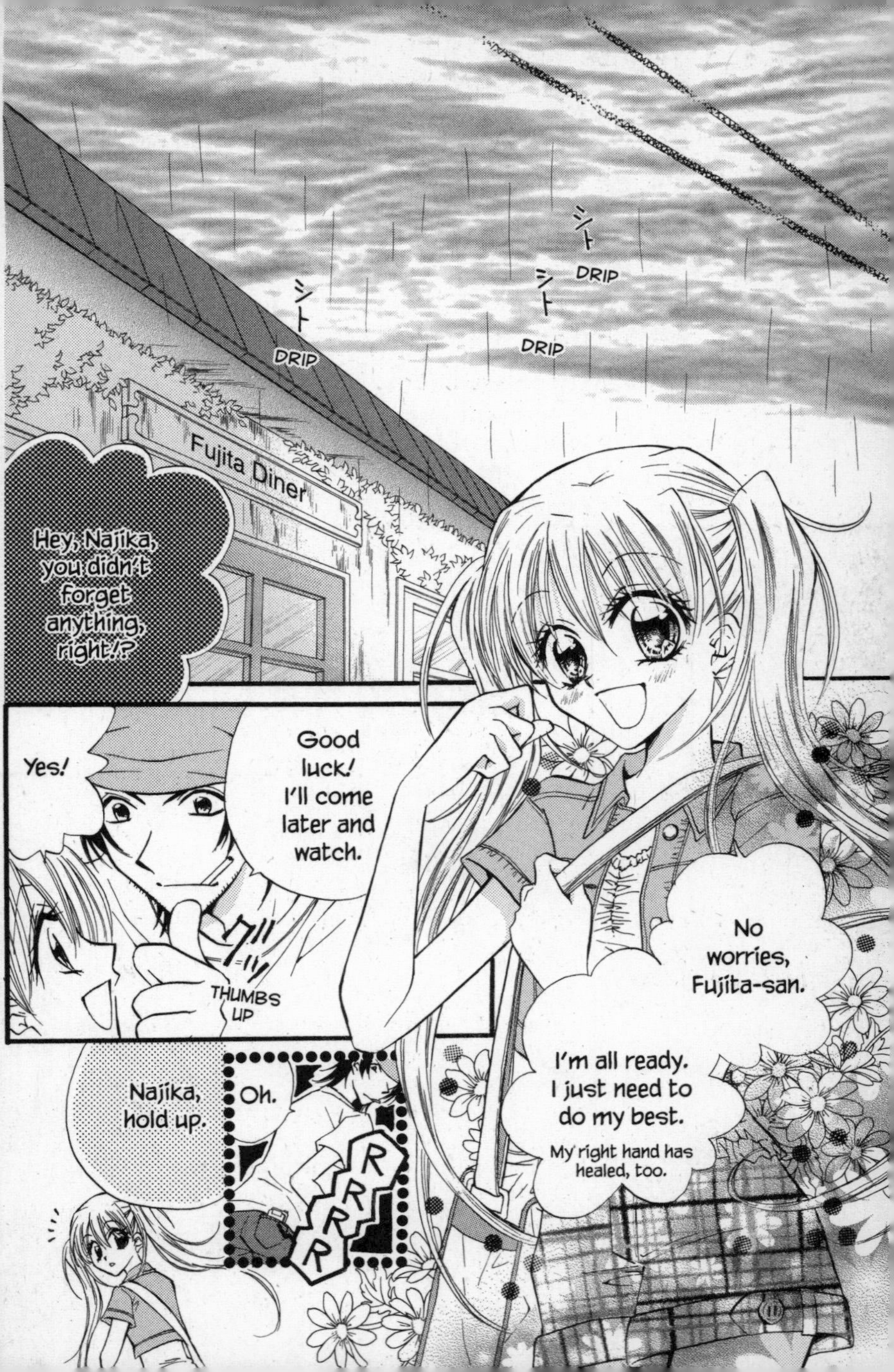
シト
DRIP
シト
DRIP
シト
DRIP
Fujita Diner
Hey, Najika, you didn't forget anything, right!?
No worries, Fujita-san.
I'm all ready. I just need to do my best.
My right hand has healed, too.
Good luck! I'll come later and watch.
Yes!
THUMBS UP
RRRR
Oh.
Najika, hold up.

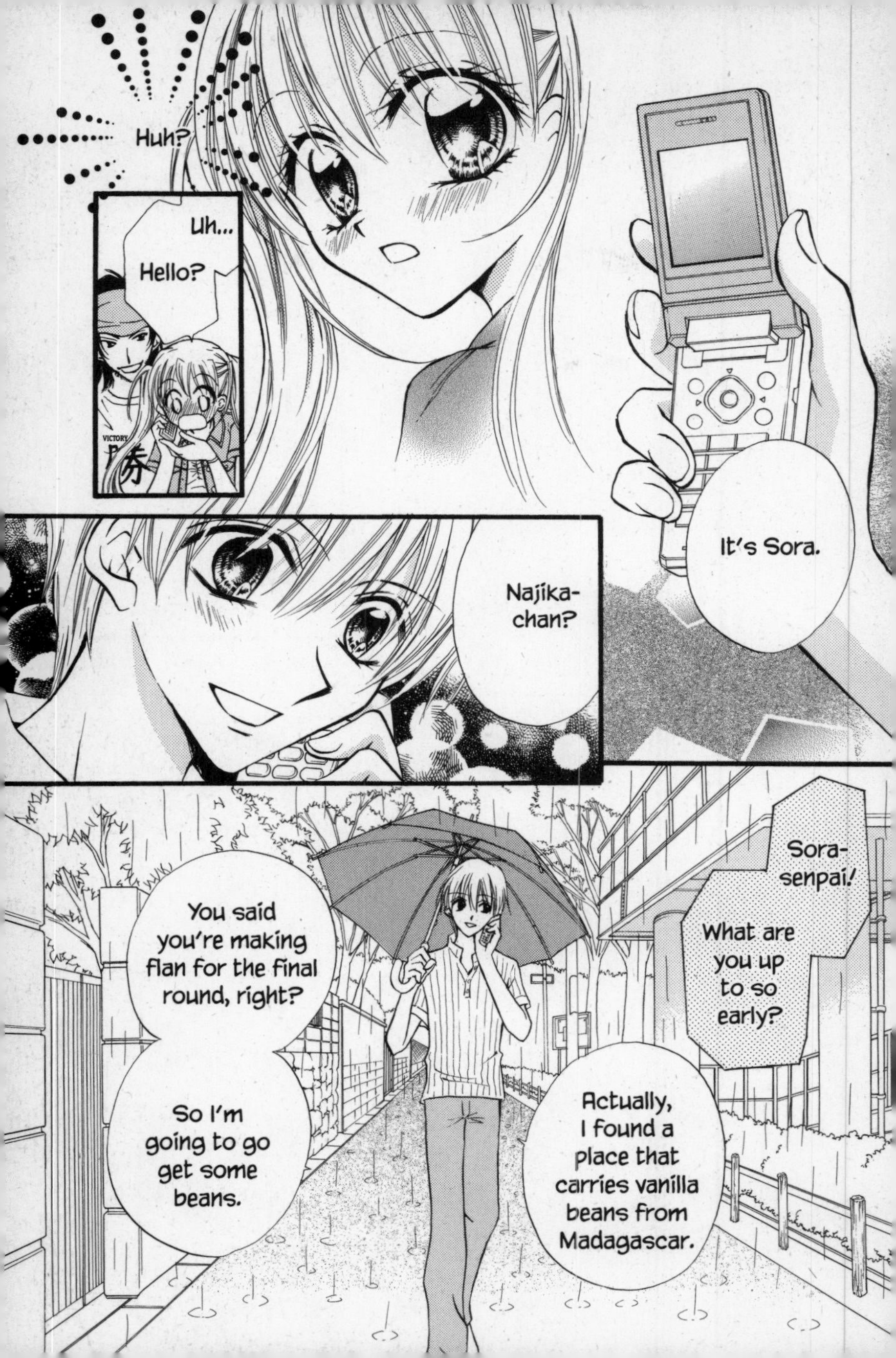
Uh...
Hello?
It's Sora.
Najika-chan?
Huh?
Sora-senpai!
What are you up to so early?
Actually, I found a place that carries vanilla beans from Madagascar.
You said you're making flan for the final round, right?
So I'm going to go get some beans.

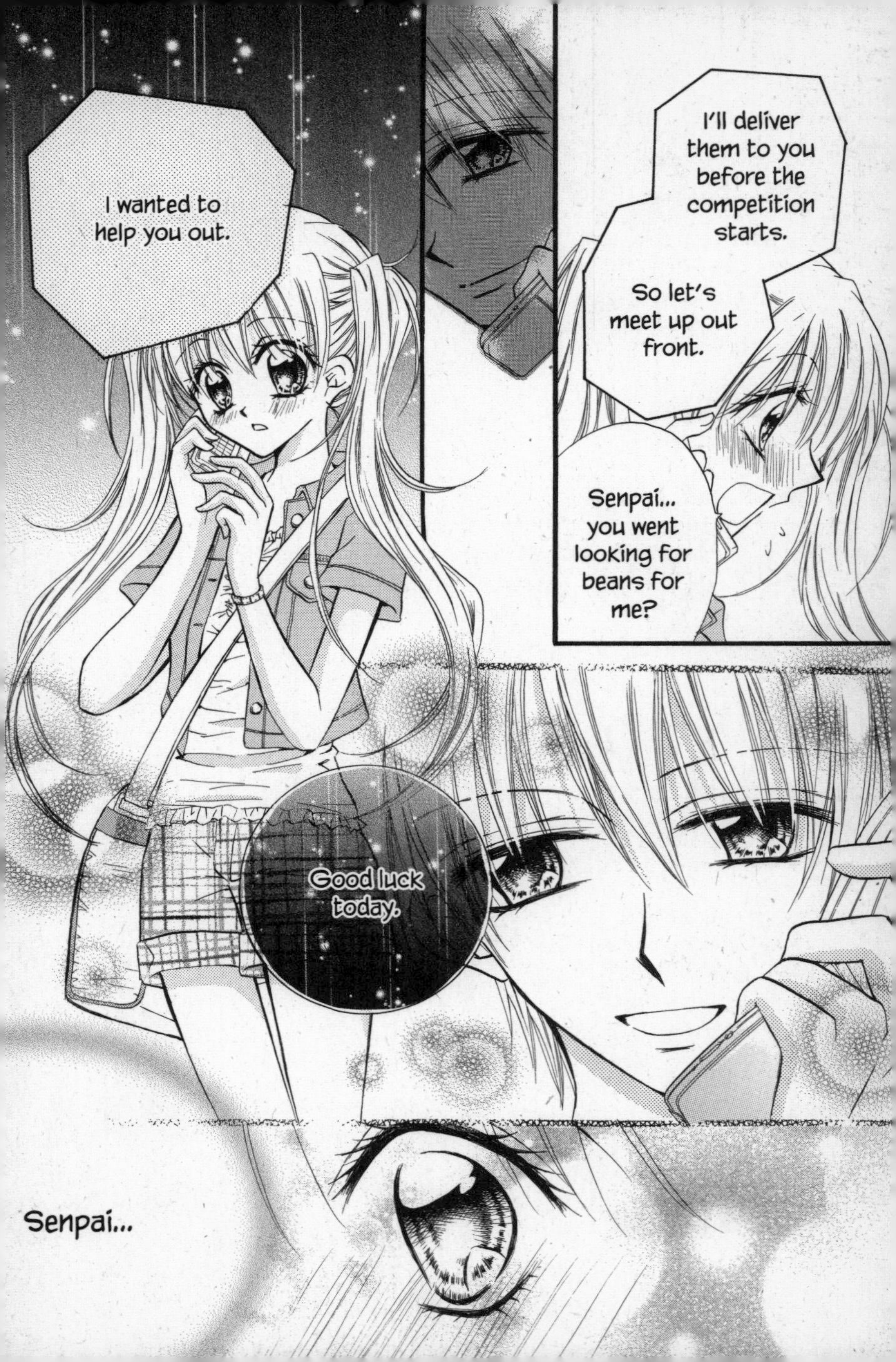
I'll deliver them to you before the competition starts.
So let's meet up out front.
Senpai... you went looking for beans for me?
I wanted to help you out.
Good luck today.
Senpai...

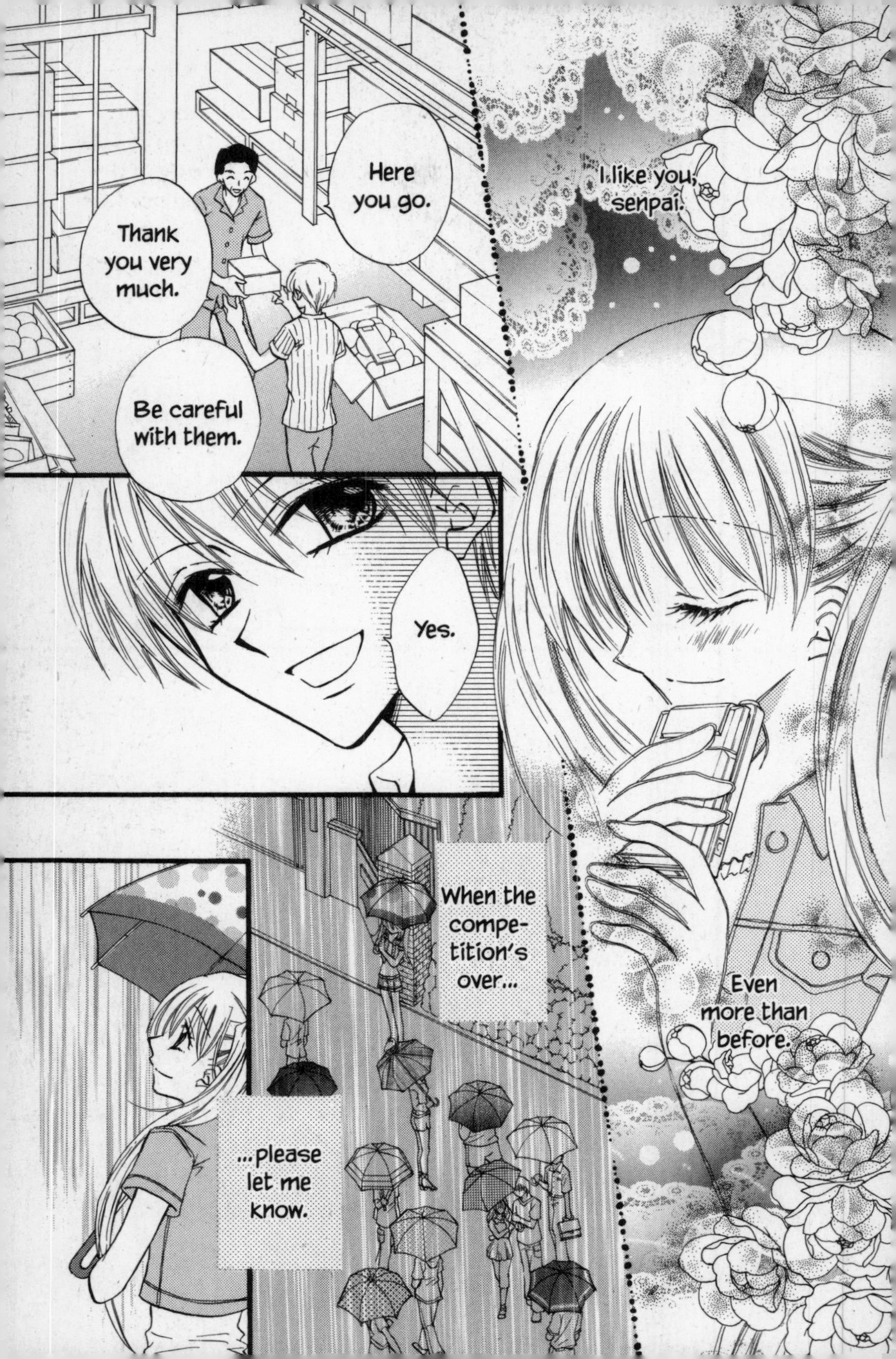
I like you, senpai.
Even more than before.
Here you go.
Thank you very much.
Be careful with them.
Yes.
When the compe-tition's over...
...please let me know.

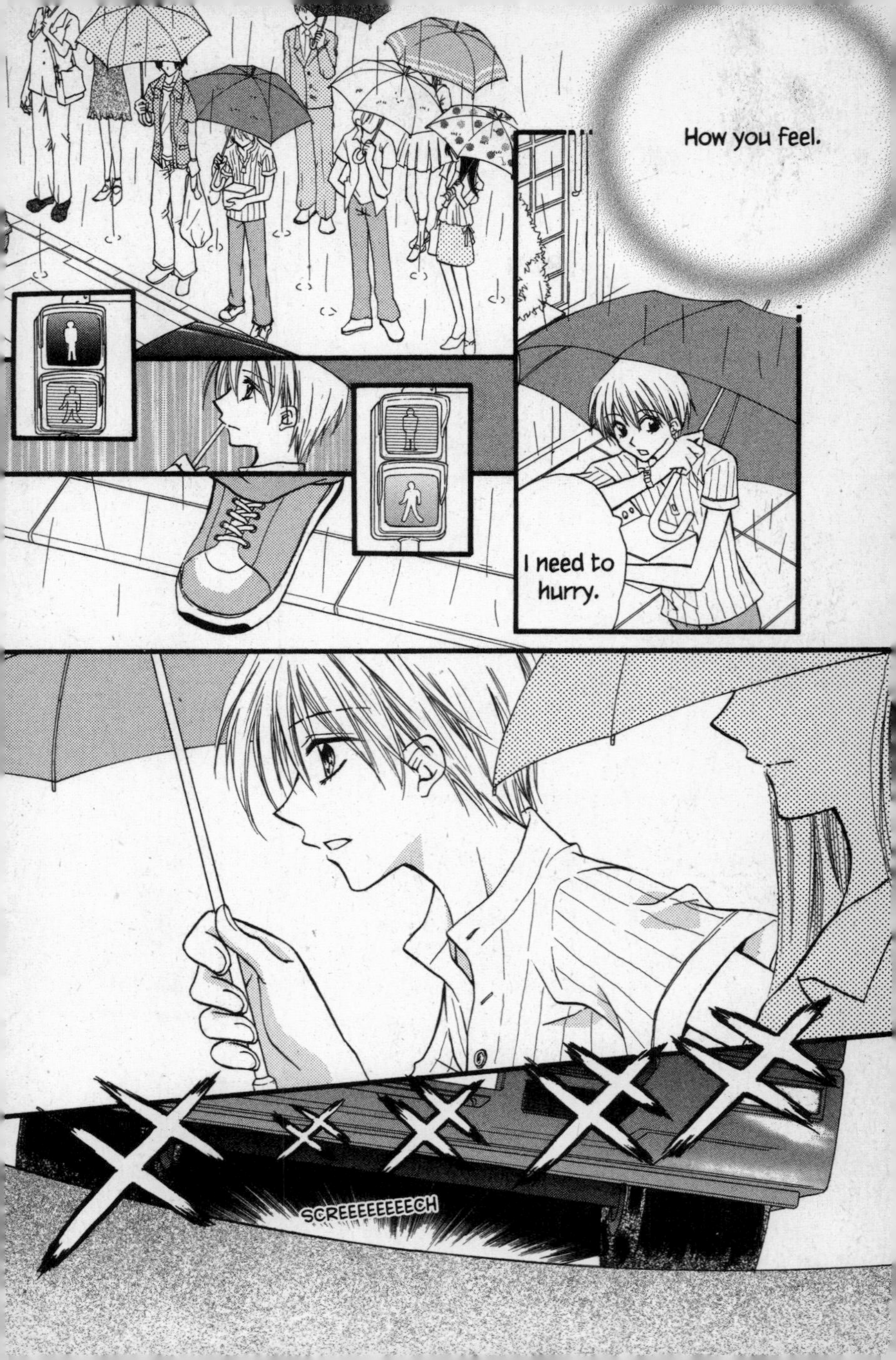
How you feel.
I need to hurry.
SCREEEEEEEEECH

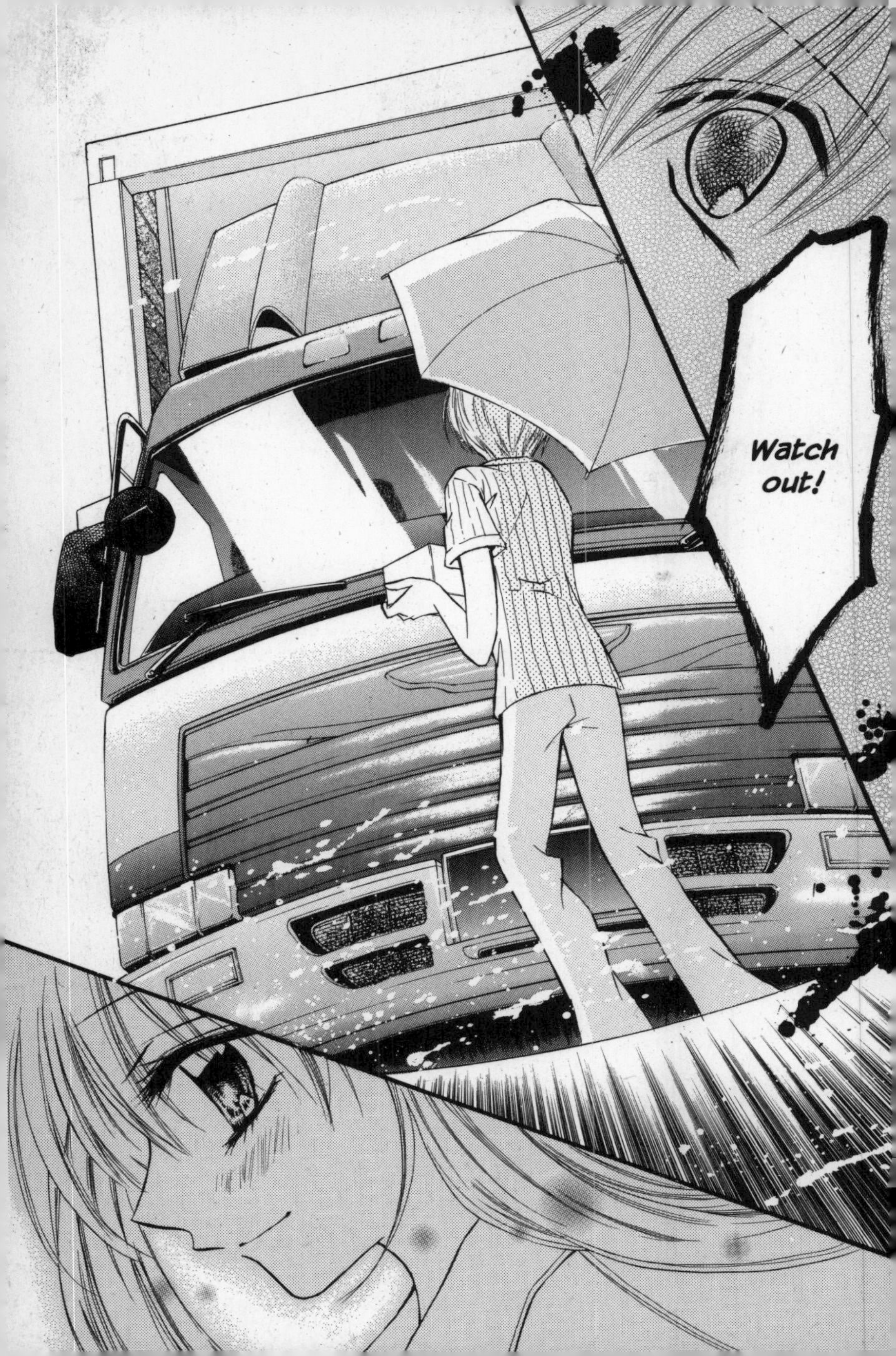
Watch out!

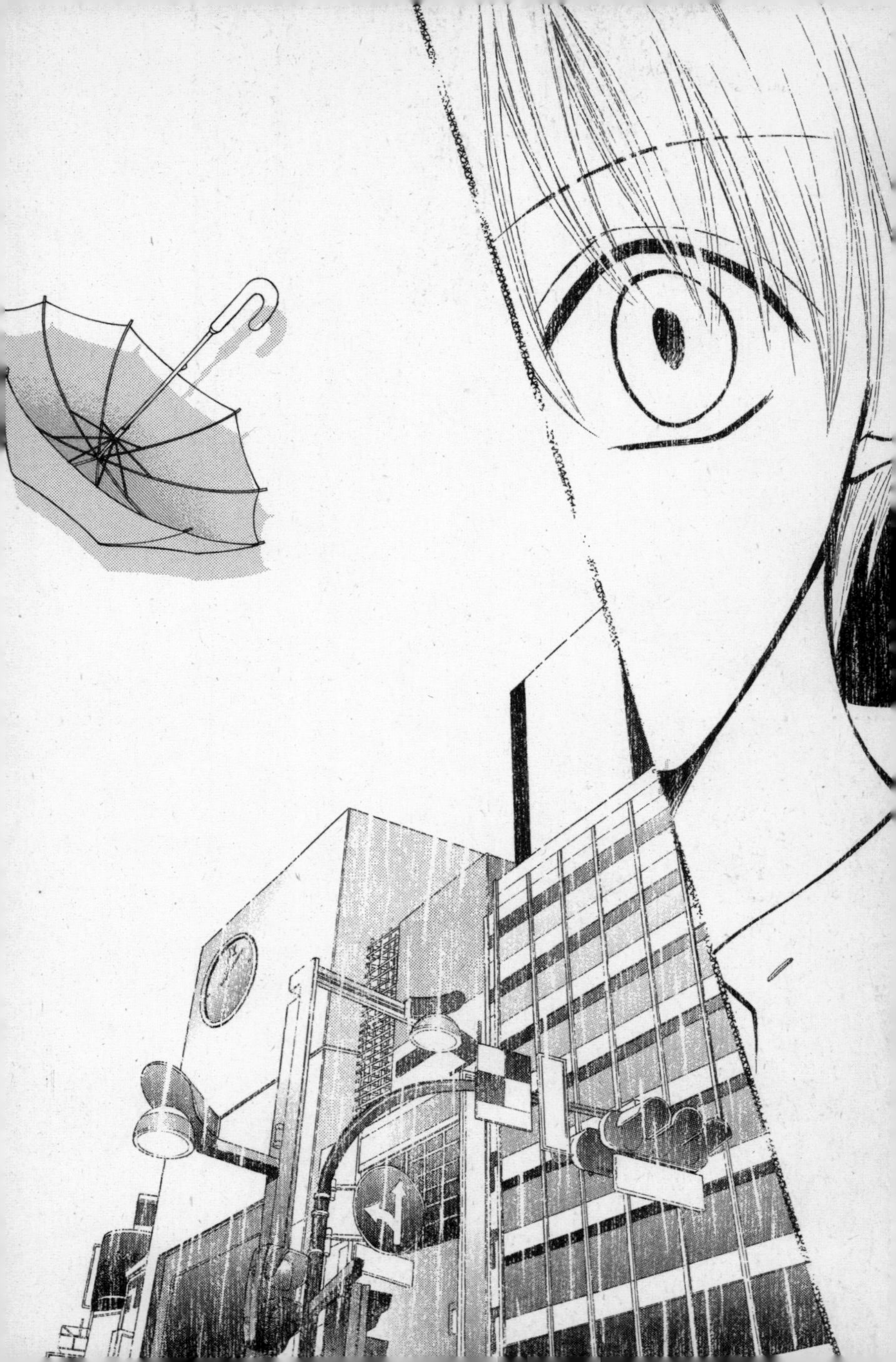

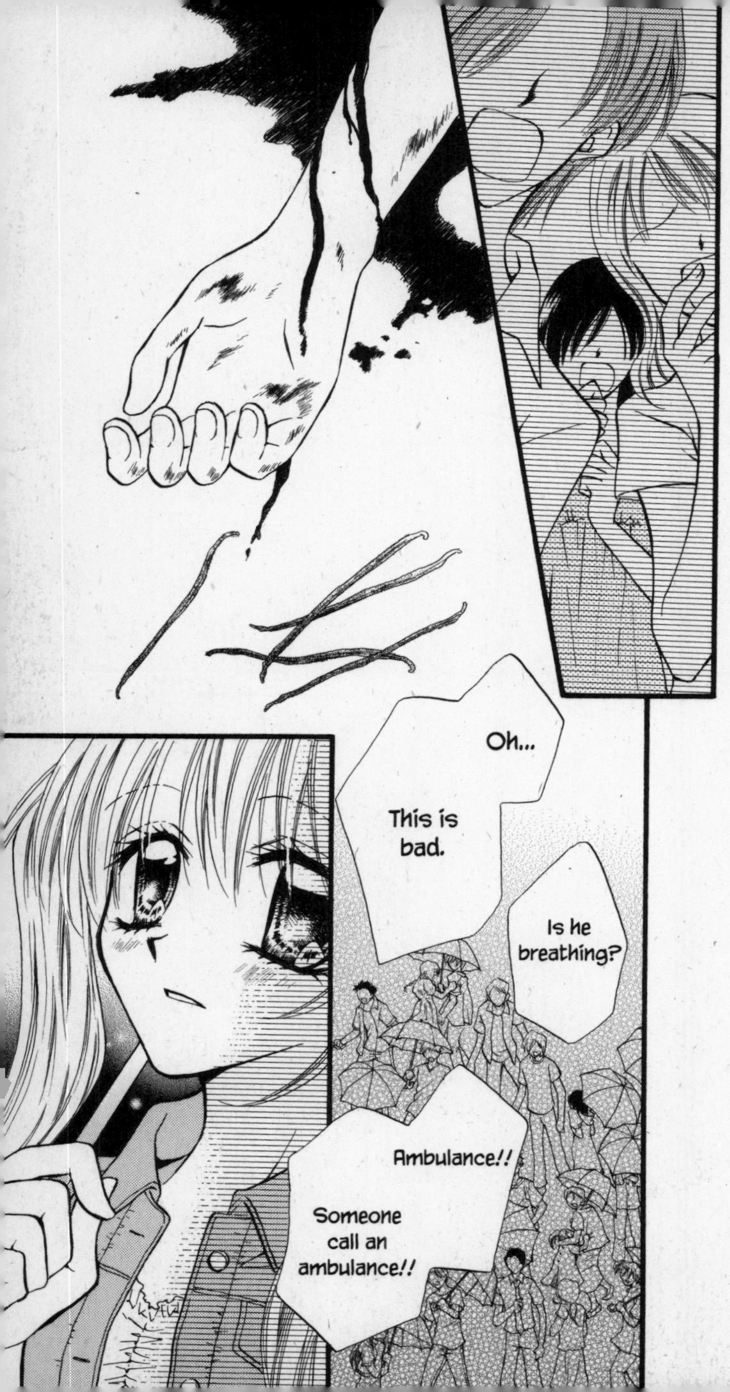
Oh...
This is bad.
Is he breathing?
Ambulance!!
Someone call an ambulance!!

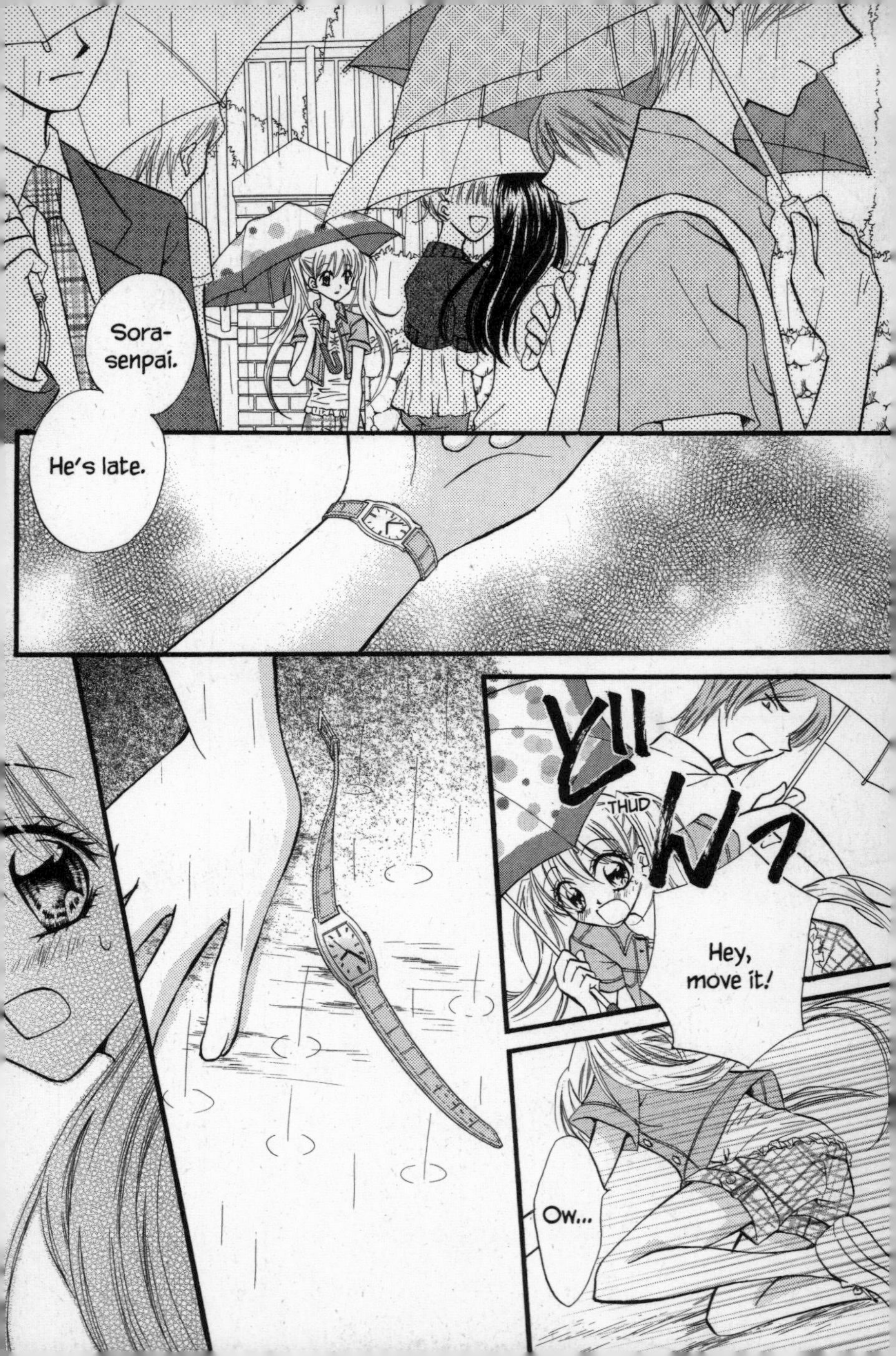
Sora-
senpai.
He's late.
THUD
Hey,
move it!
Ow...

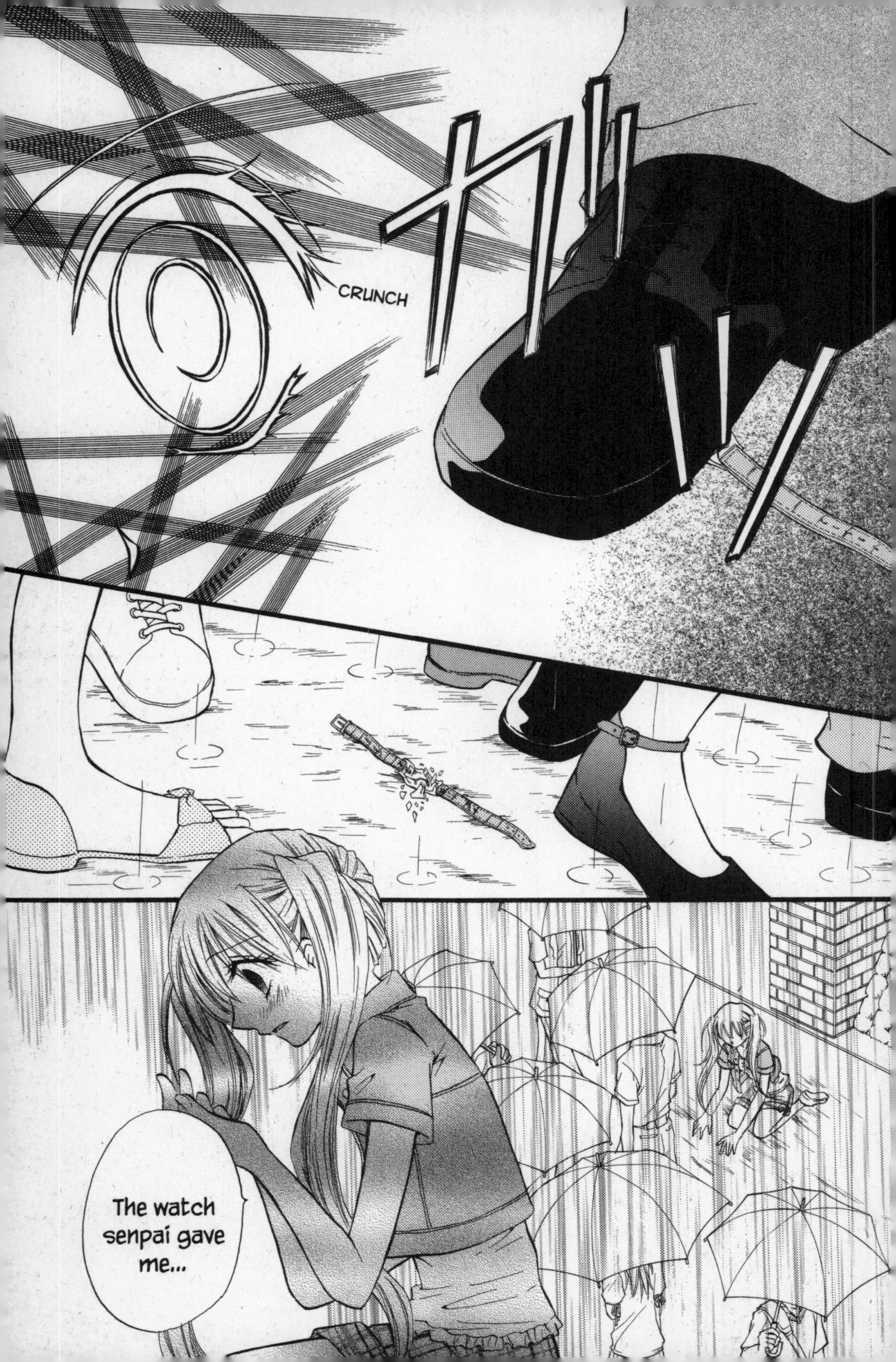
CRUNCH
The watch senpai gave me...

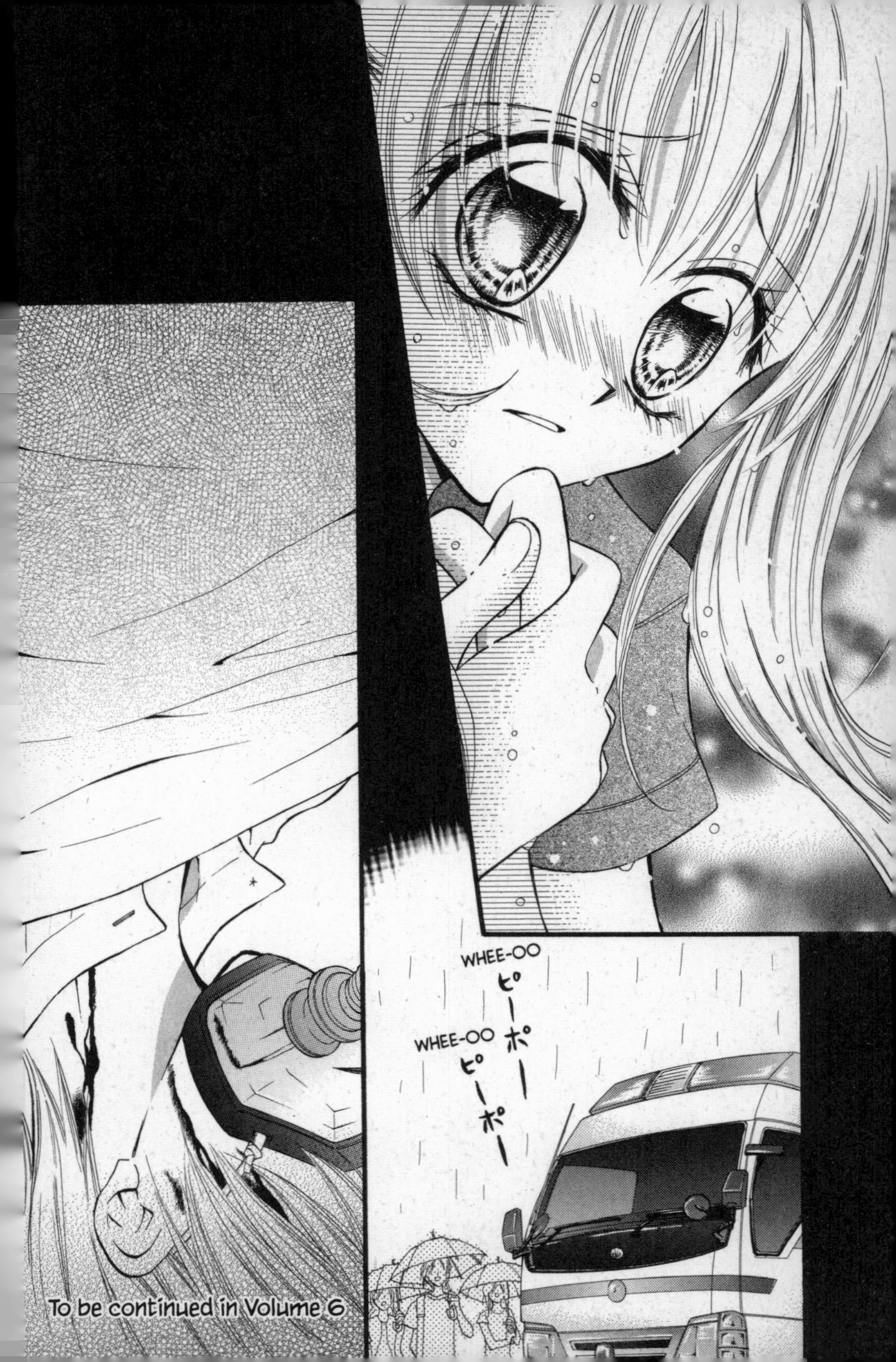
WHEE-OO
ピーポー
WHEE-OO
ピーポー
To be continued in Volume 6

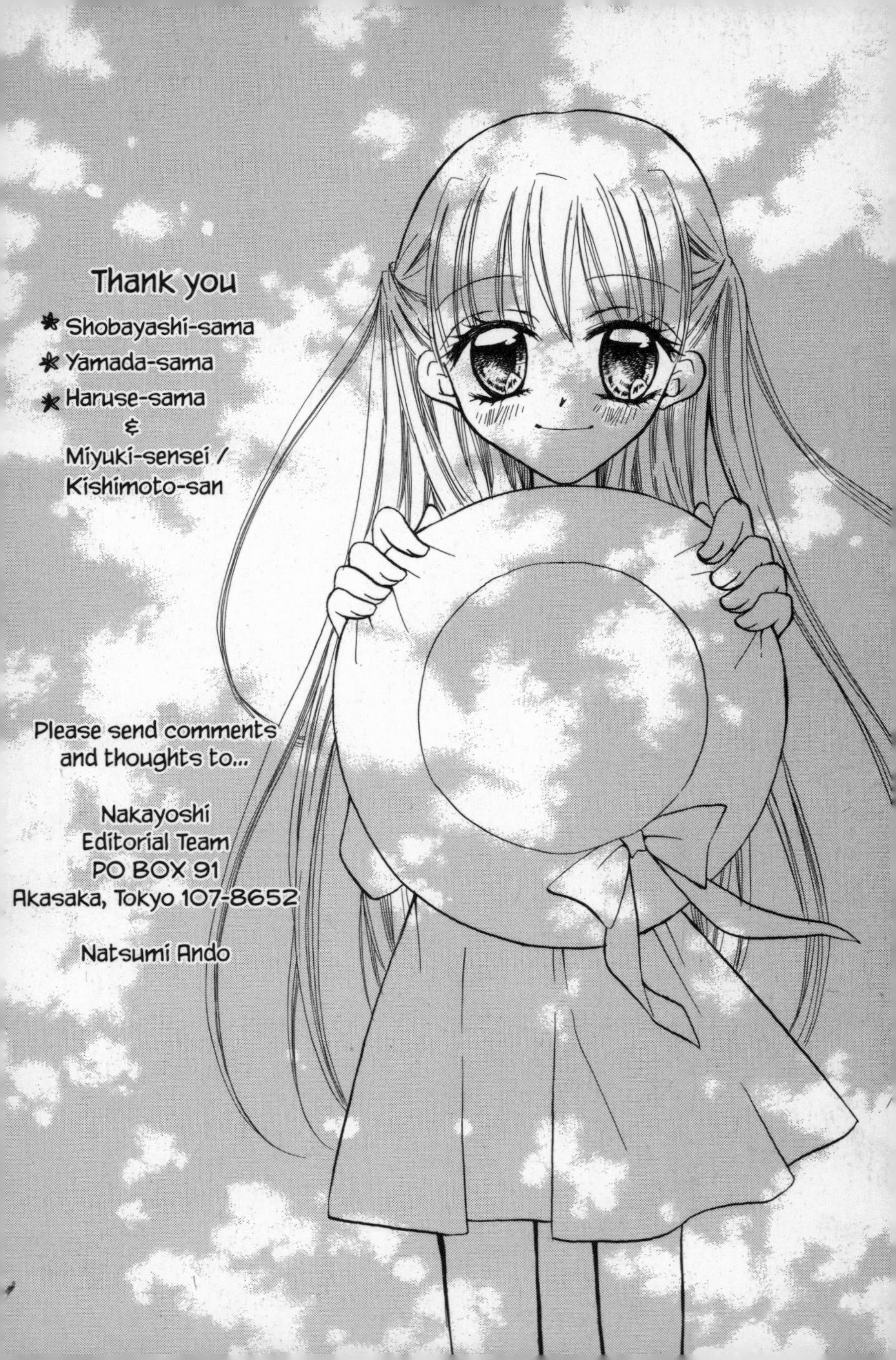
Thank you
Shobayashi-sama
Yamada-sama
Haruse-sama
&
Miyuki-sensei /
Kishimoto-san
Please send comments and thoughts to...
Nakayoshi Editorial Team
PO BOX 91
Akasaka, Tokyo 107-8652
Natsumi Ando

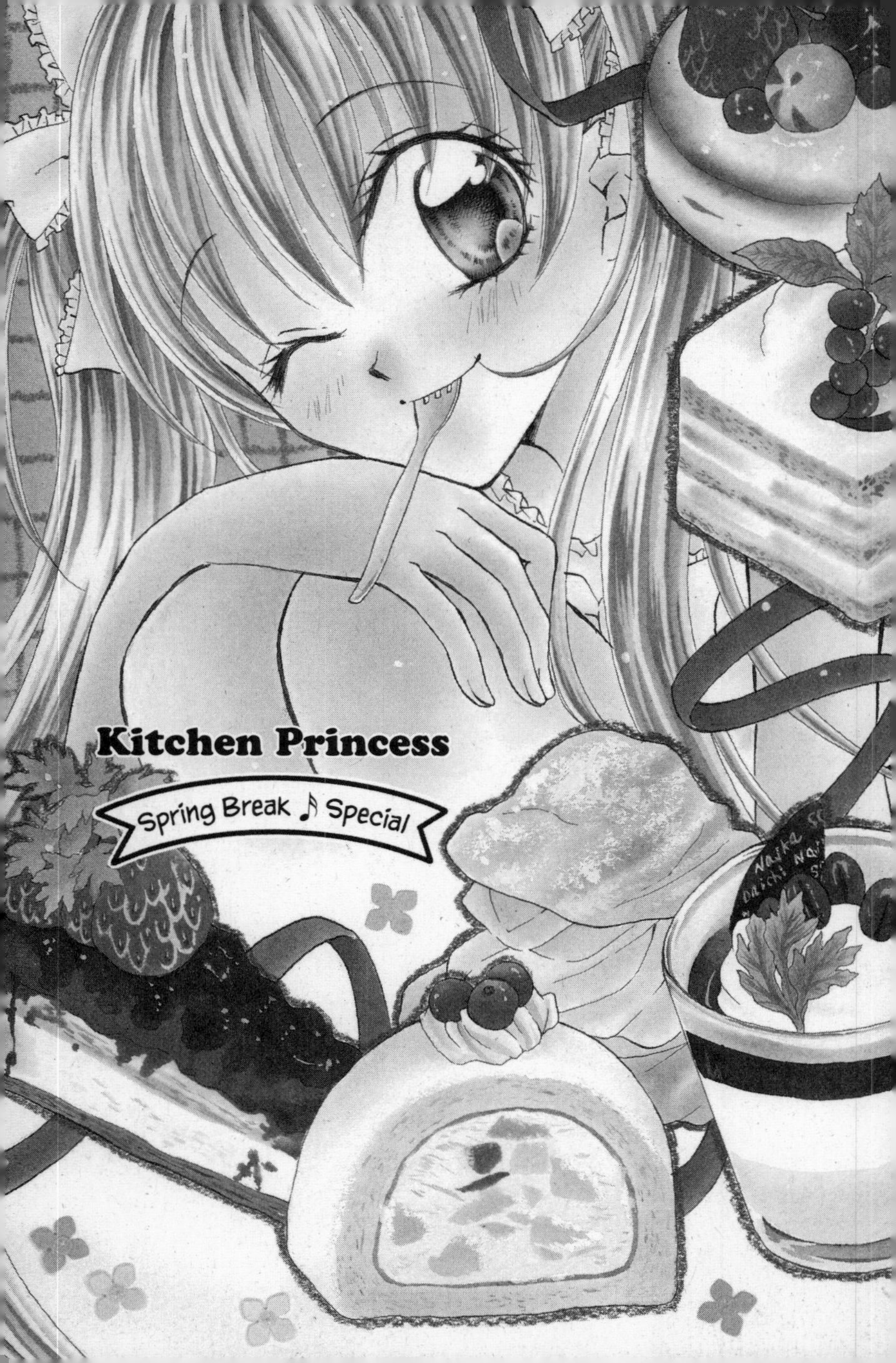
Kitchen Princess
Spring Break ♪ Special

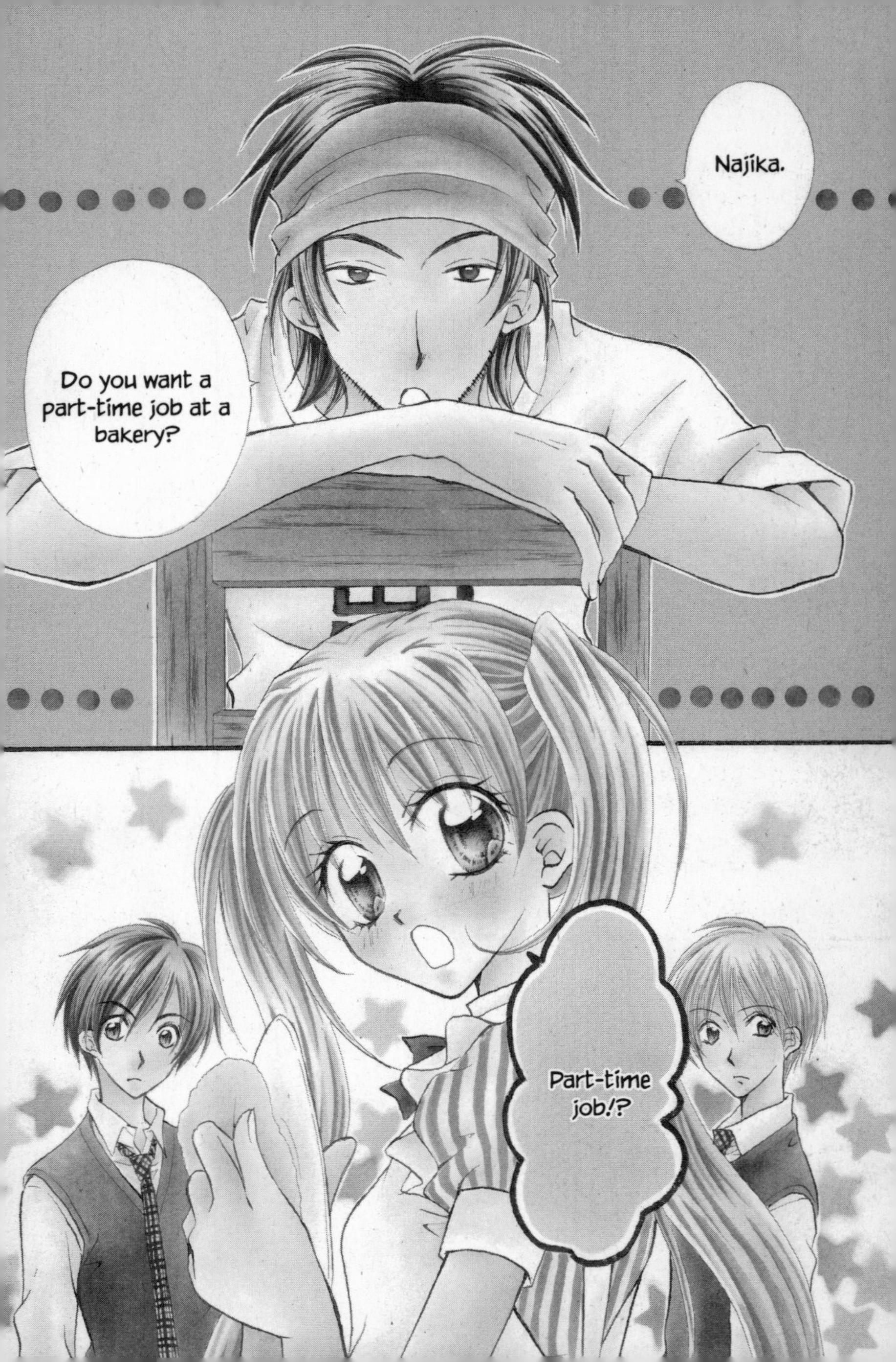
Najika.
Do you want a part-time job at a bakery?
Part-time job!?

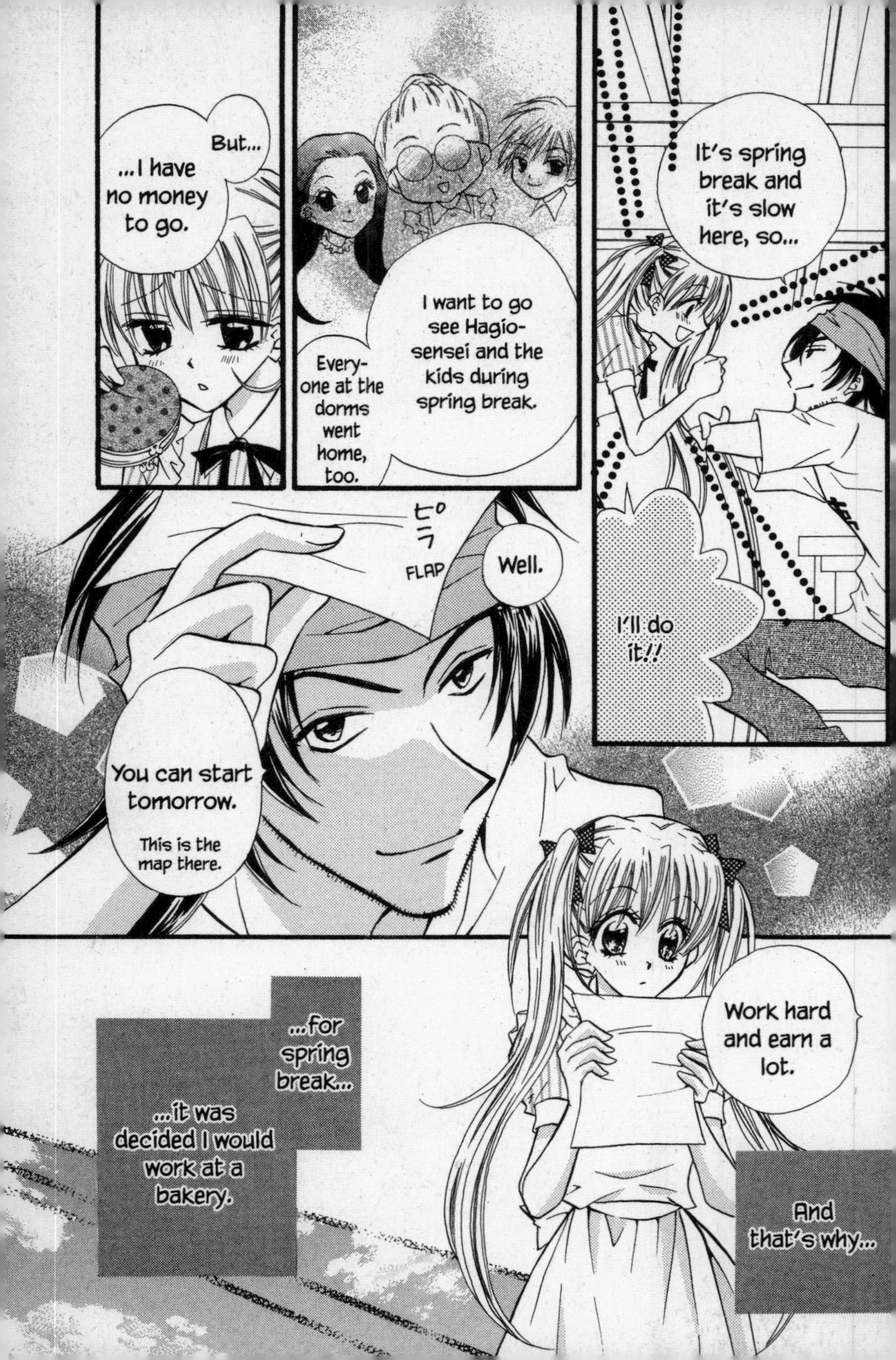
It's spring break and it's slow here, so...
I'll do it!!
I want to go see Hagio-sensei and the kids during spring break.
Everyone at the dorms went home, too.
But...
...I have no money to go.
Well.
ピラ
FLAP
You can start tomorrow.
This is the map there.
Work hard and earn a lot.
And that's why...
...for spring break...
...it was decided I would work at a bakery.

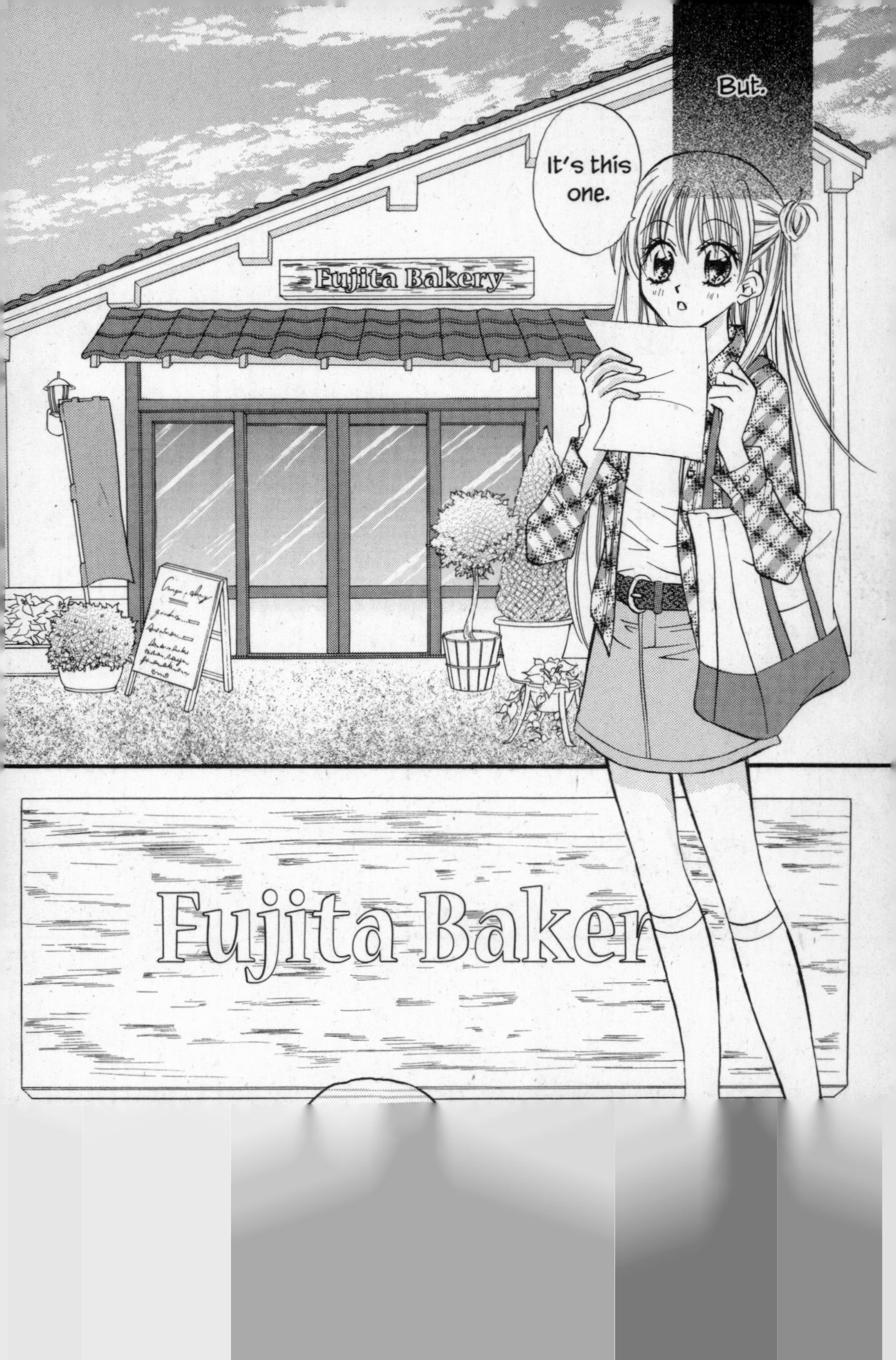
But.
It's this one.
Fujita Bakery
Fujita Baker

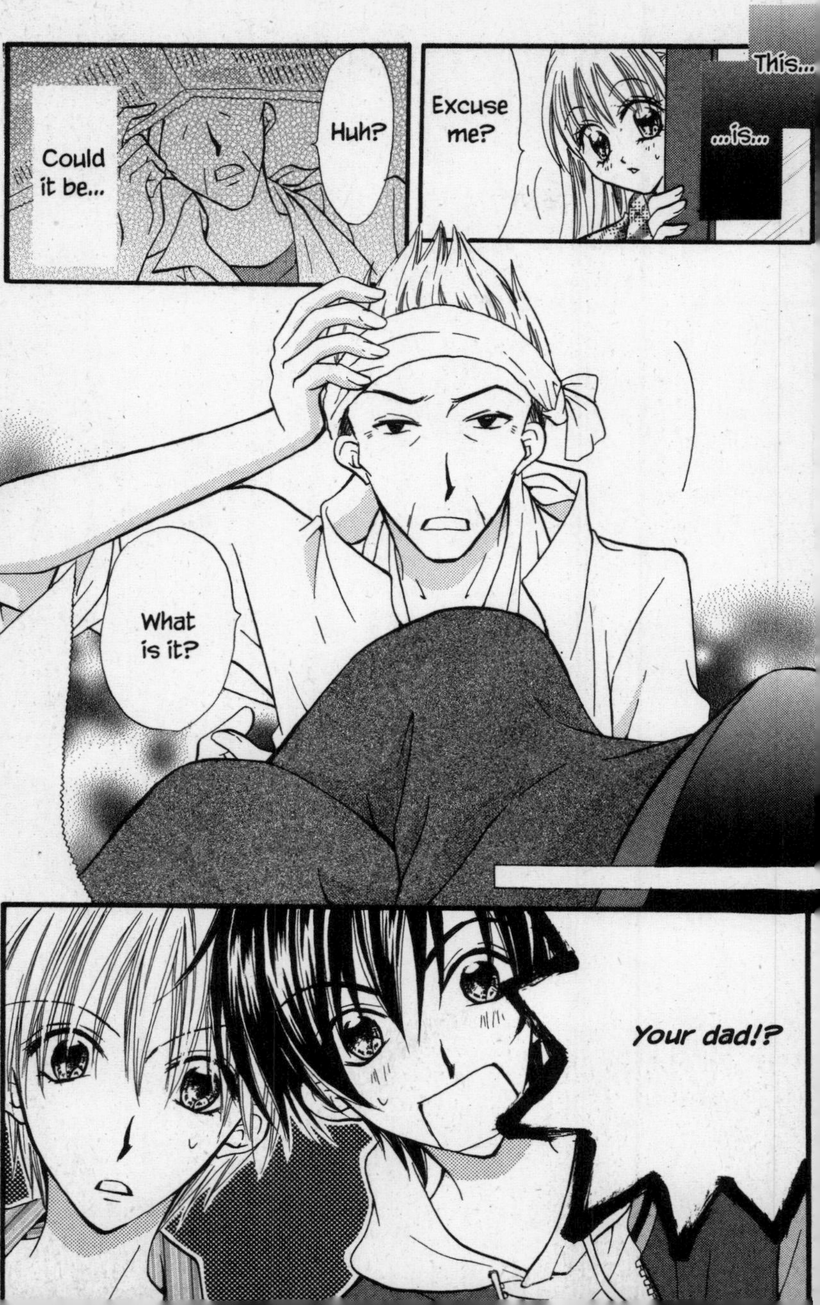
This...
...is...
Excuse me?
Huh?
Could it be...
What is it?
Your dad!?

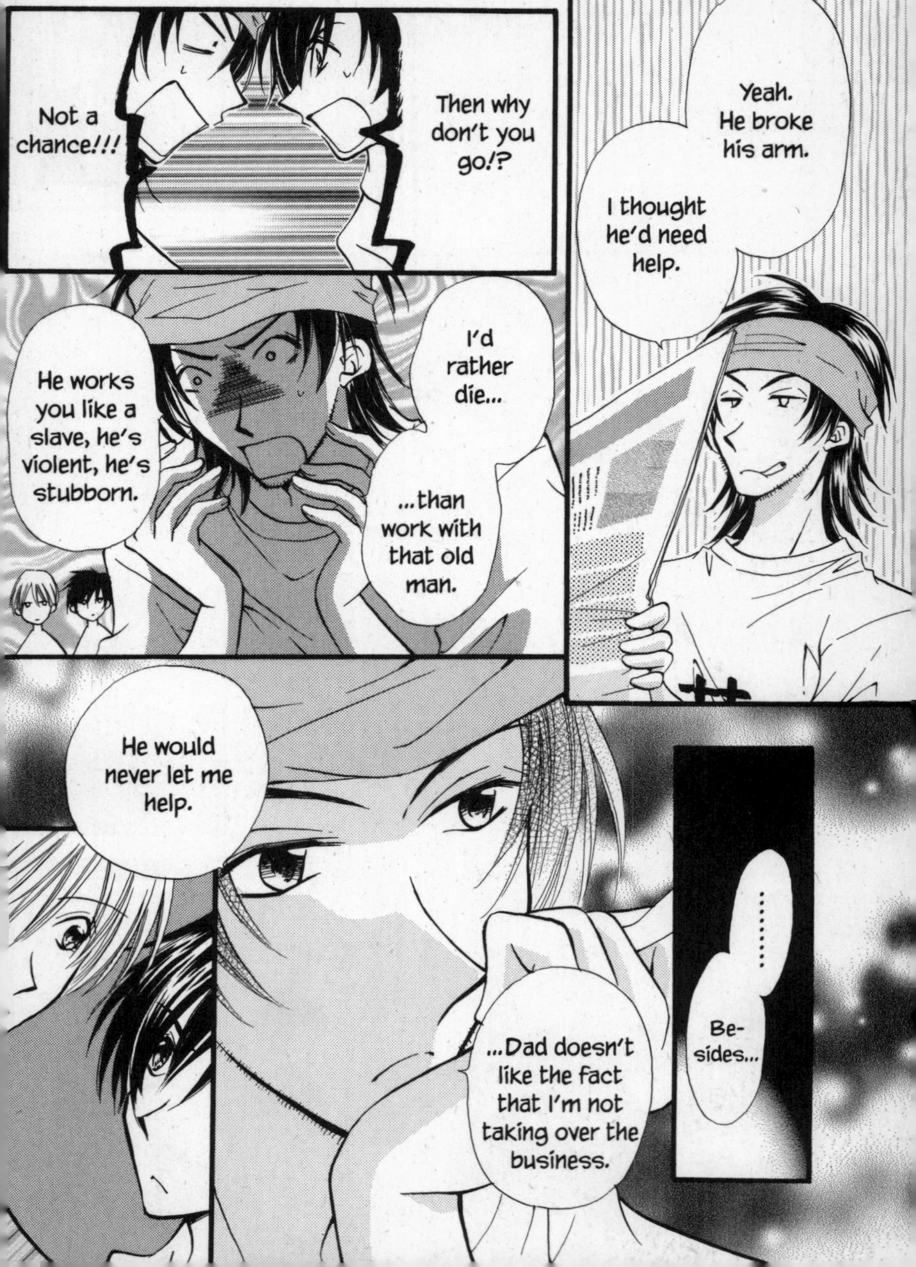
Yeah. He broke his arm.
I thought he'd need help.
Then why don't you go!?
Not a chance!!!
I'd rather die...
...than work with that old man.
He works you like a slave, he's violent, he's stubborn.
......
Be-sides...
...Dad doesn't like the fact that I'm not taking over the business.
He would never let me help.

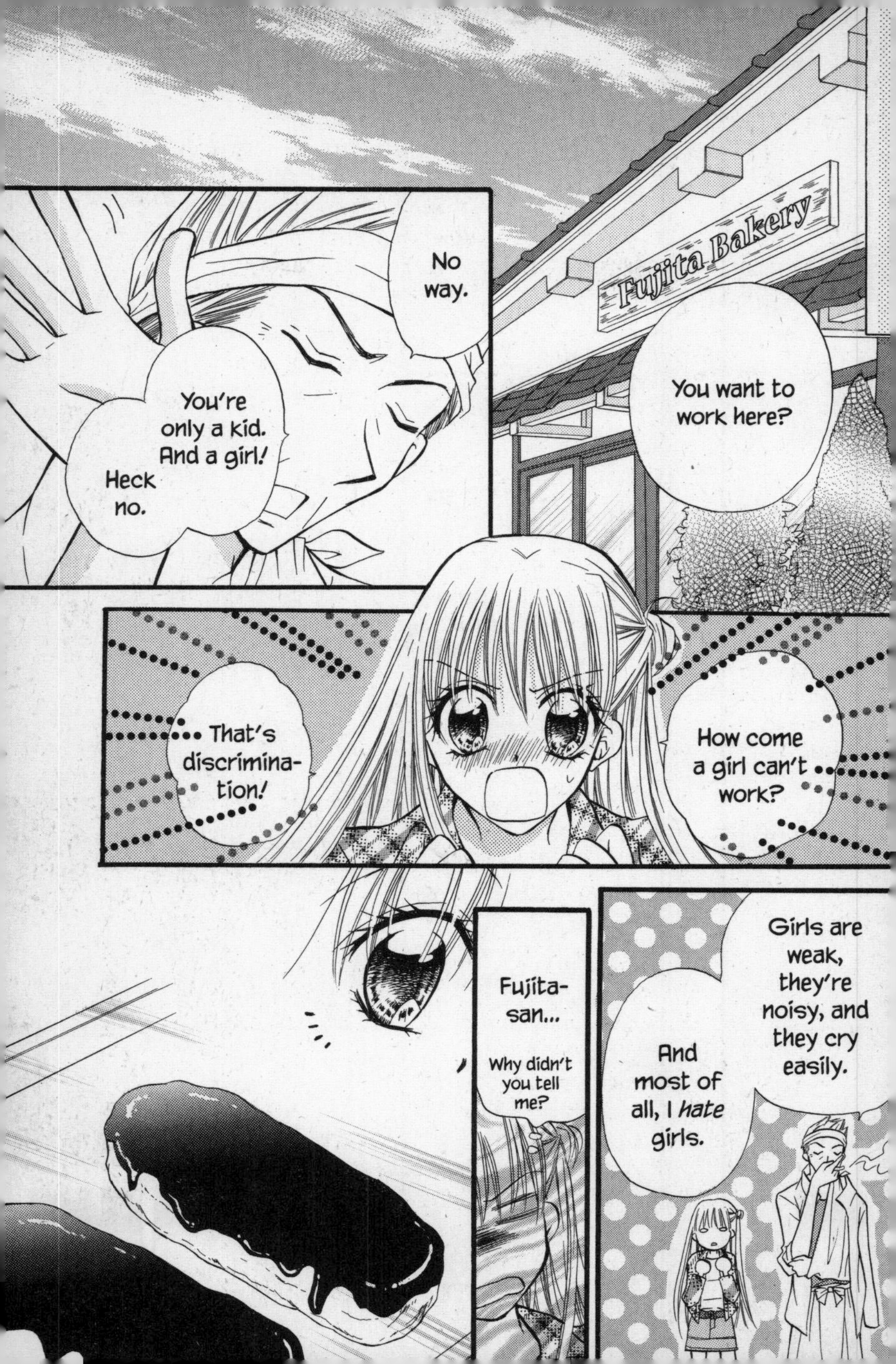

Fujita Bakery
You want to work here?
No way.
You're only a kid. And a girl!
Heck no.
How come a girl can't work?
That's discrimination!
Girls are weak, they're noisy, and they cry easily.
And most of all, I *hate* girls.
Fujita-san...
Why didn't you tell me?

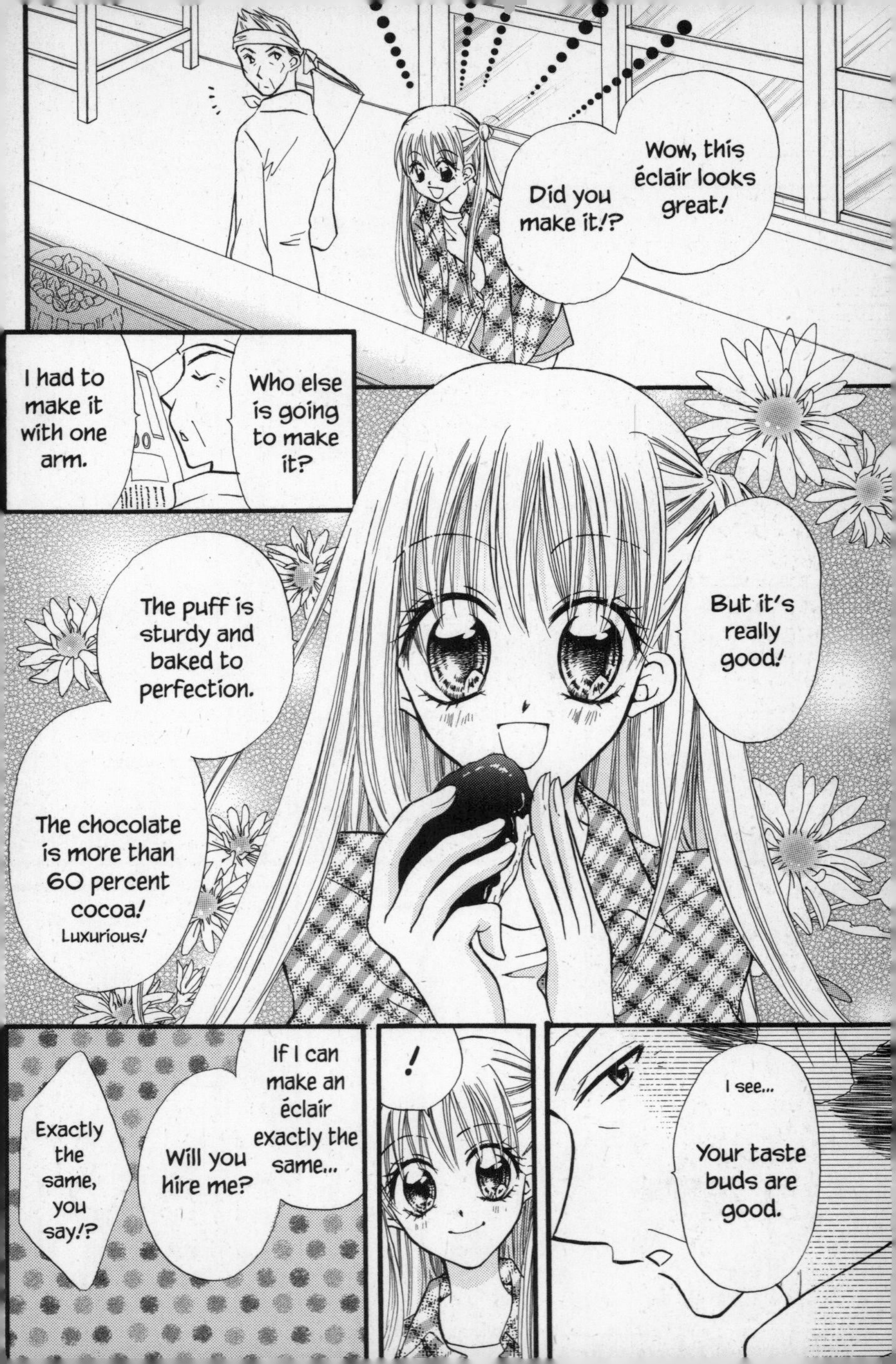
Wow, this éclair looks great!
Did you make it!?
Who else is going to make it?
I had to make it with one arm.
But it's really good!
The puff is sturdy and baked to perfection.
The chocolate is more than 60 percent cocoa!
Luxurious!
I see...
Your taste buds are good.
!
If I can make an éclair exactly the same...
Will you hire me?
Exactly the same, you say!?

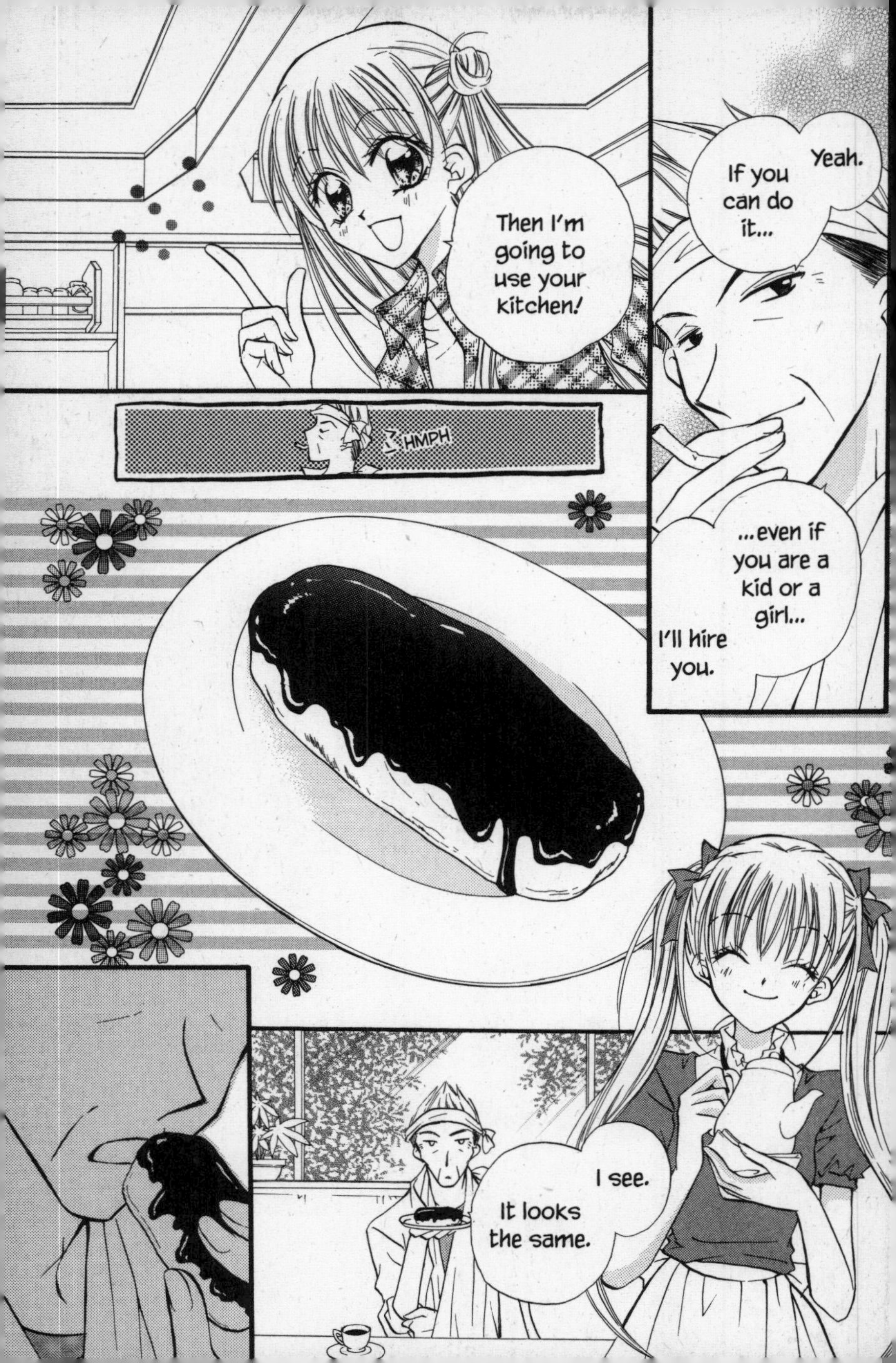
Yeah.
If you can do it...
...even if you are a kid or a girl...
I'll hire you.
Then I'm going to use your kitchen!
HMPH
I see.
It looks the same.

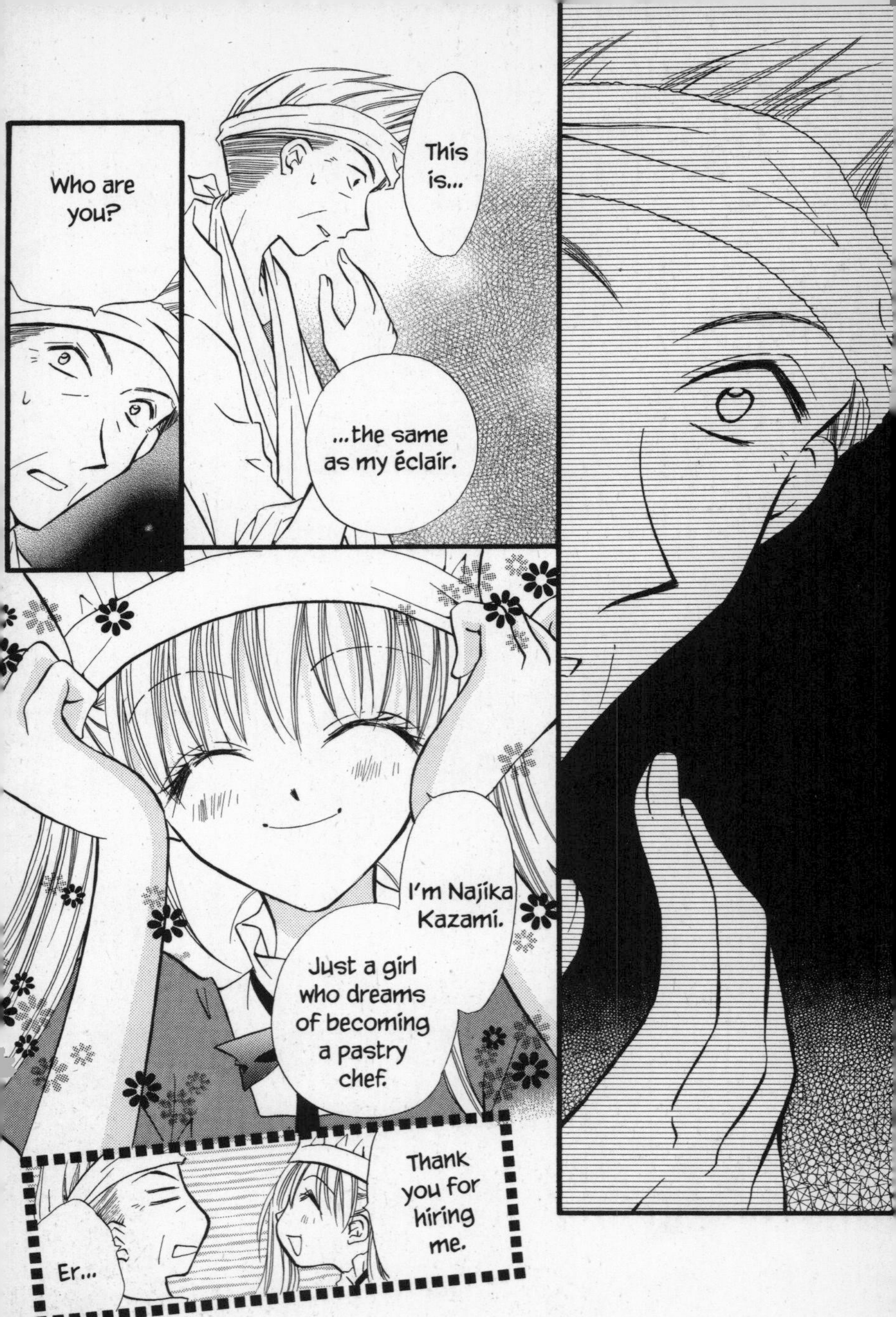
This is...
...the same as my éclair.
Who are you?
I'm Najika Kazami.
Just a girl who dreams of becoming a pastry chef.
Thank you for hiring me.
Er...

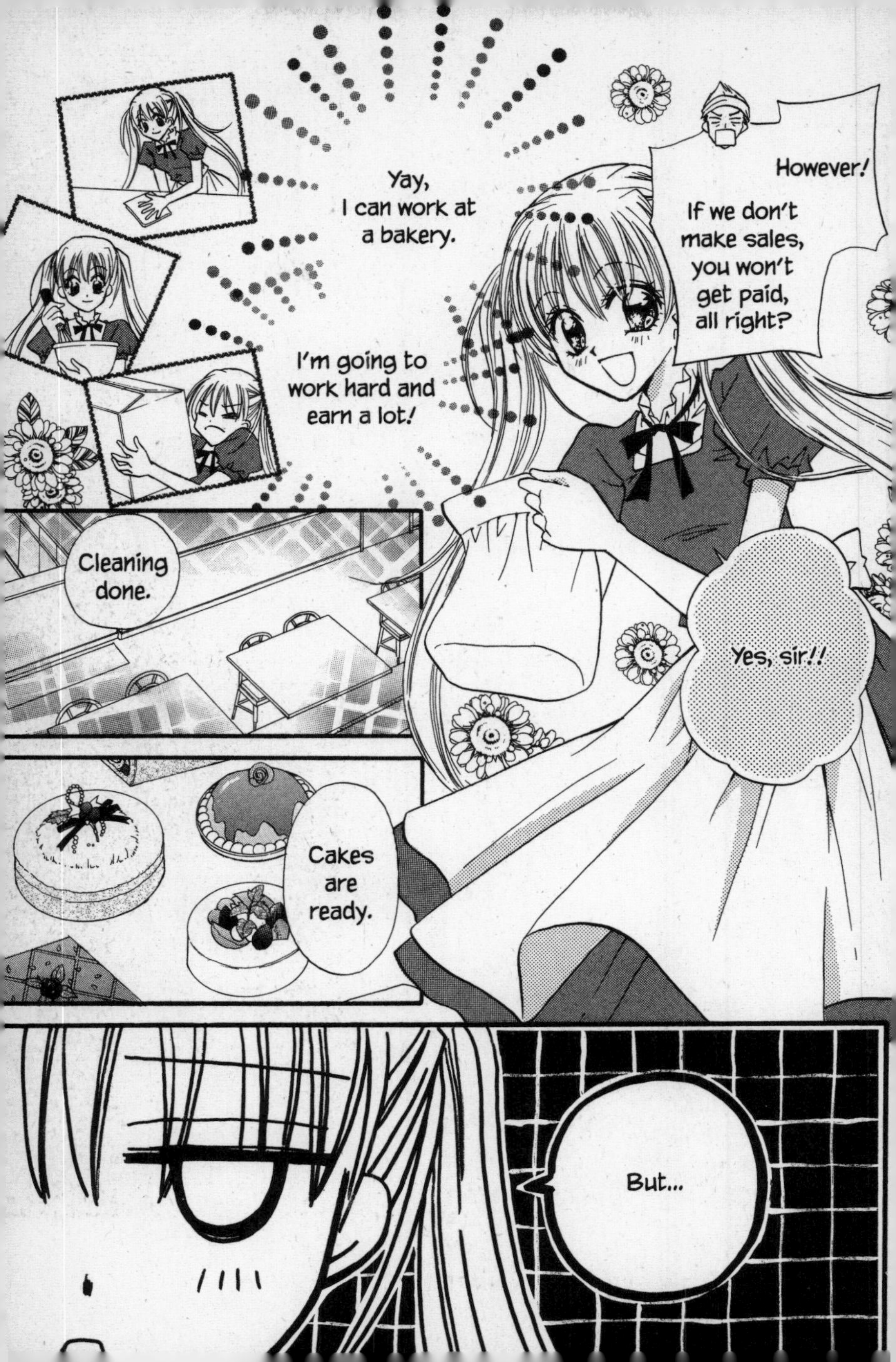
Yay, I can work at a bakery.
I'm going to work hard and earn a lot!
However! If we don't make sales, you won't get paid, all right?
Yes, sir!!
Cleaning done.
Cakes are ready.
But...

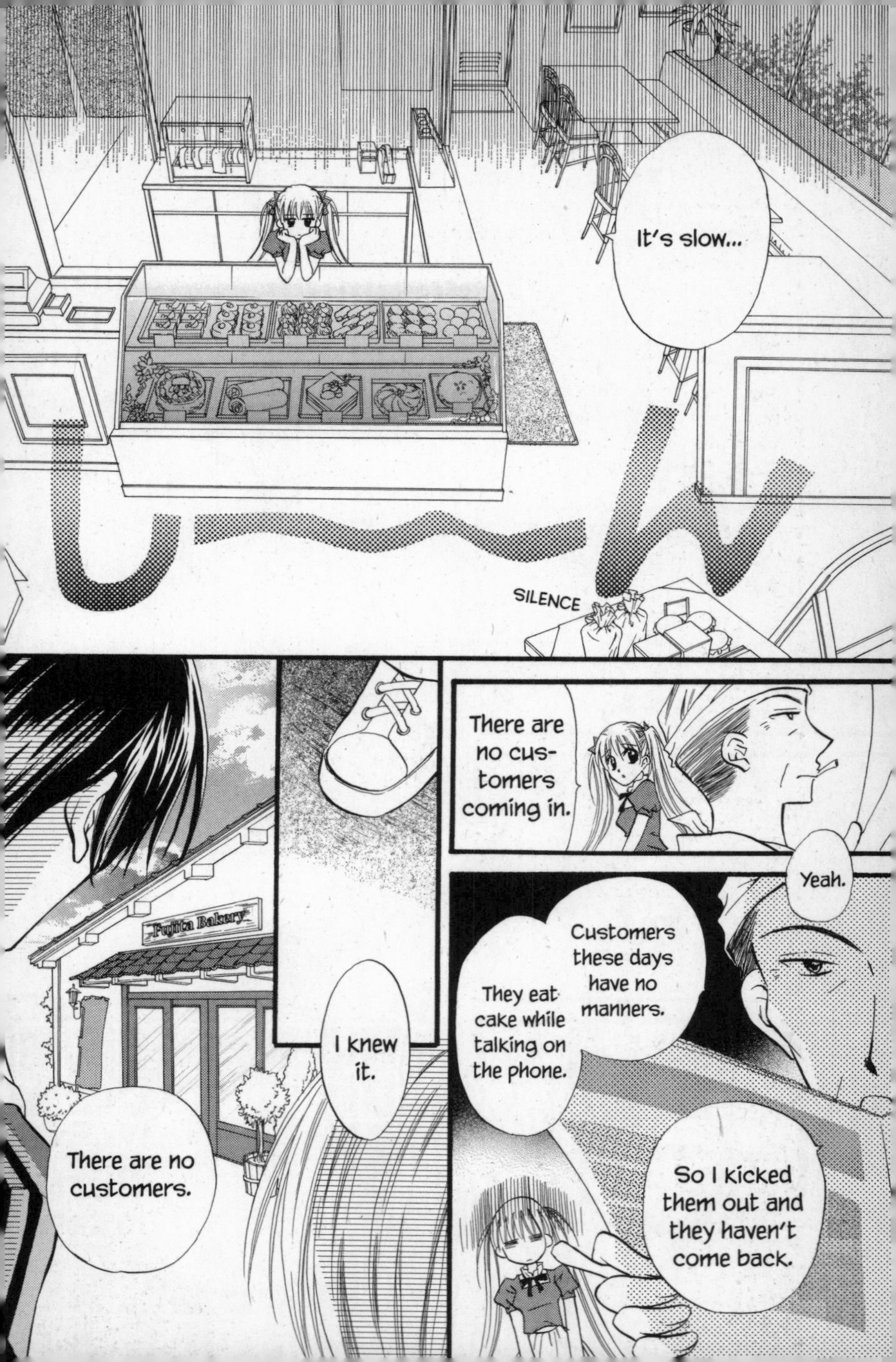
It's slow...
SILENCE
There are no customers coming in.
Yeah.
Customers these days have no manners.
They eat cake while talking on the phone.
So I kicked them out and they haven't come back.
Fujita Bakery
I knew it.
There are no customers.

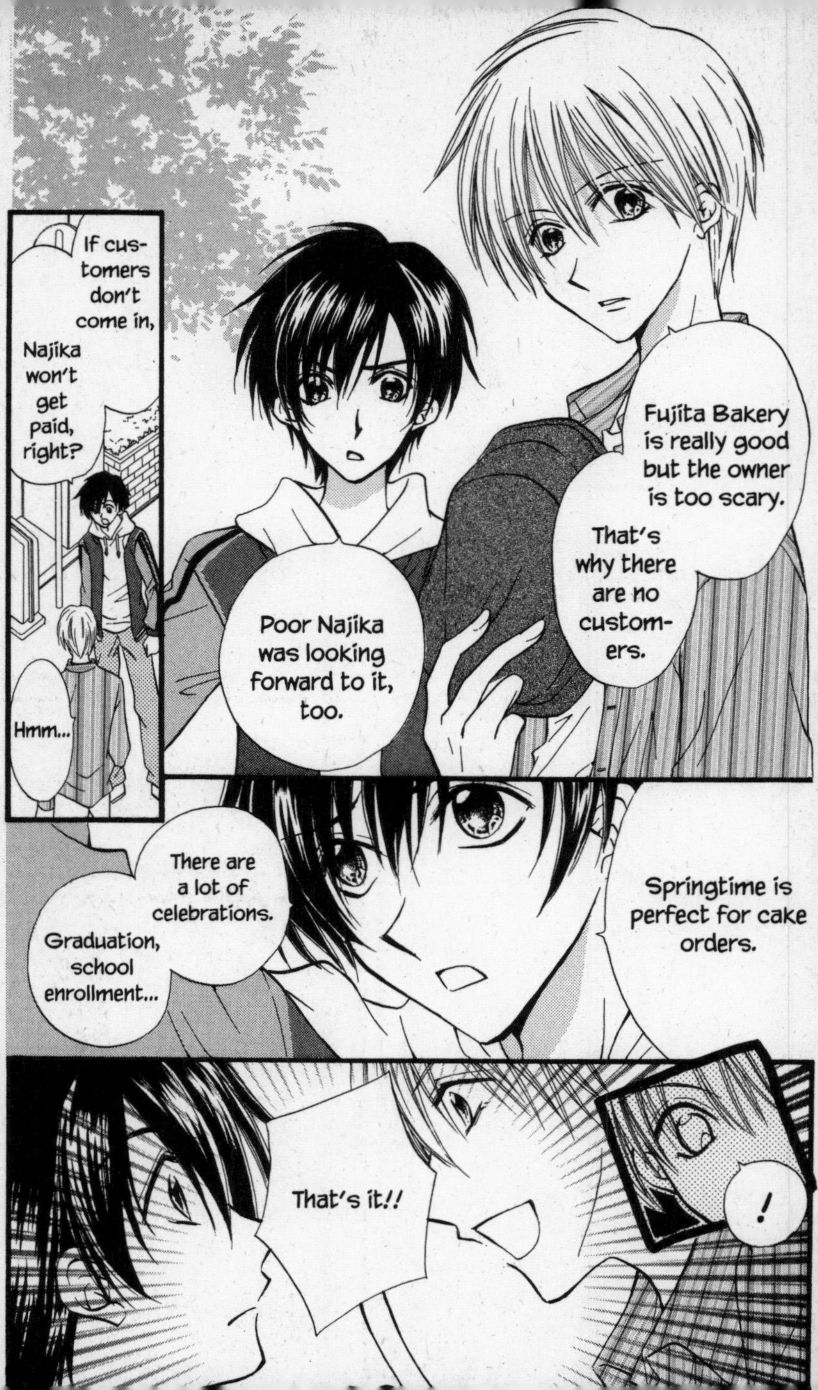
Fujita Bakery is really good but the owner is too scary.
That's why there are no customers.
Poor Najika was looking forward to it, too.
If customers don't come in, Najika won't get paid, right?
Hmm...
Springtime is perfect for cake orders.
There are a lot of celebrations.
Graduation, school enrollment...
!
That's it!!

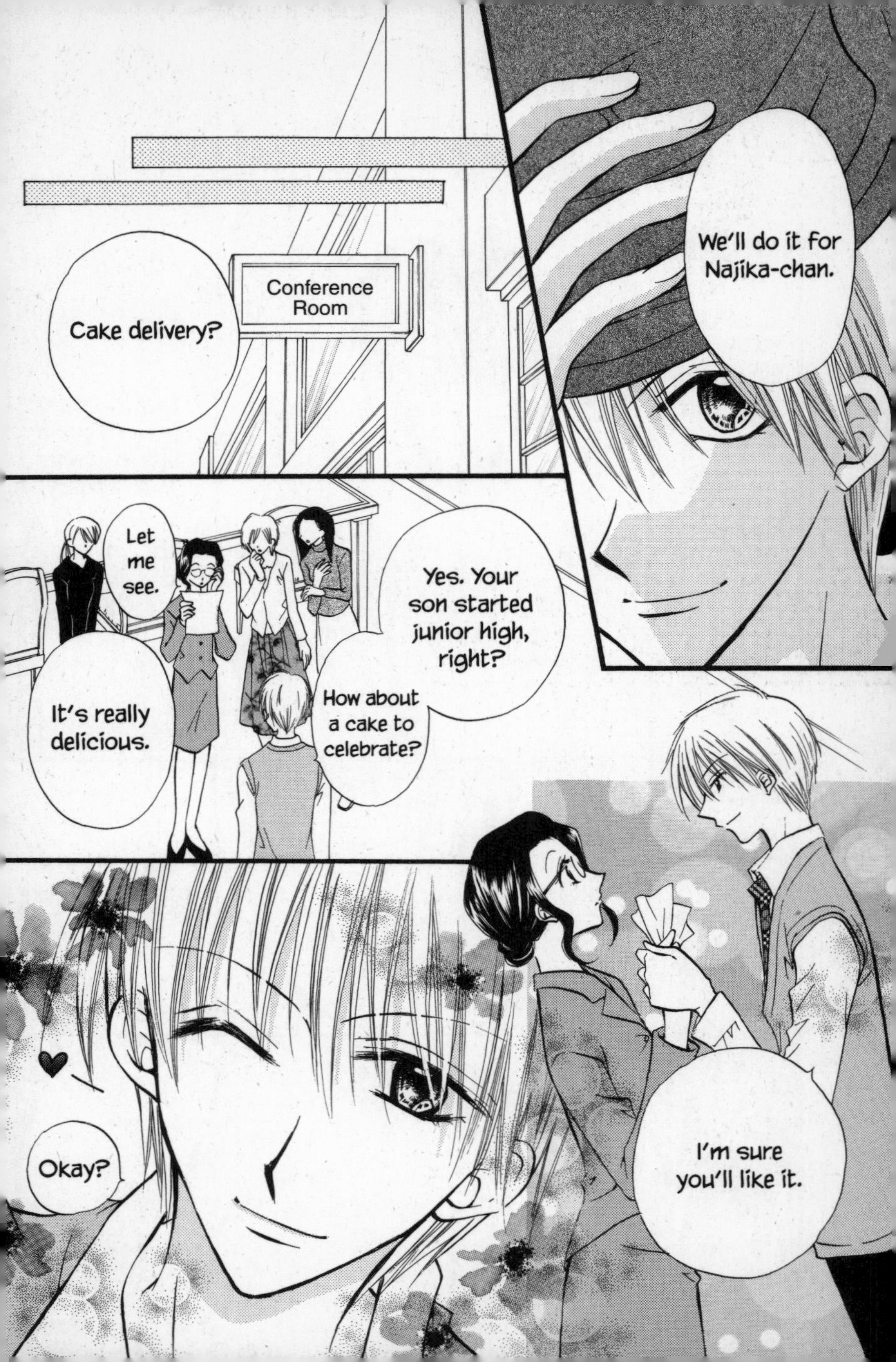
We'll do it for Najika-chan.
Conference Room
Cake delivery?
Yes. Your son started junior high, right?
How about a cake to celebrate?
Let me see.
It's really delicious.
I'm sure you'll like it.
Okay?

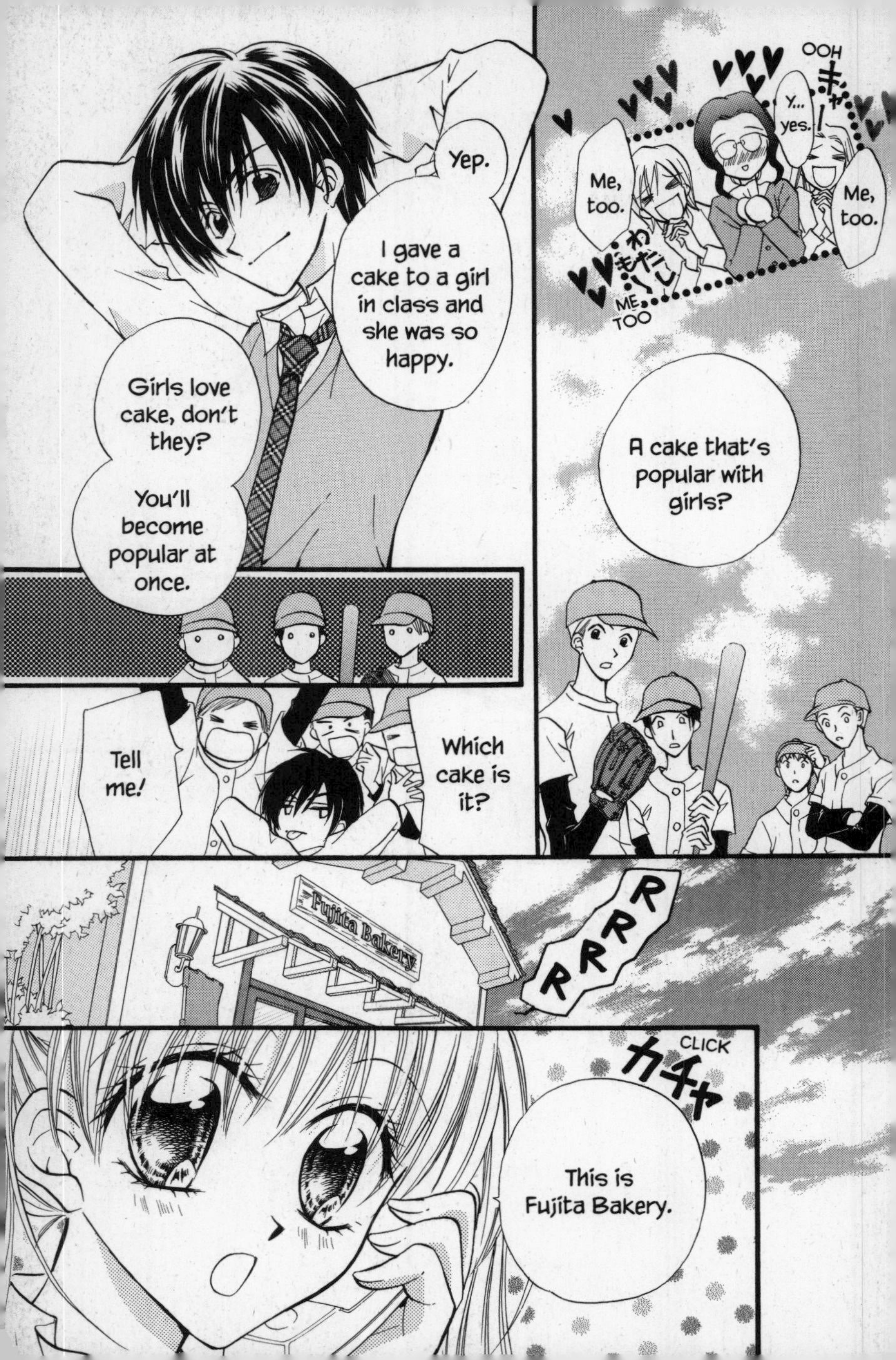
OOH
Y... yes.
Me, too.
Me, too.
ME TOO
Yep.
I gave a cake to a girl in class and she was so happy.
Girls love cake, don't they?
You'll become popular at once.
A cake that's popular with girls?
Which cake is it?
Tell me!
Fujita Bakery
RRRRR
CLICK
This is Fujita Bakery.

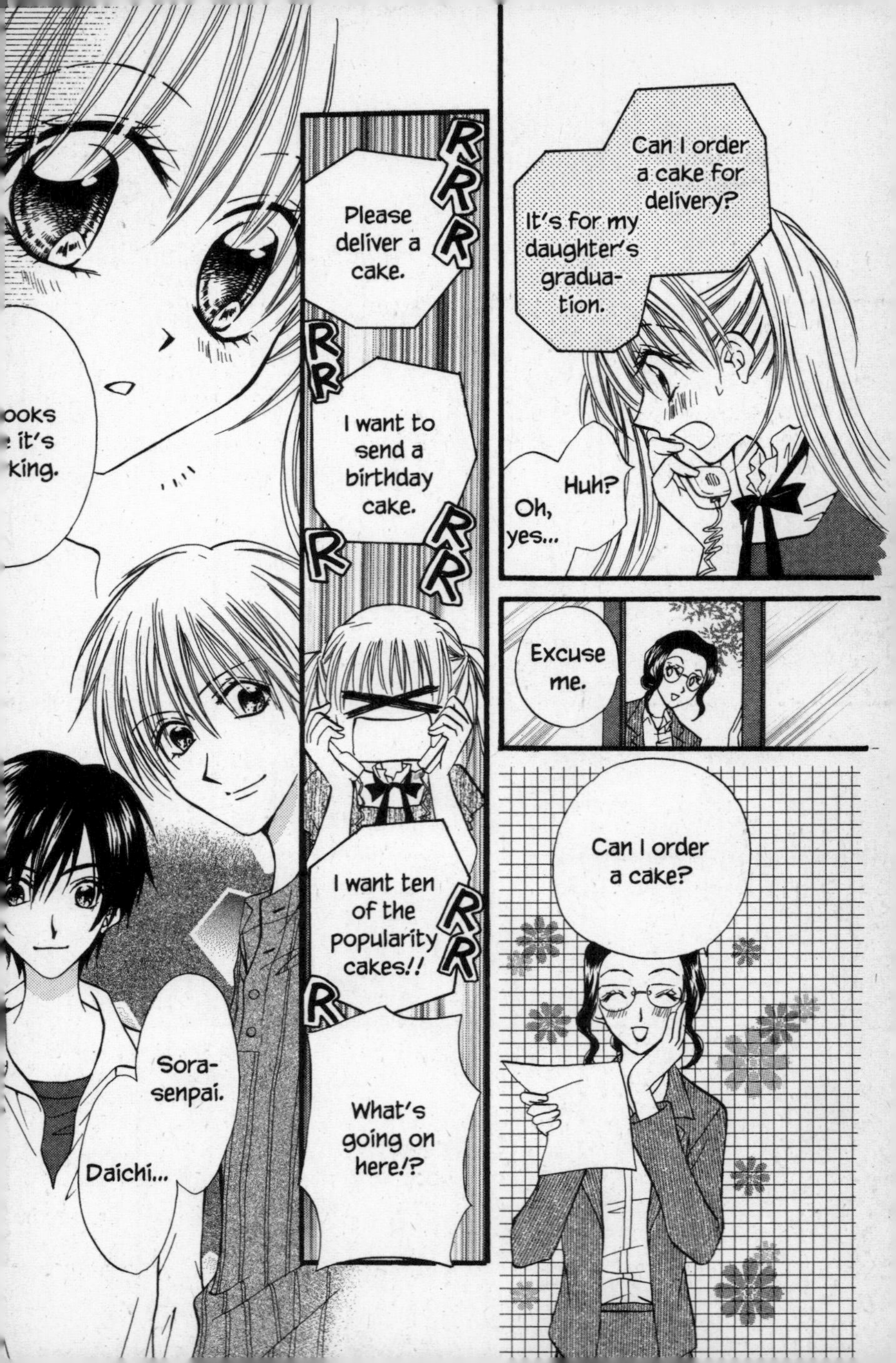
Can I order a cake for delivery?
It's for my daughter's graduation.
Huh?
Oh, yes...
Excuse me.
Can I order a cake?
RRR
Please deliver a cake.
RR
I want to send a birthday cake.
RRR
I want ten of the popularity cakes!!
RRR
What's going on here!?
ooks it's king.
Sora-senpai.
Daichi...

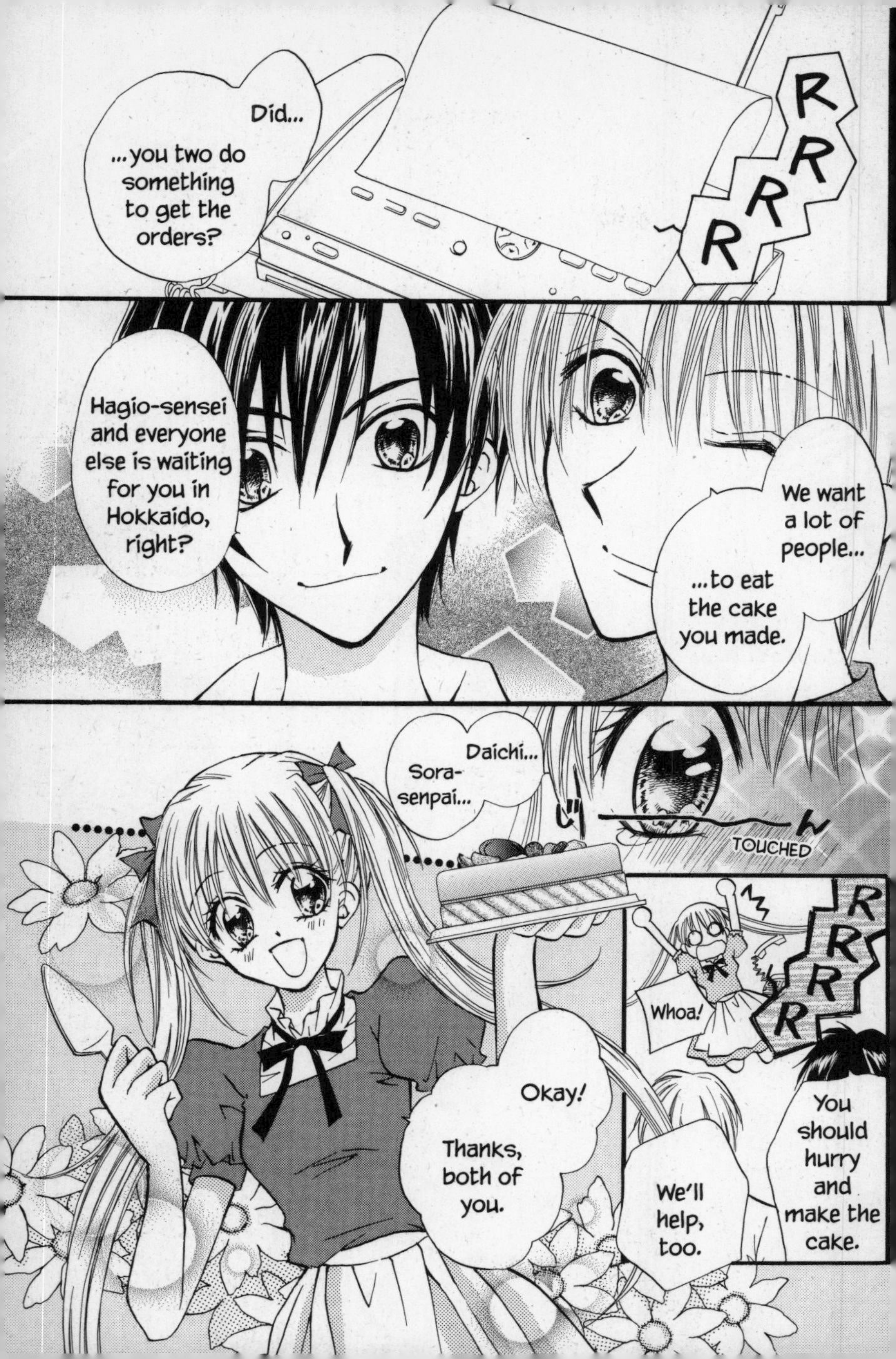
RRRR
Did...
...you two do something to get the orders?
We want a lot of people...
...to eat the cake you made.
Hagio-sensei and everyone else is waiting for you in Hokkaido, right?
Daichi...
Sora-senpai...
TOUCHED
RRRR
Whoa!
You should hurry and make the cake.
We'll help, too.
Okay!
Thanks, both of you.

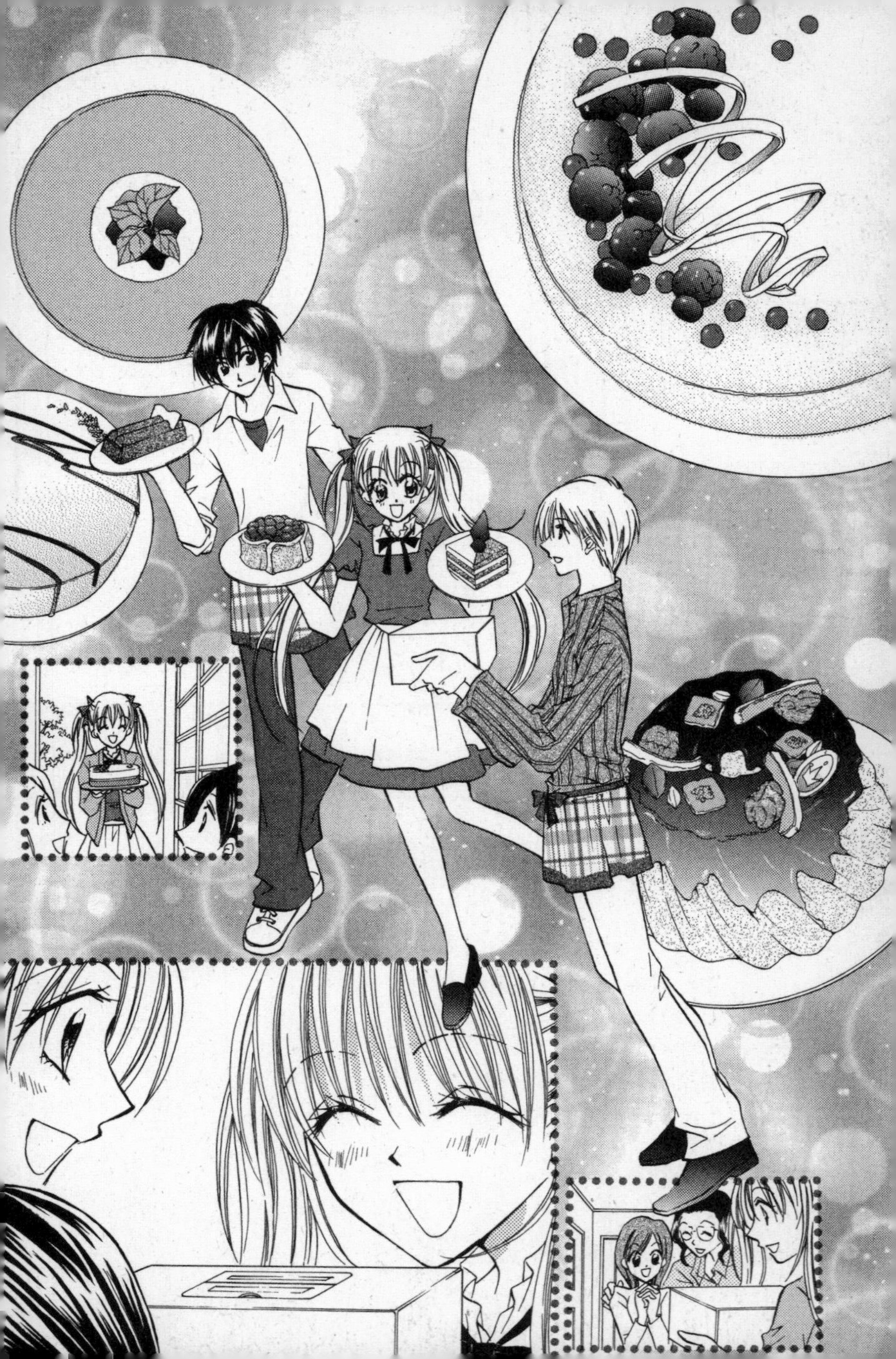

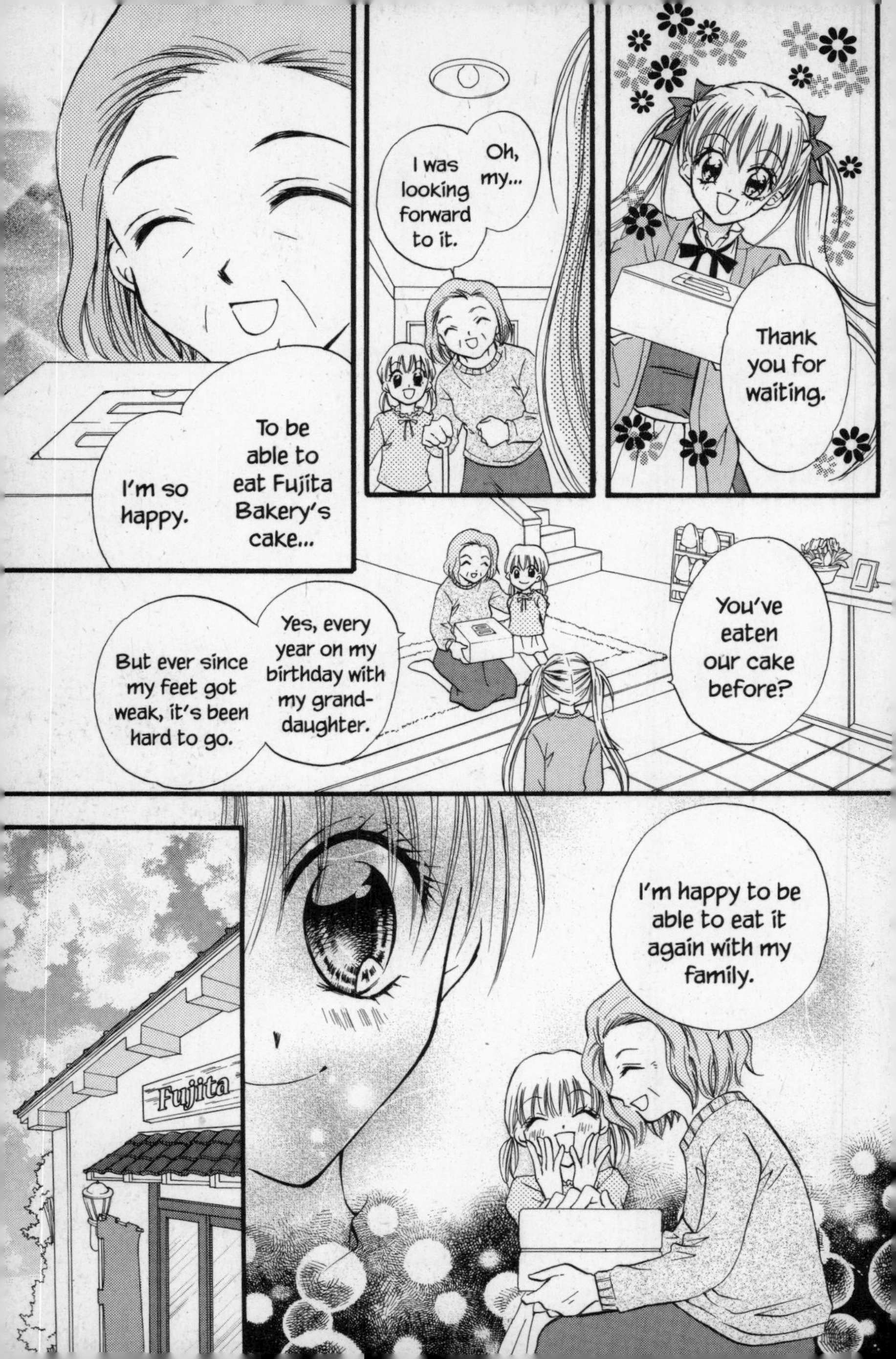
Thank you for waiting.
Oh, my...
I was looking forward to it.
To be able to eat Fujita Bakery's cake...
I'm so happy.
You've eaten our cake before?
Yes, every year on my birthday with my grand-daughter.
But ever since my feet got weak, it's been hard to go.
I'm happy to be able to eat it again with my family.
Fujita

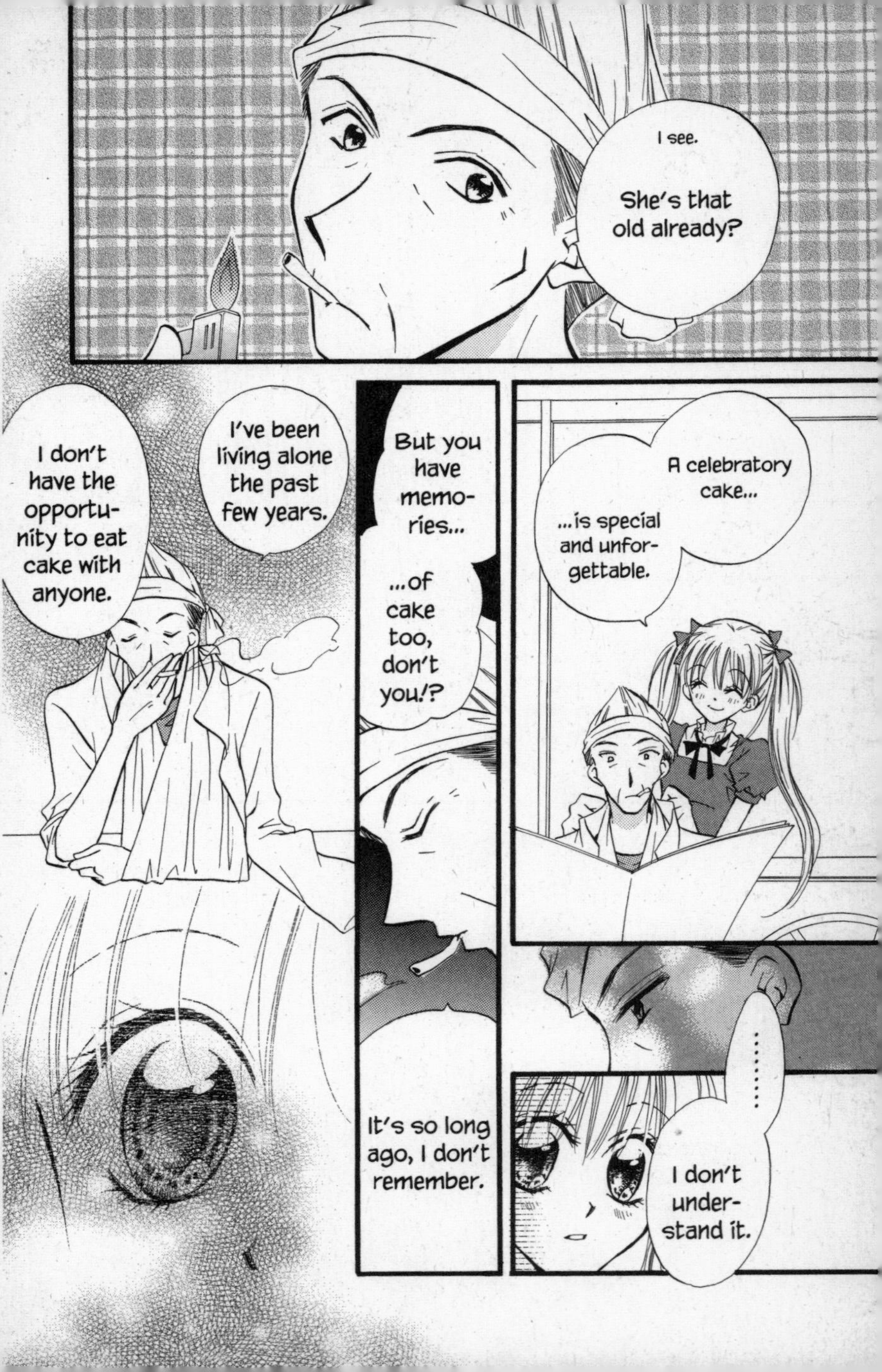
I see.
She's that old already?
A celebratory cake...
...is special and unforgettable.
......
I don't understand it.
But you have memories...
...of cake too, don't you!?
It's so long ago, I don't remember.
I've been living alone the past few years.
I don't have the opportunity to eat cake with anyone.

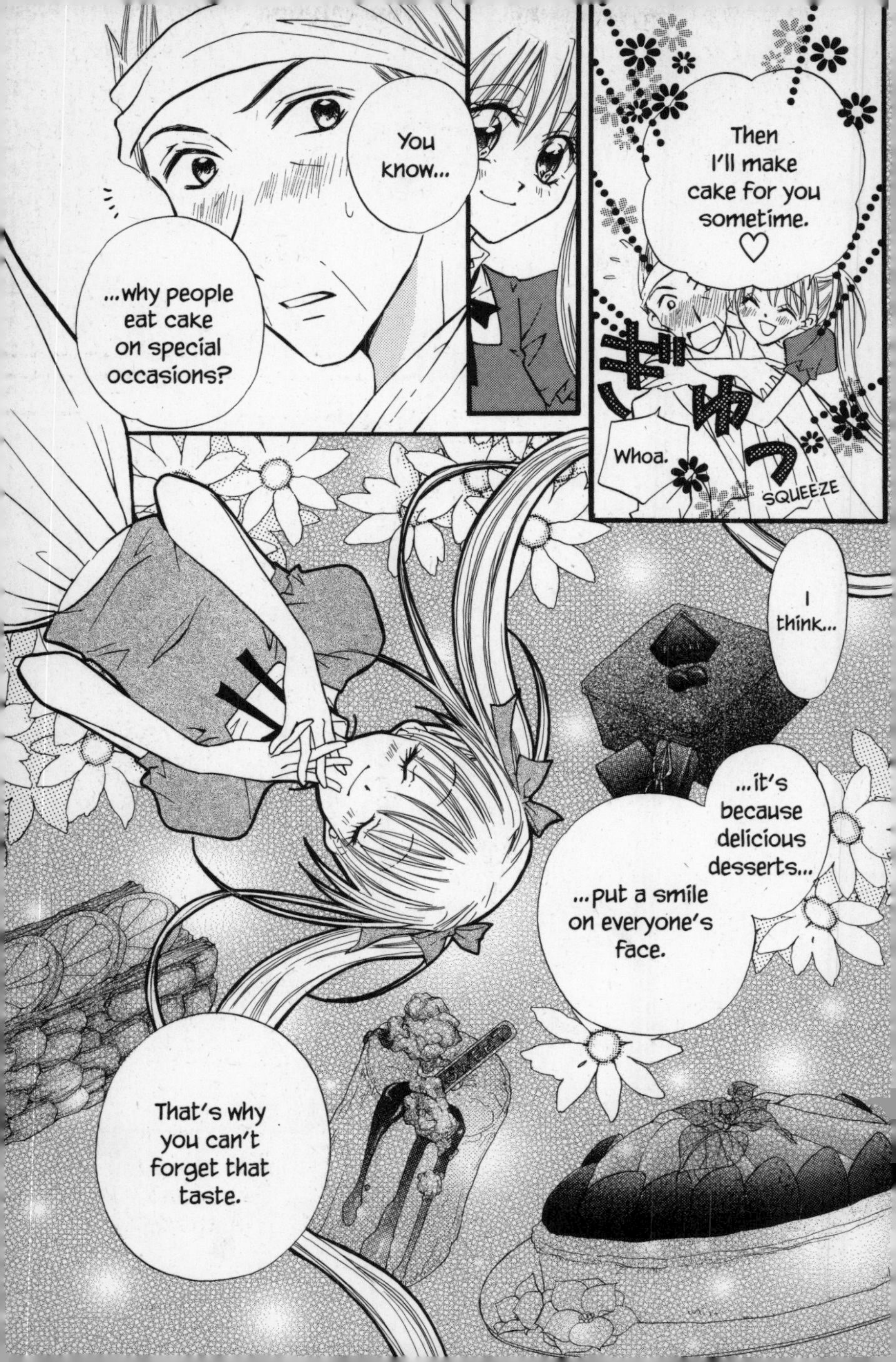
Then I'll make cake for you sometime. ♡
Whoa.
ぎゅっ
SQUEEZE
You know...
...why people eat cake on special occasions?
I think...
...it's because delicious desserts...
...put a smile on everyone's face.
That's why you can't forget that taste.

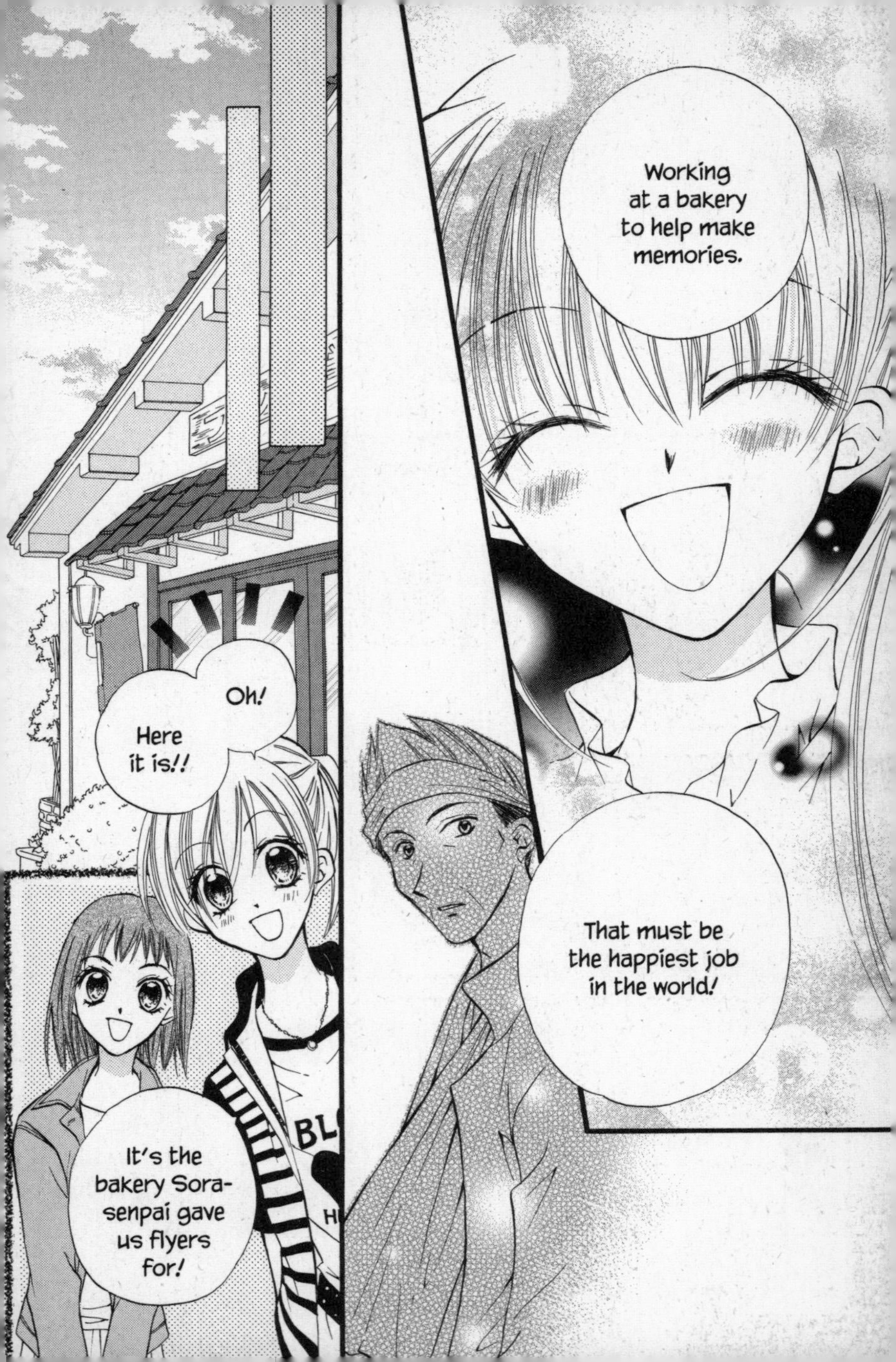
Working at a bakery to help make memories.
That must be the happiest job in the world!
Oh! Here it is!!
It's the bakery Sora-senpai gave us flyers for!

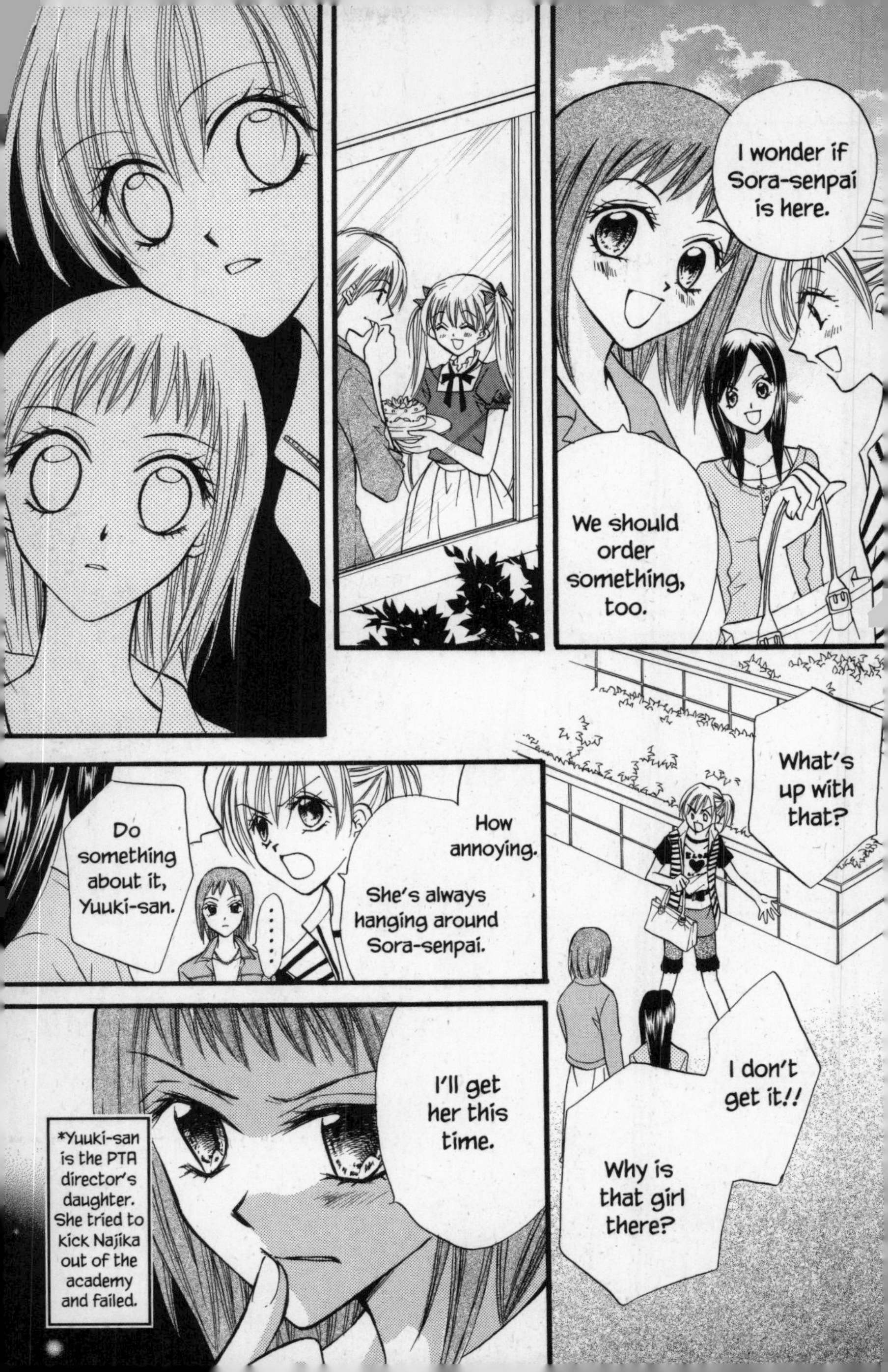
I wonder if Sora-senpai is here.
We should order something, too.
What's up with that?
I don't get it!!
Why is that girl there?
How annoying.
She's always hanging around Sora-senpai.
Do something about it, Yuuki-san.
......
I'll get her this time.
*Yuuki-san is the PTA director's daughter. She tried to kick Najika out of the academy and failed.

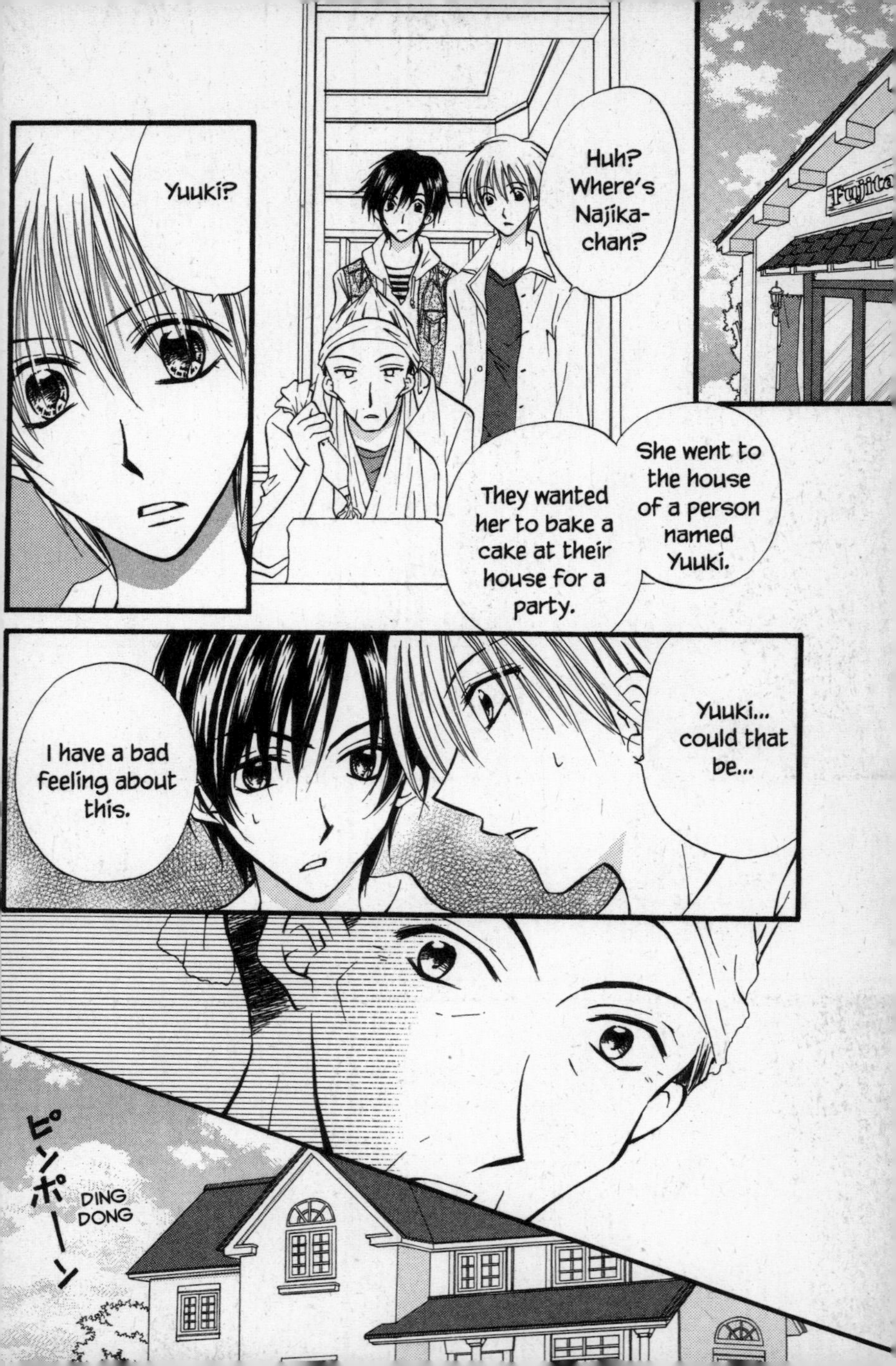

Fujita
Huh? Where's Najika-chan?
She went to the house of a person named Yuuki.
They wanted her to bake a cake at their house for a party.
Yuuki?
Yuuki... could that be...
I have a bad feeling about this.
ピンポーン
DING DONG

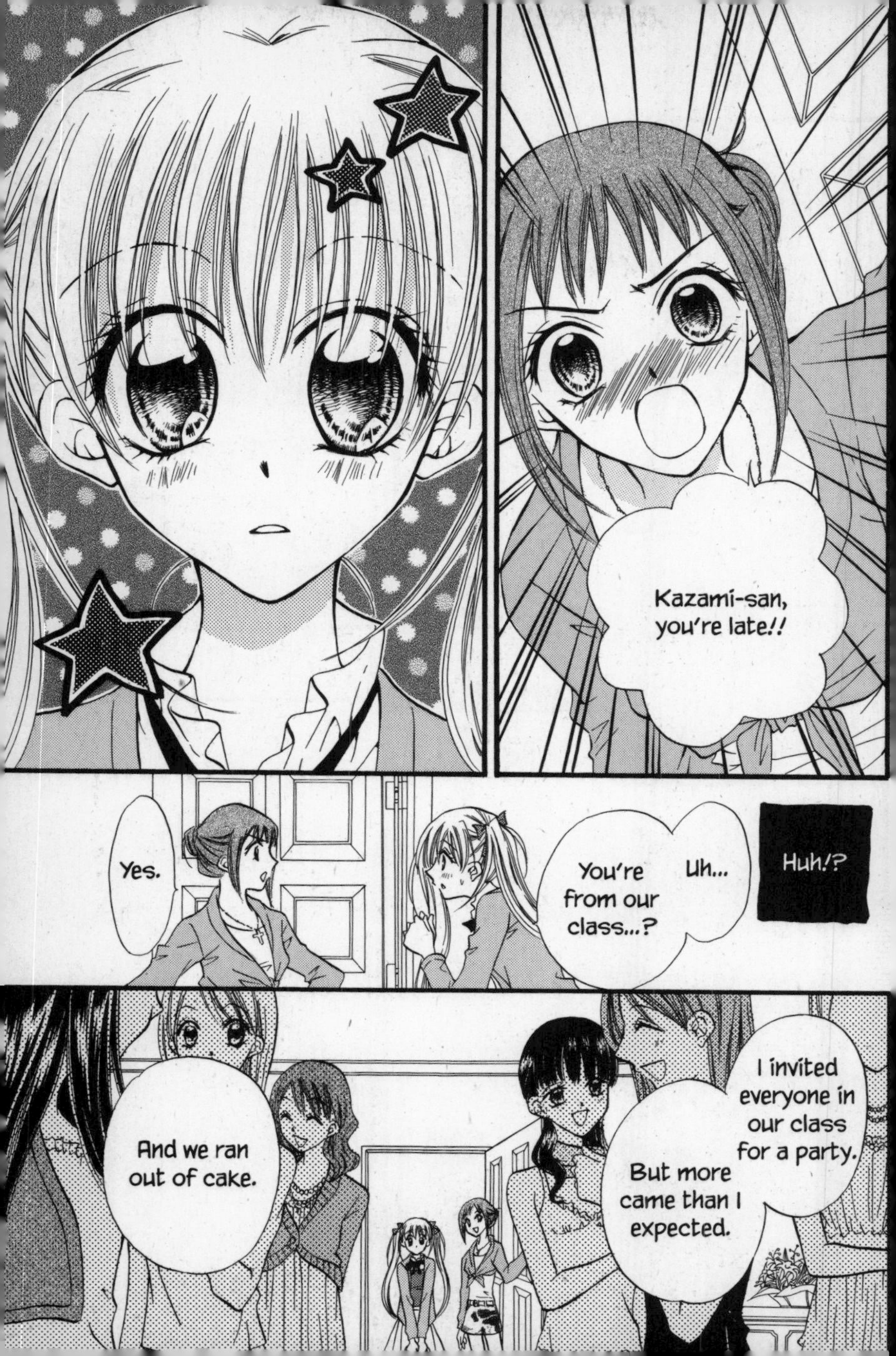
Kazami-san, you're late!!
Huh!?
Uh...
You're from our class...?
Yes.
I invited everyone in our class for a party.
But more came than I expected.
And we ran out of cake.

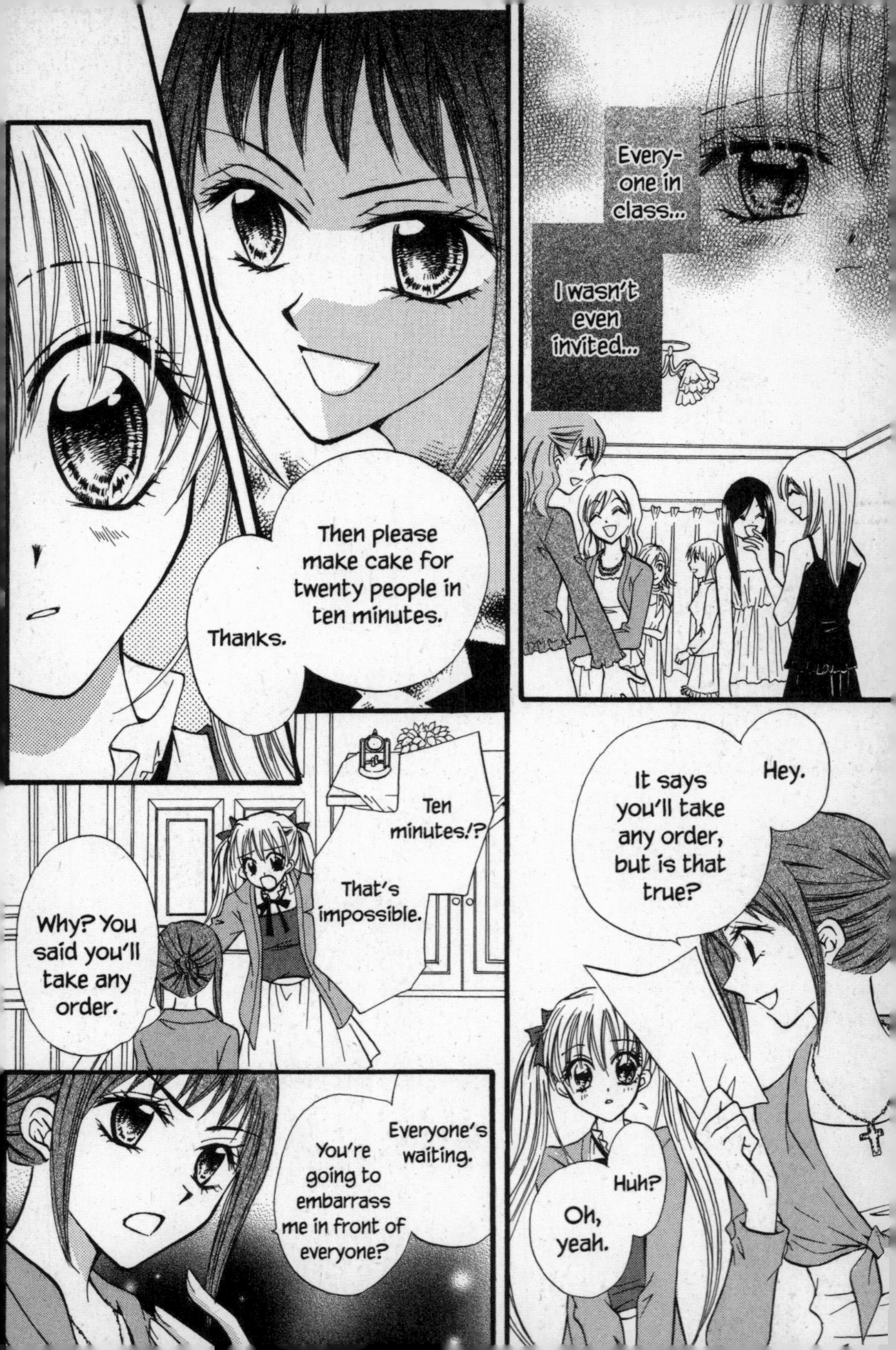
Every-one in class...
I wasn't even invited...
Then please make cake for twenty people in ten minutes.
Thanks.
Hey.
It says you'll take any order, but is that true?
Huh?
Oh, yeah.
Ten minutes!?
That's impossible.
Why? You said you'll take any order.
Everyone's waiting.
You're going to embarrass me in front of everyone?

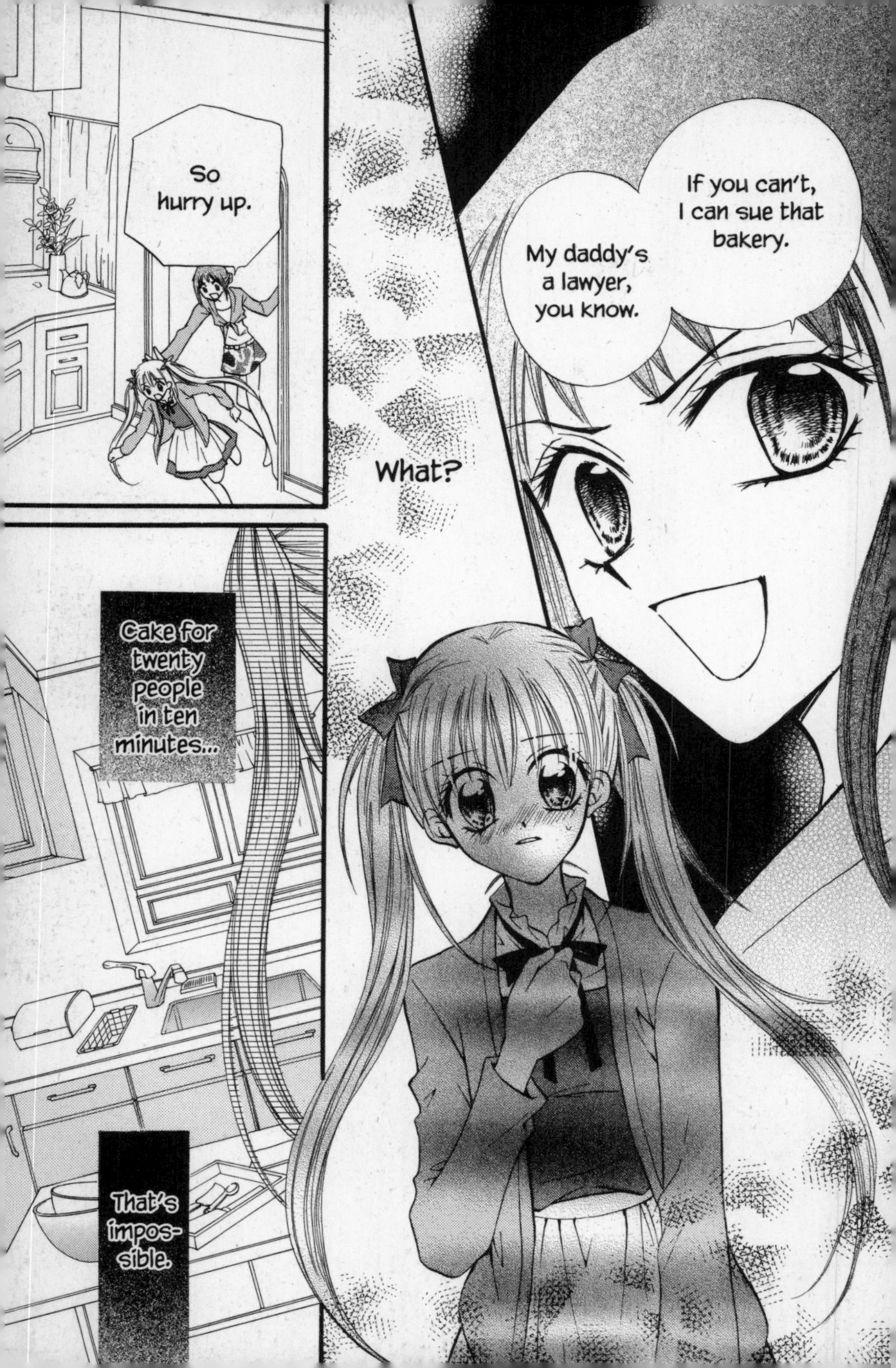
If you can't, I can sue that bakery.
My daddy's a lawyer, you know.
What?
So hurry up.
Cake for twenty people in ten minutes...
That's impossible.

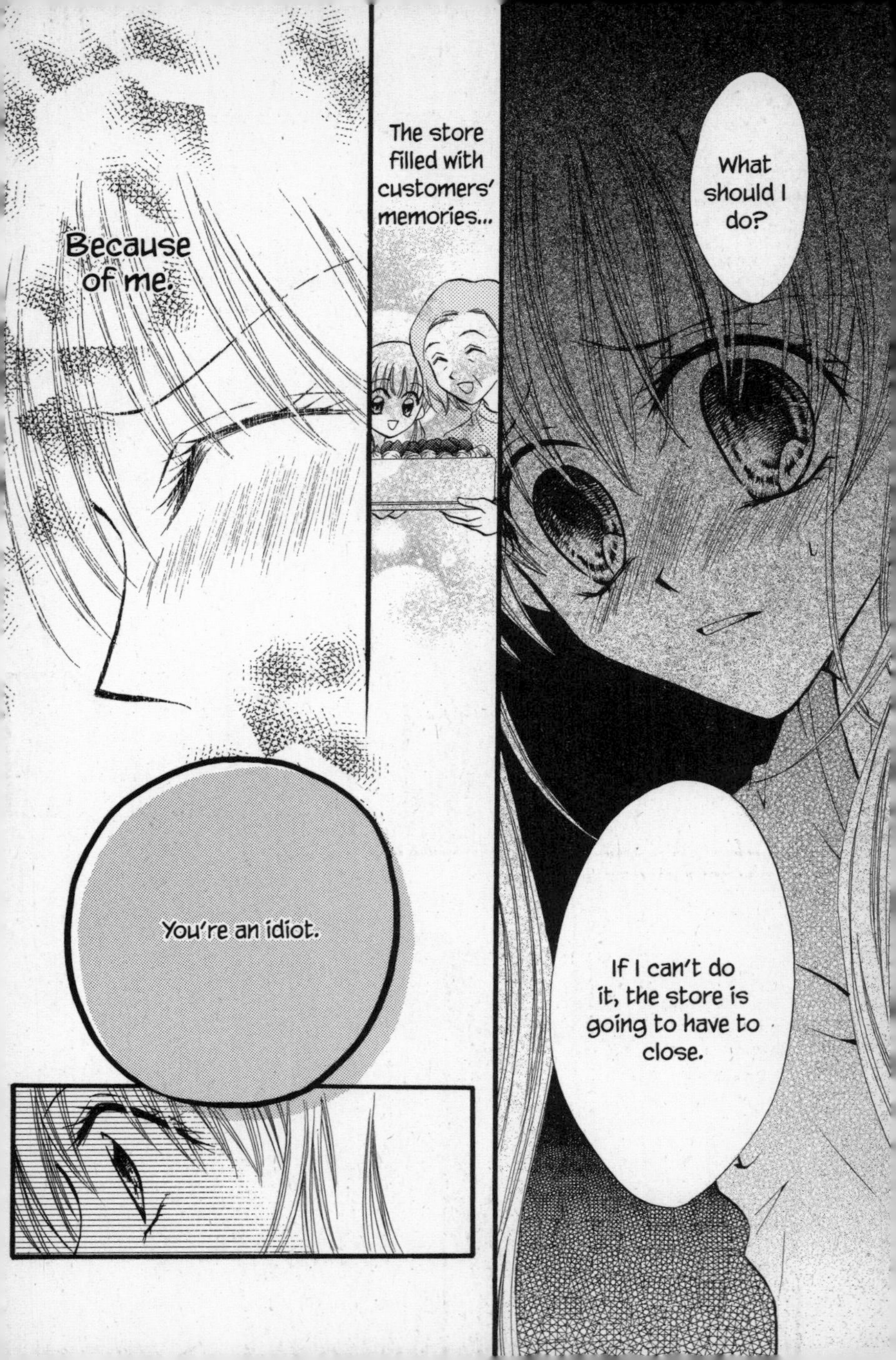

What should I do?
If I can't do it, the store is going to have to close.
The store filled with customers' memories...
Because of me.
You're an idiot.

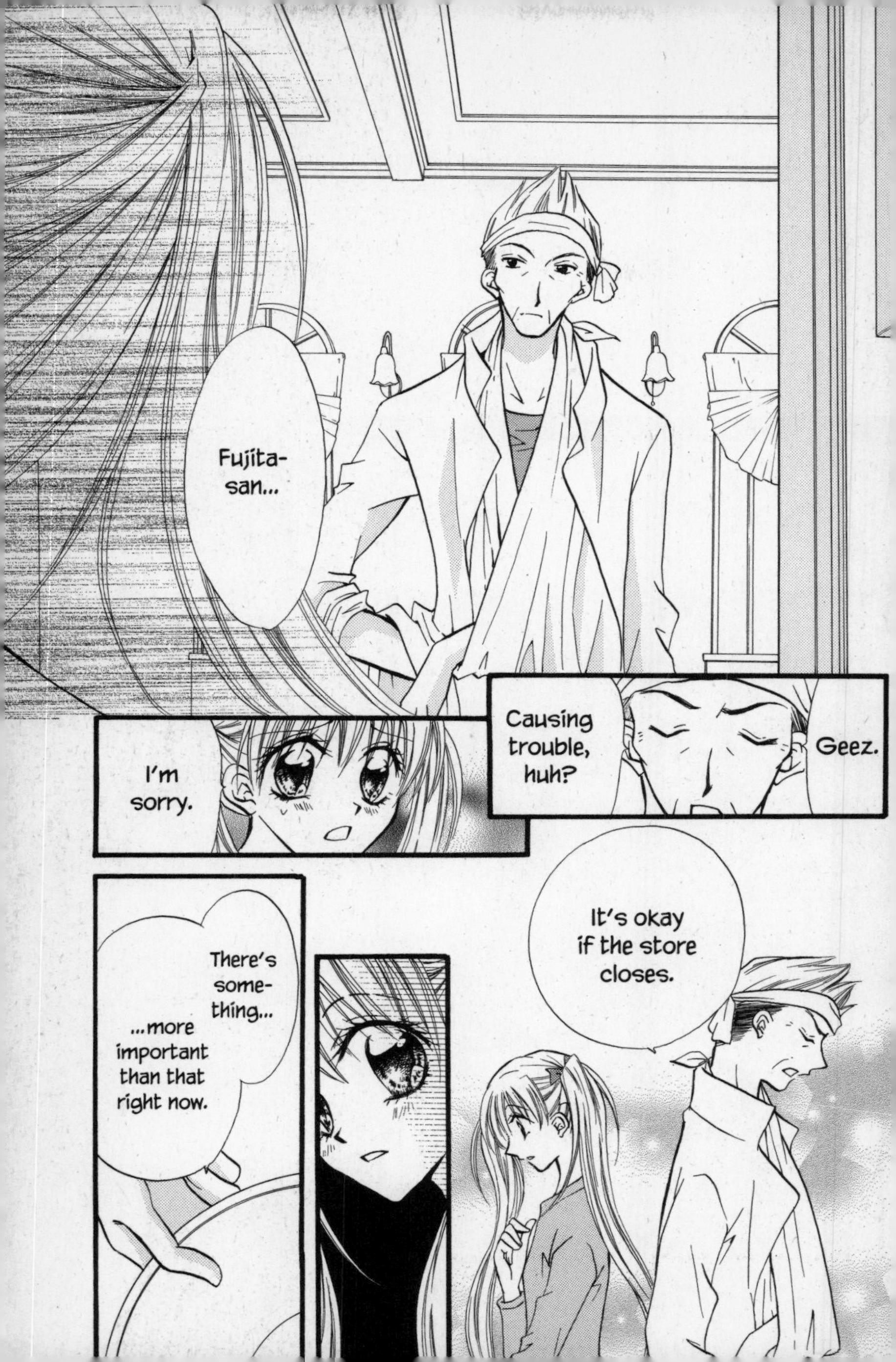
Fujita-san...
Geez.
Causing trouble, huh?
I'm sorry.
It's okay if the store closes.
There's some-thing...
...more important than that right now.

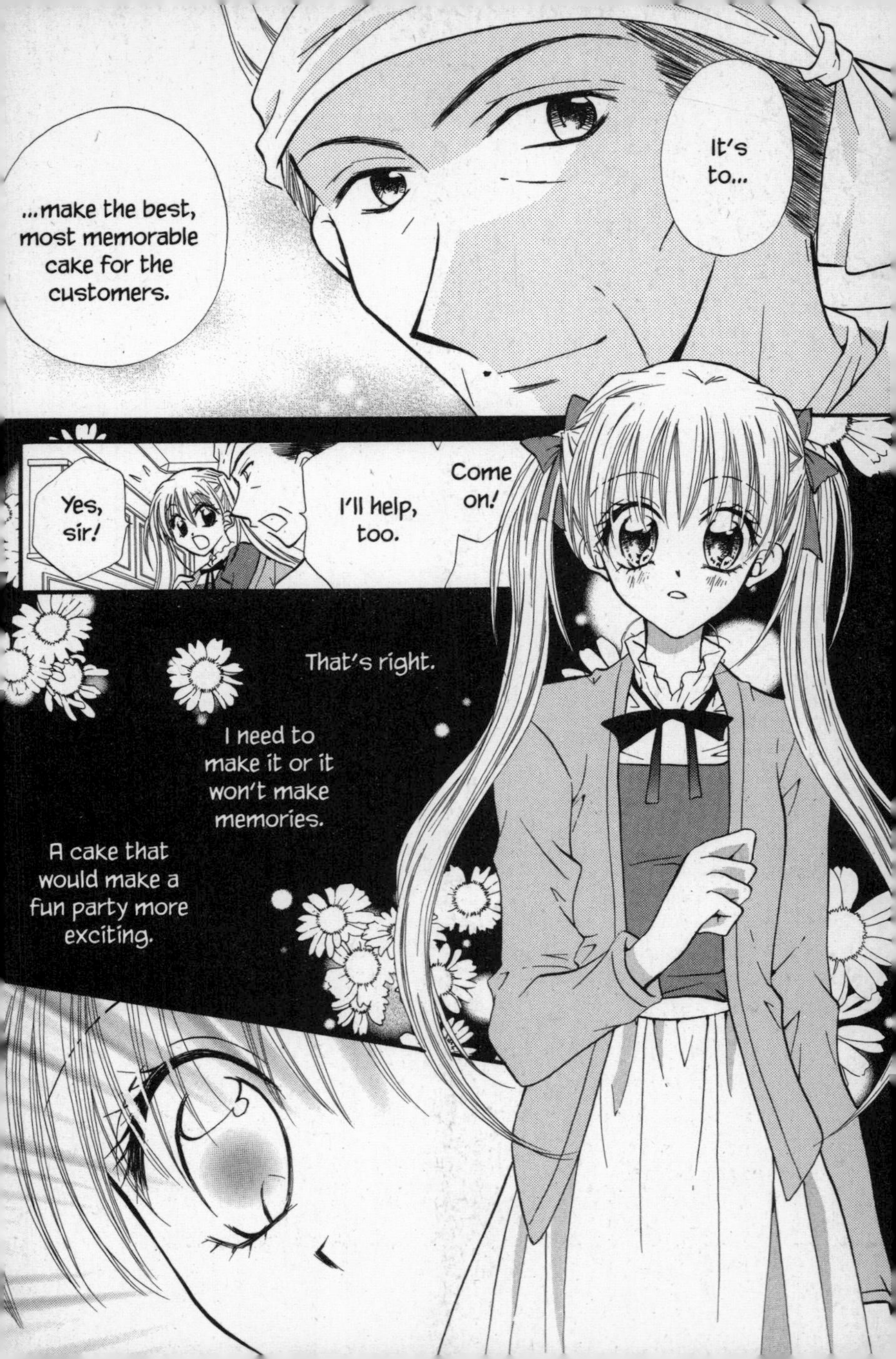
It's to...
...make the best, most memorable cake for the customers.
Come on!
I'll help, too.
Yes, sir!
That's right.
I need to make it or it won't make memories.
A cake that would make a fun party more exciting.

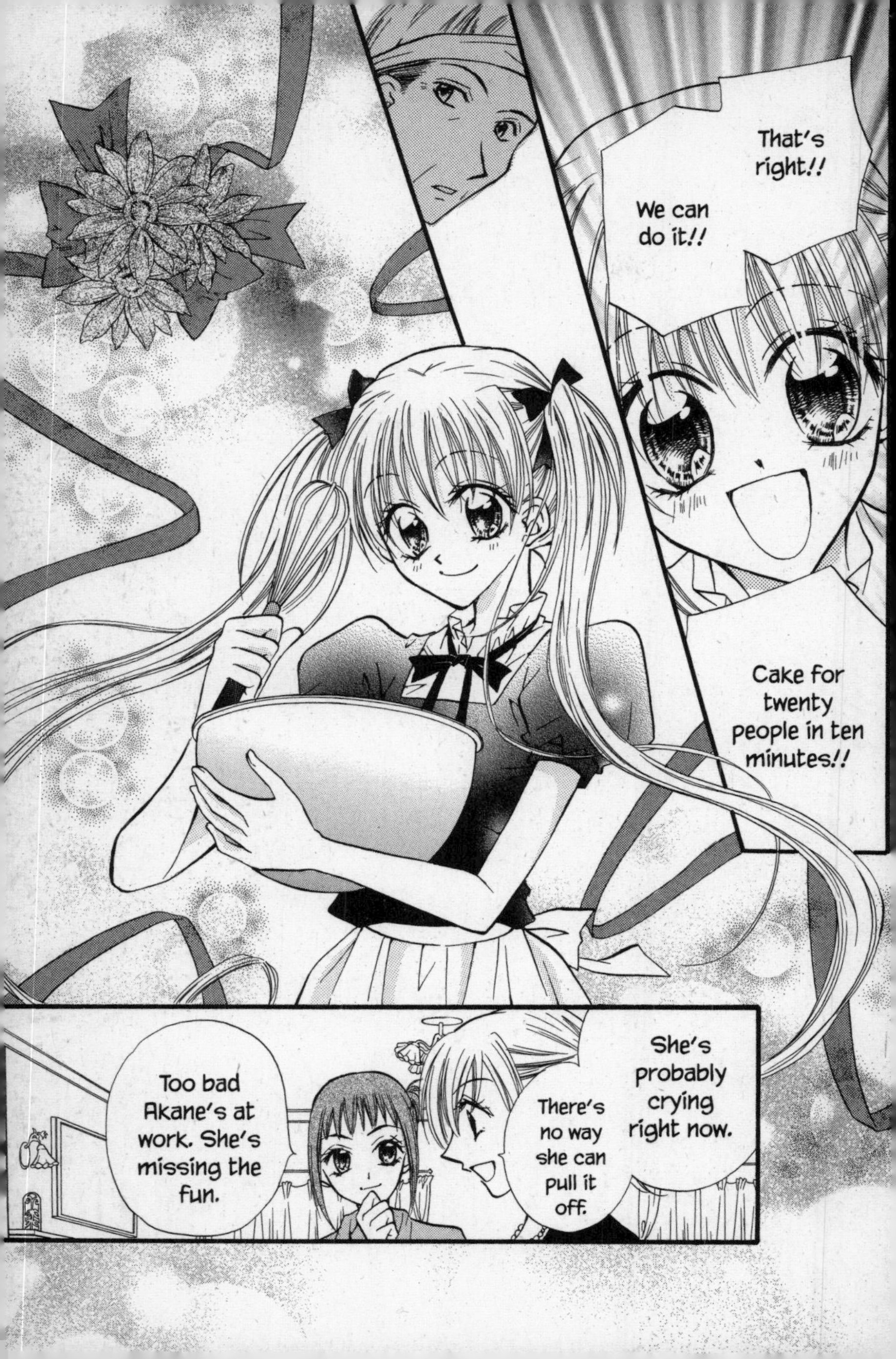

That's right!!
We can do it!!
Cake for twenty people in ten minutes!!
She's probably crying right now.
There's no way she can pull it off.
Too bad Akane's at work. She's missing the fun.

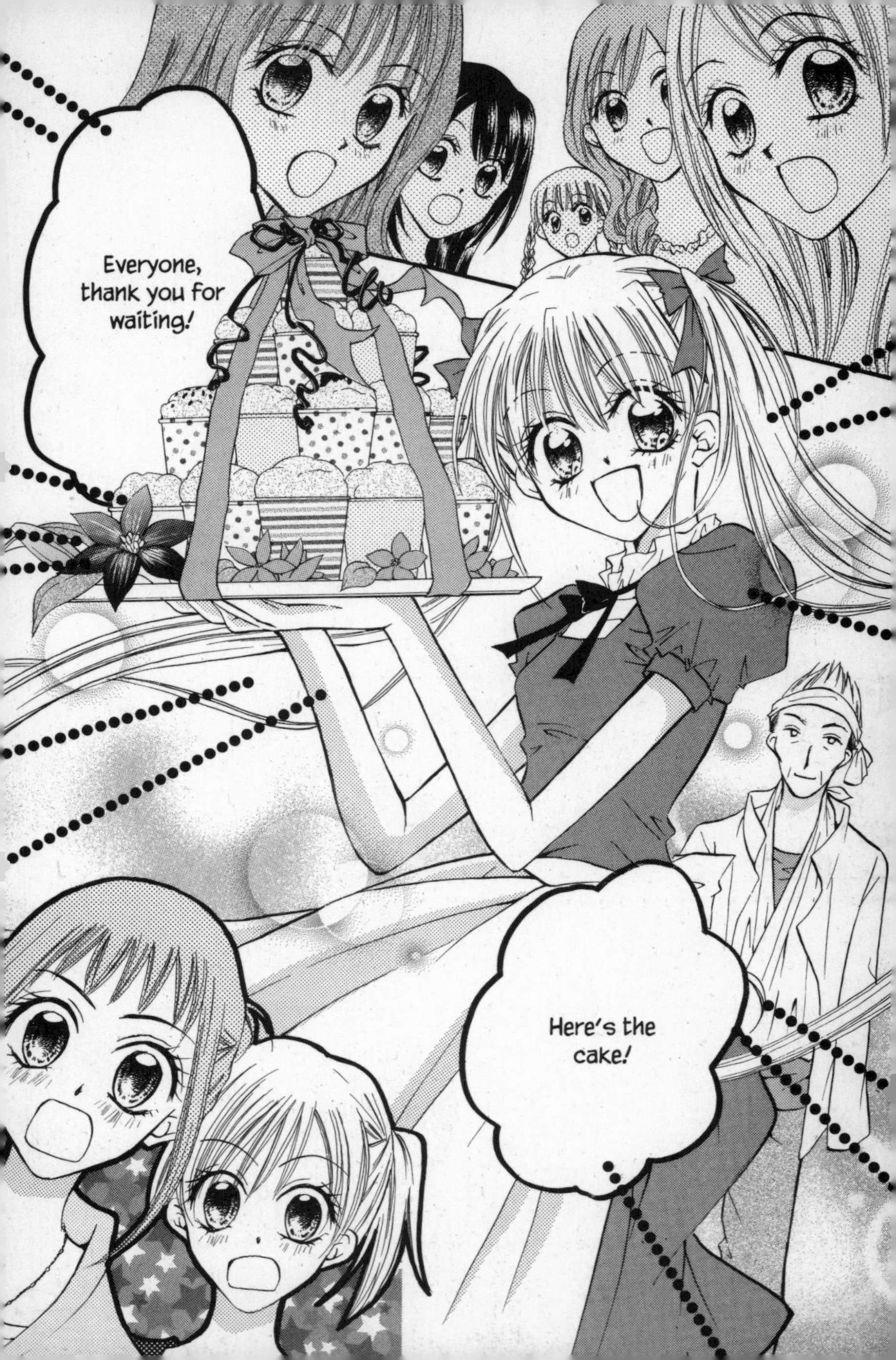
Everyone, thank you for waiting!
Here's the cake!

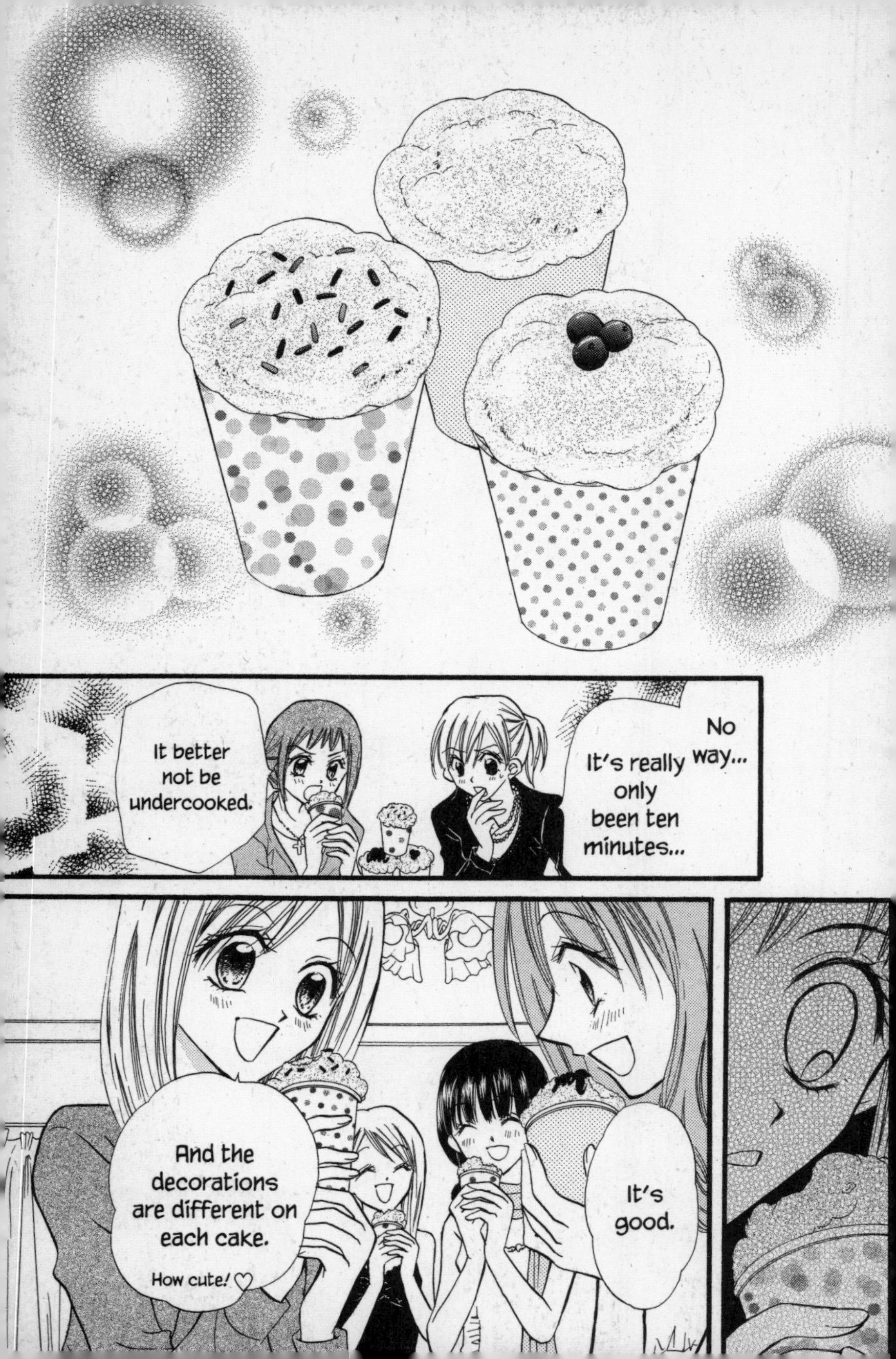
No way... It's really only been ten minutes...
It better not be undercooked.
It's good.
And the decorations are different on each cake.
How cute! ♡

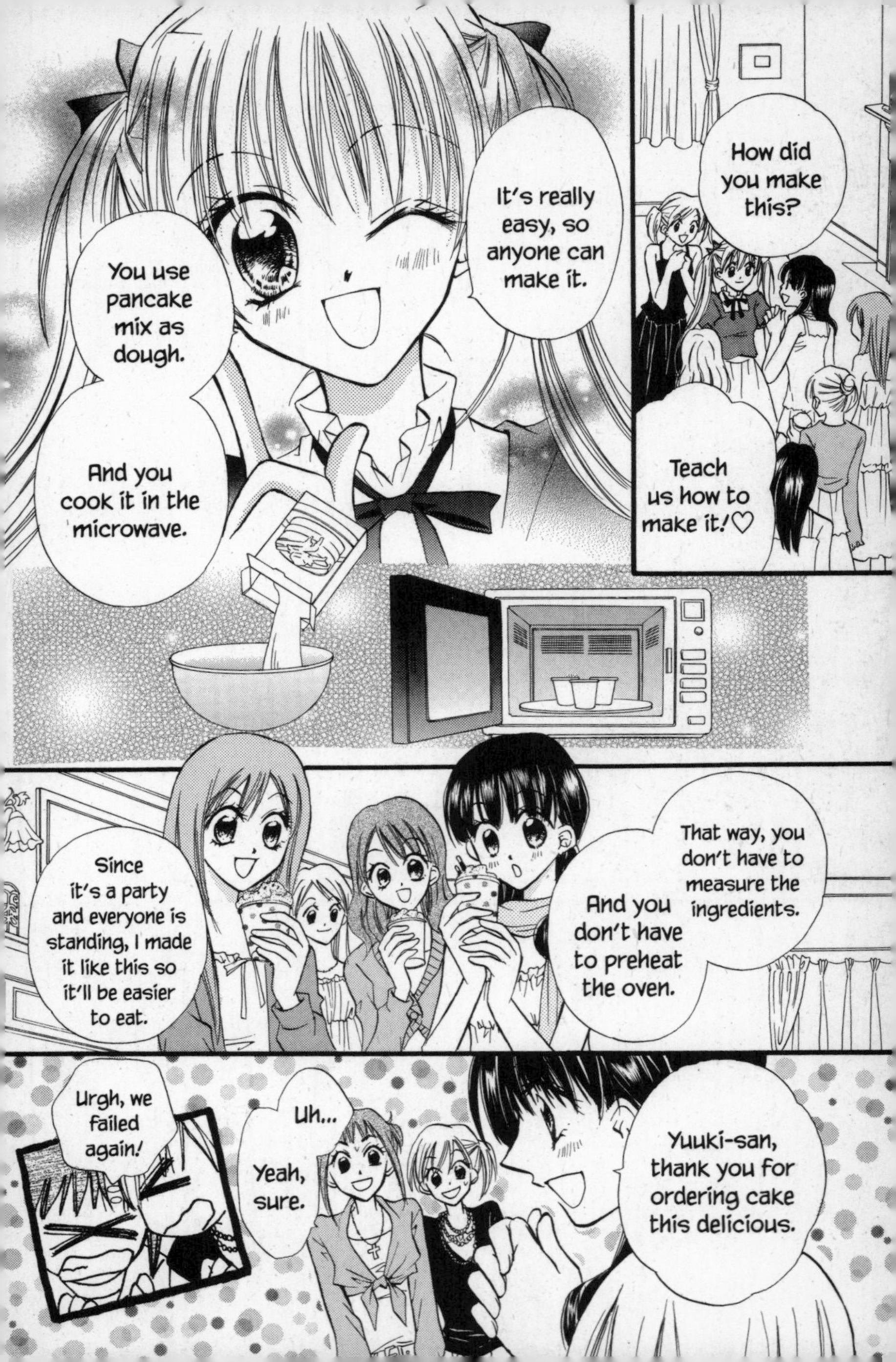
How did you make this?
Teach us how to make it!♡
It's really easy, so anyone can make it.
You use pancake mix as dough.
And you cook it in the microwave.
That way, you don't have to measure the ingredients.
And you don't have to preheat the oven.
Since it's a party and everyone is standing, I made it like this so it'll be easier to eat.
Yuuki-san, thank you for ordering cake this delicious.
Uh...
Yeah, sure.
Urgh, we failed again!

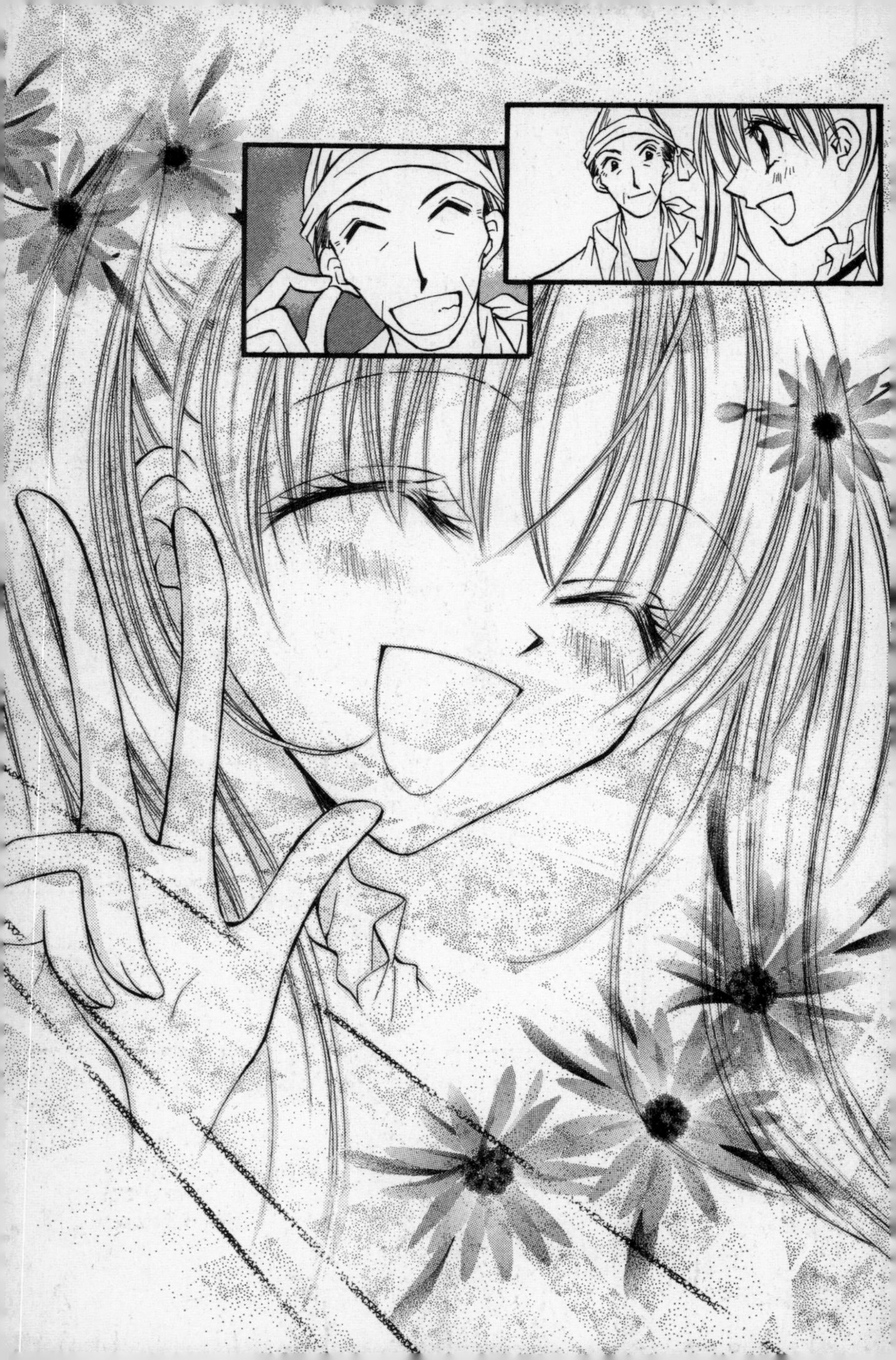

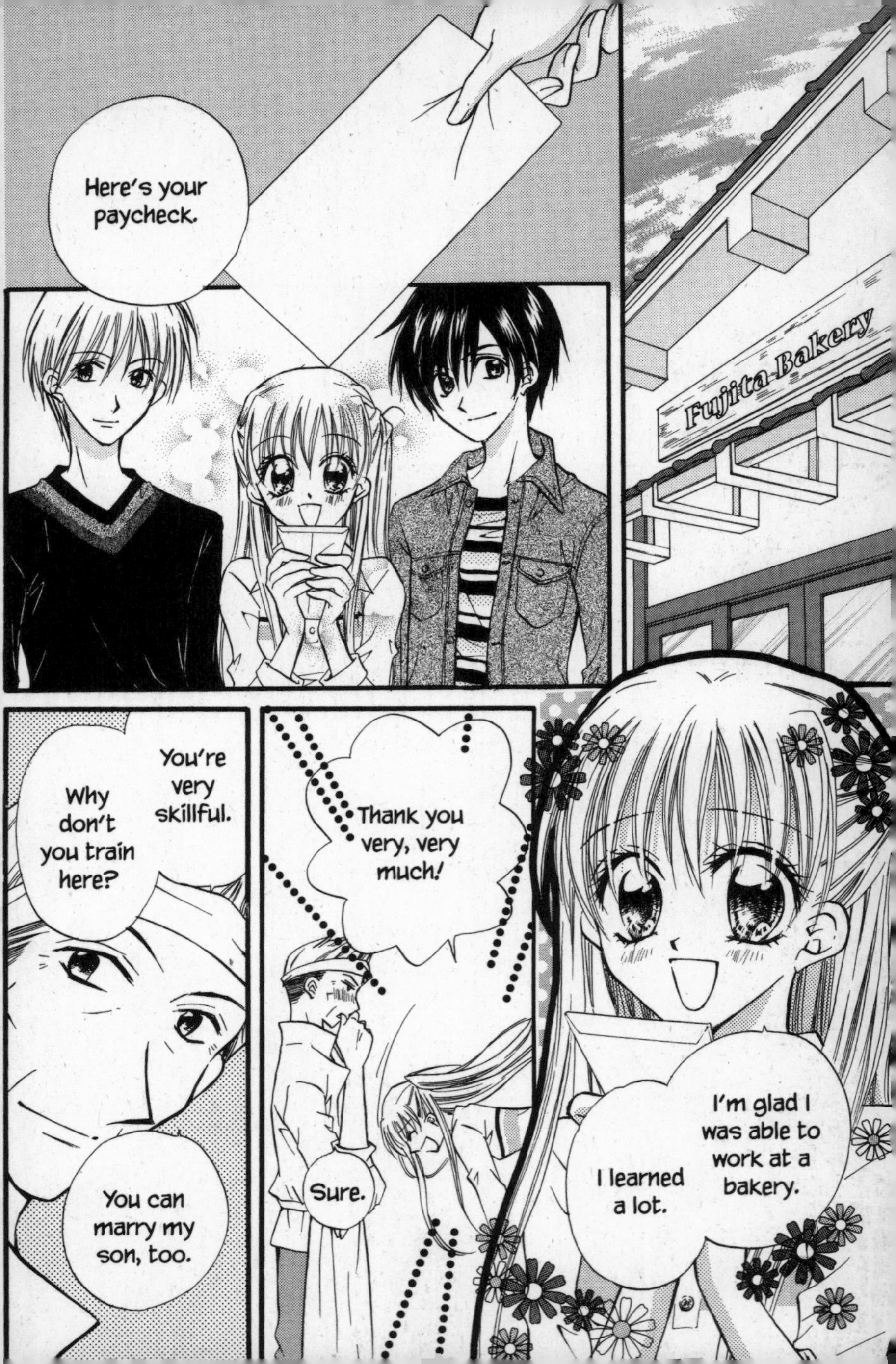
Fujita Bakery
Here's your paycheck.
I'm glad I was able to work at a bakery.
I learned a lot.
Thank you very, very much!
Sure.
You're very skillful.
Why don't you train here?
You can marry my son, too.

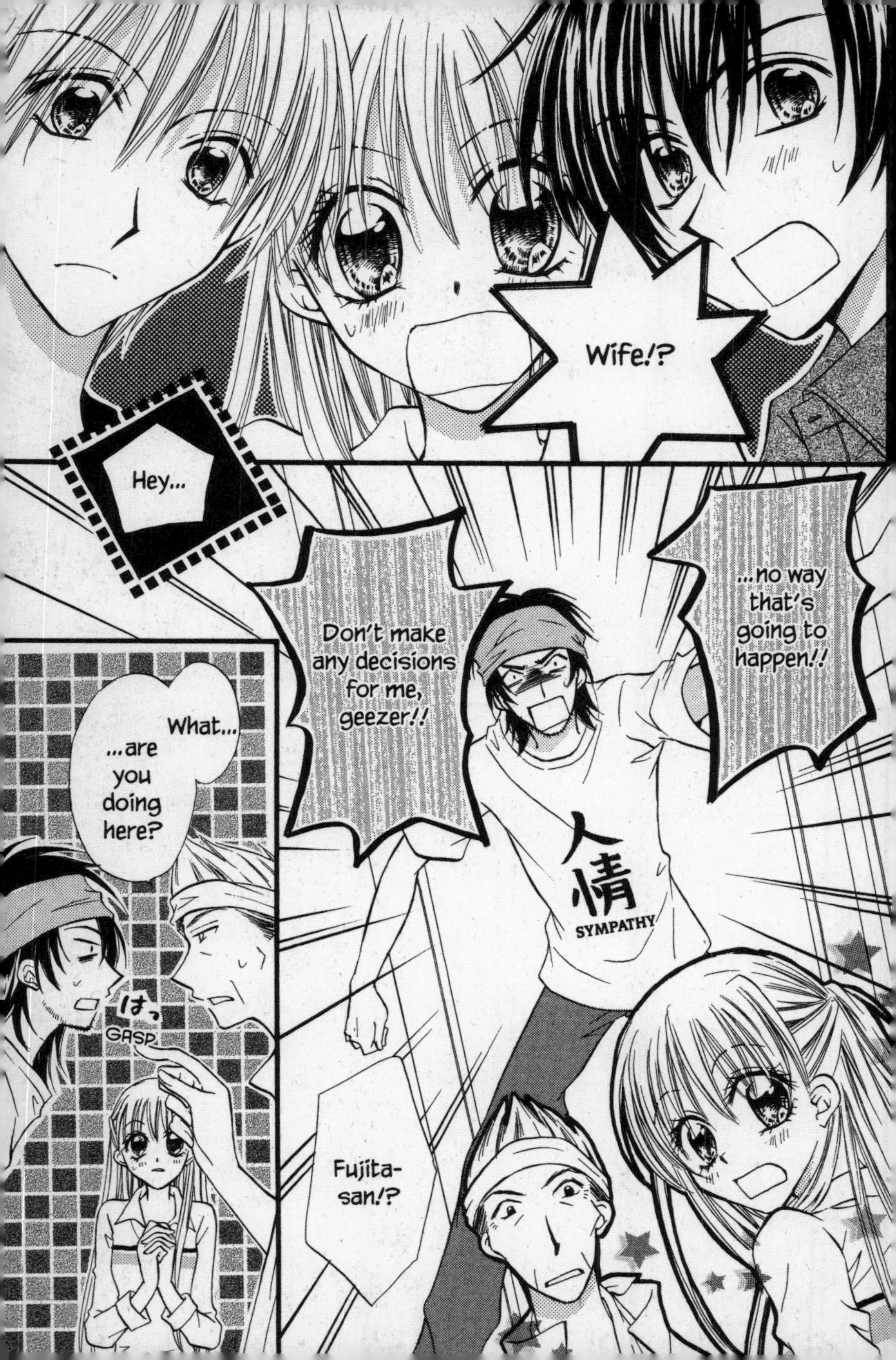
Wife!?
Hey...
...no way that's going to happen!!
Don't make any decisions for me, geezer!!
人情
SYMPATHY
Fujita-san!?
What... ...are you doing here?
はっ
GASP

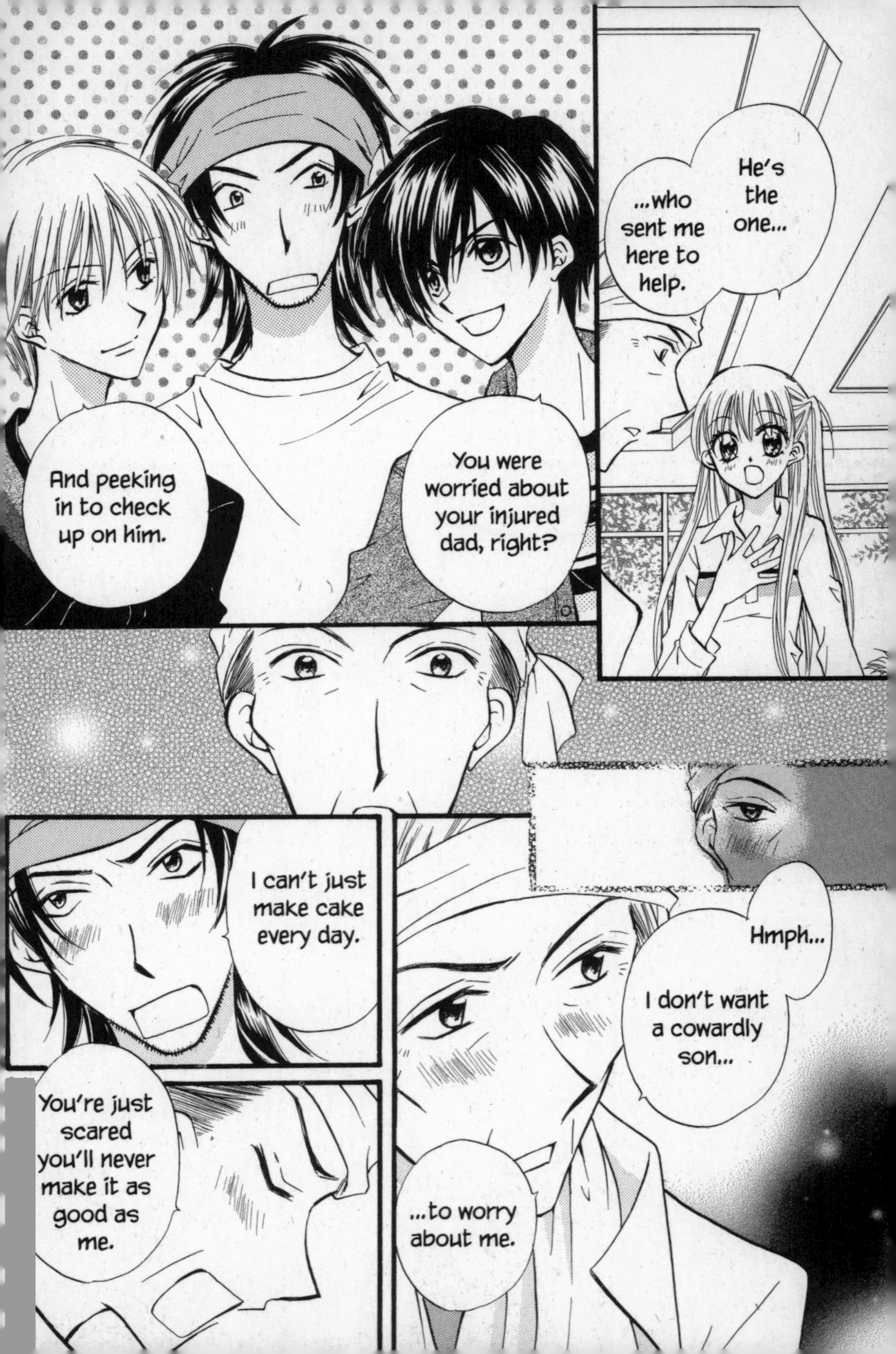
He's the one...
...who sent me here to help.
You were worried about your injured dad, right?
And peeking in to check up on him.
Hmph...
I don't want a cowardly son...
...to worry about me.
I can't just make cake every day.
You're just scared you'll never make it as good as me.

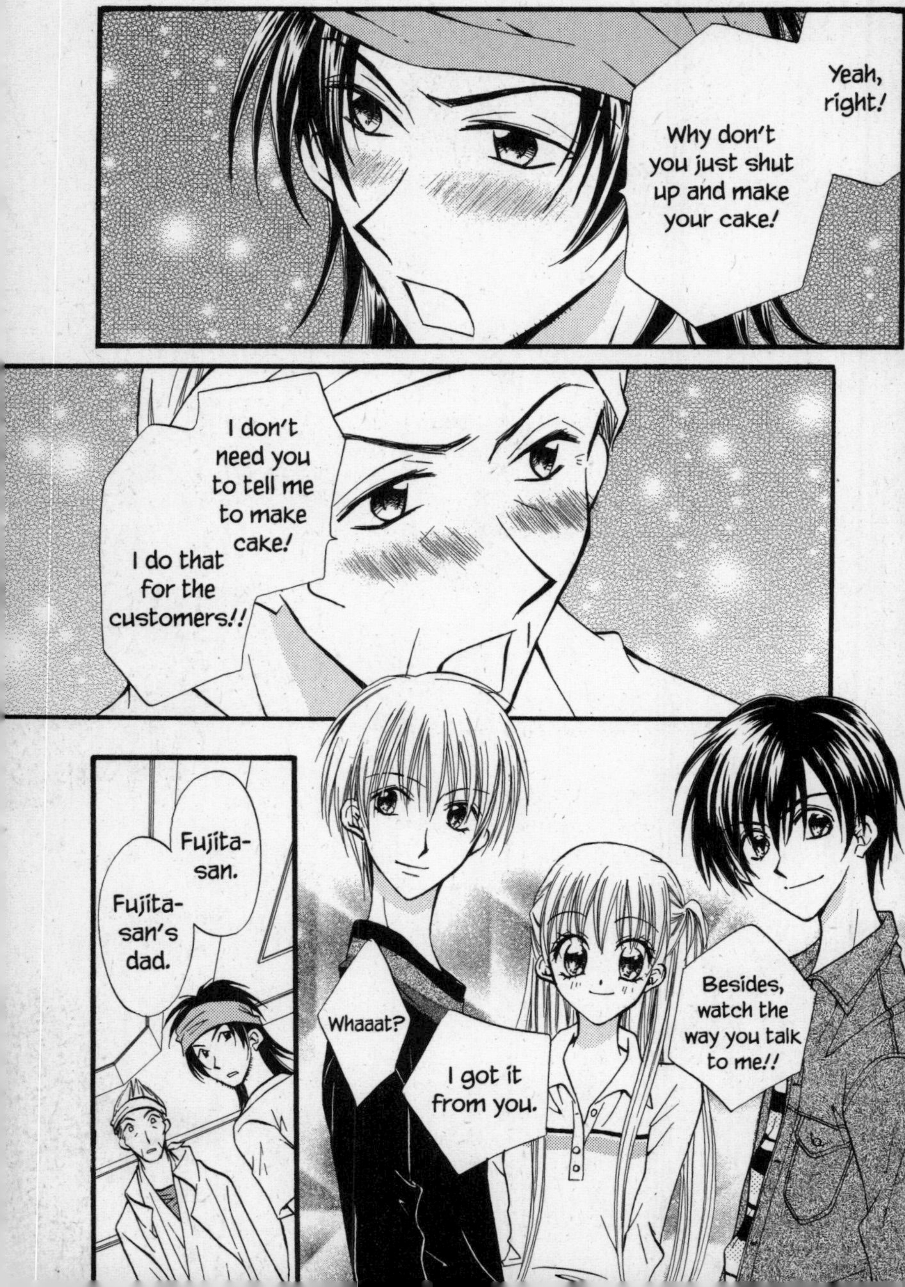
Yeah, right!
Why don't you just shut up and make your cake!
I don't need you to tell me to make cake!
I do that for the customers!!
Besides, watch the way you talk to me!!
Whaaat?
I got it from you.
Fujita-san.
Fujita-san's dad.

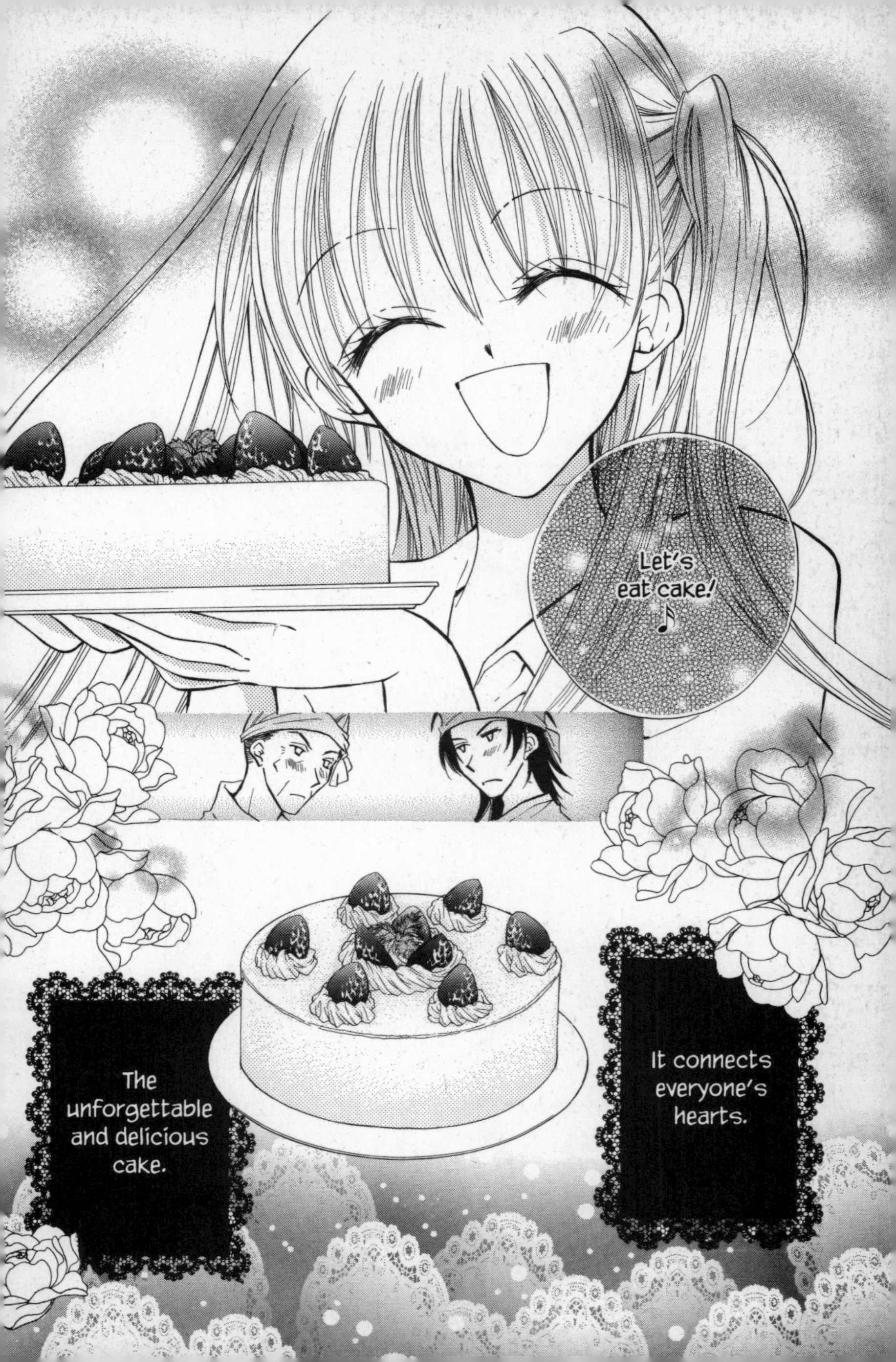
Let's eat cake! ♪
It connects everyone's hearts.
The unforgettable and delicious cake.

Kitchen Palace

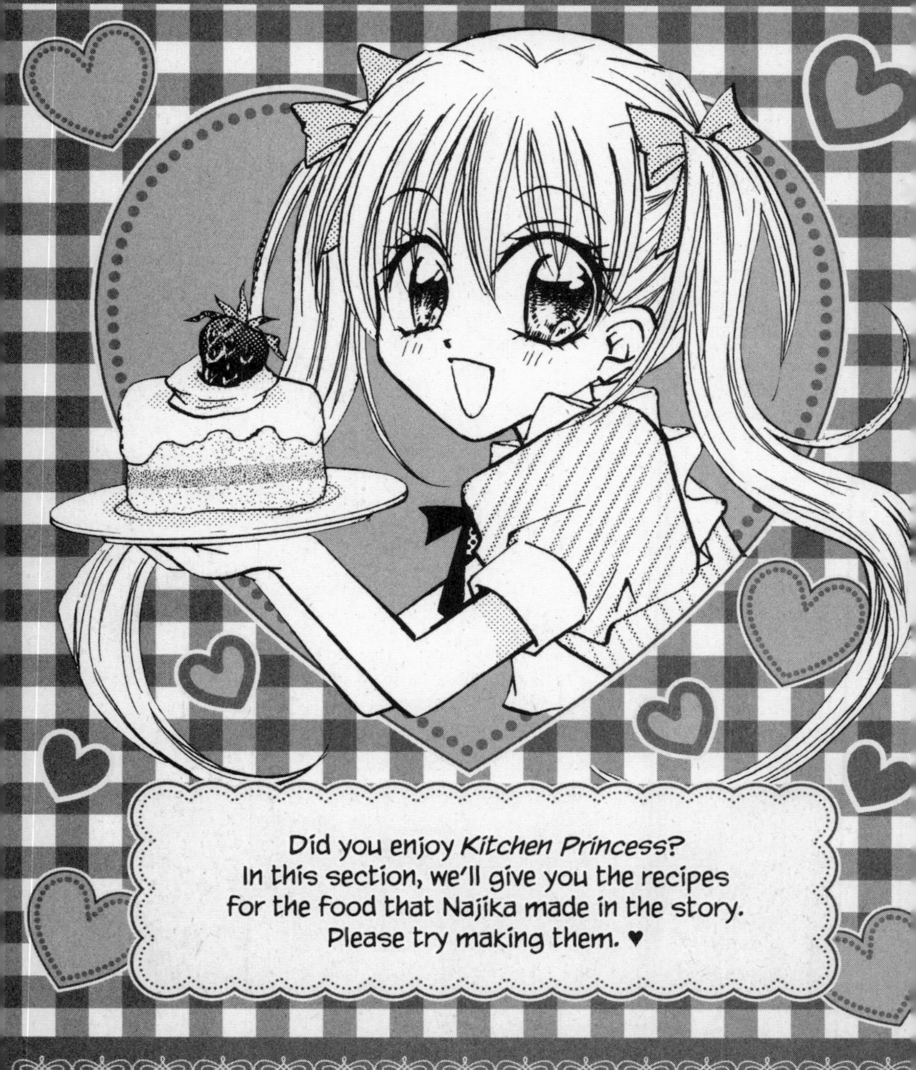

Did you enjoy *Kitchen Princess*?
In this section, we'll give you the recipes
for the food that Najika made in the story.
Please try making them. ♥

Strawberry Tart

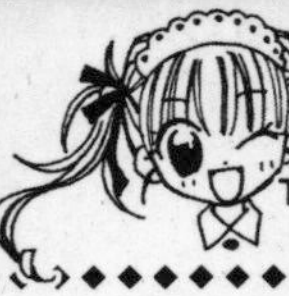

You can use whipped cream or cream cheese in place of the custard. ♥

Tip from Najika!

◆◆◆How to Make◆◆◆

Custard

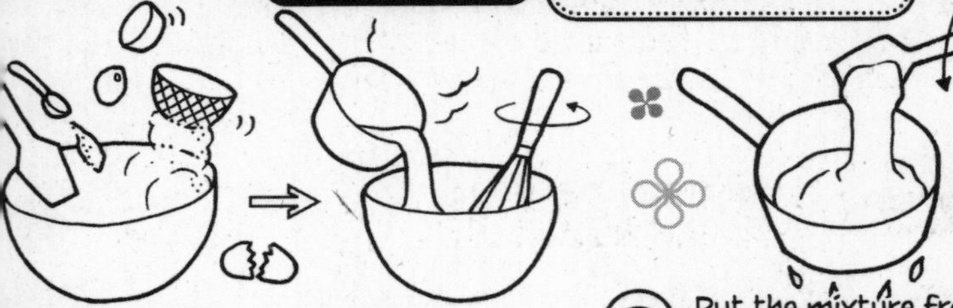

1 In a bowl, mix the egg yolk, sugar, and sifted flour with a ooden spoon. Heat the milk until it's st about to boil, and then add to the owl. Whisk well.

2 Put the mixture from step 1 into a saucepan and simmer over low heat. Stir like you're scooping the mix from the bottom of the pan.

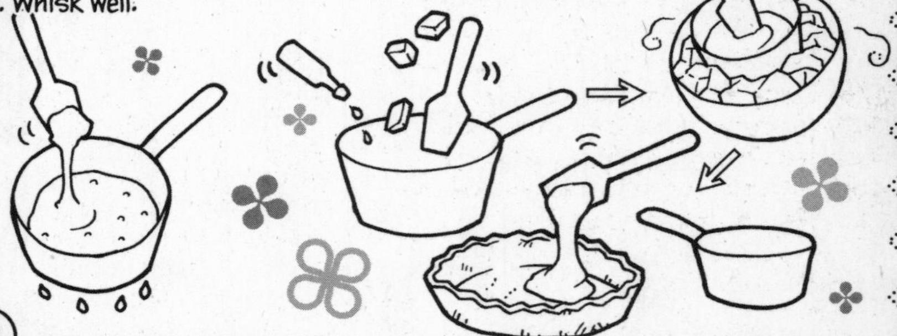

3 When bubbles start forming in the cream and t thickens, you can take t off the heat. If lumps form, you should crush hem.

4 Cut up the butter into small pieces and put them in the pan from step 2. Add some vanilla, too. Once butter is melted, place the saucepan in a big bowl filled with ice and stir until completely cooled. Once cool, pour into the tart dough.

A tart topped with blueberries and raspberries is a must-have snack in France during the spring!

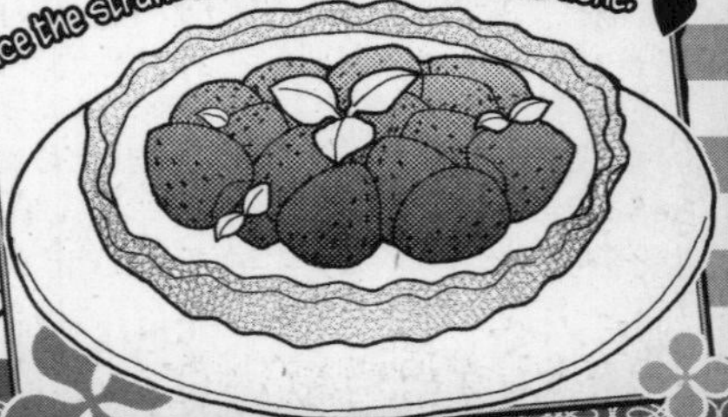

Place the strawberries on top and you're done. ♥

Strawberry Tart Makes 6-inch diameter tart

Tart Dough: 3-1/2 tablespoons unsalted butter, 3 tablespoons sugar, 1 egg yolk, 1 cup sifted flour, a little bit of milk (optional)

Custard: 1 egg yolk, 3 tablespoons sugar, 2 tablespoons sifted flour, 3/4 cup milk, 2 tablespoons unsalted butter, a little bit of vanilla

Fruit for decoration: 1 container of strawberries

How to Make — Tart Dough

1 Leave out the butter at room temperature so it softens. In a bowl, mix the butter and sugar with a whisk. When it becomes creamy, add the egg yolk and whisk some more.

3 Sprinkle flour on the board and on the rolling pin. Roll the dough into a round flat piece about 8 inches in diameter and 1/4 inch thick. Place the dough in a pie plate and use your fingers to make it fit. Cut off the extra dough from the sides and poke holes in the base using a fork.

2 Sift flour into the bowl from step 1 and mix. When the dough becomes crumbly, make one big lump with your hands. If the dough doesn't stay together, you can add milk to make it a little moist.

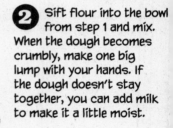

4 Bake in oven at 180 Cels (approx. 350 F). for 25 minutes. Cool on a cooling rack

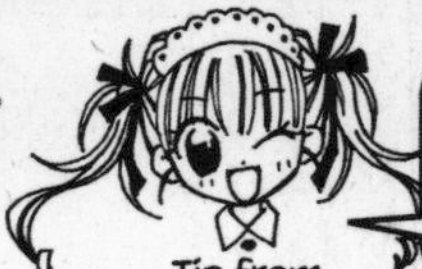

Tip from Najika.

Since the recipe used in the competition is a little difficult, I will introduce a version of it that you can make at home.

4 Add black sesame and the mixture from step 1 to the bowl from step 3. Mix well.

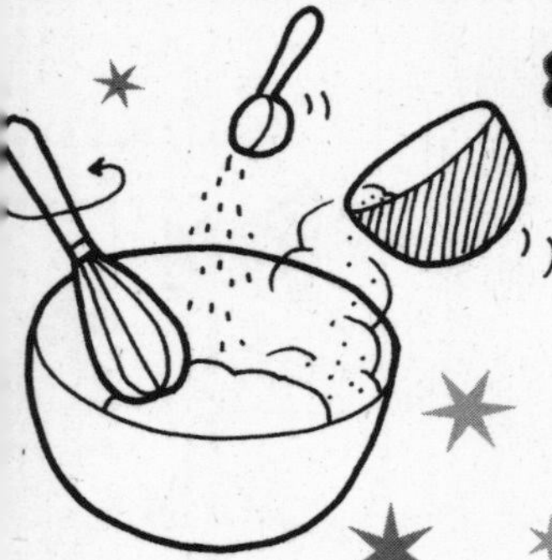

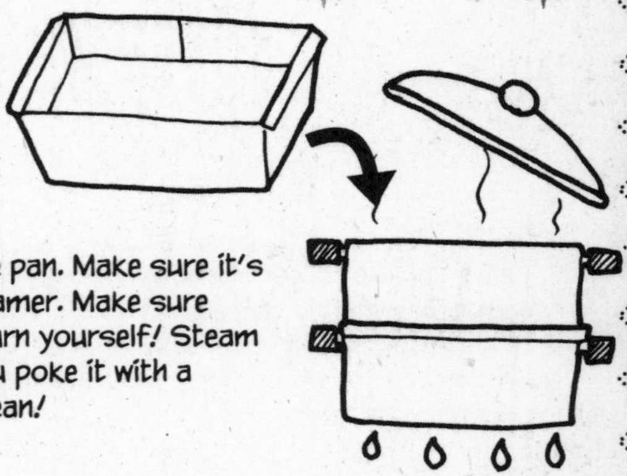

5 Pour the dough into the pan. Make sure it's even. Place it in the steamer. Make sure you stop the heat and don't burn yourself! Steam for 15 minutes. It's done if you poke it with a toothpick and it comes out clean!

If you use nrefined sugar (brown sugar, cane sugar), it becomes richer and tastes very good. ♡

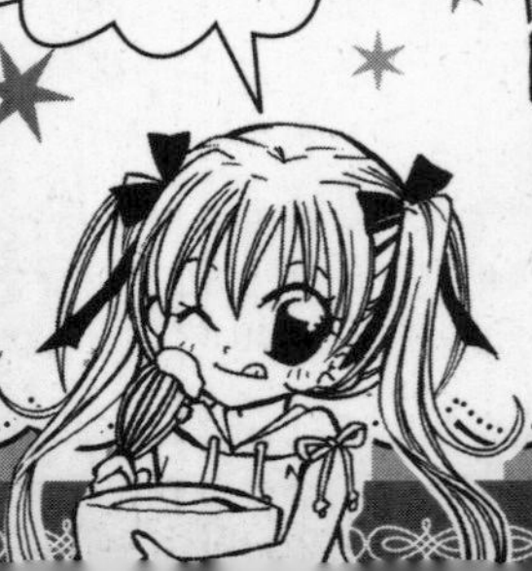

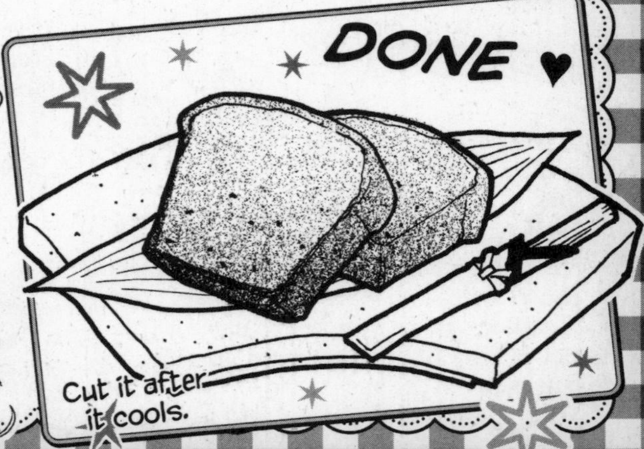
DONE ♥
Cut it after it cools.

Black Sesame Castella Makes 1 6x3 inch castella

2/3 cup sifted flour, 2 teaspoons baking powder, 2 eggs, 3 tablespoons sugar, 5 tablespoons black sesame (crushed)

How to Make

Preparation

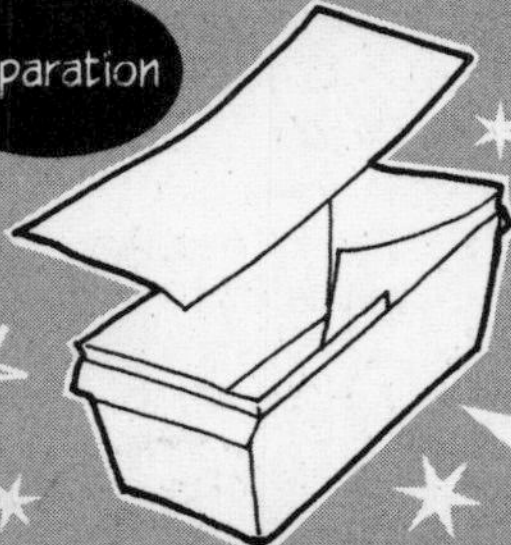

Cut out wax paper to cover the sides and the bottom of the cake pan.

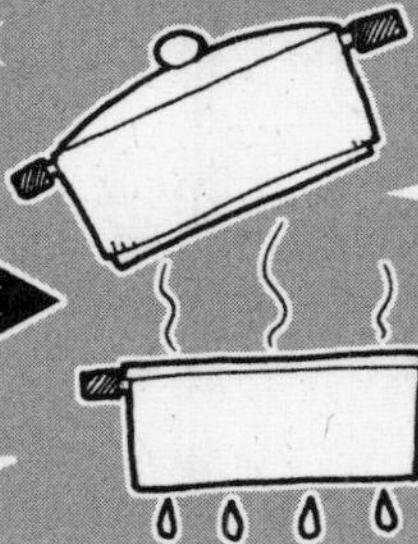

Put a lot of water in a steamer and have it ready over medium heat.

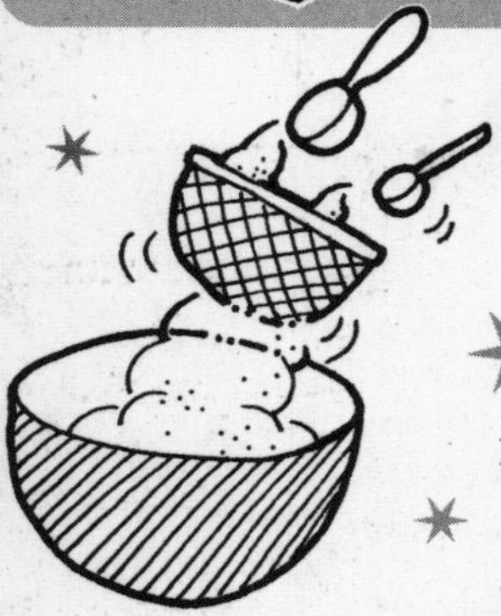

1. Sift the flour and baking powder together.

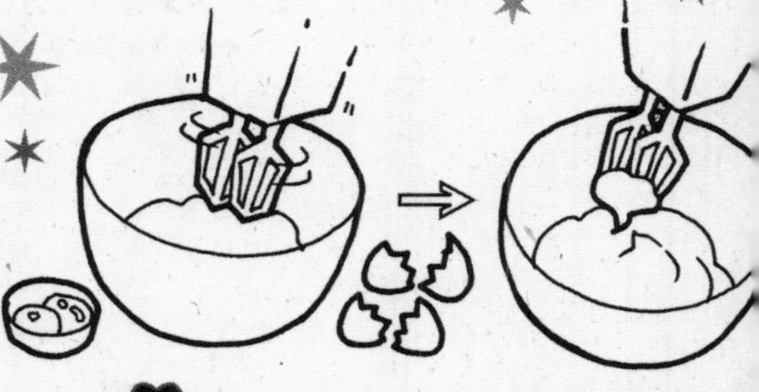

2. Put the egg whites in a bowl and mix until it stands up. It'll be easy and fast if you use a hand mixer.

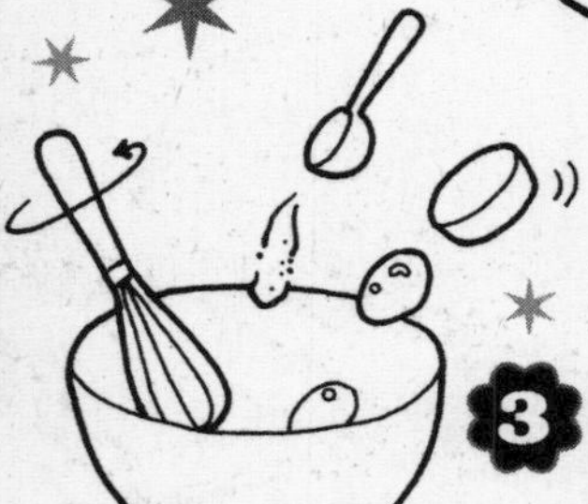

3. Add egg yolks and sugar to the bowl from step 2 and whisk.

Recipe 22: Crepes

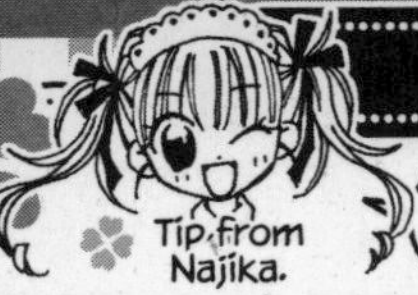

Tip from Najika.

Make them carefully, one by one.

Crepes Makes 4 or 5 about 7 inches in diameter

½ cup sifted flour, 2 teaspoons sugar, a little salt, 1 egg, ½ cup milk, 1 tablespoon unsalted butter, some jam, cream, and chocolate sauce, some butter for the frying pan

◆How to Make◆

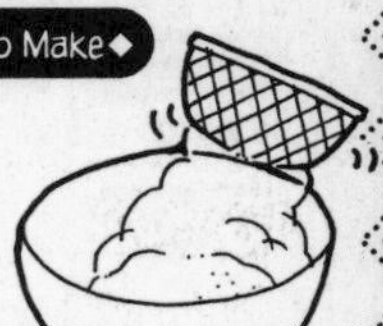

1. Sift flour into a bowl.

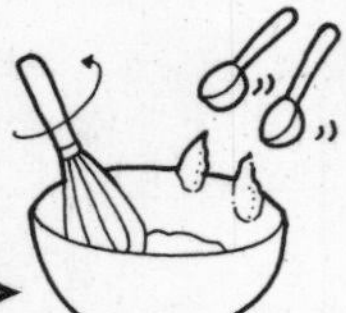

2. Add sugar and salt and mix.

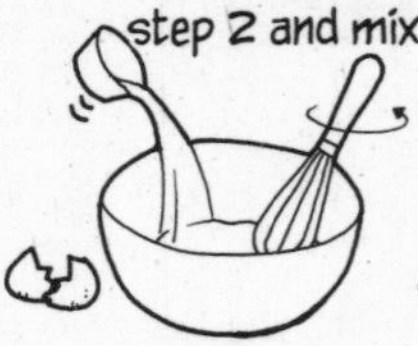

3. Whisk the egg separately and add it to the bowl from step 2 and mix.

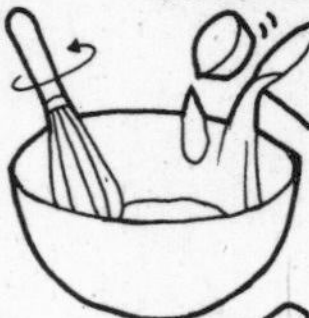

4. Microwave butter for 1 to 2 minutes, then add the butter and milk to the bowl from step 3. Mix well.

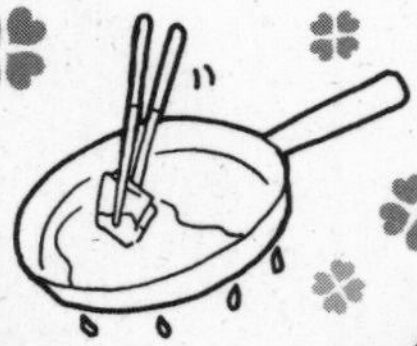

5. Put a frying pan (better if it's nonstick) over low heat and melt butter in it. Use a paper towel to spread it and remove any excess butter.

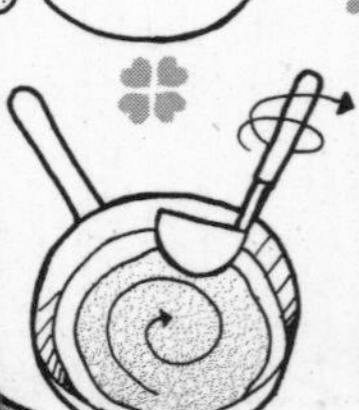

6. Pour the batter in the frying pan and use the ladle to spread it in a circular motion.

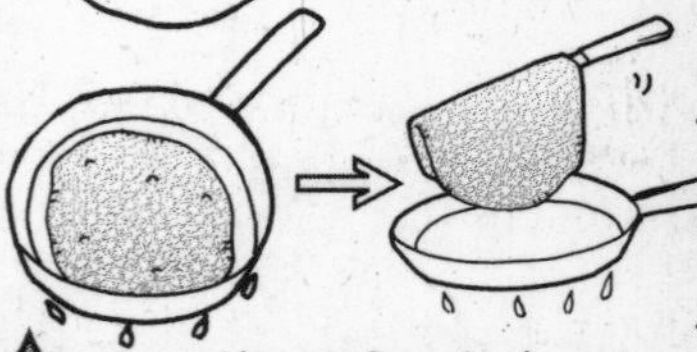

7. Once the surface is dry, use a spatula to pick up the crepe and flip it over. Fry it for half a minute then remove it from the pan, careful not to rip it. Repeat as necessary until you run out of batter.

8. Fold it in fours and add jam, cream, or chocolate sauce. Enjoy.

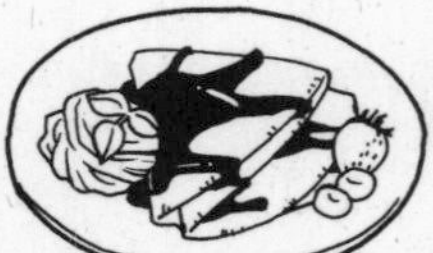

Once you master crepe making, you can try making the milk crepe! After you make about 15 or 20 crepes, place whipped cream between them and stack them up.

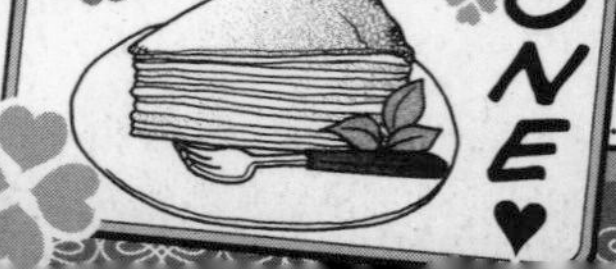
DONE♥

Recipe 23: Soufflé Ice Cream

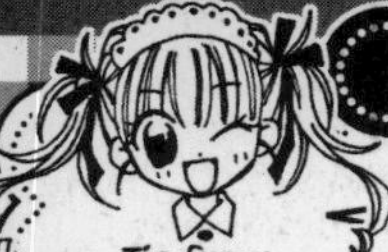

Tip from Najika.

If you use a hand mixer, it'll be really easy!

Soufflé Ice Cream Makes 4 servings
3/4 cup whipping cream, 2 eggs, 3 tablespoons sugar, some vanilla

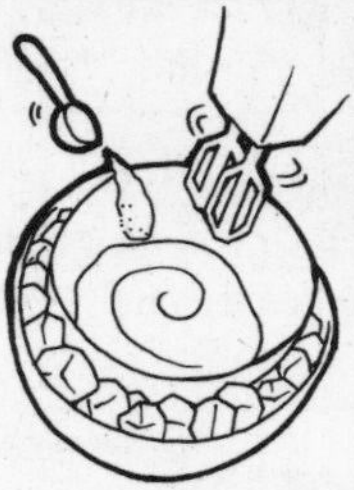

How to Make

1 Place ice in a big bowl. Put a smaller bowl over the ice and add whipping cream and sugar. Mix well until it's stiff.

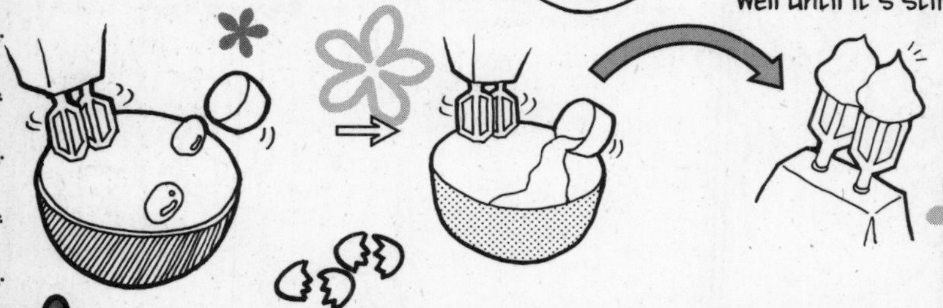

2 Separate the egg yolks from the egg whites. Place in separate bowls. Mix the egg whites until stiff like a meringue.

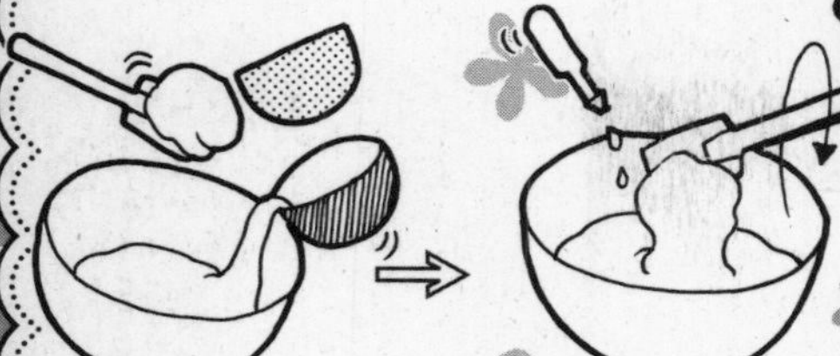

3 Add the egg whites from step 2 to the bowl from step 1. Stir quickly using a spatula. Add vanilla. It's ready when there are no lumps.

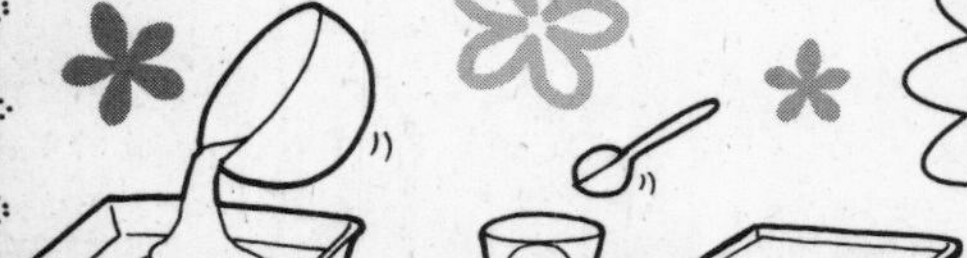

4 Pour the mix from step 3 into a container and put it in the freezer. After two hours, you can scoop it out and eat it.

The meringue makes it soft and delicious. You can serve it with fruit, or even pie or cake! It melts fast, so make sure you enjoy it as soon as you scoop it out.

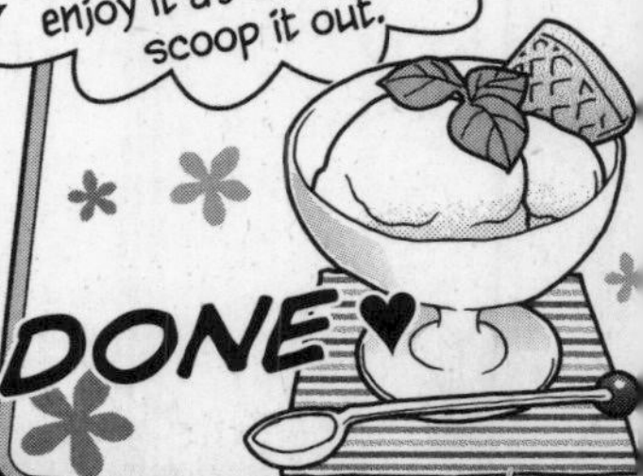
DONE♥

Special Recipe: Cupcakes

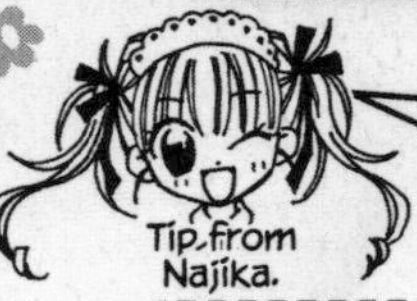

Tip from Najika.

You can make this in a short amount of time. It can be topped with whipped cream or fruit as well as other decorations!

Cupcake Makes 4 to 5

1 egg, 2/3 cup milk, 3 tablespoons sugar, 1-1/2 cups pancake mix

How to Make

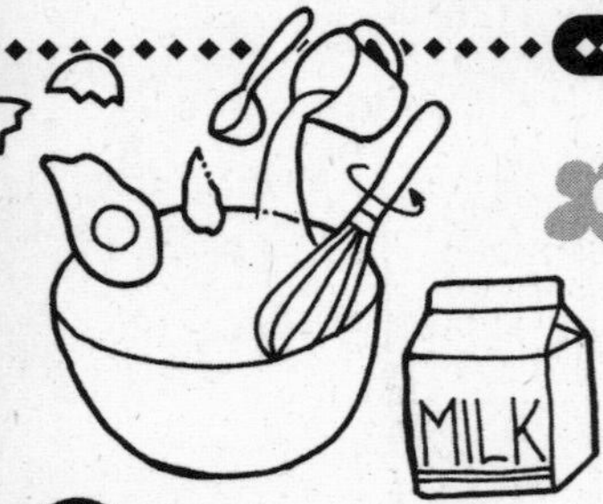
MILK

1. Add egg, milk, and sugar to a bowl and mix.

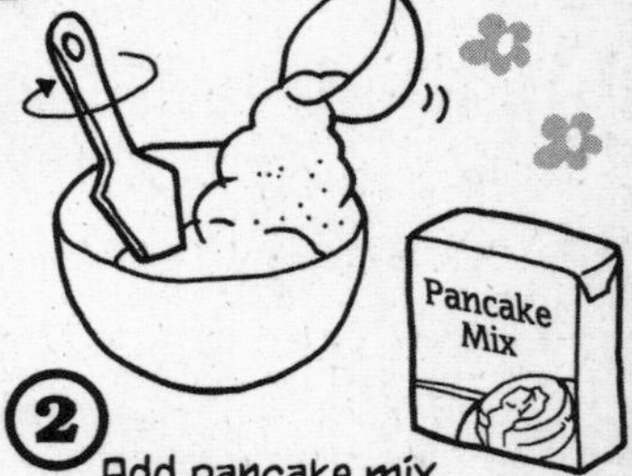
Pancake Mix

2. Add pancake mix and stir well.

3. Pour into paper cups, filling each halfway. If you add too much batter, it'll overflow when you cook it, so be careful.

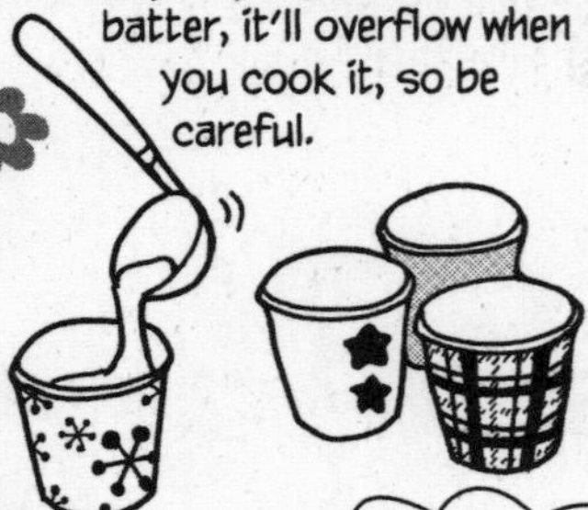

4. Put the paper cups from step 3 into the microwave and heat (approx. 4 to 5 minutes in a microwave). It's done when you poke it with a toothpick and it comes out clean!

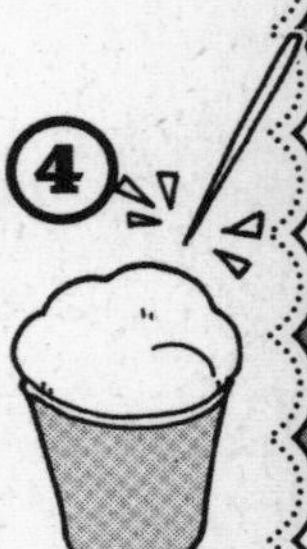

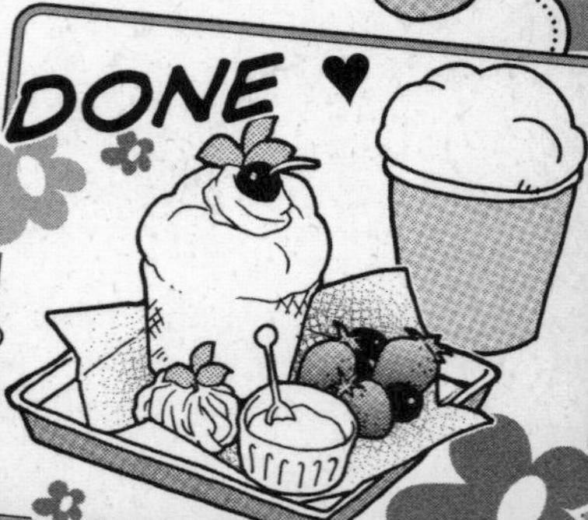
DONE ♥

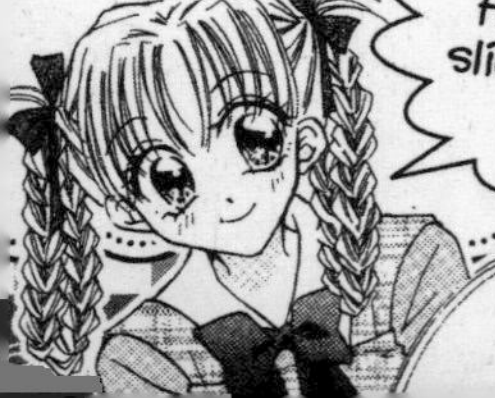

You can add chocolate chips, dried fruit, nuts, or banana slices to the batter and make different kinds! ☆

Kitchen Princess

From the Writer

Hello! This is Miyuki Kobayashi.

Kitchen Princess has won the 30th Kodansha Manga Award. I am very grateful and happy for receiving this award. This is thanks to all our readers. Thank you very much! My heart is full of appreciation. I hope to continue to make *Kitchen Princess* more interesting, so please keep rooting for me!

Now to talk a little bit about Volume 5. I think most of you are surprised by the sudden turn of events. But actually, this was decided when I first thought of the plot for *Kitchen Princess*. Still, I got teary eyed when I was writing the story...The story will start moving in a different direction, so please don't miss it. I would love to hear your comments, too!

And I like this volume because the special story, my personal favorite, is included.

Finally, I would like to thank Natsumi Ando-sensei, our editor Kishimoto-san, Saito-san from the editing team, our former editor in chief Nouchi-san, and current editor in chief Matsumoto-san.

I'll see you again in Volume 6!

About the Creator

Natsumi Ando

   She was born January 27th in Aichi prefecture. She won the 19th
Nakayoshi Rookie Award in 1994 and debuted as a manga artist. The title
she drew was *Headstrong Cinderella*. Her other known works are *Zodiac
P.I.* and *Wild Heart*. Her hobbies include reading, watching movies, and
eating delicious food.

Translation Notes

Japanese is a tricky language for most Westerners, and translation is often more art than science. For your edification and reading pleasure, here are notes on some of the places where we could have gone in a different direction in our translation of the work, or where a Japanese cultural reference is used.

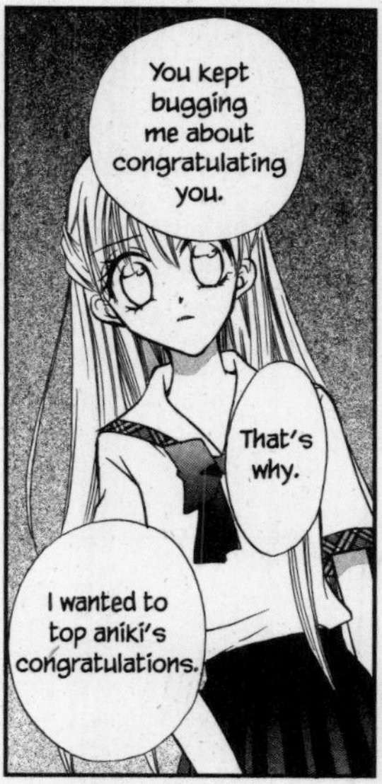
You kept bugging me about congratulating you.
That's why.
I wanted to top aniki's congratulations.

Aniki, page 12

Aniki is a term for "older brother," usually used by boys (or girls who are tomboys) in their younger teens. It is less honorific than "onii-chan" and "onii-san."

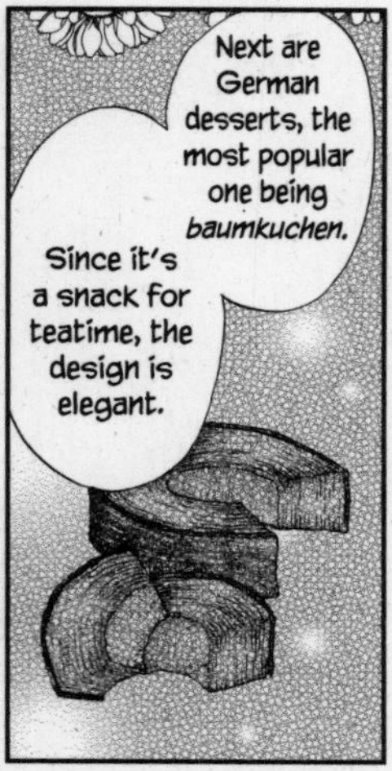
Next are German desserts, the most popular one being *baumkuchen.*
Since it's a snack for teatime, the design is elegant.

Baumkuchen, page 24

Baumkuchen is a kind of layered cake that originated in Germany. It is now very popular in Japan. Inside, the cake has golden rings that give it its name, which, literally translated, means "tree cake."

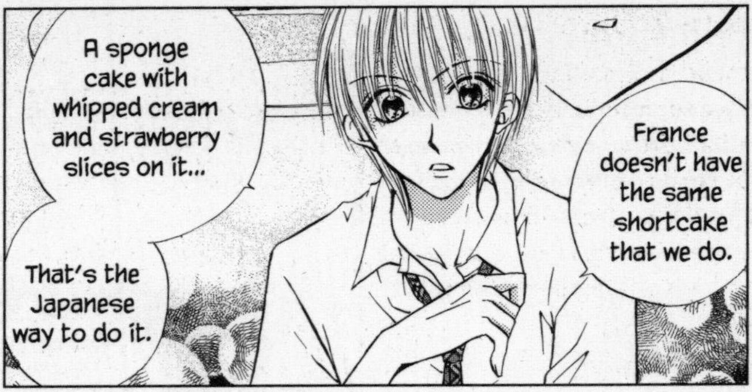
France doesn't have the same shortcake that we do.
A sponge cake with whipped cream and strawberry slices on it...
That's the Japanese way to do it.

Strawberry shortcake, page 31

What the Japanese call strawberry shortcake does not use shortcake as it is known in the West, but instead uses a sponge cake, with whipped cream and strawberry slices in the middle and a strawberry on top. It is the most popular type of cake in Japan. The sponge cake has almonds in it and is more moist than shortcake. The cream is typically butter cream or crème mousseline.

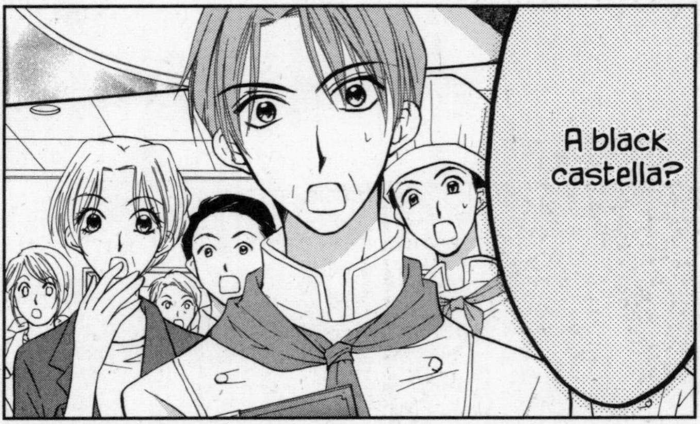
A black castella?

Black castella, page 60

Everyone is surprised with Najika's castella because usually castellas are light tan on the inside and a darker brown on the outside.

Muscovado, page 61

Muscovado, or Barbados sugar, is an unrefined sugar with a heavy molasses flavor. Dark brown in color, it is coarser and thicker than other brown sugars. It gets its flavor from the sugar cane juice it is made from, rather than having molasses added later, like most brown sugars.

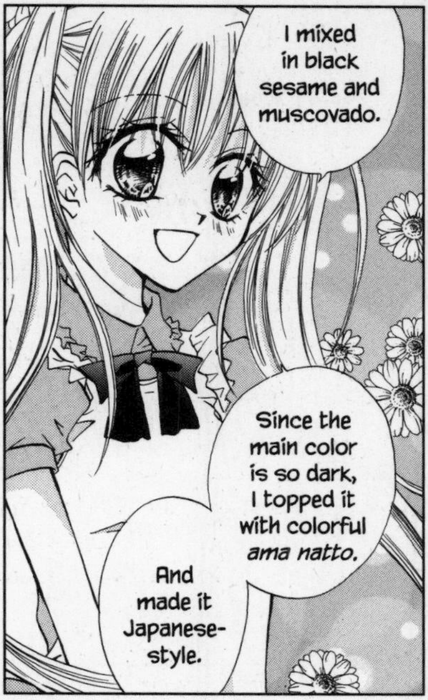
I mixed in black sesame and muscovado.
Since the main color is so dark, I topped it with colorful *ama natto.*
And made it Japanese-style.

Ama natto, page 61

Ama natto literally translates to "sweet fermented soybeans," but it is not actually made of fermented soybeans. It is beans and chestnuts sweetened with sugar. *Ama natto* is made by boiling the beans and chestnuts in sugar water, covering them with sugar, and then drying them.

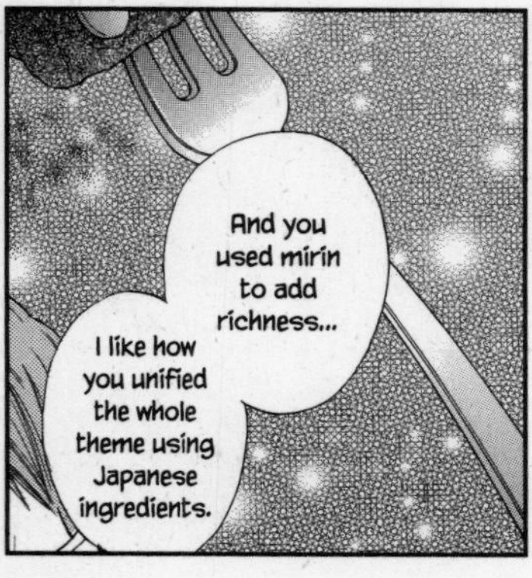
And you used mirin to add richness...
I like how you unified the whole theme using Japanese ingredients.

Mirin, page 62

Mirin is a kind of sweet rice wine that is used as a condiment. Sometimes mirin is used for cooking in place of sugar or soy sauce. It is also popular in cooking fish, because it masks the fish odor.

Chef names, page 63

If you've been reading the artist's and writer's notes in *Kitchen Princess*, you will notice that the two chefs have the same names as *Kitchen Princess*'s editor in chief and editor.

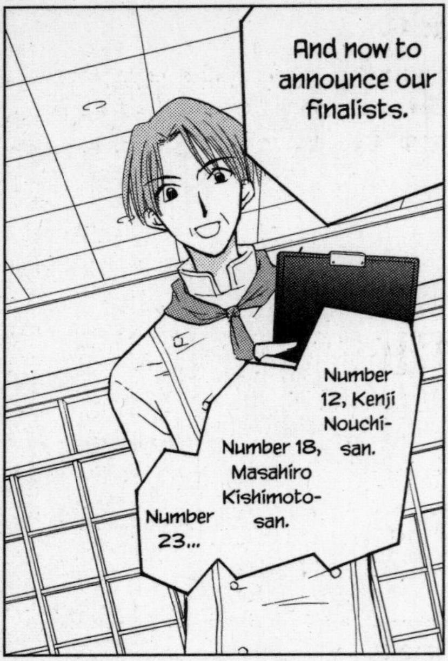
And now to announce our finalists.
Number 12, Kenji Nouchi-san.
Number 18, Masahiro Kishimoto-san.
Number 23...

Screen tone, page 68

A screen tone is a patterned sticker sheet that manga artists use to decorate their art. There are hundreds of patterns, with new ones coming out every so often.

Glasses photograph book, page 68

It's now very trendy in Japan for girls to wear glasses, and a publisher in Japan published a photo book featuring teen idol girls wearing glasses. The artist is hoping for a similar photo book featuring different aprons so she can use it as a reference in making her illustrations.

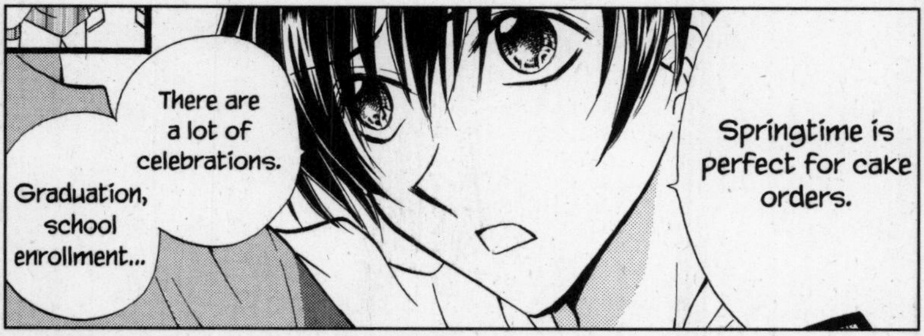
Springtime is perfect for cake orders.
There are a lot of celebrations.
Graduation, school enrollment...

Graduation and school enrollment, page 153

The new school year starts during the spring in Japan. The previous year ends in March, then students have a week or two of Spring Break before beginning the new school year. That's why Daichi says that during spring, there are a lot of graduations and a lot of new school enrollments.

Preview of Volume 6

We are pleased to present you a preview from volume 6 of *Kitchen Princess*. Please check our website (www.delreymagna.com) to see when this volume will be available in English. For now you'll have to make do with Japanese!

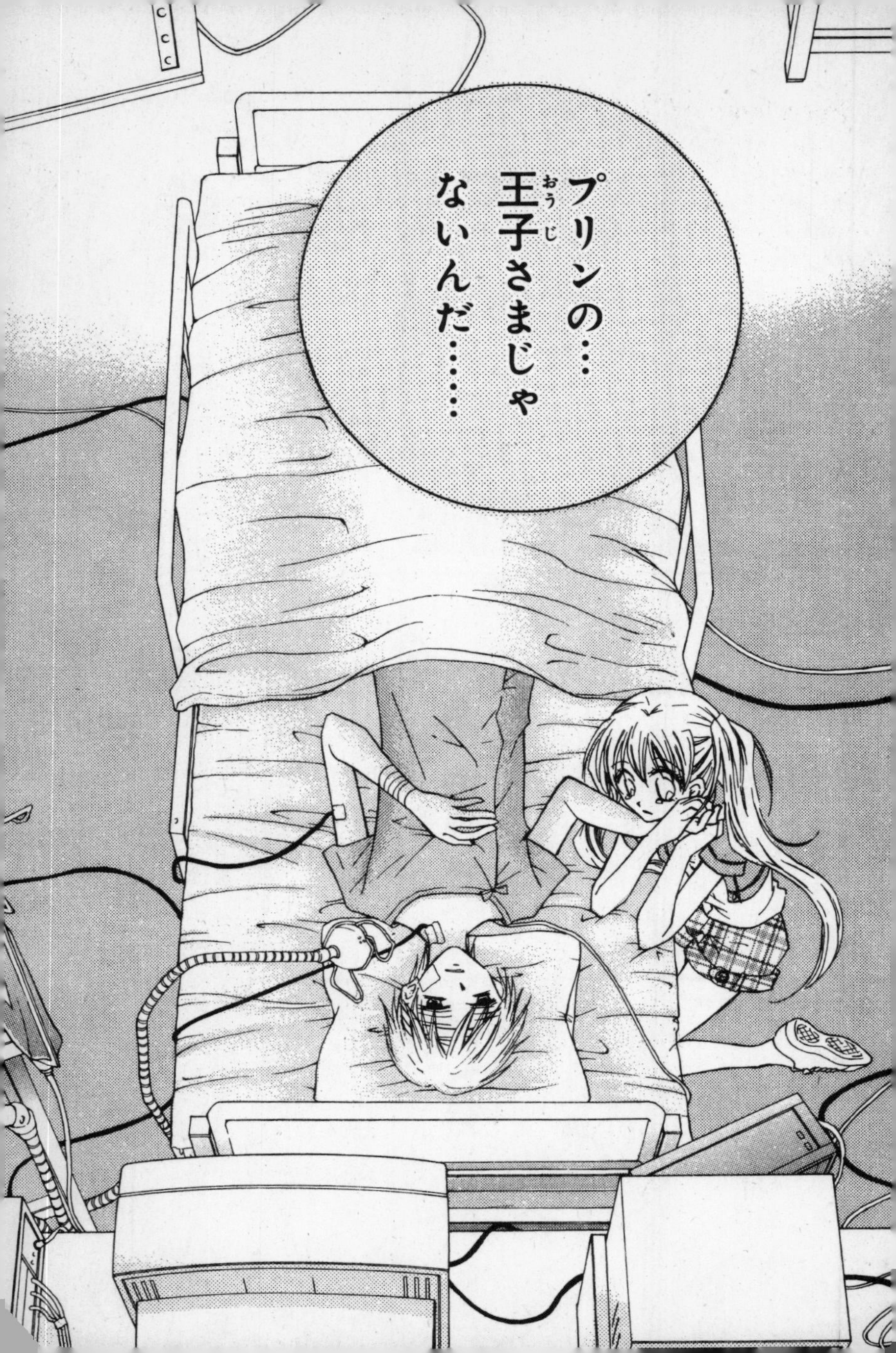
プリンの…王子さまじゃないんだ……

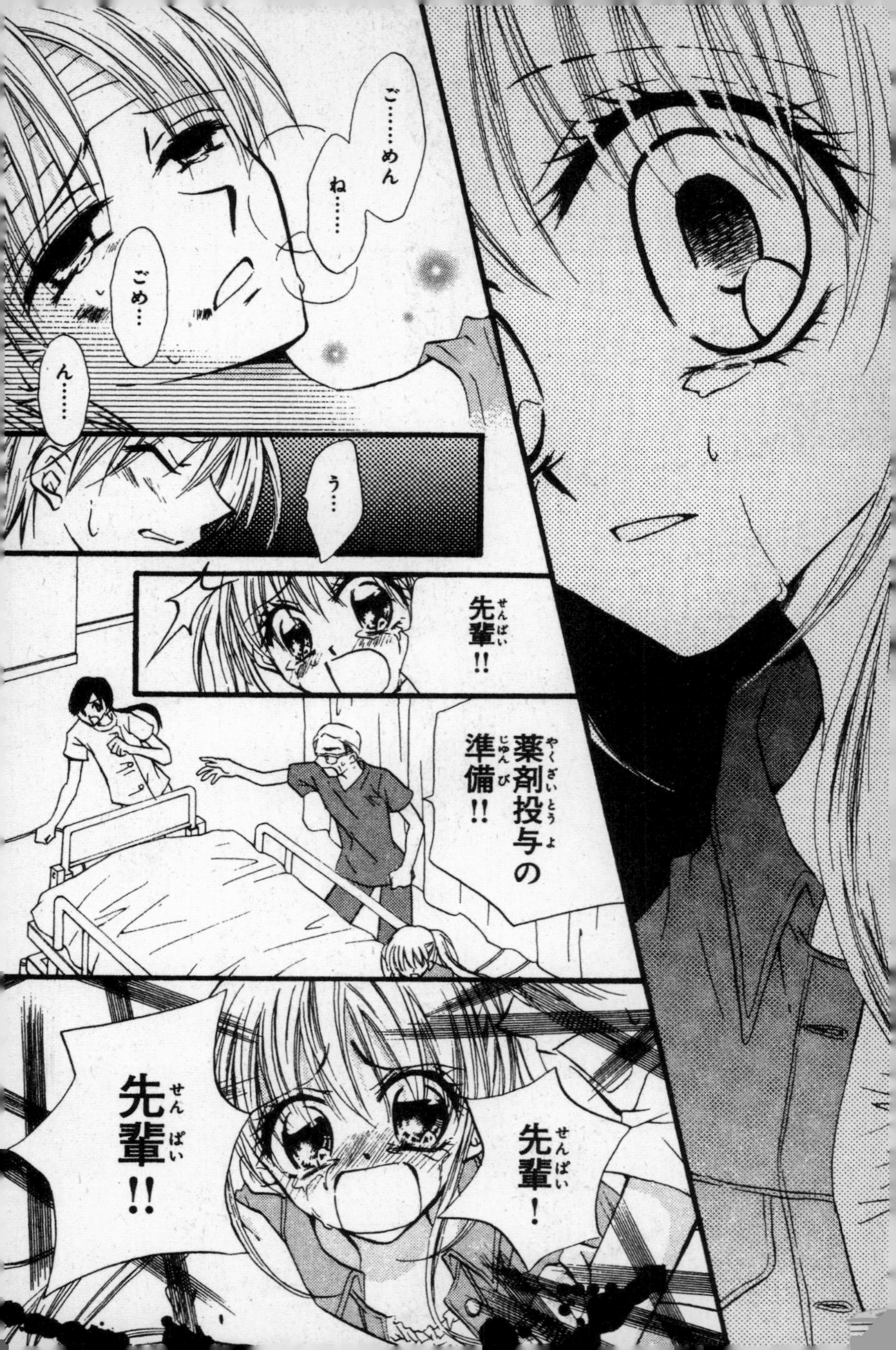
ご……めんね……
ごめ…
ん……
う…
先輩!!
薬剤投与の準備!!
先輩!
先輩!!

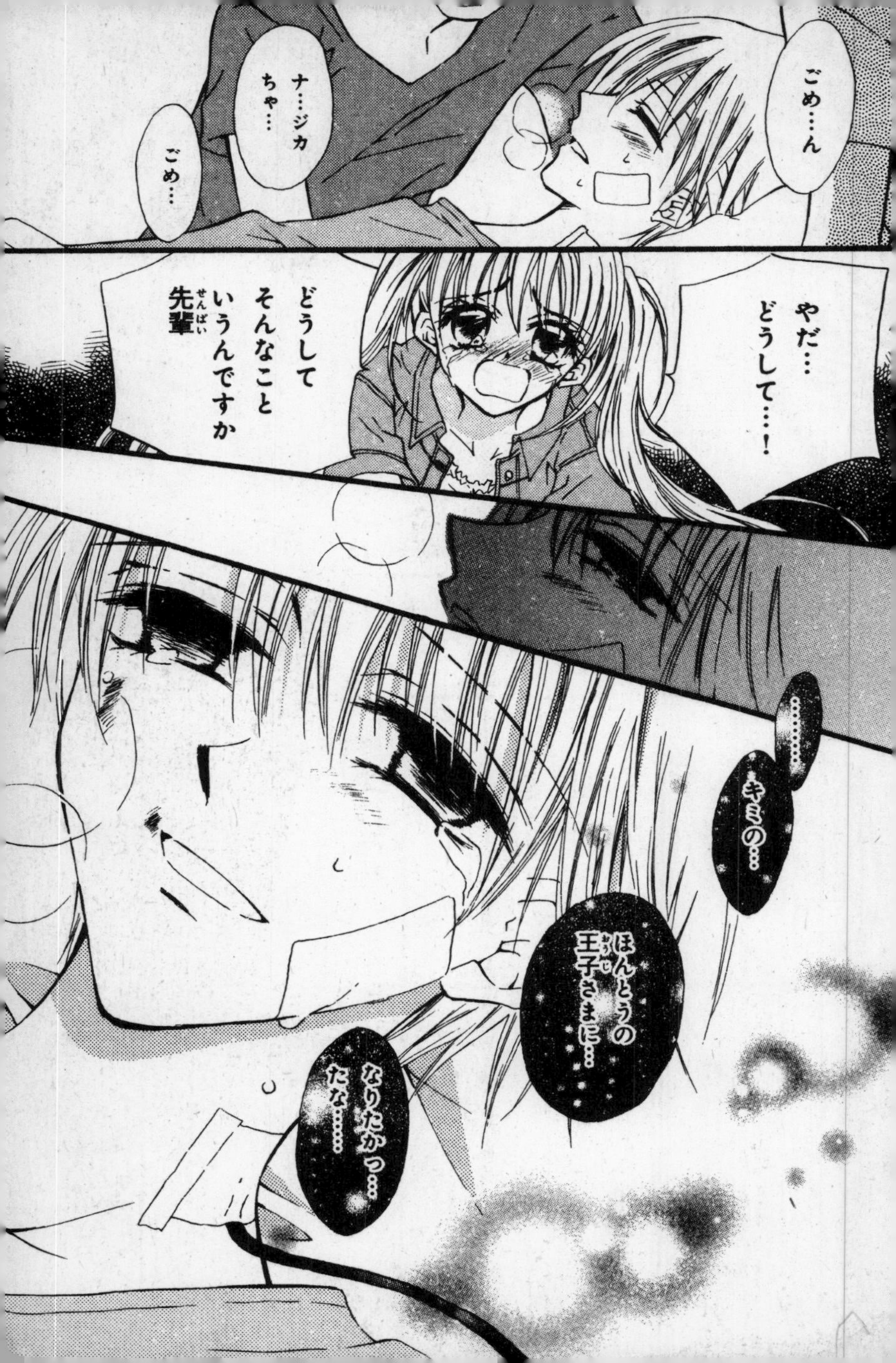
ごめ…ん
ナ…ジカちゃ…
ごめ…
やだ…どうして…！
どうしてそんなこというんですか先輩
……
キミの…
ほんとうの王子さまに…
なりたかっ…たな……

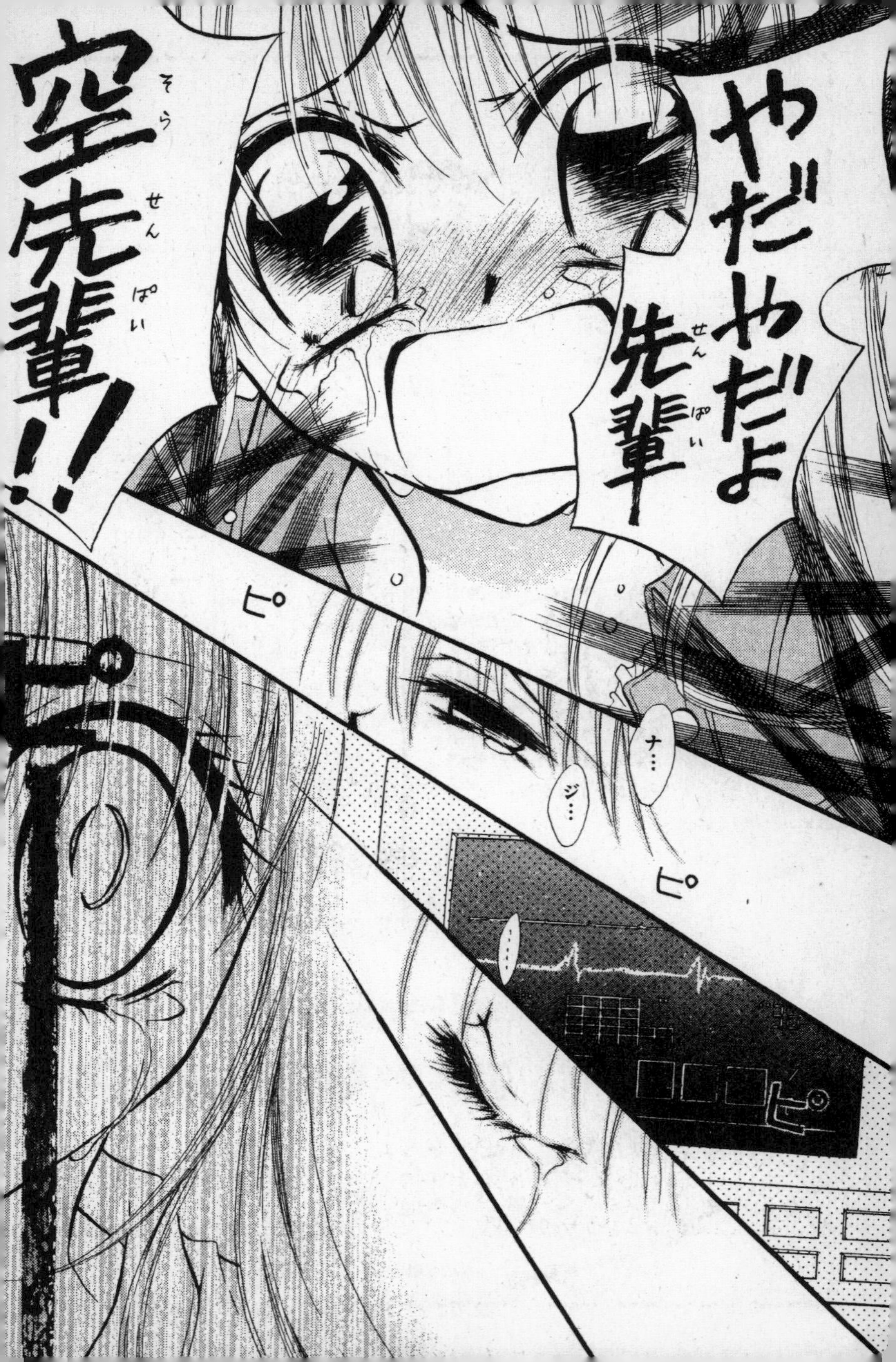

やだやだよ先輩
空先輩!!
ナ…
ジ…
ピ
ピ
…
ピ

BY MACHIKO SAKURAI

A LITTLE LIVING DOLL!

What would you do if your favorite toy came to life and became your best friend? Well, that's just what happens to Ame Oikawa, a shy schoolgirl. Nicori is a super-cute doll with a mind of its own—and a plan to make Ame's dreams come true!

Special extras in each volume! Read them all!

VISIT WWW.DELREYMANGA.COM TO:
- Read sample pages
- View release date calendars for upcoming volumes
- Sign up for Del Rey's free manga e-newsletter
- Find out the latest about new Del Rey Manga series

RATING T AGES 13+

TOMARE!

止まれ

[STOP!]

You're going the wrong way!

Manga is a completely different type of reading experience.

To start at the *beginning,* go to the *end!*

That's right! Authentic manga is read the traditional Japanese way—from right to left. Exactly the *opposite* of how American books are read. It's easy to follow: Just go to the other end of the book, and read each page—and each panel—from right side to left side, starting at the top right. Now you're experiencing manga as it was meant to be!